This Wired Home

SECOND EDITION

The Microsoft® Guide to Home Networking

Alan Neibauer

PUBLISHED BY
Microsoft Press
A Division of Microsoft Corporation
One Microsoft Way
Redmond, Washington 98052-6399

Library of Congress Cataloging-in-Publication Data
Neibauer, Alan R.
    This Wired Home : The Microsoft Guide to Home Networking / Alan Neibauer.-- 2nd ed.
       p. cm.
    Includes index.
    ISBN 0-7356-1158-0
  1. Home computer networks--Amateurs' manuals.   I. Title.

  TK5105.75.N45   2000
  004.6'8--dc21   00-057856

Printed and bound in the United States of America.

2 3 4 5 6 7 8 9   QWTQWT   5 4 3 2 1 0

Distributed in Canada by Penguin Books Canada Limited.

A CIP catalogue record for this book is available from the British Library.

Microsoft Press books are available through booksellers and distributors worldwide. For further information about international editions, contact your local Microsoft Corporation office or contact Microsoft Press International directly at fax (425) 936-7329. Visit our Web site at mspress.microsoft.com. Send comments to *mspinput@microsoft.com*.

For Microsoft Press
Acquisitions Editor: Christey Bahn
Project Editor: Sally Stickney

For nSight
Project Manager: Susan H. McClung
Copy Editor: Chrisa Hotchkiss
Technical Editors: Don Lesser, Mannie White,
    Doug Slaughter, Eric Brewer, Timothy Upton

Contents

Acknowledgments XIII
Introduction XV

Part 1

Getting Started

Chapter 1
Why Set Up a Network?   3

Sharing an Internet Connection 4
 Don't Worry if the Line Is Busy 5
 Getting Your Money's Worth from Your ISP 6
 Getting the Most from Broadband 6
 The Bottom Line 7
Sharing Printers 7
 Putting the Printer Online 10
 The Bottom Line 10
Sharing Files and Folders 11
 Avoiding the Floppy Shuffle 11
 Making Files Easy to Find 11
 Keeping Documents Current 12
 Working Together 12
 Safeguarding Important Documents 13
 The Bottom Line 14
Sharing CD-ROMs and Removable Drives 14
 Escaping the CD Shuffle 14
 Adding Zip to Your Life 15
 The Bottom Line 16
Communicating with Others 16
 Using an Electronic Intercom 16
 Sending Mail, Messages, and Reminders 17
 Staying in Touch 18
 The Bottom Line 18

Playing Family Games 18

Setting Up for Multiplayer Gaming 18

The Bottom Line 19

Bridging Macs and PCs 19

Making It Educational 20

Chapter 2
Getting Connected Without a Network   21

When Sharing a Printer Is Enough 21

Using Printer Switches 22

Putting It on Automatic 25

Making a Direct Connection 29

One Simple Cable Is All It Takes 30

Installing the Free Software 31

Choosing a Protocol 33

Setting Up a Direct Cable Connection 35

Using a Direct Cable Connection 40

Using Direct Cable Connection with Windows 2000 41

Other Software for Direct Connections 46

Another Way to Share Files and Printers 47

Going Wireless with Infrared 52

What to Do with an Old CPU 54

The Bottom Line 56

Chapter 3
Planning a Network   57

A Little Network Preamble 57

Deciding on Network Control 59

Setting Up a Level Playing Field 59

Putting Someone in Charge 62

Deciding on the Connection 65

Understanding Networking Software 68

Network Drivers 68

Network Operating Systems 68

The Bottom Line 69

Part 2

Installing the Hardware

Chapter 4
Ethernet Networks   **73**
Types of Cable 74
Fiber Optics 78

Chapter 5
Non-Ethernet Networks   **81**
Setting Up a Phone-Line Network 82
   The Pros and Cons of Phone-Line Networks 83
   Choosing a Phone-Line System 85
Using Wireless Network Devices 87
   The Pros and Cons of Going Wireless 88
   Choosing a Wireless System 89
Setting Up a Power-Line Network 91
   The Pros and Cons of Power-Line Networks 92
USB Direct Cable Networks 96
Bridging Network Types 100

Chapter 6
Installing Network Cards   **103**
Are You Network-Ready? 103
Working Without Cards 104
Cook It Yourself or Order Out? 106
   Installing a Network Card Yourself 106
   Finding Someone Else to Do It 106
Buying and Installing a Network Card 108
   It's All in the Cards 108
   Catching the Right Bus 109
   The Whole Kit and Caboodle 112
   Where to Shop? 113
   Playing the Card Game 114
   Installing the Card 115
   Installing ISA Cards 117

Chapter 7
Running the Cables   **121**

Running Cables Within a Room 121

Running Cables Between Rooms 121

    Running Cables Between Adjacent Rooms 122

    Running Cables Between Nonadjacent Rooms 122

Using Twisted-Pair Cables 123

    Making the Grade 123

    Hubless Networking 124

    Locating the Hub 124

    Making Your Own Network Cables 126

Using Thin Ethernet Coaxial Cable 127

    Making Your Own Coaxial Cable 130

    Good Cabling Equals Good Networking 130

Accessorizing Your Installation 131

Expanding Your Network 132

Alternatives to Hubs 135

The Bottom Line 137

Part 3
Setting Up the Software

Chapter 8
Installing the Software   **141**

Installing Network Drivers 141

    Loading Drivers Automatically 142

    Installing Drivers Manually 143

    Installing Drivers for Non–Plug-and-Play NICs 145

    Checking Hardware Conflicts 147

Configuring Windows for Networking 148

    Adding the Network Client 150

    Installing Protocols 152

    Selecting Network Services 155

    Identifying Your Computer on the Network 156

    Configuring TCP/IP 158

Welcome to the Neighborhood! 163

    Accessing the Network in Windows 95 and Windows 98 163

    Accessing the Network in Windows Me 165

    Accessing the Network in Windows 2000 165

Troubleshooting 166

    Exploring the Network Neighborhood 166

    Checking Network Settings 166

    Diagnosing Hardware Conflicts 167

Chapter 9
Creating Profiles   169

What's in a Profile? 169

Turning on Profiles 170

Adding Users 172

    Adding Users When You Log On 172

    Adding Users Through Control Panel 173

    Changing User Settings 175

Logging On as a Different User 175

    The Microsoft Family Logon 176

    Locating Your Folders 177

Changing Passwords 178

    Surviving Password Forgetfulness 178

    Deleting All Profiles 179

Windows 2000 Profiles 182

Chapter 10
Learning to Share   187

Turning On File Sharing 187

Sharing and Accessing Network Resources 189

    Sharing Drives 190

    Sharing Folders 192

    Accessing Shared Disks and Folders 193

    Making Sharing Easier 200

    Working with Remote Files 204

Sharing with Windows 2000 215
  Turning On File Sharing 215
  Sharing Drives 216
  Sharing Folders 218
Sharing Programs 219
  What Can Be Shared? 219
  Running a Program Remotely 220
  Sharing a Data File 220
Backing Up Important Files 222
  Using Removable Disks 223
  Storing Files Remotely 224
  Using Microsoft Backup 224
Summary 228

Part 4

Running the Network

Chapter 11
Printing Across the Network

231

Sharing Printers 232
  Let the Printer Beware! 232
  Setting Up Printer Sharing 233
  Installing a Printer 234
  Handling Problem Printers 236
  Sharing a Printer 237
  Separating Print Jobs 238
  Sharing Printers in Windows 2000 240
  Accessing a Shared Printer 241
  Selecting a Different Printer on the Network 243
Connecting Printers Directly to the Network 244
  Setting Up a Pocket Print Server 245
  Setting Up an External Print Server 247

Chapter 12
Communicating Over the Network 251

Sending and Receiving Pop-up Messages 251
    Starting WinPopup 252
    Installing WinPopup 254
    Using WinPopup 254
Creating Your Own Post Office 258
    Mail Servers and E-Mail Clients 258
    Using Microsoft Mail Postoffice 260
    Installing Microsoft Mail Postoffice 260
    Sending and Receiving E-Mail 267
Communicating Using Outlook 271
    Selecting the Mail Service 272
    Working with Profiles 273
    Using the Outlook Address Book 275
Using a Shareware Mail Server 282

Chapter 13
Going Online Through the Network 291

Internet Sharing Alternatives 293
    Getting Ready to Share a Modem 295
    Making Sure TCP/IP Is Installed in Consumer Windows 295
    Making Sure TCP/IP Is Installed in Windows 2000 297
Using Modem-Sharing Software 297
    Installing Windows Internet Connection Sharing 298
    Setting Up the Client Computers 303
    Running the Internet Connection Setup Wizard 304
    Internet Connection Sharing with Windows 2000 308
    Other Software Solutions for Internet Connection Sharing 309
Using Internet Sharing Hardware 311
    Sharing Broadband Internet 312
Internet Security 318
    Turning Off Internet File Sharing 319
    Creating a Firewall 319

Chapter 14
Playing Games   **323**

Solo vs. Network Games 323
- Preparing for Network Play 324
- Selecting Games for Network Play 324
- Installing Games for Network Play 326

Playing Games on the Network 326
- Hearts 327
- Flight Simulator 2000 330
- Watching Out for Pitfalls 333

Part 5

Extending the Network

Chapter 15
Setting Up a Web   **337**

Creating a Web Site with Personal Web Server 340
- Installing Personal Web Server 341
- Using Personal Web Manager 342
- Creating Your Home Page 344
- Accessing Your Home Page 348
- Using Your Guest Book and Drop Box 349
- Publishing Documents on Your Site 352
- Creating a Web Site with Windows 2000 355

Creating Web Pages with Microsoft Word 356
- Using the Web Page Wizard 357
- Now It's Your Turn 361
- Working with Web Pages 363

Chapter 16
Networking PCs and Macs   **373**

Planning for Networking 373
DAVE: A Mac-Based Solution 376
- Configuring TCP/IP on the Mac 376
- Installing DAVE 379

Accessing the Mac from a PC 383

Accessing the PC from a Mac 384

Communicating on the Network 388

Sharing a Printer 389

A Windows-Based Solution 390

Preparing Your Macintosh 390

Using PC MACLAN in Windows 394

The PC MACLAN Print Server 401

Sharing Files as a Web Server 403

Sharing a Windows Printer 405

Sharing an Internet Connection 409

Windows Internet Connection Sharing 409

Using a Proxy Server 410

The Best of Both Worlds 413

Chapter 17
Networking for Road Warriors   **415**

Packing for the Road 416

Dialing In to Your ISP 418

Creating an Additional Dial-Up Networking Connection 420

Connecting to Your Home Network 423

Installing Dial-Up Server 423

Installing the Dial-Up Server Software
in Consumer Windows 425

Installing the Dial-Up Server Software in Windows 2000 427

Preparing Your Consumer Windows Laptop 428

Preparing Your Windows 2000 Laptop 431

Accessing a Home Computer Remotely 432

Keeping in Touch with Family 432

Starting a Meeting 436

NetMeeting on a Network 437

Using the Microsoft Internet Directory 438

Chatting in NetMeeting 439

Using the Whiteboard 440

Working Together on Programs 444

Sending and Receiving Files 445

Controlling a Home Computer Remotely 446

Chapter 18
Your Future Home Network 449

Controlling Your Wired Home 449

Getting Wired for the Future 453

Wiring for High-Speed Internet Access .456

    ISDN 457

    Satellite Internet Access 458

    DSL 459

    Cable Modems 459

The Everyday Web 460

Convergence Appliances: Devices of the Future 461

Index 463

Acknowledgments

Many people deserve my thanks and appreciation for making this book a reality. My thanks to Sally Stickney who served as project editor, coordinating everyone's efforts and keeping the entire process on track, and to Sue McClung, of nSight, who served as project manager.

I also want to thank the technical editing team of Don Lesser, Mannie White, Doug Slaughter, Eric Brewer, and Tim Upton, and copyeditor Chrisa Hotchkiss, for checking and rechecking this book for accuracy. Because of them, you can be sure that every step and instruction does exactly what it's supposed to do.

Thanks also to Joel Panchot at Microsoft, who redesigned the graphics for the book; Joanna Zito, the production specialist who laid out the text and graphics on the pages; proofreader Jan Cocker; and editorial assistants Rebecca Merz and Elina Pellebon.

My thanks also to Christey Bahn, acquisitions editor, to Claudette Moore, my agent, and to Laura Sackerman, managing editor.

Thanks also to James Mustarde at Allied Telesyn for use of the excellent AT-FS716E 16-port Ethernet switch, Intel Corporation for use of their AnyPoint Phoneline Home Network, and to WatchGuard, Netopia, and ZyXEL for their broadband Internet routers.

Finally, my thanks, love, and devotion to Barbara, the woman I am blessed to call my wife and best friend. We had our first date more than 37 years ago, walked down the aisle in marriage three years later, and have never ended the honeymoon.

Introduction

Try to imagine a future in which you can share files, printers, a telephone line, and a modem from every room of your home. Whether you're at home or somewhere around the world, you can see and talk to other members of your family on a video display without getting out of your chair or making an expensive phone call. You can play games with your family and help with homework even when you're away on business. But this scenario really isn't the future. It's the present, and these technological advances are made possible by something called computer networking.

Connecting your home computers on a network is neither difficult nor expensive. Anyone can do it at little cost. In fact, you can get some of the benefits of setting up a network just by purchasing a single cable that costs less than $20. You can get almost all the benefits of networking for under $100. And if you have Microsoft Windows, you already have the necessary software, and the networking capability is *free*. (What a nice word!)

In the old days—maybe as far back as 10 years ago—networking was indeed expensive and difficult. You had to know a lot and spend a good deal of money to set up a network. But that was then. Today, if you hear someone say that setting up a network is too complicated, point out that it's the new millennium and things have changed.

In this book, you'll learn all about connecting your home computers on a network, from simple file-sharing solutions involving a single cable to more advanced systems that hook up your entire home. You'll learn about networks that run with cables and without wires, and you'll learn how to harness the free networking capabilities of Windows. You'll be able to choose the networking solution that's best suited to your own home and needs, even if you have both Windows and Apple Macintosh computers that you'd like to connect on a network.

Windows itself comes in various flavors. Several versions of Windows are designed for home and small-office computing, and these versions are classified as Consumer Windows. These include Microsoft Windows 95, Microsoft Windows 98, and Microsoft Windows Millennium Edition (Me). I'll refer to Consumer Windows in this book whenever a feature or technique is common to all those versions of Windows. When I discuss a feature that's applicable to specific versions of Windows but not all Consumer Windows programs, the specific versions will be mentioned in the text.

Other versions of Windows are designed for business computing. These include Microsoft Windows 2000 and its older relatives, Microsoft Windows NT Server and Microsoft Windows NT Workstation. Windows 2000 comes in a couple of versions itself—Windows 2000 Professional and Windows 2000 Server. Windows 2000 Server, Windows NT Server, and Windows NT Workstation are aimed at medium and large corporate networks and they're beyond the scope of this book. Windows 2000 Professional, however, can be used as a desktop operating system in the home as well as business, so I'll discuss its use in home networking in this book. When you see a reference to Windows 2000 in this book, it means Windows 2000 Professional.

Chapter 1 shows you why it pays to connect your home computers on a network, and it describes the main benefits of networking, such as sharing printers and files, sending and receiving e-mail, and playing family games. In Chapter 2, you'll discover some quick and inexpensive ways to share printers and files even without a network. (This is where the $20 cable comes in.)

In Chapter 3, you'll find out about the different types of networks and the different ways that you can connect your computers: with and without cables. With this information, you'll be able to start making some initial decisions about your future home network.

Chapter 4 covers the most popular type of network, called *Ethernet*, in which computers are connected by cables. Then in Chapter 5, you'll learn about alternatives to Ethernet, including connecting computers using your existing telephone system, using the power lines that run through your home, using totally wireless radio transmission, and using special cables that connect computers by their universal serial bus (USB) ports.

Chapter 6 covers the selection and installation of an important piece of equipment called the *network interface card* (NIC). If you don't feel comfortable opening the case of your computer to install a new card, you'll find out about adapters that connect to the USB port, and how to choose a card and then have someone install it for you.

In Chapter 7, you'll see how to connect your computers with cable. Here, you'll learn more about the types of networking cable and how to run wire from room to room within your home. Chapter 8 guides you through the process of installing the software you need to get your network up and running.

Sharing a computer and its resources with other members of the family is the subject of Chapters 9, 10, and 11. In Chapter 9, you'll learn how to create and use profiles that let each family member maintain his or her own custom settings on the same computer. In Chapter 10, you'll find out how to share documents, graphics, programs, and other files .with the members of your family over the network—one of the best reasons to set up a network. You'll also learn how to back up files for safekeeping. Sharing printers is covered in detail in Chapter 11. Thanks to your network, you'll be able to use any printer in your home across the network, without having to move disks or printers from room to room.

Chapter 12 is all about family communications—using the network to send messages to one another. You'll learn how to send quick pop-up messages and how to create a home post office.

In Chapter 13, you'll discover the ultimate in sharing: how to set up your network so that every member of the family can surf the Internet at the same time through a single telephone line and modem, or by sharing a high-speed cable or digital subscriber line (DSL) connection.

In Chapter 14, the accent is on entertainment, showing you how to play computer games on your network that encourage communication and competition and can also be just great fun.

Chapter 15 contains all the information you need to set up your own family Web. Each family member can have his or her own Web home page by using software that comes free with Windows. Family members can then use a Web browser to surf the family Web just as if they were connected to the Internet.

In Chapter 16, you'll learn how to connect Windows and Apple Macintosh computers on one network so that you'll be able to share files, printers, and even an Internet account.

If you travel for business or pleasure, you'll certainly want to read Chapter 17. There, you'll learn how to stay in touch with the family and access your home computer and network while you're on the road.

Finally, in Chapter 18, you'll explore the exciting future of networking. You'll find out what's happening in home automation, learn about alternatives for high-speed Internet, and discover what the future might have in store for your home network.

Use this book as your personal guide to creating and using a family network. And have some fun while doing it! If you have any questions about setting up your network, you can contact me at alan@neibauer.net.

Part 1

Getting Started

Chapter 1
Why Set Up a Network?   **3**

Chapter 2
Getting Connected Without a Network   **21**

Chapter 3
Planning a Network   **57**

Chapter 1

Why Set Up a Network?

Families used to fight over which TV program to watch or who would get the car on Saturday night. Now they struggle over who gets to use the phone lines. Your kids want to chat with their friends online, you want to do some research, and your spouse wants to sell some concert tickets on an online auction site. Your family might also argue over the color printer or who gets to use the Zip drive to store a large file.

With television, the kids can watch one set in one room while you enjoy your favorite program on another set in a different room. But when you have more than one computer in the house, the solution isn't quite as simple because only one person at a time can get on the Internet or play that great new game on CD-ROM.

In this chapter, you'll learn how you can avoid these problems by *networking*—that is, connecting two or more computers to the same system. You'll also learn about other advantages of networking. For example, your family can play computer games together, you can help your children with their homework, and you can foster communication and a sense of family, even when family members are away from home.

See Also

In Chapter 18, you'll look into the future and see how networking will change the way you live and work.

Sharing an Internet Connection

If you have only one phone line and one Internet account, you know what it's like when several people in the house are competing for the same dial tone. Try to access the Internet while someone else is on the phone, and you won't be able to connect. Even if you have two phone lines, you still have a problem. Most Internet service providers (ISPs)—the companies through which you connect to the World Wide Web—let only one person per account log on at a time, regardless of the number of screen names or e-mail accounts you have. To add another user, you'd need to set up a second ISP account as well, and that would start to get expensive: two phone bills each month and two ISP charges. (See "The Buzz on ISPs" sidebar.)

Note

Sharing an Internet account is subject to the terms of the ISP agreement. You should check your member agreement before sharing an account.

When you connect your home computers to a network, everyone in the house can share a single phone line and a single ISP account. You can have everyone chatting online, browsing the Web, and even downloading software, all at the same time. Unfortunately, such sharing also has some drawbacks:

- Browsing and downloading might be a little slower when someone else is connected. However, at least you're online, and you don't have to wait all night for the phone to be free.

The Buzz on ISPs

To connect to the Web, you need an ISP, whose phone number your modem dials to go online. Countless providers exist; some of the largest are America Online (AOL), AT&T Worldnet, CompuServe, and MSN.

Although many types of ISPs exist, they generally fall into two categories: those that require special software and those that don't. Some ISPs don't require special software because they use a Microsoft Windows feature called *Dial-Up Networking*. This feature allows you to dial up to connect to a network—in this case, the Internet. Other ISPs make you use their own special software and their own dial-up services. Once you're connected through these ISPs, however, you have full access to the Internet through their menus. A few other services let you choose whether to connect by using Windows Dial-Up Networking or by using their software.

- Sharing an Internet connection might not work with some Internet providers. Some require their own special software and won't let you connect using the Windows Dial-Up Networking feature (explained in the sidebar "The Buzz on ISPs").

- You might need to buy special software or hardware to let you share a phone line and an Internet account. The good news, however, is that the software is inexpensive and might even be free if you have the latest version of Windows.

Note

Microsoft Windows 98, Second Edition, Microsoft Windows Millennium Edition (Me), and Microsoft Windows 2000 all have modem-sharing features built in. With these programs, you don't have to buy any additional software or hardware to share a phone line and an Internet account.

Don't Worry if the Line Is Busy

Nearly all new computers come with built-in modems, so you'll probably have a separate modem for each computer in your home. But to avoid dueling over a dial tone, you can connect your home computers in a network and designate a modem on one of them to be *shared*—that is, used by family members on other computers connected to the network. If one modem is faster than the others, such as an ultra-fast cable modem, it makes sense to share the fastest connection. You'll learn how to share modems and Internet accounts in Chapter 13, but for now, let's see how sharing a modem on a network can help.

Suppose your computer has the modem that's being shared. Here's what can happen. Another family member working on a computer connected to the network opens a Web browser or uses an e-mail program. The browser or e-mail program goes online using your modem. If your modem isn't connected to the Internet, it dials in and becomes connected. It's as though the other family member reached into your room and dialed the phone with your modem.

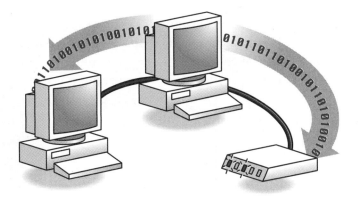

•

If you're already using the shared modem, other family members on the network just share the ride. They don't have to dial in because the connection to the phone company is already made. When they go online, they won't hear a phone dialing; they just connect.

What if your computer isn't turned on? No problem. Other family members can still go online using their own modems, as long as the line is free.

Getting Your Money's Worth from Your ISP

Because of the way sharing works, a second or third person connecting to the Internet doesn't even have to log on to the ISP. The person wouldn't have to enter a user name or password and wouldn't have to wait until a connection is made. The browser or e-mail program just slips in line with others that are already connected.

As far as the ISP is concerned, you're using only one account, so you pay for only one account. If your ISP offers unlimited use, you don't have to worry. But if your ISP gives you only so many hours for free and charges for additional time, sharing is an even better idea. If two people are on at the same time for one hour, their use counts only as one hour, not two.

Getting the Most from Broadband

If you connect to the Internet through a DSL (digital subscriber line) or cable modem, sharing the connection with your entire family is a tremendous money-saver.

Typically, DSL and cable Internet service cost more than dialup accounts—sometimes twice as much. The modems used to connect to a DSL or cable ISP don't come cheap. Most computers come with an analog modem already installed, and you can purchase 56-KB analog modems for less than $50 these days; DSL and cable modems, on the other hand, can cost several hundred dollars. In fact, you usually have to lease or purchase the DSL or cable modem from your ISP to make certain it's compatible with their system.

Even if you could buy a compatible DSL or cable modem at your local store, you couldn't just plug it into a phone line or cable jack to connect it. Your system has to be set up to communicate with your DSL or cable ISP, often through a home visit by an ISP technician. So even if you have high-speed Internet access, chances are that not every computer in the house will have a DSL or cable modem attached to it and will be able to use the high-speed connection. That's a pity, because both DSL and cable Internet accounts are so fast—from 5 to 40 times faster than a traditional modem—they are perfect for sharing among more than one user.

With a network, you can share that expensive DSL or cable modem and that costly DSL or cable Internet account. Everyone on the network can access the high-speed account at the same time, with little or no decrease in performance. You don't need to lease or purchase a separate modem for each computer, and you won't need to pay your ISP to set up each computer in the house.

DSL and cable modems connect to a computer through a network Ethernet port, so they are already network-savvy. The ISP technician has to configure the computer attached to the modem to communicate over something called an IP (Internet Protocol) address. If you have the ISP connect their modem directly to the network, you'll have to pay a monthly charge for each IP address that they set up. By connecting the modem to a network yourself, as you'll learn how to do in this book, you can save these extra charges and make the high-speed account available to everyone.

The Bottom Line

The easiest way to share a phone line and modem is to get a free or inexpensive program and install it on your computer. You'll learn how to get and use such programs in Chapter 13. With Windows 98, Second Edition, Windows Me, and Windows 2000, the software is built in.

Sharing Printers

Suppose you have a laser printer connected to your PC, but the kids have a color printer on theirs. If you weren't on a network and wanted to print in color, you'd have to take the following steps:

1. Put the file on a disk.
2. Take the disk to the kids' computer.
3. Print the document on their machine—assuming, that is, that their computer has the program needed to print.

The other option would be to do this:

1. Unplug the color printer from the kids' machine.

2. Carry the printer over to your computer.

3. Unplug your printer and plug in the kids' printer.

4. Install the necessary printer driver on your computer if it's the first time you've used the kids' printer.

5. Print the document.

6. Reverse the procedure to return the printer.

There must be a better way!

When you've set up a network, anyone on the network can connect to any printer, even if the printer is attached to another computer. You don't need to transfer files or printers from computer to computer. These are some of the advantages of using printers on a network:

- If you have only one printer, everyone on the network can use it.

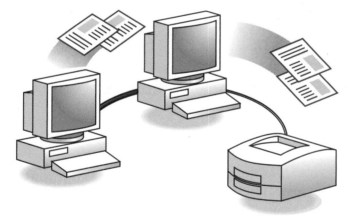

See Also

You'll learn how to share printers in Chapters 2 and 11.

• If you have more than one printer, you can just pick the one you want to use.

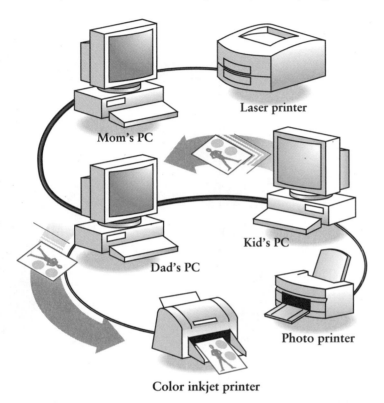

Color inkjet printer

When your computers are on a network, your kids can print their documents on your color printer just by following these simple steps:

1. Select Print from the File menu.

2. Choose the printer they want to use.

3. Click OK.

If your printer is in use, the document just waits in line until the printer is free.

Putting the Printer Online

Normally, a printer is connected to a computer through its printer port. By connecting the printer to the network, however, everyone can access the printer through the network.

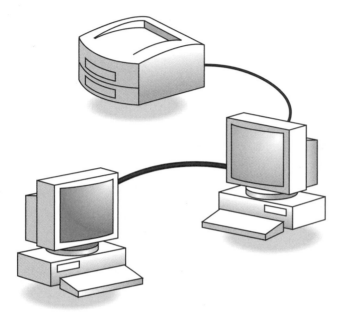

What's the benefit of connecting a printer directly to the network? As long as the printer is turned on, anyone on the network can use it. When a printer is attached to a computer, that computer must be on as well.

Connecting a printer to the network also saves you from the potential problems that can occur when you use your computer's printer port for more than one device. In addition to a printer, you might have an Iomega Zip drive, scanner, and other hardware connected to the printer port, which is also called the *parallel port*. Usually, everything works fine. But if you try to use two devices at the same time, you're asking for trouble. If you were to print a document while accessing your Zip drive, for example, your system might freeze. By connecting the printer directly to the network, you avoid this problem by not having to attach it to the parallel port.

The Bottom Line

Networking can save you the expense of buying another printer and the trouble of shuffling disks and printers between computers. You can use any printer that is attached to a computer on the network, getting the most from your investment.

Sharing Files and Folders

If you have more than one computer in the house, sooner or later, you'll need to share files between them. Your spouse might be using your computer to write a letter, for instance, when you'd like to work on a document that you've saved on your hard disk.

If you're not on a network, here's what you have to do before you can begin working:

1. Ask your spouse to stop working for a moment.

2. Copy the file to a floppy disk—assuming it fits on one.

3. Go to another computer in the house, and copy the file from the floppy disk.

Avoiding the Floppy Shuffle

When your computers are on a network, though, you can grant other network users permission to access files and folders located on your machine. If others have granted you access, you can get to files on their hard disks, too. You just access the files as though they were on your own system. You can copy or move a file from one system to another, and you can even delete a file. Not only do you avoid shuffling floppies, but you can also easily move files around that are too large to fit on a floppy.

Does this mean that all your personal files are available for everyone to read? Not at all. You can control who has access to your files and whether others can just read them or also change and delete them.

Making Files Easy to Find

Because files don't have to be moved from one machine to another, you can designate set locations for certain documents. For example, you can store all the household budget information on the computer in the family room, save investment information on the computer in the spare bedroom, and put miscellaneous files on the kids' machine.

When you need a certain type of document, you'll know exactly where to find it. And if you can't remember which computer the file is stored on, you can search for it on the network by using the handy Find command on the Start menu. (In Windows 2000, you use the Search command on the Start menu.)

Keeping Documents Current

"But it's no big deal to copy a file to a floppy," you might be thinking. Maybe not. But even if the inconvenience of copying the file doesn't bother you, you might end up with "version nightmare." Here's a scenario that might sound familiar.

You have your budget on the computer in the den and you want to work on it in the spare bedroom, so you copy it to a floppy and move it to the hard disk on the bedroom computer. You make some additions, a few changes, one or two deletions, and then save the budget on the bedroom computer's hard disk. As you're working, your spouse decides to make a few changes to the version of the file in the den. So now you have three versions of the budget: the one on the bedroom computer, the one on the floppy, and the one on the den computer. And of course none of them match.

When your computers are on a network, you can just access the computer in the den from any other computer in the house, making changes to the budget in its original location. If someone else tries to access the file while you're working on it, that person gets a message saying that the file is in use. Once you're done with the file, you can be sure that anyone who uses it after you will be working with the most recent version.

Working Together

Because networking allows you to share files, you can collaborate with other family members. After you make changes to the budget, for example, your spouse can review what you've done. You can take a look at your child's homework, suggest some improvements, and then let your child make the corrections before printing it out.

Most word processing programs help you collaborate by tracking revisions. *Revision marks* in the document show the text you think should be deleted, rather than actually deleting it. They can also indicate—with a color and formatting—text you've added. Figure 1-1 shows a document that's been edited with revision marks: changes are easy to see, and they can quickly be incorporated into the final document. You can also add a *comment*, a short note that doesn't appear on the screen but is indicated by a color or an abbreviation. To display the comment, you simply point to the color or the abbreviation, and the text appears in a small pop-up box.

A comment

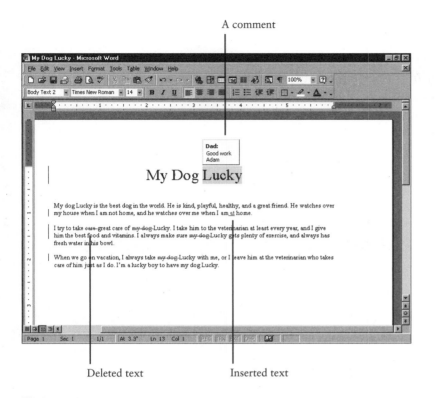

Deleted text   Inserted text

Figure 1-1.
Collaborating on a document on the network.

Safeguarding Important Documents

While you want only one *working* copy of a file, you can make *backup* copies on other machines. That way, if a hard disk goes berserk and the original file is corrupted or lost, you'll always have a safety net.

You should always back up important files. You can copy them to a Zip disk or, if they're small enough, to a floppy disk. If the original file gets damaged, all you have to do is retrieve the backup. When you're on a network, you can also back up files to another hard disk on the system, taking advantage of the larger disk drives found on newer computers. Moving a file from one networked computer to another is faster than making backups on a tape or a series of floppy disks. In addition, the backup version is available to everyone on the network.

The Bottom Line

When you set up a network, you save time and trouble by sharing files, while maintaining privacy and security. You can avoid multiple versions of the same file, locate files easily, and back up files for safekeeping. As your disk becomes full, you can avoid upgrading to a larger disk by storing your files on a computer that has extra room, a feature that saves you money and time.

See Also

You'll learn how to share documents in Chapter 10.

Sharing CD-ROMs and Removable Drives

CD-ROMs and removable drives, such as Zip drives and Superdisks, are a real boon to computer users. They store vast amounts of information, and they're fast, safe, and convenient. These days, most computers come with CD-ROM drives and many also come with removable disk drives.

Escaping the CD Shuffle

Many folks keep an encyclopedia or some other reference CD in their CD-ROM drive at all times. When they need to look up a word, find a map, or do some research, the information is quick and easy to access.

Most computer programs, such as the Windows program itself, are supplied on CDs to save space. (Windows, for example, would fill hundreds of floppy disks.) When you're working with a program or doing some magic on the computer, you might need to access the CD. Take Microsoft Office 2000, for example. When you install Office, just the main parts of the program are usually copied to your hard disk. When you want to use a feature that hasn't been installed, Office automatically looks for the CD so that it can access the necessary information. If the CD isn't in the drive, you then have to insert it. This would mean removing the encyclopedia or other CD from the drive and inserting the Office CD. When you finished installing the Office feature, you'd once again have to swap CDs.

With a network, you can access any CD on any computer on the network. So that means you can leave the CD for your encyclopedia or other program in the drive of one machine and access it from any other.

Adding Zip to Your Life

A Zip drive is one of the greatest add-ons you can get for your computer. The newest Zip disks, the storage media used in Zip drives, can store up to 250 MB of information—all on a cartridge small enough to fit in a shirt pocket!

Of course, Zip disks aren't the only high-capacity disks available. Superdisks, for example, are popular with iMac computer users. Because the iMac computer doesn't include a built-in floppy disk, many users purchase a Superdisk drive that plugs into the iMac's universal serial bus (USB) port and that can store 120 MB of data on one easy-to-carry disk. In addition, Iomega Clik! drives can store 40 MB per disk, and Jaz drives can store up to 2 GB of data on a removable cartridge.

You can also consider a rewriteable CD drive, called a CD-RW. A CD-RW lets you record information on a CD that can be used in almost any computer. You might not be able to directly record information on a CD-RW that's attached to another computer on the network, but you can easily transfer your files over the network so that they can be recorded on the CD. You can then use the CD on any computer that has a CD drive, which is far more common than Zip, Jaz, and Clik! drives, Superdisks, and other forms of removable media.

Removable disks are great for backups and for transferring files that are too large to fit on a floppy. They're also terrific for storing those files you don't need often but still want to have around. Anyone on the network can access a removable drive that's attached to one of the computers. They can access files from the drive and save files to it.

Some removable drives are built into the computer. When the drive is attached to the computer's parallel port, though, you have to be careful. No one can access the drive while that machine is printing.

You can also use removable drives that plug into your computer's USB port. These drives are the easiest to connect. They don't interfere with printers and other devices connected to the parallel port, and they can be plugged in without restarting the computer. You can also use USB devices on both PCs and iMac computers, so you can share the drive with computers even if they aren't connected to a network.

See Also

You'll learn how to share disks in Chapter 10.

The Bottom Line

You can save money by buying one removable drive and sharing it with other members of the family, and you can access files on a CD without swapping CDs in your own machine.

Communicating with Others

With everyone on a separate computer and, perhaps, connected to the Internet, you might think that there would be less personal communication in the family. Although that is a possibility, people have complained about that sort of problem since the invention of record players (now CD players, of course), television, and video games.

Networking might not bring the family closer together physically, but it does foster its own brand of communication.

Using an Electronic Intercom

By using a system known as instant messaging (IM), you can find out whether a friend across town—or around the world—is online and send a message that pops up on that person's screen. You can also send pop-up messages within the family network, as a sort of electronic intercom. The software for this comes with Consumer Windows (Microsoft Windows 95, Windows 98, and Windows Me), but not Windows 2000. You can download pop-up messaging software from the Internet that can be used with Windows 2000.

WinPopup

Messages Help

Message from Dad to Barbara
on 11/16/99 8:30:45PM

Are you doing your homework?

Current message: 1   Total number of messages: 1

If your computer is equipped with microphones and speakers, you can also speak to each other through the network, and if your computers are equipped with cameras, you can even see each other.

Sending Mail, Messages, and Reminders

But what if the people you want to send messages to aren't online? In the old days, you'd send them letters or leave messages on their answering machines. With networks, you can send or receive e-mail between networked computers by simply creating a Microsoft Post Office. (The software comes with Windows 95 and Windows 98, but not Windows Me or Windows 2000.) Just as you can send e-mail to someone over the Internet, you can send e-mail to another computer in your home so that your message appears in that computer's inbox.

Using software that you can download from the Internet, you can also leave electronic "sticky notes" on other peoples' computers, as long as their computers are turned on. The notes appear on their desktop.

Note

Some sources for sticky-note software include Netnote from Alshare (*http://www.alshare.com/*) and Stickynote from Phord Software (*http://www.phord.com/stickynote.html*).

```
Barbie --
Call Adam as soon as you get
in.
Dad

4/27/99 1:34 PM
```

Staying in Touch

It's never been easier for traveling family members to stay in touch. By using a laptop computer to dial in to the network at home, they can send and receive e-mail, transfer files, and even update their calendars. And once again, the software used to make the connection comes with Consumer Windows and Windows 2000.

The Bottom Line

Networking opens all sorts of communication channels that might otherwise be closed. You can send quick notes that appear directly on the screen of other computers, and you can create a more sophisticated post office for sending and receiving home e-mail—just like Internet e-mail. The family can share a calendar to keep track of important events, birthdays, and other family happenings. And when someone is on the road or away at school, the family connection can be maintained.

See Also

You'll learn how to communicate over the network in Chapter 12.

Playing Family Games

As the old saying goes, "The family that plays together stays together." And that's another strong case for networking. Play is a form of communication, and families can use computer games to enhance their quality time together. Kids love to play action games on their computers, while parents might enjoy more cerebral pastimes such as bridge, hearts, or chess.

Setting Up for Multiplayer Gaming

On a network, family members can go head-to-head in games of all sorts, many of them inexpensive or even free. Each member of your family can be sitting at a different computer but interacting in a virtual environment in which you can see each other, compete against each other, or even cooperate with each other against a common foe. You can all be racing on the same track or moving around some science fiction landscape trying to mutually solve a puzzle.

Games on the network can also keep score for you automatically, so there's no arguing over who's right or wrong, who shot first, or who's cheating. Many games will even remember the score, enabling you to pause and pick up later where you left off, or keep a running record for everyone to see.

The Bottom Line

Through interactive game playing, the entire family can share adventures without leaving the house. You'll draw the family closer together even when you're all playing in different rooms. You can compete individually or in teams, and you can have more than one game going if not everyone wants to play the same one.

See Also

You'll learn how to play games on the network in Chapter 14.

Bridging Macs and PCs

Why can't we all just learn to live together and share? Because there are PCs and there are Macintoshes. Like the legendary Hatfields and McCoys, these two types of computers just don't naturally get along. They use different operating systems and store information on disk in different ways. A Mac doesn't use Windows unless you add special hardware and software, and the programs you get with or purchase for your PC or Mac can't be run on the other machine.

Popping a floppy out of your Mac and into your PC, for example, doesn't mean you'll be able to use it in the PC. In fact, an entire new breed of Mac, the colorful iMac computer, doesn't even come with a floppy drive.

Note

Macintosh computers with floppy disks do have the capability to read and write to PC-formatted disks. But you can't read a Mac disk in a PC unless you get special software.

That doesn't mean that PCs and Macs can't live together in harmony. When your computers are connected on a network, your PCs and Macs can indeed talk to each other. You can share files and printers; you can even share an Internet account.

Although you can't use the same program with each type of computer, many programs come in two versions. You can get Office, for example, in both Windows and Mac versions. So if you write a document with Microsoft Word or a spreadsheet with Microsoft Excel on your PC, someone else in the house can read and edit the document or spreadsheet on his or her Mac.

See Also

In Chapter 16, you'll learn how to connect your PCs and Macs together on the network.

Making It Educational

By connecting your computers on a network, you'll also learn more about computers and software. You'll become familiar with the role networks play in society because all networks, large and small, enjoy the same benefits, but just on different levels. If you have children who are old enough, let them share in the process of setting up the network. They can help make decisions, run wires, even help install software. The experience will give them an edge in school and maybe even point them toward a career.

One way or another, connecting your home computers on a network is a time-saver, a money-saver, and just a smart move. In the following chapters, you'll learn how to design, install, and use a home network, but first, you'll learn how to accomplish some basic networking tasks without having to set up a network.

Chapter 2

Getting Connected Without a Network

Now that you're all hyped up about networking, here's a small surprise: sometimes you might not need a network at all. Perhaps you're interested in sharing a printer and occasionally transferring some files between computers, but you don't want to play games or send and receive e-mail among the family. Maybe you'd rather communicate in person, the old-fashioned way. While you'll be missing out on the many other benefits of using a network if you choose not to hook one up, you can still share printers and files, which is the subject of this chapter.

When Sharing a Printer Is Enough

If you're considering sharing a printer, take a look at the distance between the computers and the printer. If they're all located in the same room, sharing the printer will be a piece of cake. You won't need to purchase expensive devices that help you share printers and you won't need to run wires from room to room.

If the computers and printers are in different rooms, your options will be a bit trickier and more costly. Printer cable is thick and not that easy to fish through walls or hide along the baseboard. In addition, because a standard printer cable shouldn't be more than 15 feet long (any longer and the signals fade on their way to the printer), you'll need to buy extra hardware if the devices you're linking are far apart. *If the computer and printer are far apart, see "Extending Your Reach," later in this chapter.*

Using Printer Switches

When two computers and a printer are near each other, the easiest way to share the printer is with a printer switch. The least expensive type is a manual switch box with a knob that you turn by hand. As shown in Figure 2-1, you connect a cable from one computer to the A side of the switch, and a second cable from the other computer to the B side of the switch. You then connect a printer cable from the printer to the printer connection on the switch. The printer connection is usually labeled *common* because it's connected to the device shared by the two computers.

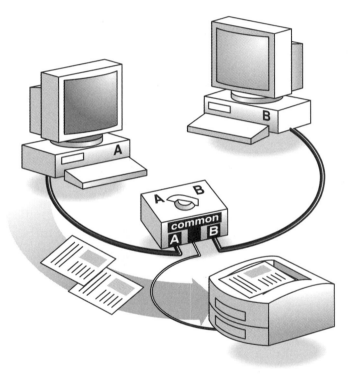

Figure 2-1.
You can connect two computers and a printer with a switch box.

When the knob is in the A position, the job you're printing flows from the A computer, through the box, and into the printer. When the knob is in the B position, the job flows from the B computer, through the switch, and into the printer. Some switch boxes can link three, four, or more computers to the same printer.

Manual switches have a few drawbacks, however. You must locate the switch so that users at both computers can reach it easily, preferably from their chairs. In addition, if either person forgets to turn the switch before trying to print a document, assumes the document has gone through to the printer, and then exits the word processor without saving the file, the document might be lost. Although all versions of Microsoft Windows will display a Printer error message, it might be too late to retrieve the document by then. Similarly, if you turn the switch while someone else is printing, you can cut off a print job in the middle. This unexpected interruption can cause another error message and generate some glares. Wait until the printer has stopped printing completely before turning the switch.

Some people used to believe that turning a manual switch while the printer was powered on could damage some printers. This might have been true in the early days of computers and printers, but it's no longer a concern with newer, more robust printers and switch boxes. Of course, if you worry about such problems, just shut off the printer before turning the switch, and then turn the printer back on.

Finally, as printers become more sophisticated and complex, you must make sure of the quality of the electrical signals going to them. Printer cables should be labeled "bidirectional" and "IEEE 1284" compliant. *Bidirectional* means that the cable is capable of carrying signals both to and from the printer, thus allowing the printer to keep the computer informed about its printing status. *IEEE 1284 compliant* means that the cable meets industry standards for quality. When you connect the cable, make sure that all connections are tight and that they can't slip off. Switch boxes not only extend the path that the signals must travel to get to the printer, but they also introduce additional connections that have to be checked. Make sure to check them regularly.

On the up side, a switch box for two computers and one printer (called a 2-to-1 switch) can cost less than $15. Use the existing printer cable to connect the switch box to the printer, and buy two additional cables (approximately $15 each) to run from the printer ports of the computers to the switch box. These cables have 25-pin male connectors at both ends, as shown here, to fit the female connectors at the back of the computer and at the switch. So for around $50, you can share a printer between two computers.

To link your computers to a printer via a switch box, see Figure 2-2 and follow these simple steps:

1. Make sure the computers and printer are turned off.

2. Disconnect the printer cable from the computer, and plug it into the "C" or "common" connection on the switch.

3. Connect either end of one of the new cables to the printer port on the back of one of the computers.

4. Connect the other end of the cable to the A connector on the back of the switch.

5. Connect one end of the other new cable to the printer port of the second computer.

6. Connect the other end of that cable to the B connector on the back of the switch.

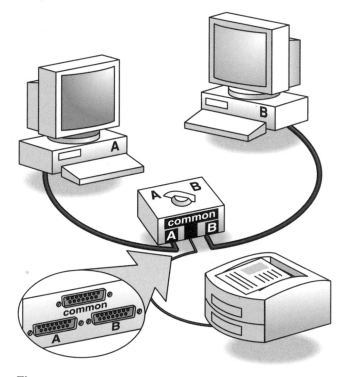

Figure 2-2.

Connecting two computers and one printer to a switch box.

You can use the same type of switch, by the way, to connect two printers (a laser printer and a color inkjet printer, for example) to one computer. Use the Add Printer Wizard in the Print dialog box (click Start, choose Settings, and then click Printers) to install both printers. Make sure to select the same printer port for both printers. Then hook up the switch box as shown in Figure 2-3. With the computer and printers turned off, connect the printers to the A and B connectors on the switch box and the computer to the C connector. It's that simple. Before you print a document, select the correct printer in the application's Print dialog box and turn the switch to that printer. There is usually a Name field with a drop-down list of printers in every application's Print dialog box. Select the list and choose the printer you want before clicking the Print button in the dialog box.

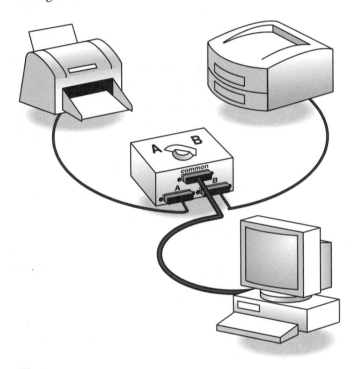

Figure 2-3.
A switch box can connect two printers to one computer.

Putting It on Automatic

Automatic switches hook up like manual switches, but there's no switch to turn. An auto-matic switch is like a traffic officer in the middle of the intersection, managing the flow of print jobs to the printer. The switch electronically watches the incoming cables for a document that needs to be printed. If the printer is busy and a document comes in from another computer, the switch holds up its hand and says, "Wait." When the printer is free, it says, "O.K., it's your turn," and sends the next print job through.

Costing between $50 and $100, automatic switches are more expensive than manual switches. Some models can handle just two computers and one printer; others can link several computers and several printers. The JetDirect auto switch, for example, made by Hewlett-Packard, can accommodate four computers sharing a single printer. To install it, you connect a cable from each computer to one of the four ports on the switch, and then connect the common port to the printer.

You can place the switch in manual or automatic mode. In manual mode, you have to press a button on the device to change printers. In automatic mode, the switch constantly scans the incoming lines for activity to the printer. It then sends the documents to the printer in the order they are received.

You can use the same switch to connect up to four different devices, such as a printer, a scanner, and a Zip drive, to one computer's printer port. In this configuration, you connect a device to each of the four ports on the switch, and then connect your computer to the common port on the switch.

When you use a switch to connect several devices to one computer, it's useful to be able to specify which device you want to use from within Windows. The JetDirect auto switch comes with the software shown here.

With this software, you can specify whether you're sharing one device among multiple computers or several devices on one computer. If you select One PC Sharing Multiple Devices, you can click Advanced and specify the device that is connected to each port.

Name and Select Devices   ✕

hp

Port	Device Name	Parallel Device
1. A	Zip Drive	Zip Drive ▼
2. B	HP LaserJet 110	HP LaserJet 1100 ▼
3. C	Canon BJC-240	Canon BJC-240 ▼
4. D	Scanner	Scanner ▼

OK

To use a device, select it by clicking the JetDirect icon on the Windows taskbar.

Note

When you add a Zip drive to the switch, you must connect it to port A so that Windows will be able to detect it properly.

We Need a Buffer Here

Not all automatic switches are created equal. Some of the inexpensive models lack a key feature that can prevent traffic tie-ups. Let's say that Tom sends a document to the printer first. While it's being transmitted and printed, you try to print a document from your computer. Because the printer is busy, your job is held up, waiting in line until the printer is free. Until Tom's job is printed and yours begins, you might not be able to exit the application you're using. You'll have the same trouble if you use a switch to connect several devices to one computer. While a job is being printed, you won't be able to access the Zip drive, for example, or scan a document using other devices connected to the switch.

The solution is a *buffer*. A buffer is simply a device that contains memory and is installed between the computer and the printer. Now, as Tom's job prints, your document is fed directly into the buffer's memory. As far as your computer is concerned, the document is off and printed, so you can go on to other work. When Tom's job is done, your document is printed from the buffer's memory.

Some automatic switches come with their own built-in buffers, or you can purchase separate buffer devices that connect between the switch and the printer.

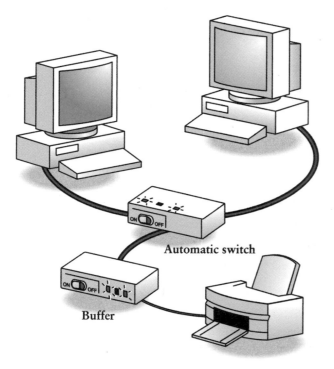

Automatic switch

Buffer

Extending Your Reach

No one wants to get up and walk into another room to flick a manual switch. Fortunately, there's a special type of automatic switch designed for use with computers that are far apart or in separate rooms. The most common model employs transmitters that are plugged into the printer port of each computer and a receiver that plugs into the printer's parallel port. The transmitters and receiver are connected with regular telephone cable. Such devices can link up to 30 computers, with a total distance between them of 2000 feet. The Max-A-Laser and Extended Systems ShareLink products are examples of these systems. Some of these systems also let you print from a computer's serial port to a parallel printer.

If you need to extend the distance between just a single computer and a printer, install a transmitter on the computer's printer port and connect a receiver to the printer or to one side of a switch, as shown in Figure 2-4. The printer signals can go a lot farther on the telephone cable used to connect the transmitter and receiver than they can on a regular printer cable. To add another computer to the configuration, just buy another transmitter.

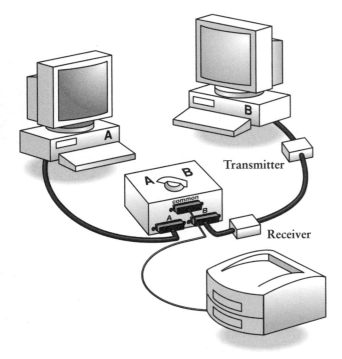

Figure 2-4.
Extending the distance to a switch.

Devices also exist that enhance the signals from your computer so that you can link it to a printer up to 50 feet away, using standard printer cable. Most of these devices plug into the computer's printer port to amplify the signal before it's transmitted down the printer cable.

Making a Direct Connection

One great benefit of networking is the capability it gives you to transfer files between two computers. But if you need to do this only occasionally and the two computers are close to each other, there's another way to hook up your computers and save some money in the process. Consumer Windows (Microsoft Windows 95, Microsoft Windows 98, and Microsoft Windows Millennium Edition) and Microsoft Windows 2000 let you connect two computers with one simple cable. That's why it's called a *direct cable connection*. With this system, you can transfer files between two non-networked computers or between a networked and a non-networked computer.

Note

You can inexpensively connect two computers together directly and get all the benefits of a network by using a special universal serial bus (USB) cable and software. See "USB Direct Cable Networks," in Chapter 5, on page 96.

One Simple Cable Is All It Takes

To set up a direct cable connection you need a cable, of course. Consumer Windows and Windows 2000 can use any of four types of cables:

- A null modem serial cable
- An Extended Capabilities Port (ECP) parallel cable
- A Universal Cable Module (UCM) parallel cable
- A Standard or Basic 4-bit parallel cable

Of these four options, the Extended Capabilities Port (ECP) parallel cable is probably your best bet. Information flows faster through parallel cables than through serial cables, and the ECP cable is cheaper and easier to find than the UCM cable. The Standard or Basic 4-bit parallel cable was popular in the past, but it's no longer easily available, and it's slower than the ECP cable anyway.

Cables used for a direct cable connection have the same type of connection on both ends because they're going into the same plug on both computers. If there's a cable connecting your parallel port to a switch box, you can try that cable, in a pinch, for a direct cable connection, but it probably won't work. The cable might look like the one you need, but it might not be able to handle the transfer of files.

When you buy the cable at the computer store, ask for "a parallel cable to use with a direct cable connection in Windows." You'll probably be given LapLink cables, named after the program that's a popular alternative to a direct cable connection.

Note

If the store doesn't have a cable for a direct cable connection and you have to transfer files right away, consider buying a file transfer program, such as LapLink, which comes with its own cable. We'll look at such options in "Another Way to Share Files and Printers," later in this chapter.

Installing the Free Software

Once you have the cable, the software you need is free and built into Consumer Windows and Windows 2000. Follow these steps to make sure that the software has been installed:

Note

These instructions are for Consumer Windows. To use direct cable connection with Microsoft Windows 2000 refer to "Using Direct Cable Connection with Windows 2000," later in this chapter.

1. Click Start on the Windows taskbar.

2. Point to Programs, and then point to Accessories on the Programs submenu.

3. In Windows 95, look for Direct Cable Connection on the Accessories menu. In Windows 98 and Windows Millennium Edition (Me), point to Communications on the Accessories submenu.

Do you see Direct Cable Connection on the menu that appears? If you do, skip ahead to the section "Choosing a Protocol." If you don't see Direct Cable Connection, you'll have to add it. You might need your Windows CD to do this, so make sure you know where it is, and then follow these steps:

1. Click Start, point to Settings, and then click Control Panel on the Settings submenu.

2. In Control Panel, double-click Add/Remove Programs.

3. Click the Windows Setup tab in the Add/Remove Programs dialog box.

4. On the Windows Setup tab, shown in Figure 2-5, click the word "Communications," but don't click the check box next to Communications or you'll remove the check mark.

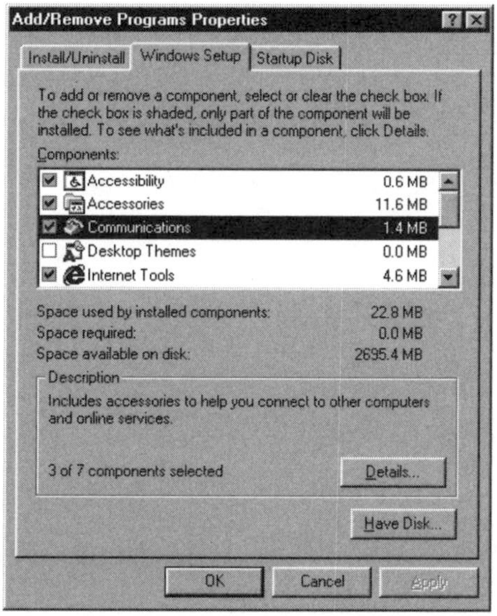

Figure 2-5.
Add Direct Cable Connection using the Add/Remove Programs Properties dialog box.

5. Click the Details button.

6. Click to select the check box next to Direct Cable Connection, as shown here.

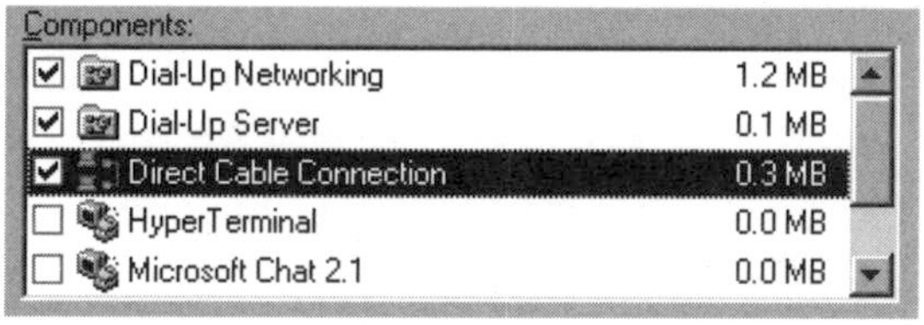

7. Click OK to close the Communications dialog box.

8. Click OK to close the Add/Remove Programs dialog box.

Here's where you might need your Windows CD. On some computers, the files that Windows needs to add more components are stored on the hard disk. If so, Direct Cable Connection will be installed and you're ready for the next stage. If the files aren't on your hard disk, you'll be asked to insert the Windows CD. Put the CD in the drive and click OK. The Direct Cable Connection feature will then be installed. You might be asked to restart your computer.

Choosing a Protocol

For two people to communicate, they must know the same language, or be awfully good at charades. The same goes for computers, but with computers, we call the shared language a *protocol*. The two computers use the same protocol to be able to understand what the other is saying.

A lot of different protocols exist, but for home networking, only three are important: Transmission Control Protocol/Internet Protocol (TCP/IP), Internetwork Packet Exchange/Sequenced Packet Exchange (IPX/SPX), and NetBIOS Enhanced User Interface (NetBEUI, pronounced net-buoy). IPX/SPX is the one you need for a direct cable connection, but it's best to make sure that all three protocols are installed in Windows, just in case you need them.

If you're running Consumer Windows, here's how to see whether the protocols are on your computer and how to install them if you need to.

1. Click Start, point to Settings, and then click Control Panel on the Settings submenu.

2. In Control Panel, double-click Network.

On the Configuration tab of the Network dialog box, shown in Figure 2-6, look for the big three—TCP/IP, IPX/SPX, and NetBEUI. If any of them aren't listed, you'll have to add them. Follow these steps to add a protocol:

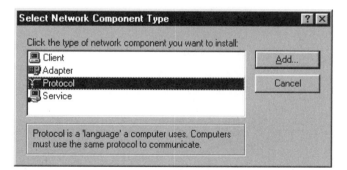

Figure 2-6.
The network components list shows the protocols that are installed.

1. In the Network dialog box, click Add to see this dialog box.

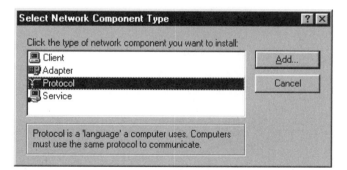

2. In the Select Network Component Type dialog box, click Protocol, and then click Add.

3. Click Microsoft in the list of manufacturers to see the options shown in Figure 2-7.

4. In the Network Protocols list, select the protocol you want to add, and then click OK.

5. Repeat steps 1 through 4 to add the other two protocols.

6. When you're done, click OK to close the Network dialog box. A message tells you that you must restart your computer for these new additions to work.

7. Click OK to restart the computer.

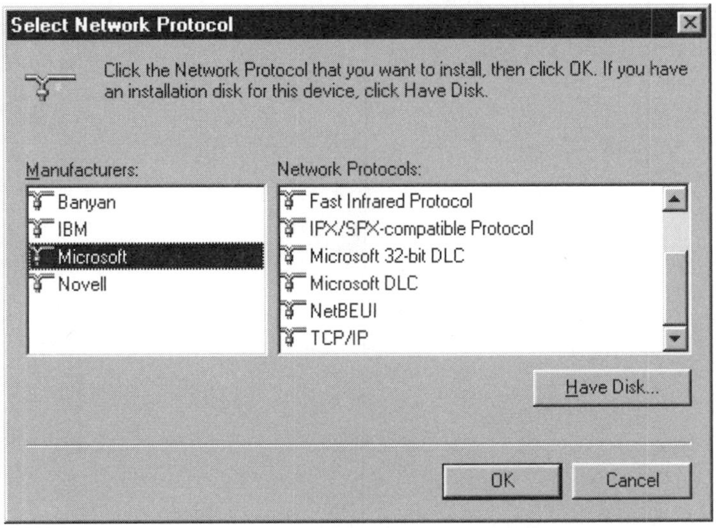

Select Network Protocol

Click the Network Protocol that you want to install, then click OK. If you have an installation disk for this device, click Have Disk.

Manufacturers: Network Protocols:

Banyan   Fast Infrared Protocol
IBM   IPX/SPX-compatible Protocol
Microsoft   Microsoft 32-bit DLC
Novell   Microsoft DLC
                        NetBEUI
                        TCP/IP

Have Disk...

OK   Cancel

Figure 2-7.
Select a protocol to install.

Setting Up a Direct Cable Connection

Now that the protocols you need are installed, you're ready to set up a direct cable connection. With the two computers turned off, plug in the connecting cable. If you're using a parallel cable, make sure the printer is off, remove the printer cable, and then plug the new cable into the printer port. If your cable is a serial cable, plug it into the computer's serial or COM port.

Now that the hardware is set up, you need to deal with the software end of things. First, you have to choose one computer to be the host and the other to be the client. The host machine contains the information you want to get to. The client is the computer you will use to access the information.

After you've chosen a host computer, you need to allow its files and folders to be shared. *Sharing* means that other users can view and work with them over a network and over the cable connection.

You can provide access to your entire hard drive or just to selected folders. Sharing your entire drive in one step makes it easy for other users to get to the files they need. If you're worried about security, you can limit another user's access to just reading and copying files but not changing or deleting them. If you want to keep another user from even seeing certain folders on your drive, it's possible to share only those folders you want to make available.

To allow access to the entire drive on the host, follow these steps:

1. Double-click My Computer on the desktop.

2. Right-click the C drive.

3. Click Sharing on the shortcut menu to open the Properties dialog box shown in Figure 2-8.

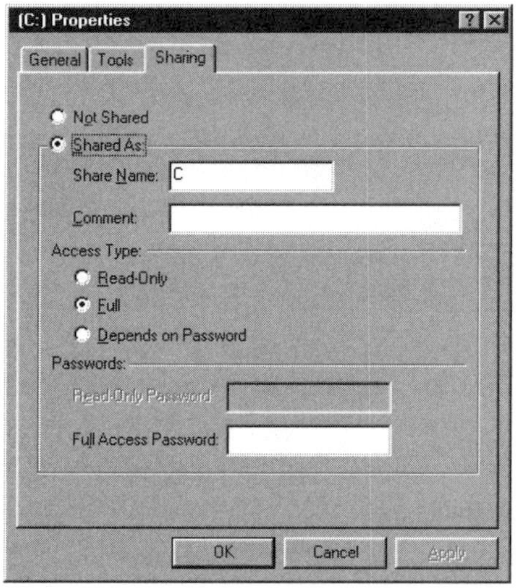

Figure 2-8.
You can change how drives and folders are shared on the Sharing tab of the Properties dialog box.

4. If Sharing doesn't appear on the Quick menu, you'll have to enable File Sharing. In Control Panel, select Network, and click the File And Print Sharing button. Select I Want To Be Able To Give Others Access To My Files, and click OK. Click OK to close the Network dialog box. You'll have to restart your computer to enable File Sharing.

5. On the Sharing tab of the Properties dialog box, click Shared As.

6. You can leave the Share Name as is, or replace it with another name that others connecting to your computer will see. You should use a descriptive name, such as "Dad's C Drive" to help others identify the computer and hard drive that is being shared.

7. In the Access Type section of the dialog box, choose the type of access you want to offer to others:

   - **Read-Only** means that the person on the guest computer can copy and look at information on the host but not delete or change the information. The person on the guest computer can't, for example, add a file to the host computer.

   - **Full** means that the person on the guest computer can do anything at all to the information on the host, including adding, deleting, or editing files.

   - **Depends On Password** determines the level of access according to the password the guest enters, either a read-only or a full access password.

8. Depending on the type of access you've chosen, enter a Read-Only password, a Full Access password, or both. If you don't want to require a password, you can leave these fields blank.

9. Click OK.

10. If you entered a password, a dialog box opens asking you to confirm it. Reenter the password, and then click OK.

   A small hand attached to the drive icon indicates that the drive is shared.

(C:)

Note

You can also choose to share only specific folders. Right-click a folder in My Computer, choose Sharing, and then set the folder's sharing properties in the Properties dialog box.

Now start the direct cable connection on the host computer by following these steps:

1. Click Start, point to Programs, and then point to Accessories on the Program submenu.

2. In Windows 95, click Direct Cable Connection. In Windows 98 and Windows Me, point to Communications and then click Direct Cable Connection on the Communications submenu.

   If this is the first time you're running a direct cable connection, you'll see the dialog box in Figure 2-9.

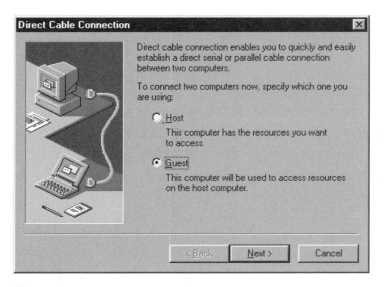

Figure 2-9.

Choose whether the computer you're using is a host or a guest.

3. Click Host and then click Next.

4. In the Direct Cable Connection dialog box, shown in Figure 2-10, select the port you're using, and then click Next.

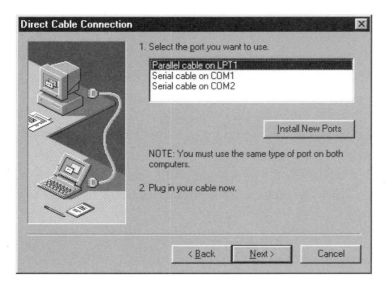

Figure 2-10.

Select the port you're using.

5. If you want to require the person using the guest computer to enter a password, select the check box labeled Use Password Protection, and then click Set Password. In the next dialog box, enter the password in both fields and click OK.

6. Click Finish.

   A message reports that the host computer is waiting for the guest computer to connect.

   Direct Cable Connection   _ □ ✕

   Status: Waiting to connect via Parallel cable on LPT1.   [Close]

   ---

7. Now follow the same procedure on the guest computer, but select Guest in the first dialog box rather than Host.

   When you click Finish, the machines connect. On both machines, you see messages that they're verifying the user name and password. Then the guest computer reports that it's looking for shared folders. Finally, the host computer shows a message, such as this one, to indicate that both computers are connected:

   Direct Cable Connection   _ □ ✕

   Status: Connected via Parallel cable on LPT1.   [Close]

The next time you start a direct cable connection on the host computer, you'll see the dialog box shown in Figure 2-11. Click Listen if you are the host and click Connect if you are the guest.

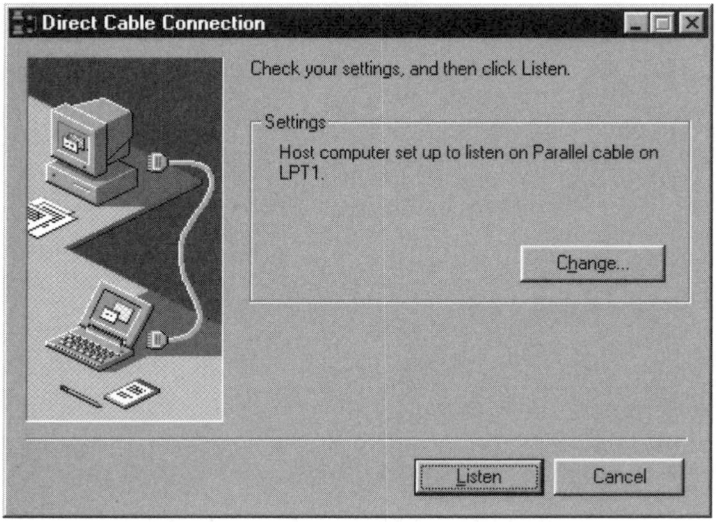

Figure 2-11.

Starting Direct Cable Connection a second time on the host computer.

Using a Direct Cable Connection

After you connect the host and guest computers, the guest computer displays a dialog box showing the shared resources on the host, as shown in Figure 2-12. The person using the guest computer can then open any shared folder to access its files and move or copy files between the two computers using the drag-and-drop method.

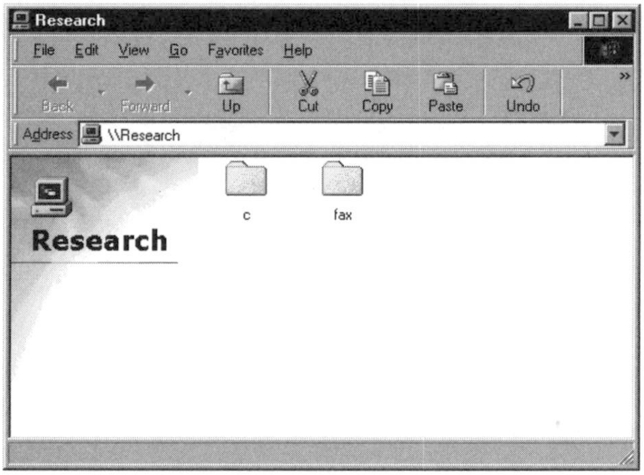

Figure 2-12.

The shared resources on the host computer are visible on the guest computer.

The host computer must leave the Direct Cable Connection dialog box open on the screen. Closing this dialog box stops the connection and causes the guest to receive a message that the connection has been closed.

Using Direct Cable Connection with Windows 2000

Setting up and running Direct Cable Connection between Windows 2000 computers is slightly different than for Consumer Windows. Direct connection is installed by default when you install Windows 2000. You do, however, have to set your computer to act as a host or guest, and you must make sure the proper protocols are installed.

First, see whether your computer is already set up as a guest or host. Remember, the host computer makes its resources available to the guest computer. The guest computer will be initiating the connection. To find out the status of your computer, take the following steps:

1. Double-click My Computer on your Windows desktop.
2. Click Network And Dial-up Connections.

If you see an icon for Direct Connection, as shown here, your computer is set up to act as the guest by connecting to another computer. If you see the icon for Incoming Connections, your computer is set up as the host.

If one or neither of the icons appears, you have to set up your computer before you make a direct connection. To set up your computer as a host from the Network and Dial-up Connections window, follow these steps:

1. Double-click Make New Connection to open the Network Connection Wizard.
2. Click Next to open the Network Connection Type box to see the options in Figure 2-13.

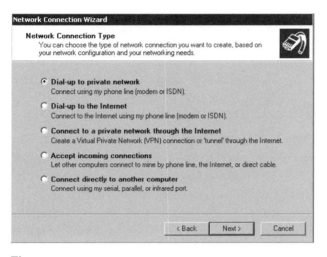

Figure 2-13.

Selecting a connection type in Windows 2000.

3. Click Connect directly to another computer.

4. Click Next to see the choices: Host or Guest.

5. Click Host and then click Next to see the Connection Device box with a drop-down list of these options:

   • Infrared Port (IRDA0-0)

   • Direct Parallel (LPT1)

   • Communications Port (COM2)

   • Communications Port (COM1)

An infrared port is normally found on laptop computers, but it might also be on or added to a desktop computer. The direct parallel port is the printer port on your computer, and the communications ports are the serial ports.

6. Select the port you want to use and then click Next to open the Allowed Users box, shown in Figure 2-14. The two types of users that automatically appear are Administrator and Guest. Select the check boxes for both options.

7. If you want to add the names of specific users, click Add. Enter the person's user name, full name, and password, and then click OK.

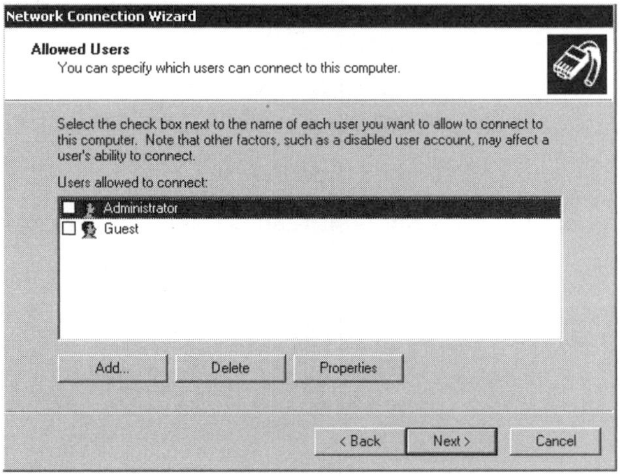

Figure 2-14.

Choosing who can allow direct connections.

8. Click Next to see that Incoming Connections has been set as the default name for the connection.

9. Click Finish.

The procedure to set up your computer as a guest is similar to the one used to designate your computer a host. Just follow these steps:

1. Double-click Make New Connection and click Next.

2. Select Connect directly to another computer and click Next.

3. Click Guest, and then click Next to see Connection Device options.

4. Select the port you want to use—it must match the port on the Host computer—and then click Next to open the Connection Availability box with the options For All Users and Only For Myself. Select the option that determines which users you want to be able to access your computer as a guest.

5. Click Next, and then click Finish.

Your computer will now be able to connect to the host computer.

Selecting the Protocol

The next step is to make sure that all the protocols are installed to enable communications between computers. To do this, follow these steps:

1. Right-click Incoming Connections and choose Properties.

2. Click the Networking tab. If the IPX/SPX option isn't shown, as seen here, continue with these steps.

> ☑ ⵛ NWLink IPX/SPX/NetBIOS Compatible Transport Protocol

3. Click Install to see a list of the network components you can add to your computer.

4. Click Protocol.

5. Click Add.

6. Click NWLink IPX/SPX/NetBios Compatible Transport Protocol.

7. Click OK, and then click Close.

8. Right-click Direct Connection and choose Properties. Click the Networking tab. If the IPX/SPX protocol isn't listed, repeat the previous steps to install it.

Turning on the Sharing Function

Before a guest can access files on a host computer, folders on the host must be made available for sharing. You can turn on the sharing function for the entire C drive or just for selected folders within the drive. For security and safety, it's best to turn on sharing only for those folders that you want other people to access.

To turn on sharing for a specific folder, follow these steps:

1. Using My Computer, open the disk drive that contains the folder you want to share.

2. Right-click the folder and select Sharing from the shortcut menu.

3. Click Share This Folder.

4. Click Permissions. In the Permissions box that appears, shown in Figure 2-15, you'll see the notation Everyone at the top and two columns at the bottom—Allow and Deny.

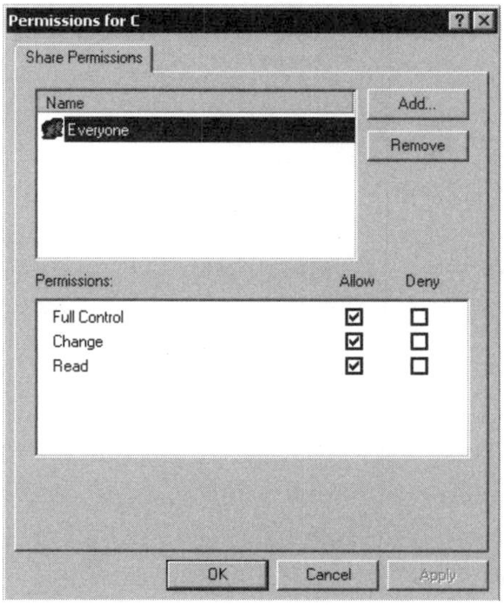

Figure 2-15.
Setting permissions for shared folders.

5. In the Allow column, select the type of permissions you want to grant users: Full Control, Change, or Read.

6. Click OK.

You can also turn on sharing for the entire disk drive so that all the folders within the drive are available for sharing. When you right-click the drive's icon and select Sharing, however, you might see that the drive is already being shared with the name C$. The dollar sign indicates that this is a special share that Windows 2000 requires. To also share the disk with guests over a direct cable, you have to create an additional new share name for the drive. To do so, click the New Share button. In the box that appears, enter a name for the shared drive and then click OK.

When you want to connect from the guest to the host, follow these steps:

1. Double-click My Computer.

2. Click Network And Dial-up Connections.

3. Double-click Direct Connection.

4. Enter your user name if it doesn't appear in the box.

5. Enter your password.

6. Click Connect. You'll see an icon on the taskbar that indicates a connection has been made.

To access the shared files on the host computer, click Start on the taskbar, and then click Run. In the box that appears, type \\ followed by the name of the computer that is serving as the host, as in \\john, and click OK. A window appears showing the shared drives and folders. You can now access the files in a folder by double-clicking the folder.

Network Paths

You probably know about the convention used to designate the location of a file, called its *path*. For example, your hard drive is C, the Windows folder is C:\Windows, and the System subfolder is C:\Windows\System.

The path to resources on a network or over a direct cable connection uses a different syntax called the Universal Naming Convention (UNC). Start the UNC with two backslashes (\\) followed by the name of the computer, as in \\Joe. To access a specific drive or folder on the remote computer, add the path to the UNC, as in \\Joe\C\Budget.

Other Software for Direct Connections

With a direct cable connection, one computer must act as the host and the other as the guest. Let's say, however, that you want to change which computer controls the flow of information. The only way to reverse the computers' roles is to break the connection between them and then reconnect.

If you want to switch the host and guest computers on the fly, you might want to consider one of the other programs designed to transfer files directly between two computers via a cable connection. Many of these programs are available free or at low cost over the Internet, so you can download them to your computer and try them out.

FastLynx, for example, can monitor more than one port for a connection with another machine also running FastLynx. With this product, you can connect two or more computers to yours at the same time. One might be connected to the parallel port, the other to the serial port.

Once installed and connected, FastLynx displays the contents of both machines on a split window with two panes, as shown in Figure 2-16. You can transfer files between machines simply by dragging them from one pane to the other.

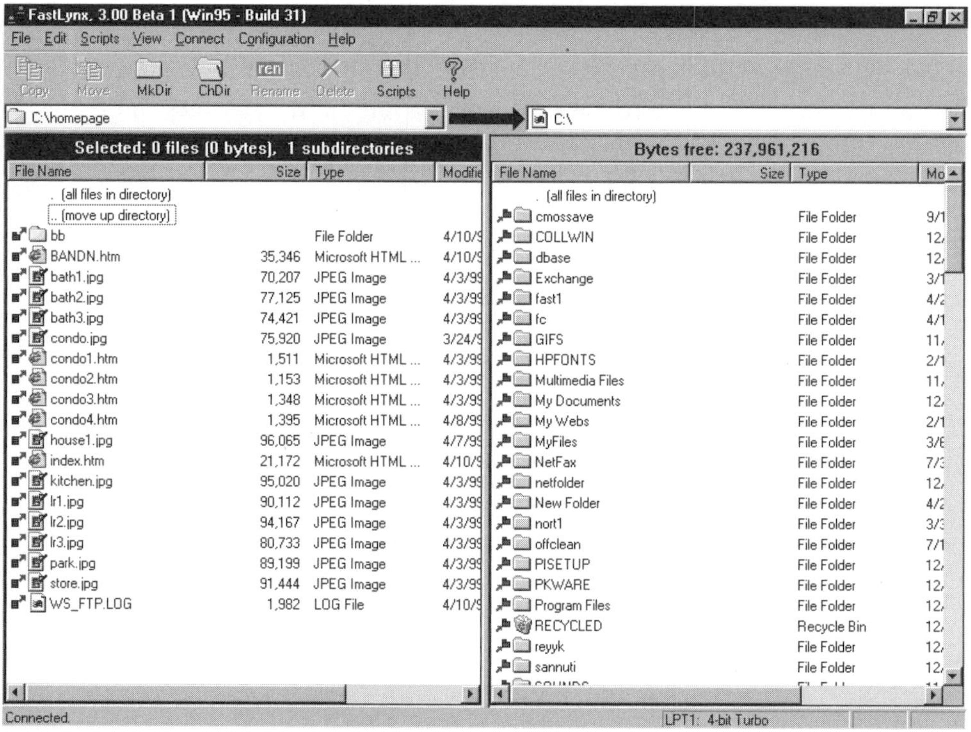

Figure 2-16.
Move and copy files in any direction with FastLynx.

FastLynx also comes in an MS-DOS-based version for older computers. The MS-DOS-based version lets you automatically switch the host and guest designations. A person on the guest computer, which FastLynx calls the *slave,* can press the Alt+S key combination to make his or her machine the host. There's also a mode that lets you copy disks between the floppy drives of both machines and to make full or partial backups of the hard drive of one machine to the drive of the other.

Note

You can get more information about FastLynx at *http://www.sewelld.com/.*

Another Way to Share Files and Printers

So far in this chapter, you've learned how to share printers and transfer files without a network. Here's yet another way to accomplish these tasks without a network.

An entire class of programs lets you remotely control one computer from another. You connect the computers through a serial, parallel, or USB cable, or through a telephone line and modem. Once the connection is made, you can transfer files and print documents on a printer linked to either computer. Some of these programs also let you control another computer remotely by connecting to it via the Internet.

See Also

We'll look at using remote control programs to share information in a network when you're away from home in "Controlling a Home Computer Remotely," in Chapter 17, on page 446.

Using remote control means that you can sit at your system and actually operate another computer you're connected to. Your keyboard and mouse control the other computer, and you see on your screen what appears on the other computer's screen.

Several programs provide these capabilities, including the following:

- Carbon Copy
- Close-Up
- CoSession Remote
- LapLink
- PCAnywhere
- Rapid Remote
- ReachOut
- Remote Desktop
- Remotely Possible
- Timbuktu

As an example of a remote control program, let's take a look at LapLink Professional, shown in Figure 2-17.

Note

LapLink and some of the other file transfer programs come complete with the appropriate cables for connecting computers.

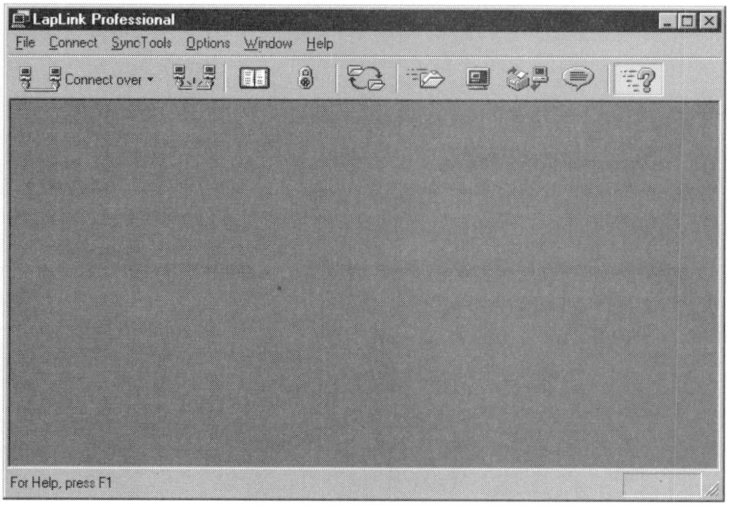

Figure 2-17.

LapLink Professional allows you to share files and printers remotely.

Your first task with LapLink, and similar programs, is to designate how the computers are to be connected. It's possible to enable more than one port so that you can connect to your computer from another computer in the home and dial in to your computer from the road with a laptop. In LapLink, you select Port Setup from the Options menu to open the Port Setup dialog box shown here.

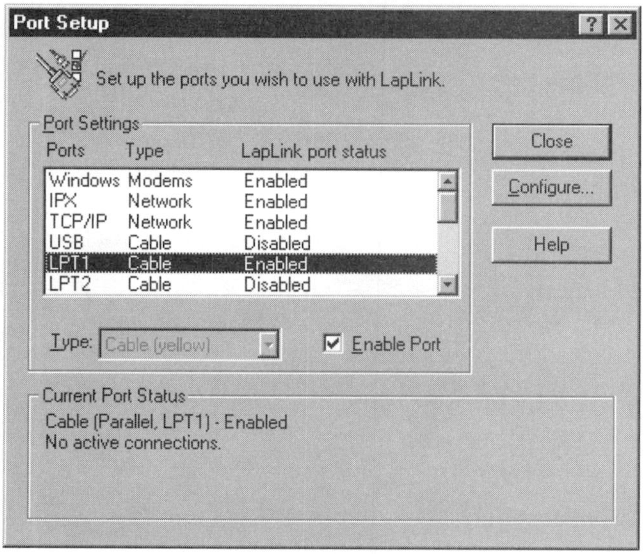

To enable the ports you want, select each one in the Port Settings list, and then select the Enable Port check box.

As with direct cable connection, you must have the proper cable to make the link work. In the Port Setup dialog box, the entry in the Type field shows the type of LapLink cable required. To connect the parallel (printer) ports of two computers, for example, use the yellow cable that comes with LapLink. If you later have problems connecting through the port, you can open the Port Setup dialog box again, choose the port, and click the Configure button to fine-tune how the port works.

By default, each time LapLink makes a connection between two computers, it lets you copy files between them. You can choose other services from the following list by selecting Connect Options from the LapLink Options menu and then clicking the Connect tab in the Options dialog box.

- **Remote Control** lets you control the other computer from yours.

- **Print Redirection** lets you print a document from your computer to the printer attached to the remote machine and from the remote machine to the printer attached to your computer.

- **Text Chat** lets you exchange messages with the person using the remote computer, just as you would in a chat room online. In fact, a chat window pops up on your screen automatically whenever the remote user sends a message, as shown in Figure 2-18.

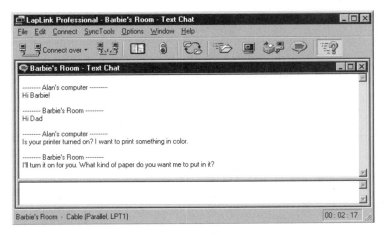

Figure 2-18.

LapLink's Text Chat feature lets you exchange typed messages between computers.

When you're ready to make the connection, start LapLink on both computers. The program automatically detects the connection you've established with the other computer and displays the disks, folders, and files of your computer and the remote computer side by side, as shown in Figure 2-19.

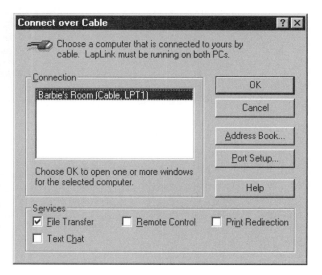

Figure 2-19.
LapLink displays the disks, folders, and files on both computers.

If LapLink is unable to detect the connection automatically, you might need to pull down the Connect menu and select Connect Over Cable. This opens the Connect Over Cable dialog box, in which you choose the remote computer to which you want to connect and the combination of services that you want available: File Transfer, Remote Control, Print Redirection, and Text Chat.

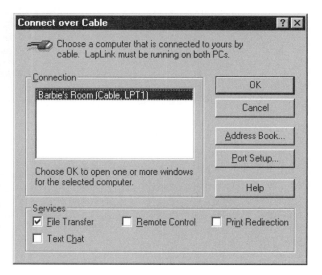

To transfer a file, open the folder on either computer containing the file as you would in Windows Explorer, and then drag the file to a folder on the other computer. In addition to moving and copying files, you can synchronize them using a feature called Xchange Agent. This feature keeps track of changes to files and makes sure that both computers have the most recent version by automatically copying that version to both computers.

Going Wireless with Infrared

Another way to transfer files among laptops is to connect them through their infrared ports. This process is easy because laptops can be connected without wires, and the software you need is built into Windows.

Follow these steps to make sure that infrared communication has been enabled on both computers:

1. Open Control Panel, and double-click the Infrared icon.

2. In the Infrared dialog box, click the Options tab, shown in Figure 2-20.

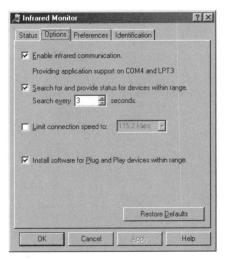

Figure 2-20.
Enabling infrared communication.

3. If the Enable Infrared Communication check box isn't selected, click it now.

4. Click OK.

5. Repeat the procedure on the other laptop to enable infrared communication.

When you're ready to transfer a file between two computers connected by infrared, follow these steps:

1. Position the computers so that their infrared ports are facing each other.

2. On the computer containing the file you want to transfer, double-click My Computer on the Windows desktop and double-click the Infrared Recipient icon, shown here.

Infrared
Recipient ...

Windows opens the Infrared Transfer dialog box, shown in Figure 2-21.

Figure 2-21.
Transferring files by infrared.

3. If more than one computer is shown in the box, click the one to which you want to send the file.

4. Click the Send Files button, select the file you want to send, and then click Open. The file will be transferred to the other computer and saved in a folder named My Received Files.

On the other computer, you can click Received Files in the Infrared Transfer dialog box to see which files have been sent to that computer by infrared.

In Windows 2000, you can also communicate over infrared using the Direct Connection feature. When you select the connection device when setting up the host and guest computers, select the Infrared Port (IRDA0-0) option.

Be My Buddy?

So far, we've talked about sharing files and printers between two computers. If you have an extra monitor, keyboard, and mouse, two people can use the same computer at once. A product named BuddyPC lets you connect two monitors, two keyboards, and two mice to one computer. Each user has his or her own Windows desktop and can run his or her own programs independently of the other.

To use the BuddyPC system, you have to install a special controller card in the computer and run a cable from the card to a small junction box. You then connect the second monitor, keyboard, and mouse to the junction box to give you a virtual computer. Some versions of the BuddyPC hardware let you run four or more virtual computers at once as long as you have a monitor, keyboard, and mouse for each.

You can get more information about BuddyPC at *http://www.buddypc.com/*.

What to Do with an Old CPU

As your computer hardware ages, you might find yourself purchasing another computer but using your existing monitor, keyboard, and mouse. You'll have the old computer left over, and it'll just sit there in the closet or basement collecting dust—unless you want to put it to good use.

Although the older computer probably won't stack up to the new one in terms of speed and resources, you might still want to use it occasionally—say, for downloading software from the Internet. That way, you can test the software for viruses before using it on your new machine. Or there could be some files or programs on your older machine that you don't want on your new computer but that you're not quite ready to delete.

By purchasing some inexpensive hardware, you can set up both your old and new computer to use the same keyboard, monitor, and mouse. You can't use both at the same time, but you can then decide which computer to use before turning on either one. If you have a removable disk drive, such as a Zip drive that plugs into the computer's parallel port or USB port, you can then use the drive to transfer files from one computer to the next.

To share a keyboard, monitor, and mouse, you need to purchase a keyboard, video, and mouse (KVM) switch and two sets of cables. You hook up the switch as shown in Figure 2-22. The switch is similar to one used to share a printer but with three connections for each computer.

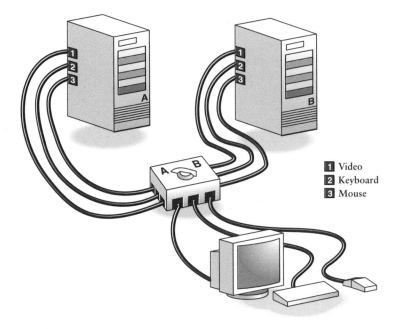

Figure 2-22.
Sharing a keyboard, monitor, and mouse between an old computer and a new one.

Your keyboard, monitor, and mouse plug into one set of connections on the switch. You then plug in a separate keyboard, monitor, and mouse extension cable between the switch and each of the computers. You then turn a switch or push a button on the front of the unit to determine which computer will be used.

The KVM switch and cables must match the type of hardware you have. Two types of connections exist for keyboards and mice: AT and PS/2. PS/2 uses small round connectors, and AT uses a large round connector for the keyboard and a D-shaped serial connection for the mouse. Although you can purchase adapters to convert one to the other, it's best to purchase the switch and cables that are ready to be connected.

The Bottom Line

In this chapter, you learned a number of ways to share files and printers, even when your computers aren't connected through a network. You can share printers with an inexpensive manual switch box or with an automatic switch. You can share files using the software built into Windows, and with some additional software and hardware, you can share both printers and files at the same time.

In the next chapter, you'll learn how to get started when you want to do more than just share a printer and transfer an occasional file. You'll learn about the types of networks you can set up and the hardware and software you'll need to connect your home computers in a network.

Chapter 3
Planning a Network

You know it's time to set up a network when just sharing a printer or transferring an occasional file doesn't cut it anymore. Networking doesn't have to be complex or expensive; you won't have to learn the history of networking or study arcane subjects such as network layers. But before you run down to the computer store and part with your hard-earned cash, you should take the time to make some basic decisions about your networking needs.

This chapter will help you decide on the type of network you want and how best to connect your computers. You'll learn the difference between a peer-to-peer network and a client/server network, and you'll find out how to decide which type of network connection will work best for your situation. But first, here's a little network preamble.

A Little Network Preamble

Before we look at ways to connect computers, you need to know about an important piece of hardware called a *network interface card*, or NIC, for short.

To connect to a network, a computer needs a NIC to handle the flow of information to and from the network. Some computers come with the NIC already built in, but most don't, so you'll have to order one when you buy your computer or add one afterward.

Most NICs fit inside a computer; others come on PC cards that plug into laptops. Also, there are some external devices that perform the same function as a NIC, but they connect to a computer's universal serial bus (USB), parallel, or serial port, as shown in Figure 3-1. As you'll learn later on, there are even special NICs for wireless networks and for networks that use the telephone and electrical lines in your home to transfer information between computers.

Network devices that plug into the USB port are perhaps the easiest to install because you don't need to open up your computer. To use your computer's USB port, you need to have Microsoft Windows 95 version 4.00.95B or any version of Microsoft Windows 98, Microsoft Windows Millennium Edition (Me), or Microsoft Windows 2000. To see which version of Windows 95 you have, right-click My Computer on the desktop, select Properties, and then look under System on the General tab of the System Properties dialog box that appears.

Caution

You can connect and disconnect many types of USB devices while your computer is turned on, but you should connect or disconnect a network USB device only when the computer is turned off. Inserting or removing a network USB device when the computer is turned on may cause your computer to stop responding and you'll need to restart it.

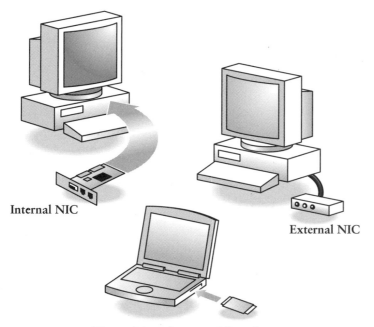

Internal NIC

External NIC

Network interface on a PC card

Figure 3-1.
Network interfaces can be internal, external, or on a PC card.

Because the type of NIC you'll need depends on how you want to connect your computers, read the rest of this chapter before you go out and buy one.

Deciding on Network Control

One of the first decisions you have to make when you're deciding how to set up your network is whether to give someone control of it. In one type of setup, called the *client/server network*, a single computer controls access to the network and serves as a central storage area for files and information. But before you decide to go this route, consider these points:

- Putting someone in charge of your network means spending more money on additional computer resources and on software that isn't free.

- Putting someone in charge dramatically increases the complexity of creating a network and the likelihood that you'll run into trouble.

Because of the potential downside to this option, consider the alternative carefully before choosing to let someone control your network.

We'll look at each of these options next, but Table 3-1 summarizes the features of peer-to-peer vs. client/server networks.

Table 3-1. Peer-to-Peer vs. Client/Server Networks

Peer-to-Peer Network	Client/Server Network
Can share files, printers, and modems	Can share files, printers, and modems
Anyone can connect to the network	Only authorized users can connect to the network
No central file storage	Central file storage
Each user sets own security	Central security
Easy setup and maintenance	More complicated setup and maintenance
Low cost	Moderate to high cost
Limited expansion	Unlimited expansion

Setting Up a Level Playing Field

When no single computer acts as the controller, you have a *peer-to-peer network*. This means that everyone on the network is equal—all are peers. Any computer on the network can communicate with any other computer on an equal basis. It also means that information flows directly between two computers without being controlled by any other, as shown in Figure 3-2.

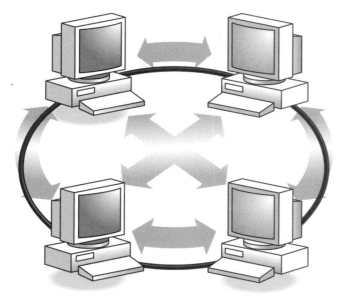

Figure 3-2.

Computers on a peer-to-peer network communicate with each other directly.

A peer-to-peer network doesn't eliminate all forms of control, however. Each person on the network can use a password to protect files and folders. You don't have to let people share your files or use your printer or modem. How other people can access your computer is entirely up to you. In fact, you can create a password that controls who can access your computer, which files they can access, and how they can use them.

See Also

For more information about using passwords, see "Accessing Resources with Passwords," in Chapter 10, on page 199.

For example, you can allow only certain folders to be shared. In fact, to protect critical Windows files, you always want to prevent the Windows folder from being shared. You can also grant *read-only rights* to a folder. This means that others on the network can look at a file in a shared folder on your computer and copy it to their computers, but they won't be able to change or delete it.

You can also grant full access, which means that everyone on the network can read, change, and delete files just as you can. Grant full access only to people you really trust and only to those folders that you want to be totally accessible.

A peer-to-peer network can also have an e-mail system. Your family will be able to send and receive e-mail messages within the network, just as they can on the Internet. But one person has to set up the e-mail system and control who has access to it.

In a peer-to-peer network, if any one computer is down—is turned off or not working—everyone else on the network can still communicate. In Figure 3-3, for example, even though two of the four networked computers are turned off, the other two computers can still share files and printers. The printers attached to computers that are off won't be available to others on the network, but you'll still be able to use the files and resources of those computers that are on.

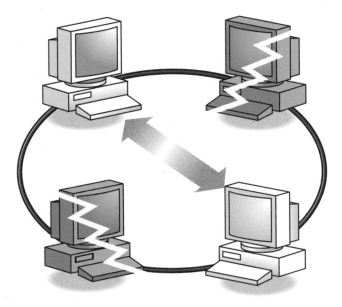

Figure 3-3.
Peer-to-peer networked computers can still communicate when other computers are turned off.

Of course, to use a printer connected to any computer on the network, the computer and printer must be turned on and working properly. Some computers, especially laptops, have a *suspend state*. After a certain period of inactivity, a computer in suspend state saves information about all open programs on its hard disk and turns off automatically. When you later turn the computer back on, the screen appears exactly as it was. If a computer on the network goes into suspend, its resources won't be available.

Other computers have an energy-saving feature that turns off only the display or the disk drive after a period of inactivity. The resources of such computers might also be unavailable when they go into energy-saving mode. Because so many different kinds of computers exist, you'll have to experiment to see how a particular computer reacts on your network.

A peer-to-peer network has no central storage location for everyone's files. If you're looking for a file that's not on your machine, you'll need to know where it is on the network or search all the computers on the network to locate the file. And if the computer that has the file is turned off, you're out of luck. You'll have to wait until it's back on to get to the file.

Still, the advantages of peer-to-peer networks—they're inexpensive and easy to set up, run, and maintain—clearly outweigh the disadvantages, particularly for home computers.

Putting Someone in Charge

As you've seen, when you want tighter control over a network, the solution is a client/ server network. The server is a single computer equipped with special software that supervises everything on the network. The clients are the computers that connect to the server. Communication among the clients must go through the server, as shown in Figure 3-4.

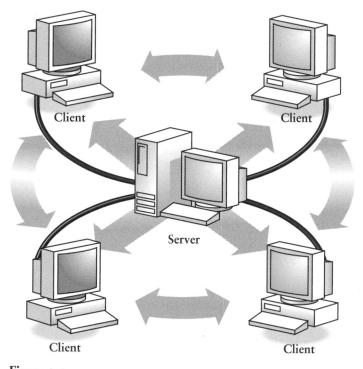

Figure 3-4.
Client computers connect through a server in a client/server network.

In most client/server networks in large offices, the server computer is usually dedicated to the task of being the server and isn't used as a regular workstation for everyday
jobs. The tasks the server has to do, and the information stored in it, are just too important to take a chance on. If the server is down, the network goes down and none of the
computers can communicate, as shown in Figure 3-5.

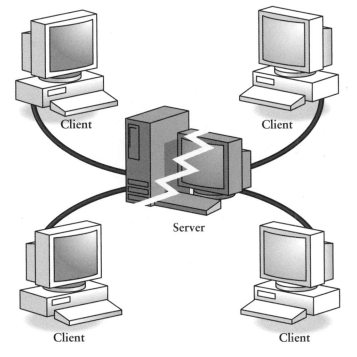

Figure 3-5.
When the server is down, the entire network goes down with it.

The server computer doesn't have to be dedicated, however, especially in a small
home office network. You can still use it as a workstation for ordinary tasks, but it's not
the best idea. Server software is much more complex than workstation software and
requires more effort and patience to keep it running. The server software also might not
include the software needed to run scanners and other devices. On the other hand,
operating a Consumer Windows (Microsoft Windows 95, Microsoft Windows 98, and
Microsoft Windows Millennium Edition) client computer on a client/server network is a
piece of cake. You pretty much just turn on the computer and start working.

A client/server network offers a number of advantages in addition to control. For example, the server can act as a central storage location that everyone on the network can reach. Because the server is always on, you can use it to store graphics, downloaded files from the Internet, and other documents that you want everyone to share. The files are always available and accessible to everyone.

You can also load and run applications from the server instead of installing them on every computer. This way, you can be sure that everyone on the network is using the same programs and can easily share files. When you want to update a program, from version 6 to version 7, for example, you need to install the update on only one machine.

And finally, the server can act as a central e-mail message center. As with an Internet newsgroup or bulletin board, you can leave messages on the server for everyone else on the network to see and respond to, as shown in Figure 3-6.

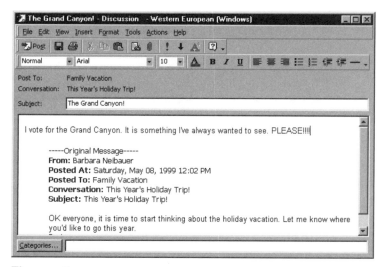

Figure 3-6.
You can also use the server computer as an e-mail message center.

Setting up a client/server network at home can be impractical, though. If you're using Consumer Windows, you can't create a server for a client/server network, although you can connect to one. In order to create a client/server network, you'll need to run either Windows NT 4.0 Server or Windows 2000 Server. Both of these programs are expensive, however, and neither is necessary for the average home network.

Note

You can set up Windows NT or Windows 2000 computers so they also have Consumer Windows, in a dual-boot configuration. You can then decide which system to use when you start your server. If you start in Consumer Windows, however, you lose the benefits of client/server computing because the server computer will be operating on a peer-to-peer basis.

A client/server network offers many advantages to the business user. But for the average home network, the two major disadvantages of the client/server setup—cost and complexity—usually outweigh the advantages. For this reason, we'll leave the client/server option to large businesses and concentrate in this book on peer-to-peer networks using Consumer Windows and Windows 2000 Professional. (For the sake of brevity, I will refer to Windows 2000 Professional simply as Windows 2000.)

Note

Although in this book I've distinguished between peer-to-peer and client/server networks, in real life, many networks are a blend of the two. You can have a client/server network set up so that if the server goes down, the other computers on the network can still communicate on a peer-to-peer basis.

Deciding on the Connection

Your next decision is how to connect the computers so that information can flow between them. Your choice depends on several factors:

- The number of computers
- The distance between the computers
- The speed you want
- How much work you want to do
- How much money you want to spend

Generally, there are five different types of network connections:

- Network cable
- Home phone line
- Wireless
- Home power line
- USB direct connection

We'll be looking at each type of network in detail in the next chapters. In the meantime, Table 3-2 summarizes the major differences among them.

Table 3-2. Comparing Network Connections

Network connection	The good	The bad	The ugly
Network cable	The fastest and most expandable type of network connection.	Requires running cable between computers.	Might require running cable through walls, ceilings, and floors; extra jacks and special hardware might also be needed.
Home phone line	Requires no cables; plugs into existing telephone wiring.	Requires a phone jack in rooms in which you want to connect to the network. Best used when there is less than 150 meters (about 500 feet) of phone line throughout the house.	Some home phone line systems are slower than network cable, although some approach the low end of Ethernet speed.
Home power line	Requires no cables; plugs into a wall outlet.	Slower than network cable.	Might be subject to electrical interference, which can break contact between network computers and result in data loss.
Wireless	Requires no cables; "broadcasts" network over the air.	Might be subject to interference from large electrical appliances; computers might have to be moved to improve performance.	Generally slower than network cable, although some approach the low end of Ethernet speed.
USB Direct Connection	Requires no internal cards to be installed; you plug a special cable into the USB ports of both computers.	Slower than network cable but faster than power line and many other types of connections.	Limited to a maximum of 5 meters between any two computers. Networks can be extended greater distances with additional hardware.

For most networks, network cable is the preferred choice because of its speed and dependability using what's called an *Ethernet* network. Ethernet is a set of specifications that determine how information is communicated across a network. Because the specifications are universally accepted, you can mix Ethernet hardware from any manufacturer in the same network. If you later need to purchase another NIC, for example, you don't have to purchase the same model that you're using on other computers. You can also use internal NICs on some computers, devices that connect to the USB ports on others, and a NIC on a PC card for a laptop.

The other types of networks are suitable when you don't want to, or can't, run cables between computers in various parts of the house. Although many telephone and wireless networks are slower than Ethernet, newer systems approach the low end of Ethernet speeds. For home networks, however, the network speed usually isn't critical. USB direct connection networks are suitable when the computers are in the same room or no further than an adjoining room.

The hardware you use with non-Ethernet alternatives, however, isn't compatible among manufacturers. If you purchase a telephone network kit from one company and need extra network cards or USB network adapters, you'll have to get them from the same company. That might be a problem if the company discontinues the product line or goes out of business—you might need to start over with new network equipment. Some non-Ethernet kits, however, do allow easy migration to an Ethernet network. For example, some adapters for telephone networks also contain Ethernet ports.

Note

High-speed DSL and cable modems require an Ethernet connection on your computer. So regardless of the type of hardware you choose for your network, you'll need an Ethernet connection as well on at least one computer to use the high-speed Internet.

As for price, although you can find starter kits of each type of network connection that include the hardware and software to network two computers for less than $100, the non-Ethernet alternatives are generally more expensive. The least expensive kits are those that contain Ethernet network cards that fit inside your computer, followed by internal telephone cards and internal wireless cards. Kits that contain adapters that plug into the USB port or that fit into the slot in a laptop computer can cost between $100 and $200 for each type of network connection. Wireless and telephone network adapters that operate at the low end of Ethernet speeds also cost between $100 and $200, but are dropping in price. Depending on your situation, the extra cost of a telephone or wireless solution might be compensated by the convenience of not having to run Ethernet wires through the house.

Understanding Networking Software

Once you decide on the type of network and connections you want, you'll need two basic types of software:

- Network drivers
- A network operating system

Network Drivers

Your NIC will come with a floppy disk or CD that contains *network drivers*, the special programs that Windows needs to access your specific NIC. The disk or CD might also include drivers for MS-DOS (the disk operating system that preceded Windows) and for other types of operating systems. Complete instructions for installing the drivers come with the interface card.

See Also

To learn more about installing drivers, see "Installing Network Drivers," in Chapter 8, on page 141.

An increasing number of NICs now adhere to the Universal Plug and Play (UPP) initiative. Instead of requiring different drivers for different types of NICs, computer manufacturers are working toward a universal standard. The goal is "one size fits all." When you install a new card in a machine running Consumer Windows or Windows 2000, the Windows system will recognize the card and load the universal drivers from the Windows CD. If the drivers aren't on the CD, you'll need the disk that came with your card.

Network Operating Systems

In addition to the network drivers, you'll also need a network operating system. This software contains the programs necessary to perform network tasks and to share files and printers. For home networks, the choice is easy. If you have Consumer Windows or Windows 2000 running, you have everything you need in Windows; you don't need to buy any other software. Consumer Windows (other than Windows 95) and Windows 2000 even have software that lets you share a modem over a network. You can also download free or inexpensive networking utilities over the Internet.

The Bottom Line

In home networking, the bottom line is clearly a peer-to-peer network using Windows. You'll get the network drivers you need with the NIC, and Windows supplies a network operating system and other networking programs for free.

To hook up your network, your best choice, in terms of speed and performance, is a wired Ethernet network. If you can't run cable from one computer to the other in your home, and want the speed of Ethernet, consider a home phone line or wireless network that operates at Ethernet speeds. If budget is a consideration, consider a slower home phone line or wireless network, or a power line carrier network. USB cable networks are great for connecting two computers in the same room, as long as both have USB ports.

In the next chapter, we'll look at wired Ethernet networks. Then we'll discuss the alternatives to Ethernet in Chapter 5.

Part 2

Installing the Hardware

Chapter 4
Ethernet Networks   73

Chapter 5
Non-Ethernet Networks   81

Chapter 6
Installing Network Cards   103

Chapter 7
Running the Cables   121

Chapter 4

Ethernet Networks

The most common type of network today uses network cabling to communicate information, and Ethernet is the most popular network of this kind. As long as the cables are connected, very little can interfere with the flow of information in an Ethernet network. In home Ethernet networks, information can travel through the cables at speeds of 10 million bits per second (Mbps) to 100 million bits per second, depending on the speed of the NIC and your cables.

These numbers might not mean too much to you unless you've waited online for a file to download. The fastest telephone modems can download files at about 53,000 bps if you have a great phone line. A file that takes 10 minutes to download from the Internet takes only a few seconds to transfer from computer to computer on an Ethernet network.

Gigabyte Ethernet

Gigabyte (1000 Mbps) speed networks are just emerging, but they are expensive. Gigabyte Ethernet requires special (and pricey) copper twisted-pair wire or fiberoptic cable. There is a type of gigabyte Ethernet that runs on coaxial cable, but only up to lengths of 25 meters.

The problem with gigabyte Ethernet is that many computers just can't keep up with the network, so you won't see the full benefit of gigabyte speeds unless you have very high-end computers.

The problem with cable is that you have to run it physically to each computer. This isn't a problem if the computers are in the same or adjacent rooms and you don't mind drilling a hole in the wall. But when your computers are spread throughout the house, running cable can be a problem, unless one of the following conditions applies to you:

- You're lucky enough to find ways to run the cable without having to pass through too many walls.

- You're building a new house.

Types of Cable

The two most common types of cable are twisted pair, also known as 10BaseT cable, and 10Base2 thin Ethernet coaxial cable. A network whose computers are connected with either of these types of cable is known as an *Ethernet network*.

Note

10BaseT is named for its original maximum speed of 10 Mbps on twisted-pair wire. 10Base2 is named because the maximum length of the coaxial cable is less than 200 meters.

Twisted-pair cable looks like telephone cable on steroids. It's a thick, round cable with connectors that look like pumped-up telephone connectors, as shown in Figure 4-1. Twisted-pair connectors, called RJ-45 connectors, and telephone connectors, called RJ-11 connectors, can't be used interchangeably.

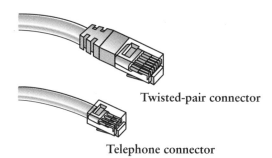

Twisted-pair connector

Telephone connector

Figure 4-1.
Network cable connectors resemble oversized phone connectors.

Twisted-pair cable comes in two types and several grades. The higher the grade, the better and more reliable the cable, but quality comes at a price.

See Also

For more about wire grades, see "Making the Grade," in Chapter 7, on page 123.

The two types of twisted-pair cables are unshielded twisted pair (UTP) and shielded twisted pair (STP). As shown in Figure 4-2, UTP cable consists of eight insulated wires, twisted together in pairs within an insulating sheath.

Figure 4-2.
Twisted-pair cable contains four pairs of insulated wires that are twisted together.

STP cable is similar to UTP but has a layer of woven copper and foil around the wires within the plastic sheath to shield them from extraneous electrical signals. STP cable is more expensive than UTP and is more difficult to work with because it is heavier and less flexible. The advantage of STP, however, is its resistance to *crosstalk*—when signals from one cable mix with signals in another cable running adjacent to it.

In most cases, when you wire a network with either type of twisted-pair cable, all the cables must converge at a device called a *hub,* as shown in Figure 4-3. The hub acts like a traffic intersection, where all roads come together and traffic can flow in any direction. This means you have to run all the network cables to a central location in the house, and the hub has to be turned on for any of the computers to communicate. As you'll learn in Chapter 6, there are several types of hubs, and you can use other devices called switches as the converging point of the network cables.

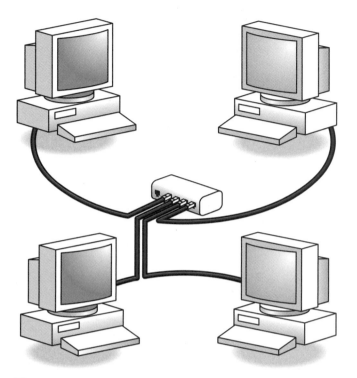

Figure 4-3.
In a network wired with twisted-pair cable, all the cables converge at a hub.

See Also

If you're networking only two computers, you don't need a hub. See "Hubless Networking," in Chapter 7, on page 124.

The 10Base2 thin Ethernet coaxial cable is an alternative to twisted-pair cable. It looks like the cable from your VCR or cable box, only a little thinner, which is why it's called thin Ethernet or just ThinNet. As shown in Figure 4-4, ThinNet is a round cable with a solid insulated wire at its core and a layer of braided metal under its external sheath. Although thinner than other coaxial cables, ThinNet is thicker than twisted-pair cable, so it's slightly more difficult to fish through walls and lay along baseboards.

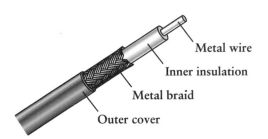
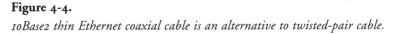

Metal wire

Inner insulation

Metal braid

Outer cover

Figure 4-4.
10Base2 thin Ethernet coaxial cable is an alternative to twisted-pair cable.

A coaxial cable network doesn't require a hub. As shown in Figure 4-5, you simply run the cable from one NIC to another. The absence of a central hub reduces the amount of cable you need to run from room to room and between floors. You can join two lengths of coaxial cable to make a longer cable, and two lengths of coaxial cable joined with a coupler are more reliable than two lengths of twisted-pair cable coupled together.

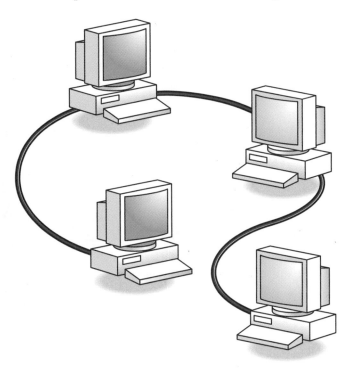

Figure 4-5.
Coaxial cable connects computers directly, without a hub.

Fiber Optics

Fiberoptic cable is growing in popularity for larger network installations and new homes. Fiberoptic cable consists of a thin glass wire through which light passes in pulses. The light pulses represent the digital information being carried over the network.

It has a low error rate and isn't susceptible to electromagnetic interference. The cable can transmit signals in the tens of gigabits per second and can handle several different gigabits of channels simultaneously, each channel on a different wavelength of light.

However, fiberoptic cable costs more than twisted pair or coaxial, and it's more difficult to install. While you shouldn't make any sharp bends when installing any type of cable, fiber optic cable is much less flexible than other types. If you need to install your own connector to the end of a fiberoptic cable, it must be attached with epoxy or by a heat process, although there are connectors that can be crimped on for emergency repairs.

As shown in Figure 4-6, fiberoptic cable contains five parts:

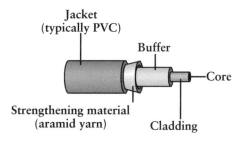

Figure 4-6.
Parts of a fiberoptic cable.

- The glass core that carries the light
- Glass cladding surrounding the core, which reflects the light back to the core so that it travels without loss of the signals
- A buffer layer that protects the core and cladding from damage
- A layer of material that strengthens the cable
- An outer jacket, such as PVC (polyvinyl chloride) plastic

Two fiberoptic cables connect the computer's NIC to the network hub, as shown in Figure 4-7. One carries information to the computer, the other to the hub for distribution to the network. For that reason, the cable is usually purchased with two fibers together in the same outer jacket.

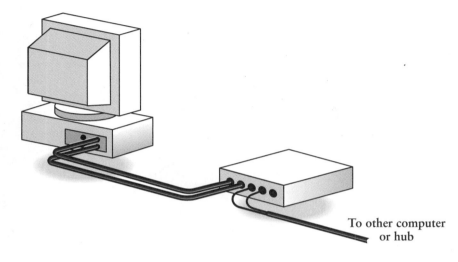

To other computer
or hub

Figure 4-7.
Connecting a fiberoptic cable.

Using some kind of cable—whether it should be twisted pair, coaxial, or fiber optic—is generally the preferred option as long as you can physically run wire between your computers. Wire is faster than the alternatives and can connect almost any distance in an office. But some environments are inhospitable to laying cable, so you may want to consider other options. In the next chapter, we'll take a look at the alternatives to a wired Ethernet network.

Note

You can mix twisted-pair, coaxial, and fiberoptic cables in the same network, but you'll need additional hardware. See "Expanding Your Network," in Chapter 7, on page 132.

Chapter 5

Non-Ethernet Networks

Ethernet has been the mainstay for small networks for many years. The inconvenience of running cables, however, is a major disadvantage if you're networking an existing home. The alternatives to Ethernet are ideal when you don't want to cut holes in walls and otherwise run Ethernet cable. These other options are perfect for renters, for example. These alternatives provide networks that run through the existing wires in your home, that run through the phone lines or power lines, or that directly connect through special universal serial bus (USB) cables. They also include completely wireless networks.

Because everything you'll learn in Chapter 8 about the software side of Ethernet networks also applies to non-Ethernet networks, this chapter focuses on the hardware you need to set up a non-Ethernet network rather than the software. You must install the appropriate network drivers, and add protocols and shared resources. All the network kits this chapter discusses include software that automates the setup and configuration process. The software installs the drivers needed to run the network and configures Microsoft Windows for the proper protocols. Most of the kits also include software for sharing your Internet connection with other family members on the network.

See Also

For more on sharing modems and Internet accounts, see Chapter 13, "Going Online Through the Network."

You can choose from many different non-Ethernet hardware combinations when you're setting up a network. With wireless and telephone networks, as with Ethernet networks, you can use an internal network interface card (NIC), a USB device, or a parallel port device. Your options are more limited with a power-line network. No USB power-line network kits are currently on the market, and you probably wouldn't want to connect an internal NIC directly to a power line anyway because it might directly expose your computer to power surges.

Setting Up a Phone-Line Network

Telephone networks operate on the principle that the phone lines running through your home can be shared. The technical term is *frequency-division multiplexing* (FDM), which means that the waves running through the phone line can be divided into separate frequencies, as shown in Figure 5-1.

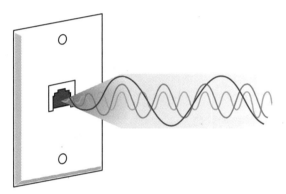

Figure 5-1.
Standard phone lines can carry three separate transmissions on different frequencies.

One frequency is used by voice and fax calls coming or going over the phone. Your home network uses a totally different frequency, so the network signals can travel through the phone line while you're using your phone to talk to someone, send a fax, or surf the Internet. You can't talk on the phone and surf the Internet at the same time, but that's true with any type of network if you have only one phone line.

A group of companies and agencies joined together in June 1998 to form the Home Phoneline Networking Alliance (HomePNA) to create standards for phone-line networks. They started with the tried and true Ethernet standard and modified it when necessary to fit into the phone-line hardware.

The Pros and Cons of Phone-Line Networks

Phone-line networks are convenient for two main reasons:

- You don't need to run any special cable.
- You can connect a computer to the network in any room that has a phone jack.

Most homes have phone jacks in the places where you'll want to put a computer anyway. After all, you'll want to use the phone to connect your computer to the Internet. The phone jack can then serve a dual purpose by also letting you connect computers on a network. If you do need another phone plug, the phone company can install it for you—for a charge, of course. You can also purchase adapters, such as the one shown here, to connect both a phone and a telephone NIC to the jack at the same time.

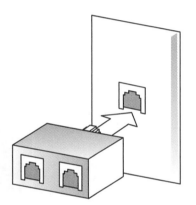

While the original telephone networks operated much more slowly than Ethernet, they cost about the same in the 1 Mbps to 2 Mbps range as Ethernet starter kits. The newer systems that communicate at 10 Mbps cost slightly more, but you can still network two computers for between $100 and $200.

If you have more than one computer in the same room, you can usually connect their NICs with phone cables directly, as shown in Figure 5-2.

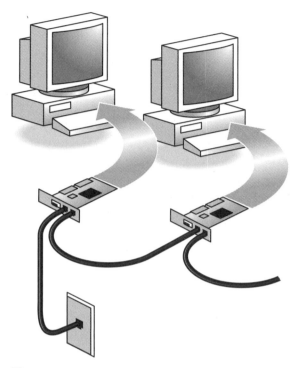

Figure 5-2.

You can link computers directly with HomePNA cards and regular telephone wire.

To connect a computer in a room without a phone jack, use a regular telephone extension wire to connect the computer to a networked machine in another room. Telephone wire is much easier to hide along baseboards than twisted-pair or coaxial cable.

Note

Some HomePNA network cards include a 10/100BaseT port in case you want to convert from a phone network to Ethernet. Connecting a cable to the port disables the NIC's phone network capabilities.

Choosing a Phone-Line System

Several companies sell phone-line network kits. The HomeLink Phoneline system from Linksys (*http://www.linksys.com*), for example, offers a choice of an internal NIC for a desktop computer, a PC card for a laptop, and an external USB model. All the adapters operate at 1 Mbps over the phone line, but they also include an Ethernet port just in case you want to change to an Ethernet network later by installing twisted-pair cables and a hub. The Ethernet port on the internal card operates at 10 Mbps, but the port on the laptop card and USB model can also run at 100 Mbps fast Ethernet speed.

Diamond Multimedia (*http://www.s3.com*) offers both a USB model that operates at 1 Mbps and an internal model that fits inside your computer and operates at 10 Mbps. The USB model includes software to let the device work with both PCs and Apple iMac computers, so you can use it to network both types of computers together. All the devices are compatible with each other.

As an example of a phone-line network, we'll look at the AnyPoint Home Network kit from Intel (*http://www.intel.com*).

Intel AnyPoint Home Network

The AnyPoint Home Network kit from Intel comes in USB and parallel port versions, each of which includes a small box for each computer. One end of the box plugs into your computer's USB or printer port through a cable; the other end of the box connects by phone wire to a phone jack. There are 1 Mbps and 10 Mbps models—the faster models cost more.

The AnyPoint software includes the drivers you'll need to network computers as well as software to share an Internet connection. After you install the AnyPoint software, the Intel AnyPoint Network Sharing and Mapping program starts each time you turn on your computer. The program presents a series of boxes in which you determine which disks, folders, and printers you want to share with others, and which disks, folders, and printers are available for use on other computers.

Figure 5-3 shows the drives that I'm allowing to be shared on an AnyPoint network. Although the floppy drive (A) isn't shared, the hard disk, removable disk, and CD-ROM can be used by others on the network. The Access column shows the type of permissions that I've granted to users.

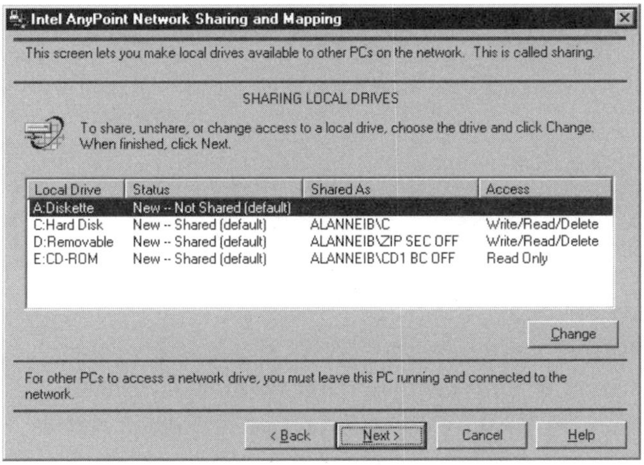

Figure 5-3.

Setting up drives to be shared.

If other computers are connected to the AnyPoint network, another dialog box will list the resources that their users have made available. The box will also let you map the resources. *Mapping* means to assign a drive letter on your computer to the resources on another computer.

In Figure 5-4, another computer, named SILVERFOX, is connected to the network. The user of that computer has made four resources available to the network: a folder, hard drives D and C, and the CD-ROM drive E.

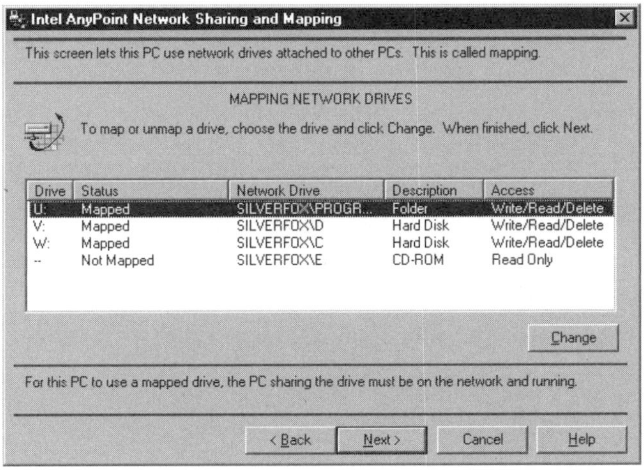

Figure 5-4.

Mapping resources on other computers.

The Drive and Status columns show that the folder and two hard drives have been mapped to your computer. Clicking Change lets you determine whether you want to map the drive and the letter assigned to it. When you open My Computer, the folder will appear as drive U, and the hard drives as drives V and W, just as if they were actual drives on your own computer.

Double-click the icon for a particular drive, for example, to display the folders and files within that drive. You can then open a file, such as a graphic or document, even though it's physically located on someone else's computer. To transfer a file to your computer, just display the file in My Computer or Windows Explorer and drag it to a drive or folder that's located on your computer.

Using Wireless Network Devices

If you don't want to string cable throughout the house, consider a wireless network, such as those that use the Home RF standard (RF stands for radio frequency). Just like a wireless phone system, a wireless network transmits information via radio waves to other computers in the house.

Wireless systems use a special interface device called a *transceiver* that takes the information you want to send to other computers and transmits it over the air. The transceiver also receives the signals coming from other computers. In some wireless systems, the transceiver fits inside your computer on an interface card, with an antenna that sticks out the back that sends and picks up the signals. Other transceivers are external, connecting to your computer through the USB or printer port. The USB versions are the easiest to set up because you don't have to open the computer to install an internal NIC or share a parallel port with a printer. Figure 5-5 shows computers communicating over a wireless network through transceivers.

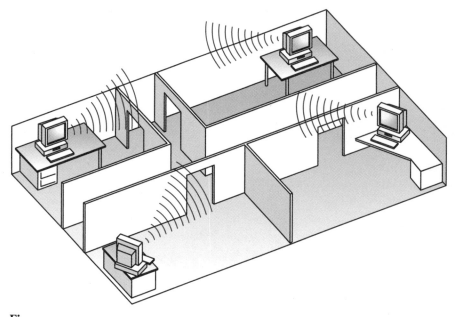

Figure 5-5.
Wireless network transceivers send and receive information on radio waves over the air.

The Pros and Cons of Going Wireless

Like phone-networking hardware, most wireless networks are slower than Ethernet but cost about the same. Newer systems operate at 10 Mbps but cost more than an Ethernet starter kit. Although they're easy to install because there are no network cables, wireless networks have several drawbacks.

Wireless networks that are designed and priced for the home function only within a certain distance, usually a radius of about 150 feet between the computers, although some models have a range of up to 250 feet. That distance should be enough to accommodate all the computers in an average-sized home, but check the documentation that came with your wireless network kit to find its range. If a computer on the network appears to be turned off, it might just be out of range. Try moving the computer closer to the others. If that fixes the problem, leave the computer in its new location.

A more common problem with wireless networks is interference from walls and large metal objects. If a computer on the network is located on the floor under a metal desk, for example, the metal might block incoming and outgoing signals. A wall with metal pipes or studs can also interfere with signal transmission, and you can't have large metal objects or huge containers of water, such as fish tanks and water coolers, between computers. Try moving the computer to another location, such as on top of the desk or to one side of it.

One final problem with wireless systems is that there are two wireless standards of communication—direct sequence and frequency hopping—and the two aren't compatible. Hardware from one company might not be compatible with hardware from another even though they both claim to meet industry standards for compatibility.

The technology that wireless systems use to create a secure network, called *spread spectrum*, divides the wireless signal into small pieces. In a frequency-hopping spread spectrum, the system switches, or hops, between several different frequencies for a specific amount of time. Both the sending device and the receiving device know the pattern, so the signals are received intact.

In a direct sequence spread spectrum, the signal is encoded with extra redundant bits of information that the receiving device can decode. The redundant bits help ensure that the information can be received successfully even if some bits are lost during the transmission.

Choosing a Wireless System

A number of companies market wireless network systems. The Intel AnyPoint Wireless Home Network system, for example, operates much like the telephone network model but has only 1.6 Mbps. It comes in both a USB version and as an internal card. The USB version includes a small box for each computer that plugs into your computer's USB port through a cable. The internal card model fits into a slot in your computer, as you'll learn in Chapter 6.

The Aviator network from WebGear (*http://www.webgear.com*) features an interface that plugs into your computer's parallel port and operates at 1 Mbps. You can purchase a kit that includes devices for networking two computers, and you can expand the network to as many as 32 machines. WebGear also markets the AviatorPro series of internal cards that operate at 2 Mbps over a range of 250 feet.

SohoWare's CableFree wireless networks (*http://www.sohoware.com*) come in two versions: an internal card and a laptop card. The system operates at 2 Mbps over a range of 250 feet.

If you have a really large home (as well as some extra cash on hand), you might want to consider a commercial-quality wireless system. Such systems cost more, but they operate at higher speeds and over a wider area than kits designed for the home. RadioLAN (*http://www.radiolan.com*), for example, sells a wireless system that achieves Ethernet speeds. Some other commercial-grade wireless systems are summarized here:

- The BreezeNet Pro system (*http://www.breezecom.com*) operates at speeds between 2 Mbps and 3 Mbps and has a range of up to 3000 feet when unobstructed, and up to 600 feet in an obstructed environment. The access point can accommodate up to 20 users per coverage area (known as a *cell*).

- The Aviator Pro wireless system (*http://www.webgear.com*) boasts a range of 500 to 1000 feet at a speed of 2 Mbps, with up to 60 users per access point.

- Cisco Aironet 340 (*http://www.aironet.com/default/asp*) wireless network supports 2048 users per access point at speeds up to 11 Mbps. Each cell covers an area up to 1500 feet.

- WaveLan Turbo (*http://www.lucent.com*) operates at 2 Mbps and can accommodate 250 users per access point. Its range is 1200 feet.

As an example of a wireless system, let's look closer at the Diamond Multimedia HomeFree network.

Diamond Multimedia HomeFree

Diamond Multimedia (*http://www.s3.com*) markets the HomeFree wireless network system that operates about 1 Mbps. HomeFree comes as either a card for laptop computers or an internal card for desktops. You can also purchase starter kits that include either two internal cards or one internal card and one laptop card. The internal NIC has a small protrusion that sticks out of your computer to serve as an antenna, and which offers a range of up to 150 feet.

Installing the HomeFree software sets up your computer to communicate over a network. It even configures the internal Industry Standard Architecture (ISA) card version to operate without conflicts.

See Also

You'll learn more about the various types of internal cards in Chapter 6, "Installing Network Cards."

The installation program also sets up HomeFree Assistant, an easy-to-use program for keeping track of the computers and peripherals being shared on the network. The HomeFree Assistant shown in Figure 5-6 shows a network consisting of two computers—Silverfox and Seg—and lists the resources that are being shared on each. You can access the drives and folders on the network through My Computer or Windows Explorer.

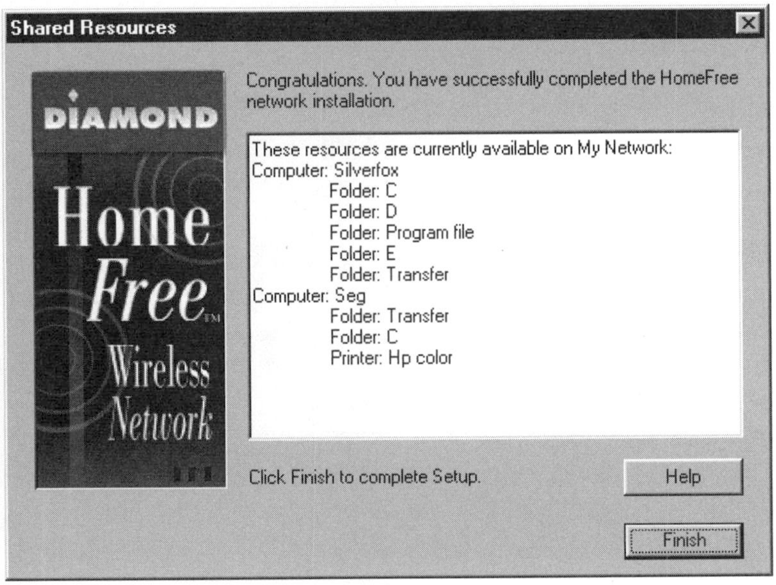

Figure 5-6.
Keeping track of a network with HomeFree Assistant.

HomeFree uses a 2.4 GHz frequency-hopping spread spectrum technology that randomly switches frequencies to prevent interference from wireless telephones and other wireless devices and networks.

Setting Up a Power-Line Network

A power-line network, called a HomePLC (Home Power Line Cable) network, sends and receives information directly through the power lines of your house, so your existing electrical wiring serves as the network cable. You don't have to run any special cable, and you can network a computer at any location that has an electrical outlet.

Here's how it works.

1. A device connects your computer to an electrical outlet.

2. Your computer sends information through that device as a low-frequency radio wave. The frequency of the radio wave normally prevents it from interfering with, or being interfered by, the regular electric current running through the wires.

3. The radio wave travels throughout your entire house until it is "picked up" by another device connected to another networked computer.

The Pros and Cons of Power-Line Networks

Some potential problems exist with this technology, however, especially if you share an electrical transformer with a neighbor.

A *transformer* is a device that reduces the huge amount of power running through the outside power lines to the voltage you need for your house. The radio waves from a power-line network travel throughout all the wiring from the electrical outlet to the transformer supplying current to your house. In some cases, the transformer serves more than one house, so your network signals actually travel through the wires of other houses or apartments served by the same transformer.

Theoretically, if the family in the apartment or house next door shares your transformer and has the same type of power-line network as you do, they could automatically be part of your family's network. To prevent this problem from occurring, power-line networks let you create a "secure" network that blocks unauthorized neighbors from your computers. You can make a secure network by building what's called a *firewall*, which limits access to your network to authorized persons only.

The other problems with HomePLC networks are electrical interference and power-line fluctuations. Although the radio waves traveling through the power lines are separate from the electric current, there can be some interference from other electronic equipment in the house, especially other power-line devices, such as those for the telephone and video equipment. Power-line fluctuations can occur when you turn on a large electrical appliance, such as an air conditioner. These fluctuations can cause a temporary loss of your network connection. Power-line networks help overcome the problem by using devices that filter out the interference before it reaches the network. As with all Ethernet alternatives, power-line technologies are constantly becoming faster and more dependable.

As an example of a power-line network, we'll look at the PassPort Powerline network kit from Intelogis (*http://www.intelogis.com*). This power-line network kit is the only one that is currently available for home use. You can learn about other systems under development at these sites:

- *http://home.earthlink.net/~videocom/*
- *http://www.alt-com.net/*

PassPort Powerline

The PassPort network kit includes two plug-in computer modules, a plug-in printer module that lets you connect a printer to the network, two special power strips, and a CD containing installation software.

To use a computer module, plug it into a wall socket and then plug a cable from the module into the computer's parallel port, as shown in Figure 5-7. Because standard power strips often contain electronic devices that could filter out network signals, be sure to plug the module directly into a wall outlet and not into a power strip. With this setup, an internal NIC isn't necessary.

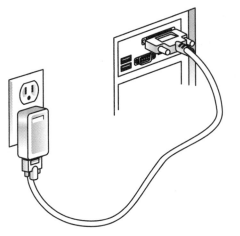

Figure 5-7.
The PassPort Powerline module links your computer's parallel port to your home wiring.

To help avoid power-line interference, use the two special power strips provided with the kit for your computer and monitor. This way, the module can occupy one plug of a dual outlet and the power strip of the other. The power strip filters out any interference from the computer and monitor.

When it senses the presence of the PassPort module, Windows automatically starts a wizard to install the drivers. Rather than use the wizard, however, click Cancel to return to your desktop, and then run the installation program on the PassPort CD.

The installation program loads the necessary drivers and configures Windows for the network, installing protocols, setting up network services, and turning on file sharing. After it restarts your computer, it installs the PassPort software too, so you don't need to do anything to configure Windows for connecting computers in a network.

To use the PassPort kit's printer module, plug your printer's parallel port cable into the module, and then plug the module into a wall outlet. The printer is now connected directly to the network rather than to an individual computer. As long as the printer is turned on, every computer on the network can access it. All you have to do is install the appropriate printer driver on each computer, following the instructions you'll find in the PassPort documentation.

Note

PassPort also includes software for sharing a single phone line and an Internet service provider (ISP) account among the computers on the network.

Once the hardware is plugged in and the software is installed, you'll be able to access the network through the Network Neighborhood icon in Microsoft Windows 95 and Microsoft Windows 98, or the My Network Places icon in Microsoft Windows Millennium Edition (Me) and Microsoft Windows 2000, on the desktop.

After you install the software and restart your computer, the PassPort Administrator program begins and asks you whether you want to create a secure network. You should click Yes even if you don't think any of your neighbors could interfere with your network. Clicking Yes starts the Secure Network Wizard, which lets you name your network and shows you the names of other computers using a PassPort Powerline device.

Click the box next to each computer that you want to allow access to your computer on the network.

Note

You'll need to create a secure network on each computer that you have attached to a PassPort Powerline device.

The PassPort Administrator window, shown in Figure 5-8, lists all the computers connected to the network. Only the systems listed under your network name and shown as Secured Devices can access your computer. If there are any computers on the same transformer that you didn't select to be in your secure network, they'll be shown in the Public Net section.

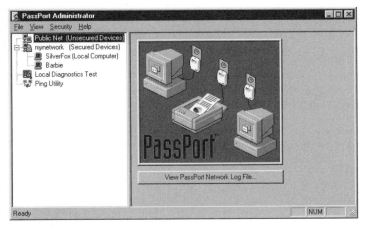

Figure 5-8.
PassPort Administrator allows you to manage and secure your home network.

If you didn't select Create A Secure Network, however, all other systems with PassPort devices on your transformer will be listed under Public Net, as shown in the dialog box below.

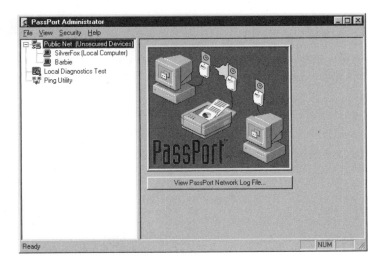

Because there are no secure devices, each of the Public Net systems has access to your computer.

Note

If you add other computers or printers to the network later, you have to run the wizard again from the PassPort Administrator's Security menu to add them to the list of allowed devices.

Expanding PassPort is easy. You can buy additional PC or printer modules and install them on other computers.

USB Direct Cable Networks

If you want to connect two computers that are in the same room and they both have USB ports, you can get all the benefits of a full network but with the convenience of a direct connection.

You can use your computer's USB ports to network computers by Ethernet, telephone, or wireless technology. When you use a USB Ethernet connection, for example, your computer has the same performance and benefits as one with an Ethernet network card installed internally. In this chapter, we'll look at special systems that network computers by connecting them directly together by their USB ports.

See Also

For information on using USB devices to connect to an Ethernet network, see Chapter 6, "Installing Network Cards."

Because the USB port is external, you can connect USB devices without having to open your computer and install an internal card. Many desktop and laptop computers include two USB ports, so you can use one port for networking and the other for a USB printer, scanner, or other device.

Note

If you have an older computer without a USB port, you can install an add-in card to give your computer USB capabilities.

If you have more USB devices than you have ports, you can purchase a *USB hub*, a device that allows multiple USB devices to be connected to one computer, as shown in the following illustration. You might even be able to combine or stack hubs to connect additional USB devices.

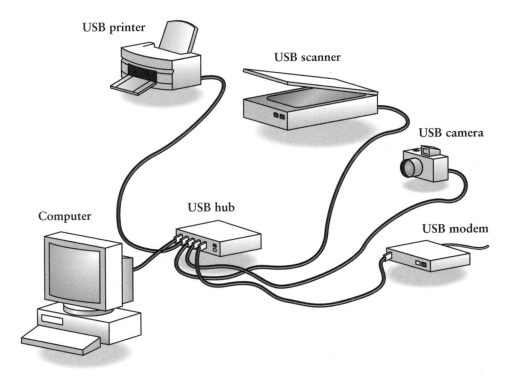

The disadvantage of connecting computers by USB cable is distance. Because USB cables can be no longer than 5 meters, the two networked computers must usually be in the same room. You can extend the distance between computers, however, by inserting a hub between them. The hub acts as a signal booster extending the distance another 5 meters. When using a hub between computers, the two machines can be up to 10 meters apart (5 meters on each side of the device), as shown here.

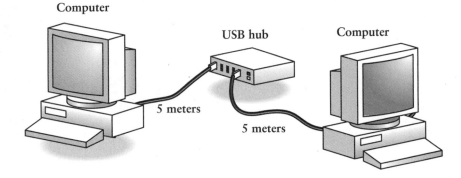

Several companies sell kits that contain a special USB cable and software for creating a two-computer network. The kits cost less than $100 and they let you share and transfer files, share Internet access, play games over the network, and share printers. Here are some examples of these kits:

- USB Direct Connect (*http://www.belkin.com*)
- EZLink USB *(http://www.ezlinkusb.com)*
- ActionLink *(http://www.actiontec.com)*

USB Direct Connect

The USB Direct Connect system from Belkin includes a device with two USB connections. The device acts as a hub, so you can connect 5-meter USB cables to each port, separating the two computers as much as 10 meters.

You can also use multiple USB Direct Connect devices to network more than two computers through their USB ports, as shown in Figure 5-9. If the computers have two USB ports, you can either daisy chain systems, going from one to the other, or connect up to eight computers to one host that has multiple USB ports or is connected to a USB hub, as shown in
Figure 5-10. When you daisy chain the devices, each computer in the chain except the first and the last must have two USB ports.

To determine how many devices you'll need, just subtract 1 from the number of computers you want to network. You'll need four devices to network five computers, for example.

Connecting two computers

Daisy chain

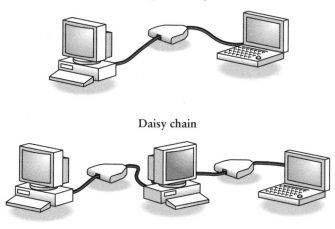

Figure 5-9.
You can determine how many USB Direct Connect devices you'll need for your network by subtracting 1 from the number of computers you have.

Host with multiple computers connected

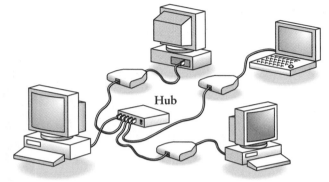

Figure 5-10.

The USB Direct Connect system can be used to network multiple computers.

You set up the system in two steps. First, you install the network drivers, and then you set up your computer to communicate over a network. The device uses the same types of protocols that must be set up for an Ethernet network, as described in Chapter 8, and the network must then be set up to share folders and files, as explained in Chapter 10.

EZLink

The EZLink system includes a hub-like device with a USB port and a built-in cable. You plug the built-in cable into the USB port of one computer, and then you run a 5-meter cable (supplied with the system) between the EZLink USB port and the USB port of the other computer to be networked. The EZLink software installs and configures your computer for the network using all the standard network protocols, although you'll have to specify which disks and folders will be shared, as described in Chapter 10.

You can also use multiple EZLink devices to daisy chain up to eight computers together, as long as each computer except the first and last have two USB ports. You can also connect up to eight computers through a series of USB hubs, with each computer connected through an EZLink device.

ActionLink

The ActionLink system includes a special 20-foot USB cable that connects directly to the USB ports of two computers. Although you can't daisy chain ActionLink systems together, you'll find them easy to set up.

The ActionLink program sets up all the necessary drivers and protocols to begin networking. Internet sharing software is built into the program, and it automatically selects the best performing computer to serve as the host—the computer that connects both systems to the Internet.

Bridging Network Types

You can use two or more different types of network connections within the same network. For example, suppose you have several computers networked using Ethernet cable, but you also have another computer in the house located where network cable can't be extended. You can install a non-Ethernet device such as a wireless or telephone adapter into that computer, and install a similar device into one or more of the networked computers.

Such a network is illustrated in Figure 5-11.

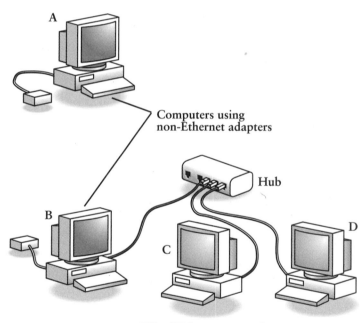

Figure 5-11.

Computers A and B can communicate with each other, but Computer A can't communicate with Computers C and D on the Ethernet network.

In this configuration, computers A and B communicate and share files over the non-Ethernet network, and computers B, C, and D communicate and share files over Ethernet. However, computer A can't communicate or share files with computers C and D because they don't share a similar network interface.

To connect two different types of networks, you need a device called a *bridge*, as illustrated in Figure 5-12. In this illustration, a wireless bridge has been connected to the network hub with an Ethernet cable. The bridge acts as a transceiver that converts wireless signals into Ethernet. Now all the computers can communicate and share files.

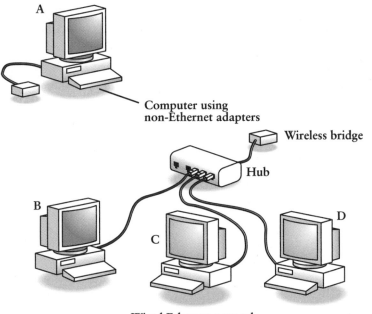

Figure 5-12.
A wireless bridge connects the wireless and wired networks so that Computer A and Computers B, C, and D can all communicate with each other.

Bridges are available for both wireless and phone networks. To ensure compatibility, you should purchase them from the same company from which you obtain your wireless or phone interfaces. Although most of the bridges have been designed for commercial-grade wireless systems and start at about $700, two bridges are designed and priced for home use.

The SohoWare NetBlaster (*http://www.sohoware.com*), for just under $300, connects computers using SohoWare CableFree 2 Mbps wireless devices to the Ethernet network. The HomeLink Broadband Network Bridge (*http://www.linksys.com*), under $200, does the same for users of HomeLink 1 Mbps phone network adapters.

Both devices act not only as a bridge to the wired Ethernet network, but they've also been designed to allow wireless or telephone network users to share a high-speed DSL or cable modem. You can connect your DSL or cable modem either directly to the bridge or to a network hub to which the bridge is connected. The systems described in this chapter let you create a network without running cables. You can share files, printers, and an Internet account through telephone or power lines, over a USB cable, or via a wireless system. Although some of them are slower than Ethernet networks, these non-Ethernet alternatives provide the same benefits as any network, and the day isn't far off when the speed and cost of non-Ethernet alternatives for the home will equal that of Ethernet networks. In the next chapter, you'll learn how to install an internal network interface card into a desktop computer.

Chapter 6

Installing Network Cards

The next step toward getting your home network going is to purchase and install the networking hardware—the network interface cards (NICs) or adapters, the hub, and the cables. If you're lucky enough to have computers with built-in network cards, you can just skip this chapter. Unfortunately, most home computers don't come with a NIC built in, so you'll have to install one yourself or hire someone else to do it.

Note

All internal cards are installed in about the same way, so you can use this chapter to learn how to install an internal card for a telephone or wireless network as well as for Ethernet.

Are You Network-Ready?

Before going any further, you might want to check to see whether your computers are already equipped with a NIC. Your machines have NICs if you purchased computers ready to be connected to a network, or if you inherited used computers that had NICs installed when you received them. If a computer is new, check its documentation or the specifications on the box the computer came in. Chances are, if your computer is network-ready, the box will say so prominently.

With a hand-me-down or used computer, check the back of the case for an RJ-45 connector, which looks like an extra-large telephone jack, or a small, metal barrel that sticks out. The large, telephone-like jack is for a twisted-pair Ethernet connection; the metal barrel is for 10Base2 Thin Ethernet coaxial cable. You can see the typical network connections on the back of a network card in the following illustration.

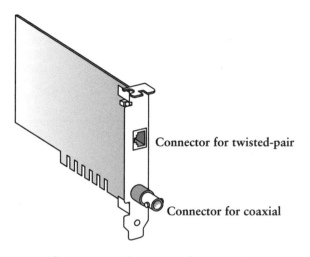

Connector for twisted-pair

Connector for coaxial

If you see neither type of connection, your computer isn't network-ready. If you see both, you're in good shape. If you see only one type of connection, it must be the correct type for the cable you'll use. Let's say you've inherited an older computer that has a NIC with just a coaxial connection. You can't connect your computer to other computers that have twisted-pair connections without replacing the NIC.

Working Without Cards

Perhaps the one aspect of setting up for networking that might make you uncomfortable is installing the NIC. As you'll learn in the section "Playing the Card Game," later in this chapter, installing a NIC inside your computer is easy, but if you'd rather not open your computer case, you can either pay someone to do it for you or consider one of the alternatives.

You can find NICs that don't have to be installed in your computer. They just plug easily into your computer's universal serial bus (USB) or printer port. Many of the USB devices are Ethernet and connect to twisted-pair wire just like an internal NIC. They have a USB connection at one end and a twisted-pair connection at the other end. You plug the adapter into the USB connection on your computer and connect a cable from the adapter to the network hub, which joins all the cables from all the NICs.

To use a USB network device, you must be running Microsoft Windows 95 version 4.00.950B or later, Microsoft Windows 98, Microsoft Windows Millennium Edition (Me), or Microsoft Windows 2000, and have at least one USB connection on your computer.

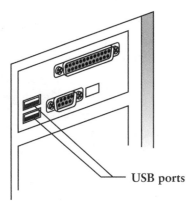

USB ports

Most of the printer port devices aren't Ethernet, however. They don't use either twisted-pair or coaxial cable but instead transmit information through the telephone line, your home's power lines, or over a radio frequency without any wires. Printer port devices are usually slower than Ethernet networks, but they're easier to install. So if you want an Ethernet network without opening up your computer, consider a USB Ethernet adapter.

Note

You can also find network interfaces that are serial port devices, but they're more expensive and can be complicated to set up. Serial port devices are recommended for businesses with older computers but not for home networks.

Networking for Broadband Internet

If you connect or are planning to connect to a DSL (digital subscriber line) or cable modem for the Internet, you'll need an Ethernet connection for the modem. If you also want to connect the computer to a home network, you'll need a second Ethernet port. You use one port for the modem and the other for your network.

You can use USB Ethernet adapters for both a network and a high-speed modem. They're ideal when you already have an Ethernet card installed on your computer and don't have or want to take up another internal slot.

Cook It Yourself or Order Out?

If you decide that the speed advantages of using networking hardware that includes an internal NIC are for you, consider installing the card yourself. There's nothing difficult or mysterious about the inside of a computer—it's just a collection of wires, circuit boards, and other paraphernalia. Lots of folks insert network cards, sound cards, and other kinds of cards themselves. They save a little money and they get the satisfaction of having faced the computer monster and triumphed.

Other folks would never operate on their computer even if you paid them. They'd rather have a professional do it. They save themselves the frustration if something goes wrong, and they have the comforting feeling that they can just take the computer back to the professional who installed the hardware for them if problems arise later.

Installing a Network Card Yourself

You don't have to be an electronics expert to install a NIC in your computer. You just need some patience, common sense, and the ability to use a screwdriver, which is about the only tool you'll need.

Of course, whenever you open a computer, you're exposing a lot of sensitive and expensive equipment. Certainly, pulling or poking the wrong part can damage your computer, but if you're careful, nothing will go wrong. A lot of wires and cables are also running around inside your computer. You can safely move wires out of the way as long as you're careful not to disconnect them.

Just keep in mind that you shouldn't open your computer with wet hands, when the computer is plugged in, or while the kids, the spouse, the television, or the telephone are distracting you.

If you have more than two computers to network, start with just two of them. Buy enough hardware for the two and no more. Setting up a network isn't difficult, but it takes some time, and it's best to get two computers communicating before you invest your whole bankroll. Starting with just two gives you time to concentrate on the basics.

If you're uncomfortable taking apart your computer to install the card yourself, however, you should consider having a professional install the hardware for you.

Finding Someone Else to Do It

If you decide not to install the hardware yourself, you'll need to have someone do it for you. That person can also set up the software drivers for your network card and configure

Microsoft Windows for the network. *Network drivers* are the programs needed for your computer to access the NIC.

See Also

If you install the card yourself, you can learn about drivers in "Installing Network Drivers," in Chapter 8, on page 141.

You may be able to find someone to come to your home to install the NIC, but the home visit will cost you extra. The less expensive alternative is to take your computer to a store that will insert the NIC; however, that solution has these drawbacks:

- You'll have to disconnect all of the cables connected to the computer, and pack up your computer to carry it to the store—which can be a real hassle.

- You'll have to do without your computer for a while.

- You'll have to consider deleting any sensitive material you have on your hard disk before you take the computer to the shop.

- You'll have to carry the computer back from the store and reconnect everything after the shop is finished working on it.

- If you have a problem with the NIC later on, you'll have to take it to the store again.

If you decide to take the computer to the store, you won't need to include the keyboard, mouse, or monitor—just the computer case itself. The shop will connect a keyboard and monitor for the installation process.

Some stores might be able to install the NIC while you wait, but others will make you drop off the computer and come back another day. It doesn't take long to install the card, but some shops are quite busy, especially around the holiday season. If you can't do without your computer for long, ask when the shop is least busy and try to schedule your visit for that time.

I'd also suggest that you go back to the same store where you bought the computer; you might get a price break on installation. When you purchase a computer at a computer superstore, for example, you can usually have a network card installed for a small flat rate. You'll save a little money and gain some peace of mind knowing that professionals who know what they're doing are working on your computer.

Note

Purchasing hardware by mail order can be a money-saving alternative if you want to install it yourself.

Buying and Installing a Network Card

You'll need to decide what to buy, where to buy it, and whether you should buy separate components or obtain everything in a kit.

It's All in the Cards

In Chapter 3, you learned about the various types of NICs and how to connect your computers. When you select hardware that includes an internal NIC, whether it works through Ethernet or the telephone line, you'll have to make sure you get the correct NIC for your computer. If you decide on an Ethernet network, the NIC you buy must be either twisted-pair or coaxial cable. Here's a recap of the choices:

- **Twisted-pair** cable looks like telephone cable on steroids, and it's by far the most popular type of cable. You'll need a hub to which cables from all of the computers connect. The hub must be turned on for any computer to communicate with another.

- **Coaxial** cable (also known as thin Ethernet) looks like cable television wire and doesn't require a hub. You run the wire from one computer to the next.

Note

You can use fiberoptic cable with the new gigabyte Ethernet cards, and it's more expandable for the future. Because fiber-optic cable is expensive and harder to install, however, it isn't commonly used for home networks.

When you buy a network card, make sure it's designed for the type of cable you select. You can play it safe by purchasing *combo cards*, which are NICs that have connectors for both coaxial and twisted-pair cables.

Next, consider whether you'll be satisfied with the usual 10 Mbps network speed of regular Ethernet or whether you want a 100 Mbps network (also called Fast Ethernet). For home networks, 10 Mbps is fast enough for now. But when the price of 100 Mbps hardware drops in the near future, slower cards and hubs might become obsolete.

Your network hub should be capable of handling the highest speed network card. Older hubs, for example, would handle communications only at the 10 Mbps speed. The hubs generally available today, however, are dual-speed hubs. This means they can accommodate network signals at both the 10 Mbps and 100 Mbps speeds. Using a dual-speed hub, you can mix 10 Mbps and 100 Mbps cards on the same network so you can always upgrade the parts of the network that you'd like to go faster.

Catching the Right Bus

The *bus* is the part of the computer that moves information around among all the components. The signals flowing in and out of the NIC and other parts of the computer flow through the bus, like traffic on city streets.

The NIC plugs into an expansion slot on the bus that's not already occupied by a video card, modem, or other device. The metal contacts in the slot mesh with the contacts on the card so that electronic information can pass between them.

Most computers today have three types of slots, as shown here:

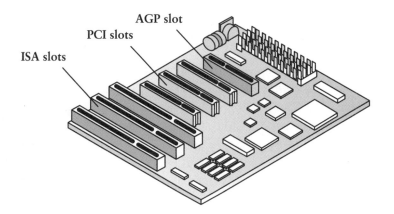

- **Industry Standard Architecture** (ISA) slots are the type used in older machines, but they're still around. They're usually black and have a plastic divider across the slot about two-thirds of the way from the end. The card fits into the slot and has a space to accommodate the divider.

- **Peripheral Component Interconnect** (PCI) slots are usually white. They're shorter than ISA sockets and have a divider about three-quarters of the way along.

- **The Accelerated Graphics Port** (AGP) slot is shorter than the PCI slots. It also has a divider, and it's set back further than the other slots. The AGP slot is used for a high-speed graphics card, so you can't use it for a NIC.

Note

Some older computers might have Extended ISA (EISA) sockets, which look like ISA sockets except that they're brown.

You must purchase the correct type of NIC for the type of slot that's open and available in your computer. You can often determine which slots are free by looking at a photograph or an illustration in your computer's manual that shows the inside of the computer. It should show you which slots are occupied and by what.

If the manual doesn't help, you might be able to tell by looking at the back of the computer for unused slots. You'll see a series of metal plates covering openings. Some of these will have connections for items such as the monitor, modem, and sound card, and others will be empty. If the computer manual shows what each type of slot is for, match up the blank plate with the slot to determine the type of slot that's empty.

If you still can't tell, open the computer and look around inside to find an empty slot on the main circuit board. If your computer doesn't have any empty slots, you'll need the type of NIC that connects to a port on the back of the computer, such as the USB port. You learned about these in Chapter 5, "Non-Ethernet Networks." *If you need help opening your computer, read the section "Installing the Card" later in this chapter.*

PCI cards are the easiest type of NIC to install inside a computer because they require the least software configuration. In most cases, they'll configure themselves when you plug them in and turn on the computer because they are *plug and play compatible*. This means that Windows senses that the card is installed and either installs the correct software by itself or prompts you to insert the disk that came with the NIC.

ISA cards are usually more complicated to install, even those that are plug and play. With ISA cards, you might have to worry about changing their settings to avoid conflicts with other cards in your computer.

Connecting Laptops

Although a few laptop computers have built-in NICs, laptops normally don't have internal slots into which you can plug a NIC. You can still connect a laptop to a network by using a network interface device on a PC Card or an external network interface device that connects to the laptop's USB port.

PC Cards are about the size of credit cards; they slide into a PC Card slot on your laptop and they work just like other NICs. The network cable connects directly to the end of the card sticking out of the computer or to a smaller cable that plugs into the card. Some cards use only twisted-pair cable, but others have adapters that can accept either twisted-pair or coaxial cable.

Installing a PC Card NIC is a piece of cake. The label on the card is on top, and the end of the card with the small holes fits into the PC Card slot, which is usually on the side of the computer. Figure 3-1, in Chapter 3, shows how a PC Card network interface fits into a laptop.

Most laptops have two PC Card slots: an upper and a lower slot. If one slot already has something in it, such as a modem, slide the NIC into the other slot. Then push the card in firmly. This pushes out a small tab on the side of the slot that you can press to remove the card.

Getting to the Hub of the Matter

If you decide to use twisted-pair cables to connect computers to a network, you'll need a hub and a twisted-pair cable for each computer. The hub serves as a central connection through which all network signals flow. The least expensive hubs are probably all you'll need for a home network. They have ports for up to five computers. You can also get hubs that handle more than five computers, but they are more expensive.

Multifunction Hubs

Before purchasing a network hub, consider whether you'd like to share a modem with everyone on the network. As you'll learn in Chapter 13, you can connect a modem, even a DSL or cable modem, so that it's available to everyone.

One way to share a modem is to connect it to one computer and let other users share it. This option is inexpensive, but it means that the computer to which the modem is attached must be turned on for other users to connect to the Internet.

The alternative is to connect the modem directly to the network hub. This way, only the hub must be turned on for anyone on the network to access the modem. This solution is more expensive because you'll need some extra hardware or software.

If you think you might want to connect a modem to a hub, you can purchase a special hub that either has a modem built in or that already contains the hardware needed to share a DSL or cable modem. These hubs cost more than a plain Ethernet hub but might be less expensive than purchasing separate modem-sharing hardware.

You'll learn more about these types of hubs in Chapter 13.

A five-port hub might also have a sixth connector called an *uplink port,* which lets you connect hubs and link them in a chain. When you need to add a sixth or seventh computer to your network, you can purchase another hub and add it to the chain.

You can get 10 Mbps hubs, 100 Mbps (Fast Ethernet) hubs, and dual-speed 10/100 Mbps hubs. The dual-speed hubs are perfect for networks that have both 10 Mbps and 100 Mbps NICs attached because you'll get the maximum speed of each NIC.

Note

As an alternative to a hub, you can use a more expensive device called a *switch*. A switch gives each connection on the network its own path to travel for faster performance.

In Chapter 7, we'll look at installing and locating hubs in more detail. You'll also learn that you can avoid using a hub altogether if you want to connect only two computers together.

The Whole Kit and Caboodle

Because of the growing popularity of networking, many manufacturers package all the essentials for setting up a small network in one box: the network kit. Ethernet kits, for example, usually include two NICs, a hub, and a couple of network cables.

The kits are a good value because they often cost less than the components purchased separately. For $50 to $100, you can buy a complete kit that gives you everything you need to connect two computers. If you need to add computers, you can purchase additional cards and cables separately. Also, you can be relatively certain that all the parts have been designed to work together. Many network kits even come with a program that sets up Windows for networking, so you don't have to do any software configuration. In addition, most of the kits come with software that lets you share one Internet connection among all the people on the network. This means that everyone on the network can browse the Internet at the same time, using one phone line and one Internet account.

See Also

You'll learn how to share Internet accounts in Chapter 13, "Going Online Through the Network."

Kits do have some disadvantages, however. Although you might be able to find a kit that includes one internal NIC for a desktop and one PC Card for a laptop computer, almost all the kits offer two cards of the same type. That's fine if that's what you need, but otherwise, you might have to purchase a card of a different type separately. The other disadvantage is that if one of the cards is defective, you might have to return the entire kit, which means you'll have to remove both cards and the hub, even if only one component is bad.

As an alternative to a kit, you can purchase each component separately. You can then buy different cards for different machines and return individual pieces if necessary. Because all Ethernet cards work together, you can even purchase NICs and hubs from different manufacturers.

Where to Shop?

Now that you've made some basic decisions about the type of components to buy, you're ready to get out the charge card and go shopping. But where?

You'll find the best prices at computer superstores—those large stores that carry only computer hardware and software—and through mail order. The superstore will have a good selection of kits and individual components, you'll be able to purchase the kit and take it home the same day, and you'll have a local place to go if you must return anything. If you can't find items locally, you should opt for buying them through mail order.

Mail-order companies and online retailers such as PC Connection, CDW, Insight, and others, also offer great prices and often a better selection than local stores. While you have to pay for shipping, most mail-order companies don't charge sales tax. They offer the same return policy as local stores and often provide overnight or two-day shipping. You'll have to install the hardware yourself, however, and it'll take longer if you have to return or exchange something.

As an alternative, you can purchase hardware at large chain appliance stores, electronic boutiques in malls, and independent computer stores. But while the prices at appliance stores might be good, you'll rarely get the sales help you need. Expect to pay slightly higher prices at electronic boutiques in malls that carry computer games, magazines, and some hardware. Again, the salespeople usually aren't computer experts, although they'll know a lot about the most awesome computer games. Also expect to pay slightly higher prices at local independent computer stores. However, at your local computer store, you'll probably find the most knowledgeable salespeople and the most helpful technical support. Try to pick a shop that's been around for a while. Plenty of little computer stores pop up, only to go out of business by the time the stoplight on the corner changes. There's nothing wrong with these places, but it's nice to have a place to go down the road if something goes wrong.

You should consider one other place as a source for computer hardware: computer shows. If you live near a metropolitan area, look for computer shows periodically at convention centers, schools and colleges, or other meeting grounds. You might have to pay a small entrance fee, but you'll have access to a wide selection of vendors and products. Some vendors simply travel from show to show, but local computer stores often send their own representatives. If you need support, you might have difficulty tracking down a traveling vendor, or one from out of town.

My recommendation? Purchase a kit from a computer superstore in your area. Check the return policy, and install and test the hardware before the return period ends. If you don't want to install the hardware yourself, have the techies at the superstore do it for you.

If there's no superstore in your area, find a local computer shop that's been around for some time. Tell them what you want and that you want to spend as little money as possible.

Playing the Card Game

If you've chosen to install the network cards yourself, a little preparation will make the job easier and faster. *If you're installing an ISA network card, refer to the section "Installing ISA Cards" later in this chapter before attempting the installation.*

Make sure you have a Phillips screwdriver; a small one will usually do. Don't use a magnetic screwdriver because the magnetism in the screwdriver might scramble information stored in computer chips.

Find a small container, such as a paper cup. You'll be removing small screws and you'll want a place to put them so they don't get lost.

While it's not necessary, you might find it handy to have needle-nose pliers available in case you drop a screw and need to fish it out of the computer. You might also need a flat-bladed screwdriver to pry off a cover plate. And you'll need a scalpel and forceps (only kidding, of course).

Next, remove rings, necklaces, and any other metal jewelry that might hang down or make contact with the inner workings of the computer. Metal is a conductor of static electricity, and necklaces can get caught inside the computer.

Now find a place to work. You should have plenty of room on all sides of the computer, so pick the center of a room or a hallway where you won't be disturbed by foot traffic. It's best to find a spot near a phone line because many manufacturers supply a telephone number that you can call for support. With the phone close to your workspace, you can describe to the support technician what you see and what you're doing.

Make sure the work area is as free from static electricity as possible. Rub your hands on your pants or skirt and touch something metal. Did you get a shock? If so, static electricity is present, and it's a danger to the components in any computer. Try working in a room without a carpet and discharge any static electricity by touching the computer case before working inside. You can also purchase an antistatic band that wraps around your wrist and connects to the computer case. Any static flows through the band to the case rather than through the delicate electronic equipment inside the case.

Leave the NIC in its antistatic packet until you're ready to insert it. Never touch the surface of the card or the metal connectors on the bottom, and handle the card only by its edges.

Installing the Card

When you're ready to start, work on just one computer at a time; don't take two or more computers apart at the same time because you might mix up their parts.

Follow these steps:

1. Unplug the computer.

   Caution

   Don't just turn off the computer or turn off the power strip it is attached to. The computer must be unplugged.

2. Unplug the wires from the keyboard, mouse, printer, scanner, and any other device. Think of this as a good opportunity to dust behind the computer and straighten out all the cables.

3. Move the computer case to a work area. Don't try squeezing in beside the desk or balancing the computer on your lap.

4. Remove the computer's cover and put any screws that you remove into the paper cup.

   If you have a desktop computer, you might need to remove only the top panel. Some cases have tabs on the back that you press to release and lift off the cover. In other cases (pardon the pun), you must remove several screws at the back of the computer and slide the case forward to remove it. If you have a tower computer that sits on the floor, you can often remove one or both side panels. Look carefully at the case to determine whether the two side panels appear to be separate from the rest of the case. If they are, you need to remove the screws only on one side and slide the panel away. Which side? Sometimes you just can't tell. If you take off one side and you don't see the row of cards and slots, replace the panel and remove the other side.

The screws you need to remove are probably near the edge of the case. Don't remove any screws from the middle, especially ones near the power supply, where you plug in the power cord, because they might hold the power supply in place.

5. Remove the metal slot cover behind the empty slot in which you plan to place the network card, as shown in Figure 6-1.

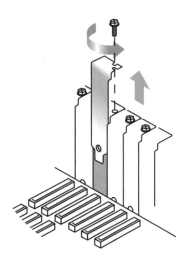

Figure 6-1.
Remove the cover plate for the slot.

You might need to either remove the screw that holds the cover in place or break off the small tab that holds the cover. Use a flat screwdriver to gently pry the cover away and then work the plate back and forth until it comes out.

6. Position the card so the connectors are toward the back of the computer. The metal back of the card will replace the blank slot cover that you've removed.

Note

If you're building a wireless network, the card might have a protrusion at the back that serves as the antenna. You might have to angle the card slightly to get the protrusion through the back of the computer before you straighten out the card so that it fits in the socket.

7. Line up the bottom edge of the card with the slot and confirm that they match. (Some ISA cards won't fill the entire ISA slot, just the front section.)

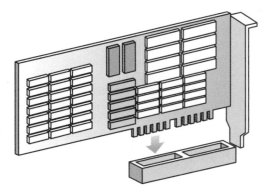

If any wires or cables are in the way, gently move them aside without disconnecting them. Although most cables inside the computer are connected snugly,
some are not, so make sure you don't dislodge the smaller and more delicate cables,
such as those that connect a CD drive to the sound card, while moving them aside
to access the slot.

8. Push the card down into the slot, exerting steady, firm pressure. As the card goes
into the slot, the metal back should slide down and fit where the plate cover was.
The top of the back should rest on the screw hole. If it doesn't, the card isn't down
all the way.

   Try not to bend the card to either side, rock it back and forth, or touch its surface. Just hold the card by its edges and apply firm, downward pressure.

9. Being careful not to drop the screw into the computer, screw the metal back of the
card into the frame of the computer. This screw is important because it keeps the
card firmly seated in the slot.

10. Replace the computer cover and be careful not to trap any wires.

11. Before putting the computer case back in its place, clean around the area, straighten
out the cables, and make sure you have no extra screws in the container.

12. Plug everything back in. Plug in the power cord last.

Installing ISA Cards

Using ISA cards often requires that you change special settings on the card, such as its
IRQ and I/O address. IRQ stands for *interrupt request*. Imagine the IRQ as a telephone
number. Each device in your computer has a different IRQ number that it uses to communicate with the computer. Your computer scans each IRQ line to see which device is
requesting service—that is, to send or receive information through the computer bus.

Only one device is allowed on an IRQ line at one time. If more than one ISA device uses the same IRQ, their signals might conflict.

Note

Some devices, such as PCI cards, can share an IRQ.

The I/O address is the location in your computer's memory where the signals from the device are stored. No two devices can have the same I/O address or their signals will conflict.

The IRQ and the I/O address of an ISA device are changed either by hardware or software. If the card's documentation tells you that the IRQ and I/O address are set up through software, you can skip this section for now.

On some older cards, you make these settings by changing a small switch or moving a jumper, which is a small device with metal prongs, as shown in Figure 6-2. There will be a plastic cap that fits over two of the prongs. The pair of prongs that the cap is on determines the IRQ that is assigned to the device. The card's documentation will show you which switch or jumper to change.

Figure 6-2.
Positioning a jumper to set the IRQ to 7.

Note

PCI plug and play cards share IRQs automatically, so no special setup is required.

Before you can pick an IRQ setting for the card, you must check to see what's available on your system to avoid a conflict. To check which IRQs are already being used, follow these steps:

1. Look at the documentation on the card for possible IRQ and I/O settings.

2. Right-click My Computer on the Windows desktop.

3. Choose Properties from the shortcut menu.

If you're using Consumer Windows, continue with these next steps to see which IRQ and I/O settings are available:

1. Click the Device Manager tab in the System Properties dialog box.

2. Double-click Computer at the top of the list.

3. Click the Interrupt Request (IRQ) button. The IRQs, usually numbered from 0 to 15, are listed.

4. Look for an unused IRQ or one that is assigned to a device you don't plan to use, such as an unused COM port. Don't worry if some IRQs are used by more than one device in the list. Some devices can share IRQs.

5. Click the Input/Output (I/O) button.

6. Check to see which of the addresses that your card can use are available.

7. Click Cancel to return to the Device Manager tab.

8. Click Cancel again to close the System Properties dialog box.

If you're using Windows 2000, follow these steps to check for available IRQ and I/O settings:

1. Click the Hardware tab in the System Properties dialog box, and then click the Device Manager button to open the Device Manager window.

2. Choose Resources By Type from the View menu.

3. Click the plus sign next to the Interrupt Request (IRQ) option. The IRQs, usually numbered from 0 to 15, are listed.

4. Look for an unused IRQ or one that is assigned to a device you don't plan to use, such as an unused COM port. Don't worry if some IRQs are used by more than one device in the list. Some devices can share IRQs.

5. Click the plus sign next to the Input/Output (I/O) option.

6. Check to see which of the addresses that your card can use are available.

7. Close the Device Manager window and then close the System Properties box.

8. Set the switches or jumpers on the card to settings that won't conflict, and then install the card and restart your system.

Your NIC is now installed. If you installed the NIC yourself, you must still install the NIC drivers and configure Windows, and that's the subject of Chapter 8. If someone else installed it, your network drivers and Windows software should also be set up and ready to go.

The next chapter covers how to run cable for your network.

Chapter 7

Running the Cables

Now that you have network interface cards (NICs) installed in your computers, you're ready to connect them with cable. Just as a chain is only as strong as its weakest link, though, your network is only as sound as the connections between computers, so you'll want to follow the suggestions in this chapter carefully to wire your network effectively.

Running Cables Within a Room

You can often run cable between devices in the same room along or even under the baseboard molding. In some rooms, you might be able to hide the cable by pushing it between the carpet and the bottom of the molding. If not, run the cable on the top of the baseboard molding. Of course, it looks best if the cable is the same color as the molding. When you get to the corner of a room, don't bend the cable sharply, even if it has to stick out slightly from the corner—sharp bends can damage the wires inside the cable so your computers cannot communicate.

Running Cables Between Rooms

Cabling together two or more computers in the same room is relatively easy, but when the computers are in different parts of the house, running cables between them can be more of a challenge.

Running Cables Between Adjacent Rooms

If you need to connect two computers that are in adjacent rooms, you can drill a hole in the wall between the rooms and feed the cable through. Of course, if the computers are on opposite sides of the same wall, you won't even have to run the cable along a baseboard. Alternatively, you can run the cable through the ceiling, between the ceiling joists. You'll then have to make two holes, one where the wire enters the ceiling in one room and another where the wire exits the ceiling in another room. If a heating duct or a return runs between rooms, you can also run the cable through it, but if you make holes in the metal to get the wire into the duct, stuff some insulation around the wire to prevent air loss around the holes and to protect the cable from the sharp metal edges.

When drilling holes through walls, be very careful not to drill through pipes and electrical wires. Consider purchasing a device from your local home center or hardware store that you can use to detect wood studs, metal pipes, or electrical cable below the surface of the wall. Drill holes only where the device indicates that no hidden items are present. If you are drilling through wallboard, you can make a preliminary hole with a small punch to determine if any obstacle lies below the surface.

If you want to connect a computer that's directly upstairs, look for a closet. You might be able to drill a hole in the closet ceiling and run the cable through it. Because floors can be 8 inches thick or more, you might have to use a coat hanger to fish the cable through. After the cable reaches the other floor, you can run it along the baseboard.

If you'd rather not drill holes in a closet, look for other wires, pipes, or ducts that go between floors. You might find some space that you can use for your network cables next to pipes or other wires. If the space you must go through is insulated, be sure to replace any insulation that you remove. In some localities, the fire code requires that all spaces between floors be insulated as a fire stop.

Running Cables Between Nonadjacent Rooms

If the computers you want to connect aren't in adjacent rooms, you might need to run cable through an attic or basement. If you have a basement or crawl space, for example, you can run cable between the first-floor rooms by drilling down through the floors in both rooms. You can then run the cable down one hole, across the basement ceiling, and up the other hole. Use an attic the same way. Drill up through the ceiling in both rooms. Run the cable up one hole, across the attic, and down the other hole. *If you need custom cable lengths, see "Making Your Own Network Cables," later in this chapter.*

Using Twisted-Pair Cables

When you're using twisted-pair cable for the network, you must run a cable from the NIC at each computer to the hub. If you purchased an Ethernet kit, you probably have a hub and two lengths of cable. You plug in the cable just as you would a telephone cable.

Note

Lengths of twisted-pair cable with connectors at both ends are called *patch cable*.

If a cable you have is too short, you can join cables end to end with a coupler, which has two female RJ-45 sockets. Couplers for network cable look just like couplers for telephone cable, only bigger.

Making the Grade

You can purchase several *categories*, or grades, of twisted-pair cable. The higher the category, the better the cable and the more stable the connection. The standard grade for home networks is called *Category 5*, or "Cat 5." Fast Ethernet, which runs at 100 Mbps, requires Cat 5 cable, but for 10BaseT, which runs at only 10 Mbps, you might be able to get away with Cat 3 or Cat 4. Most stores sell only Cat 5 cable because the price difference between categories is negligible for short patch cables. Another category of cable, called Cat 5e, falls between Cat 5 and Cat 6 in price and quality. You won't need to use Cat 6 or Cat 7 cable in a home because they're designed for high-speed networks that must span long distances.

Note

Cat 2 cable is used to wire alarm systems and telephone lines. While Cat 3 and Cat 4 wire can be used for 10 Mbps networks, use Cat 5 whenever possible to achieve the best performance.

You can purchase twisted-pair cable in various lengths and colors. Most local stores carry only one or two colors, such as gray and white, but additional colors are available through mail order. You can also get cables that have molded or booted ends; they have plastic or rubberized material that covers the connection between the wire and the plug. This reinforcement strengthens the connections and makes them more suitable for installations where you'll be frequently removing and reinserting cables.

Hubless Networking

If you want to network only two computers, you can avoid using a hub by connecting their NICs with a special cable called a *crossover* or *cross-pinned* cable. You plug one end of the crossover cable into the NIC of one computer and plug the other end into the NIC of the other computer. No other hardware is required, and the cable can even be 100 feet long or more. A crossover cable is inexpensive; a 10-foot cable might cost $20 or less. Unfortunately, crossover cables aren't that easy to buy because few computer stores carry them.

If you go to a computer store to purchase a crossover cable, make sure you don't get a regular patch cable, the standard cable for networking. A crossover cable has two of its wires switched, so it's different from a regular network cable.

If you can't find a crossover cable at the local computer superstore, try ordering one from a mail order company, such as Data Comm Warehouse (*http://www.warehouse.com/ datacomm/*). You can also go to a small, local computer store where they might know about networking and make one for you.

Tip

Because crossover and regular patch cable look the same, you might want to wrap a small piece of duct tape or adhesive tape on one end of the crossover cable and write *crossover* on it. This label will help you distinguish the crossover cable from your regular patch cables.

Locating the Hub

When you want to connect three or more computers or connect a printer directly to the network, you'll need a hub. Consider a hub even when you need to connect only two computers. Hubs are so inexpensive that buying one might cost less than having a crossover cable custom made. Before connecting the hub to the network, however, consider its placement.

Note

You'll need a hub for any Ethernet network of three or more computers that uses twisted-pair cable, even networks with computers using external universal serial bus (USB) Ethernet adapters.

The hub must be plugged into an electrical source for power, so make sure it's near an outlet. You might also want to connect the hub to an outlet that isn't controlled by a wall switch, as you might leave the hub turned on at all times. The hub needs some air circulating around it, so don't put it in a cabinet or drawer, and be sure to keep it away from direct sunlight, heat, radios, fluorescent lights, or transmitters of any kind that can cause interference.

The main trick in placing a hub is to make it convenient to all your computers so that you can easily connect cables from the computers to the hub, passing through the fewest number of walls, floors, and rooms. If you're connecting two computers that are in the same room, just place the hub near an electrical outlet and run the cables from each computer to the hub. If you're connecting computers in adjacent rooms, locate the hub near the hole you've made between the rooms.

If you live in a one-story house with a basement, consider placing the hub in the basement. You can drill down through the floor in each room that has a computer and run cables down to the hub in the basement.

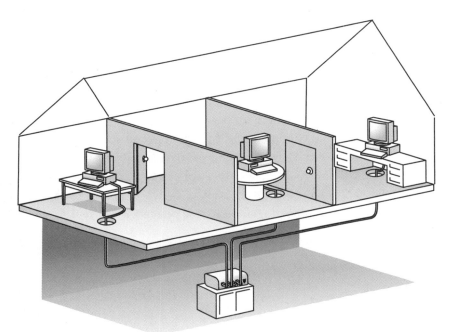

Because you have to run separate wires from every computer to the hub, sometimes the central location where you'd like to place the hub isn't ideal, especially when you have to run the cable through walls and along baseboards. Select a location that requires the least amount of cable and the least amount of fishing through walls, floors, and ceilings.

Making Your Own Network Cables

If you have a lot of wiring to do, you might want to consider making your own patch cables. That way, you can get cables that are just the right length and you can save some money, too. Rather than purchase patch cable that already has connectors on both ends, you can purchase bulk cable—long lengths of twisted-pair wire without any connectors. Although you must usually buy lengths of 250 feet or more to get bulk cable, cable at that length is relatively inexpensive. A 250-foot roll of bulk cable can cost about the same as two 50-foot patch cords. Buying bulk cable in even longer lengths, 500 or 1000 feet, is even cheaper per foot.

Note

You can also purchase patch cable, cut one end off to make it the proper length, and install a connector on the end yourself.

In addition to bulk cable, you'll need a supply of connectors and two special tools—a *stripper* and a *crimper.* The stripper cuts away the coating around the cable so that you can place the wires inside in a connector in a specific order. The crimper tightens the connector onto the wires. Complete kits of connectors and tools aren't expensive, but some dexterity is required in stripping and crimping the cable.

Another option when you are running cables through walls is to install Ethernet sockets. These are like phone sockets, but they're for network cables instead. They help to create a more attractive look and avoid clutter, especially if you plan on selling your home in the future. If you install network sockets, you can even purchase models that don't require a crimping tool. To install them, you'll need only a stripper to expose the wires in the cable and a faceplate that holds the socket on the wall, as shown in Figure 7-1. Some faceplates can hold two, four, or even more plugs. You'll need one of these faceplates for the location where all the cables connect to the hub.

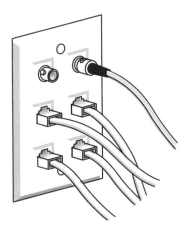

Figure 7-1.

Connecting cables to a faceplate.

Note

If you're running cable along baseboards, you can purchase surface-mounted jacks that at-tach directly to the baseboard. You then plug the patch cable into the jack. Because the cable and jacks are on the surface, you do not need to make holes in your walls, and it is easier to rewire than are cables and jacks installed in the wall.

Using Thin Ethernet Coaxial Cable

When you use coaxial cable, you don't need to connect the network cables at a hub. In-stead, you simply connect cables from one NIC to another to form a continuous chain.

At the end of each length of coaxial cable is a male BNC connector (short for several different terms, including barrel node connector, British Naval Connector, and Bayonet Neill-Concelman). The connector has a pin in the center and an outer ring that rotates. If you look into the end of the connector, you'll see that this ring has two grooves.

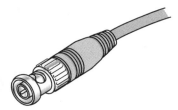

The BNC male connector attaches to a BNC female connector, which has two small stubs and no outer ring.

You join the male and female connectors by inserting the male connector into the female connector so the stubs fit into the grooves, and then rotating the ring on the male connector clockwise to lock the connectors together.

To connect a cable to a NIC, you attach it to a T-connector and then attach the T-connector to the NIC. The T-connecter has a BNC male connector at the base and a female connector at the end of each arm.

You slide the male BNC connector of the cable onto one arm of the T and then rotate the connector clockwise so that it locks into place.

If you're connecting together only two computers, you connect the other end of the cable to the T-connector attached to the second machine. If the machines are in adjacent rooms, you attach one end of the cable to the computer in one room, bring the cable through the wall, and connect it to the T-connector on the other computer. So for two computers, you'll need two T-connectors, one length of cable, and two terminators.

As you'll see in the following diagram, one arm of the T on each computer won't be connected to a cable, but you can't leave it empty because that would cause the electronic signals to be lost. So you must attach a terminator to each unused arm of the T.

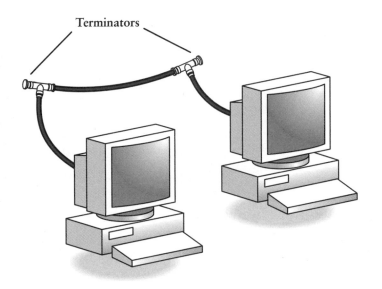

Terminators

After you've connected the cable to the T-connector, slide the T-connector onto the connector on the NIC and rotate it clockwise until it locks into place.

Just picture the network as a chain of computers with a coaxial cable running from the computer at the start of the chain to the computer at the end of the chain. Adding additional computers to the chain is easy. You can add them to the unused connections at the ends of the chain or insert them in the middle of the chain. To insert a computer in the middle of the chain, just take the coaxial cables from the computers on both sides and connect them to the T-connector on the new computer.

If at all possible, use continuous lengths of cable from one computer to the next. Connections are the most commonplace for problems to occur, so eliminate as many as possible to make sure your network runs well. If you don't have a length of coaxial cable long enough, you can join cables end to end, the same way you'd use an extension cord. To join them together, you can use the two arms of a T-connector without attaching the connector at its base to anything. You can also use a barrel connector, which is the top part of a T-connector that has the two BNC female connectors.

Making Your Own Coaxial Cable

You can create your own custom lengths of coaxial cable by using bulk cable and connectors. There are even "twist-on" connectors that you can attach to the end of bulk coaxial cable without having to do any crimping. These connectors work like the twist-on connectors you can use on cable TV wire. Bulk thin Ethernet coaxial cable is about $80 for 500 feet, and twist-on connectors are only about $2 each.

If you want to run coaxial cable through walls, you can also purchase male connectors, sockets, and faceplates, which resemble cable TV outlets.

Good Cabling Equals Good Networking

Now that you're familiar with the basics of cabling your network, here are some overall rules that you should consider.

Use Continuous Lengths

It's always best when the twisted-pair cables running from computers to the hub or the coaxial cables running from computer to computer are continuous lengths. Although you can join two cables end to end with a coupler, the connections at the coupler can come loose, and moisture or dust can disturb the contacts. Therefore, the coupler is the first place to look if something goes wrong with the network and the problem seems to be in the cable. Don't place the coupler in a wall, in case it needs to be reached or replaced.

Prevent Bends at Sharp Angles

As you run the cable, don't bend it at sharp angles. If you have to go around a corner, for example, don't bend the cable so that it folds or creases, and don't pull the cable tight. The wires inside cables are strong and flexible, but bending a cable back and forth during installation or sharply folding it in the corner of a room can break one of them. Although these wires might not break immediately, they can deteriorate over time.

Keep a Tidy Appearance

To preserve the appearance of your rooms, try to run cable in a wall or above the ceiling whenever possible. Try to avoid running it on the outside of a wall, along the baseboard. Many businesses have ceilings that are dropped just so network and other cables can easily be run from room to room, but you don't usually have that luxury in a home. If you must run cable along a baseboard or up a wall, secure it to the surface. Rather than nail or staple directly into the cable, use U-shaped nails that you've purchased at a hardware store or home center. Never put a cable where it can be tripped over or kicked, and never put it under the carpet where it can be stepped on. Although you might find it tempting to run the cable under an area rug rather than around the perimeter of a room, continuously walking over it, rolling over it with a chair, or vacuuming over it can wear down the cable and eventually ruin it. And no matter how thick your carpet is, you'll soon see the telltale sign of a cable bulging through.

Don't Force Cables

If you have to drill a hole in a wall to run the cable, make the hole larger than the connector at the end of the cable. Never force a cable through a smaller hole because you could damage the connector on the end. In fact, always be particularly careful with connectors at the end of the cable. The plug at the end of a twisted-pair cable has small metal contacts and a plastic tab that helps hold the plug in place. Don't step on the end or break off that tab. Also, take care to avoid cutting or bending the small wire at the end of a coaxial cable.

Use a Fish or a Coat Hanger

The worst part of running wire is fishing it through walls: getting it to go from one location to another when you can't see where it's going. Sometimes fishing cable is easy, such as when you have to run it between two adjacent rooms, but sometimes fishing is so frustrating that you'll want to give up and send mail by carrier pigeon.

If you have trouble feeding the cable through a wall, you can open a metal coat hanger and push one end through. Alternately, you can purchase a fish at a hardware store. It contains a coil of metal that you can unwind as needed. Once you get the coat hanger or fish through the wall, tie the end of the cable to the end of the hanger or fish, and then pull the cable through the other end.

Accessorizing Your Installation

No matter which type of cable you use, you can purchase all sorts of accessories to help hide it throughout the house. The most common of these are raceways and floor cable covers. Raceways, shown in the following diagram, are usually made of a nonconductive material like vinyl, and they attach to walls, ceilings, or floors to hide cable and keep it safe. Most raceways have curves for the corners of rooms to keep the cable from bending too sharply, and they are ideal for use with surface-mounted jacks.

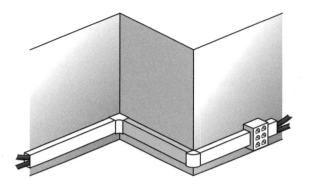

Floor cable covers are plastic or rubber, and they cover a cable that might otherwise be stepped on. Depending on their design, you run the cable through them or under them.

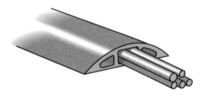

Many companies sell bulk cable, connectors, and the other accessories you'll need for a professional cabling job in your home. Unfortunately, most computer stores, even superstores, carry only a small selection of cabling supplies. An alternate source for the parts you'll need is a mail order catalog such as Data Comm Warehouse.

Because you must order the materials and wait for them to arrive, it pays to plan your detailed cable layout in advance. You can run lengths of string where you plan to run the cable to get measurements. You can also make the holes in advance and use the string later to fish the cable through the walls.

Expanding Your Network

As your needs and your family grow, you might want to add more computers to the network. As you've seen, adding computers to a network that uses thin Ethernet coaxial cable is easy; just remove the terminator at one end of the chain and connect the cable from the additional computer. But networks connected by twisted-pair cable must have enough ports on the hub for all the computers that you want to connect. If you have a five-port hub, for example, you can connect only five computers. When your twisted-pair cable network exceeds the hub's capacity, you have two choices. You can purchase a hub that handles more computers, or you can link two or more hubs together.

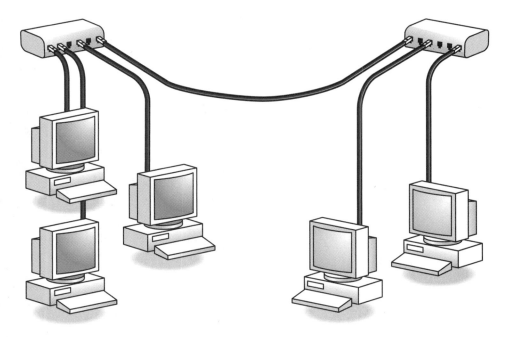

The two hubs you connect aren't required to be in the same room of your house, so you can also consider using two hubs to connect different branches of your network where it's difficult to run cables or to avoid running multiple cables along the same path. In Figure 7-2, two hubs are used to simplify a household network. With two hubs in different areas of the house, you need to fish only one wire between the areas.

Most of the ports on the hub are designed to be connected to a NIC using a standard twisted-pair cable. You can't use a regular cable to connect regular ports of two hubs. As a solution, many hubs have an extra connector called an *uplink port,* which lets you connect hubs and link them in a chain. This port is designed so that you can connect it to a regular port of another hub to connect them together. In some cases, a switch on the hub changes a port from regular to uplink. Here are four different ways to connect two hubs.

If both hubs have an uplink port, you have two choices:

• Use a regular twisted-pair cable to connect the uplink port of one hub to any regular port on the second hub. This system allows up to nine computers to be on the network if you have two five-port hubs with separate uplink ports.

• Use crossover cable to connect the uplink ports of both hubs together. With this configuration, you can have 10 computers networked with two five-port hubs with separate uplink ports.

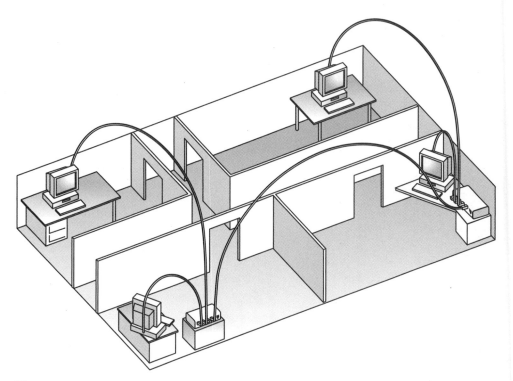

Figure 7-2.

Connecting hubs in different parts of the house.

If only one hub has an uplink port, do the following:

- Again, use a regular twisted-pair cable to connect the uplink port of one hub to any regular port on the second hub. This system allows up to nine computers to be on a network of two five-port hubs, one of which has a separate uplink port.

If neither of the hubs has an uplink port, you must use this method:

- Use a crossover cable to connect any port on one hub to any port on the other hub. This technique allows up to eight computers to be networked with two five-port hubs.

Note

If your hub does have an uplink port, check the hub's documentation. In some hubs, the uplink port shares the same resources as a regular port—usually the one next to it. This means that if you plug a cable into the uplink port to connect the hub, you can't use the shared port for a workstation. So if you have a five-port hub with an uplink port that shares resources, using the uplink port means that only four computers can be connected to the hub.

You can even connect some hubs on twisted-pair networks with thin Ethernet co-axial cable. The documentation for your hub can tell you which type of cable and which ports to use.

If you have a hub that contains one or more coaxial connections, by the way, you can use it to combine twisted-pair and thin Ethernet cable in one network. As shown in Figure 7-3, connect the free end of the coaxial cable to the coaxial port of the hub.

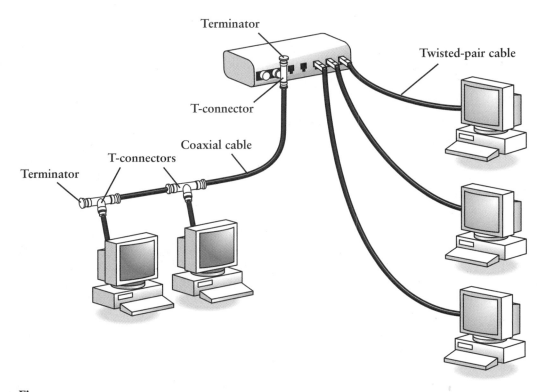

Figure 7-3.
Combining twisted-pair and coaxial networks.

Alternatives to Hubs

Most of the inexpensive hubs on the market are called *passive hubs*. They simply provide a means of linking all the computers together through twisted-pair cable.

No matter how many passive hubs you have linked together, all the computers and hubs are seen as one network, and all the computers are competing for the same space on the network cable, called the *bandwidth*. This situation is like driving along a narrow, one-lane highway with a high speed limit. No matter how fast you allow cars to travel, the road can handle just so much traffic before a traffic jam occurs.

If several computers try to access the network at the same time, a collision can occur between the information traveling through the cable. Such a collision slows down the entire network and might even result in some lost data.

One of the first options you should consider for increasing the performance of a small network is to replace the hub with a *switch* or *switching hub*. Switches work by transmitting information only to the computer it's being sent to. With a switch, the network appears to have a separate connection to each of the computers, so you get the full performance and speed from each device. Think of a switch as a mechanism that opens up the traffic to multiple high-speed lanes, with each lane going to a separate destination—one specific computer. You simply remove the hub from your network and replace it with a switch; no additional setup or configuration is required.

You can consider other types of hubs and devices as well, but many are rather costly for a home network. A device called an *active hub* can amplify the signal to allow greater distances, and an *intelligent hub* can manage the network transmissions to increase performance. A *stackable hub* uses a special high-speed bus to carry network signals from one hub to another. A *repeater* allows the distance between devices to be extended by amplifying the network signal, and a *bridge* connects two sections of a network together so that each appears as its own network without competing for the same space on the cable.

Boost Performance with Switches

Switches cost much more than a hub. They start at about $100 but are well worth the investment if you have a busy home network.

As an example, my own network consisted of a 5-port and an 8-port hub linked together in one location and an additional 5-port hub in another location. When all my computers were running and the family was busy sharing files, printers, and modems, performance dropped noticeably. It would sometimes take an unusually long time to access a resource on the network, and someone would occasionally get an error message that the network or a specific resource wasn't available.

I replaced the two linked hubs with one 16-port switch—a model AT-FS716E from Allied Telesyn. Not only did the error messages no longer appear, but the performance of the network also increased dramatically.

Switches are available with anywhere from 5 to 24 ports, and you can link together as many multiple switches as you can hubs. You can get 5-port switches that cost less than $150 from companies such as Allied Telesyn, D-Link, Linksys, and SMC.

The Bottom Line

Connecting your computers can be easy, but the location of your computers can sometimes pose some challenges. In most cases, you can find ways to run cables that avoid making too many holes in the walls and running cables where they are unsightly.

In this chapter, you learned how to connect computers using twisted-pair cable (with and without a hub) and how to use coaxial cable. In the next chapter, you'll learn how to install the software that gets your network up and running.

Part 3

Setting Up the Software

Chapter 8
Installing the Software 141

Chapter 9
Creating Profiles 169

Chapter 10
Learning to Share 187

Chapter 8

Installing the Software

Now that you've installed the network hardware, you're ready to deal with the software. Your network interface card (NIC) won't do you any good unless you configure Microsoft Windows to use it and to communicate with other computers on the network.

In this chapter, you'll learn how to install the software that controls your NIC and that allows your computer to communicate with the rest of the network. Before you do anything else, however, check the manual that came with your hardware. Some types of network hardware require a number of steps to set them up. Others come with a completely automatic setup program. Once you've run the setup program, you're ready to connect to your network without any further configuration.

Although not every networking system is automatic, many have their own special way of installing drivers and configuring Windows. So it pays to look at the hardware manual first and run any installation program the manufacturer provides.

Installing Network Drivers

Network drivers are the first software you have to install. These are files that Windows needs to communicate with your NIC. If a disk or CD came with your hardware, it probably contains the network drivers.

Drivers are installed in one of three basic ways, depending on the type of hardware.

- **The Good** Automatically, with plug-and-play devices that Windows recognizes and that provide the easiest installation

- **The Bad** Manually, with Windows or special software that comes with the hardware
- **The Ugly** Manually, with non–plug-and-play network cards that require special configuration to avoid hardware conflicts

Loading Drivers Automatically

If you installed a plug-and-play NIC, Windows senses that the card is installed and loads the software for it. For some network devices, the drivers are already on your hard disk. For others, they need to be copied from the Windows CD. (Have the CD handy, just in case.) In still other cases, the drivers will be on the disk that came with the hardware.

To install the drivers for your NIC on a Windows system, follow these steps:

Note

Depending on the version of Windows your machine is running, different wizard pages than the ones described next might appear, but the general process is the same regardless of the Windows version.

1. Turn on your computer and watch the screen.

    Windows, sensing that a new card has been installed, briefly displays the New Hardware Found message on the screen and then starts the Add New Hardware Wizard. This wizard takes you step by step through the process of installing the drivers. The first page of the Add New Hardware Wizard identifies the new hardware that has been detected.

Note

If Windows doesn't detect your card, go to Control Panel and double-click Add New Hardware in Consumer Windows (Microsoft Windows 95, Microsoft Windows 98, and Microsoft Windows Millennium Edition), or Add/Remove Hardware in Microsoft Windows 2000. Keep clicking Next and following the directions that appear until the wizard finds the card in your system.

2. Click Next.

3. The next wizard page asks whether you want Windows to search for new drivers or whether you want to select the driver from a list. Choose to search for new drivers, and then click Next.

4. Select the check boxes next to one or more of these locations to look for the drivers: Floppy Drive, CD-ROM, Microsoft Windows Update, and Specific Location.

5. If your NIC came with a floppy disk, select Floppy Disk and insert the disk in the floppy disk drive. If the NIC came with a CD, select CD-ROM and insert the CD in your CD-ROM drive. If you select Microsoft Windows Update, you'll need to have an active Internet connection because this option will open the Windows Update Web site. If you select Specific Location, you'll need to type the path of the drivers, such as D:\WIN98.

6. Click Next to have the wizard look for the appropriate drivers.

7. The next wizard page shows where the drivers are located.

8. Click Next, and then click Finish.

After the drivers are installed, you'll be asked whether you want to restart your computer. The drivers won't be recognized properly until you restart, so click Yes.

Installing Drivers Manually

If the Add New Hardware Wizard doesn't detect your NIC, you can load the drivers manually.

Installing Drivers Manually in Consumer Windows

To install NIC drivers manually in Consumer Windows, follow these steps:

1. Double-click My Computer on the Windows desktop.

2. In the My Computer window, double-click Control Panel.

3. In Control Panel, double-click the Network icon.

4. Click Add to see the Select Network Component Type dialog box shown here.

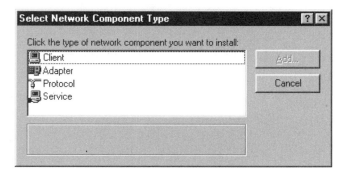

5. Click Adapter in the list, and then click Add to open the Select Network Adapters dialog box shown in Figure 8-1. On the left side of the dialog box is a list of manufacturers whose drivers are provided with Windows.

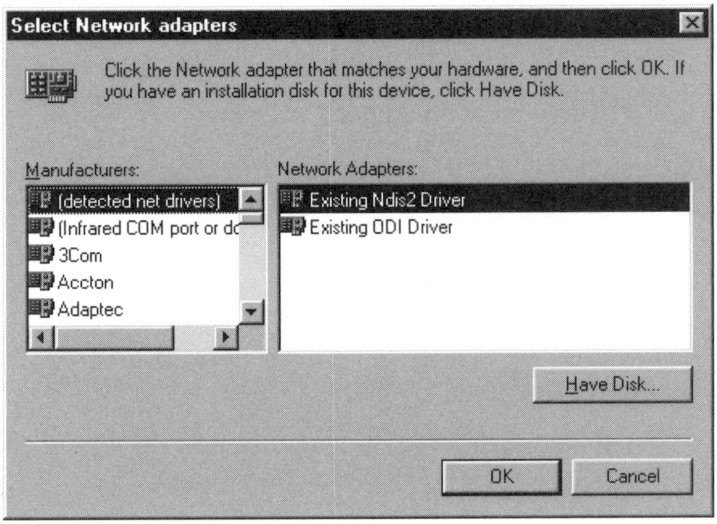

Figure 8-1.
The Select Network Adapters dialog box allows you to select the make and model of your NIC.

6. From the list of manufacturers, select the manufacturer of your NIC. On the right side of the dialog box, you see a list of network adapters made by the manufacturer.

7. From the Network Adapters list, select your card model.

8. Click OK.

9. Click Yes when Windows prompts you to restart your computer.

Installing Drivers Manually in Windows 2000

If you're using Windows 2000, follow these steps to install NIC drivers manually:

1. In Control Panel, double-click Add/Remove Hardware.

2. Click Next twice. Windows displays a list of devices. Click Add A New Device and then click Next.

3. Select No, I Want To Select The Hardware From The List, and then click Next to display the Hardware Type list, which is shown in Figure 8-2.

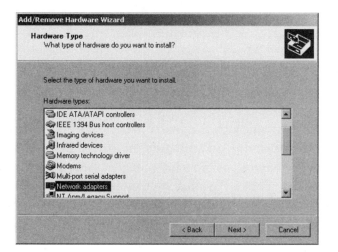

Figure 8-2.
Choose the type of hardware you want to install using the Add/Remove Hardware Wizard.

4. Choose Network Adapters and then click Next. On the left side of the dialog box is a list of manufacturers whose drivers are provided with Windows.

5. From the list of manufacturers, select the manufacturer of your card. On the right side of the dialog box is a list of network adapters made by the manufacturer.

Note

For both Consumer Windows and Windows 2000, if your manufacturer or card isn't listed but the card came with a disk or CD that contains the drivers, click Have Disk in the Select Network Adapters dialog box and navigate to the disk or CD.

6. From the Network Adapters list, select your card model.

7. Click OK.

8. Click Yes when Windows prompts you to restart your computer.

Installing Drivers for Non–Plug-and-Play NICs

In Chapter 6, you learned how to install an Industry Standard Architecture (ISA) card and how to set switches and jumpers if the interrupt request (IRQ) and input/output (I/O) addresses need to be set on the card itself. Some ISA cards, however, let you change these settings using software. Such cards come with a setup or installation program on disk that either makes the settings for you or guides you through the process.

Tip

If other devices are already using all your IRQ addresses, you might encounter difficulties when setting up an ISA card. Exchanging the card for another ISA NIC might not solve the problem—you might need a PCI card or an external network device that connects to your universal serial bus (USB) or printer port.

Run the installation program that came with the software. The program might automatically check out your system and assign the best settings to the card. If the program asks you to select the settings, however, cancel the program so that you can check out which IRQs and I/O addresses are free. The NIC manual should include a list of the possible addresses to which you can set your card. Here's a quick reminder about how to find out which of these are actually available.

Checking the IRQ and I/O Addresses in Consumer Windows

If you're using Consumer Windows, check the IRQ and I/O addresses by following these steps:

1. Right-click My Computer on the Windows desktop, and choose Properties from the shortcut menu.

2. Click the Device Manager tab in the System Properties dialog box.

3. Double-click Computer at the top of the list of devices.

4. In the Computer Properties dialog box, make sure the Interrupt Request (IRQ) option is selected on the View Resources tab.

5. Look for an unused IRQ. You might also be able to use the IRQ assigned to an unused serial port.

6. Select the Input/Output (I/O) option.

7. Check to see which address your card can use that's not already used.

8. Click Cancel twice to return to the desktop.

9. Run the installation program that came with the card and select an IRQ and I/O address not in use by another device.

Checking the IRQ and I/O Addresses in Windows 2000

If you're using Windows 2000, check the IRQ and I/O addresses by following these steps:

1. Right-click My Computer on the desktop and choose Properties.

2. On the Hardware tab, click Device Manager.

3. Select Resources By Type from the View menu.

4. Click the plus sign next to Interrupt Request (IRQ).

5. Look for an unused IRQ. You might also be able to use the IRQ assigned to an unused serial port.

6. Click the plus sign next to Input/Output (I/O).

7. Check to see which address your card can use that's not already being used.

8. Close the window.

9. Run the installation program that came with the card and select an IRQ and I/O not in use by another device.

Checking Hardware Conflicts

After you install the drivers, you should confirm that no hardware conflicts exist. Here's how to do it:

1. Right-click My Computer on the Windows desktop, and choose Properties from the shortcut menu.

2. In Consumer Windows, click the Device Manager tab in the System Properties dialog box. In Windows 2000, click the Device Manager button on the Hardware tab.

If your network device isn't working properly, you'll see an exclamation point or X next to its name. Follow these steps to troubleshoot the problem:

1. In the list of devices on the Device Manager tab, click the name of your NIC under Network Adapters. In Consumer Windows, click Properties. In Windows 2000, click the Properties button on the toolbar.

In the Properties dialog box for your network device, look in the Device Status section of the General tab. If you see a message that says "This device is either not present, not working properly, or does not have all the drivers installed," you have either a bad card or a conflict.

2. Click the Resources tab. The Conflicting Device List section shows where the conflict is occurring.

Try rerunning the card's installation program and selecting other settings, and if that doesn't work, change the settings manually in the device's Properties dialog box.

Changing the settings yourself is a last-ditch option. There's no guarantee that you'll get the NIC to work, and you could create a new conflict with another device, such as a modem or printer, causing that device to fail as well. If you do want to try changing the settings manually, follow these steps:

1. On the Resources tab of the Properties dialog box, make a note of which settings are being used.

   This information will allow you to restore the original settings, if necessary. Restoring the original settings won't do anything for the NIC, but it might restore some other device that you disabled by changing settings manually.

2. Click the Use Automatic Settings check box to clear it.

3. In the Resource Type list, click the setting you want to change.

4. Click Change Settings.

5. In the dialog box that opens, change the setting, and then click OK.

Restart your computer and test all your devices. If the new device doesn't work, repeat the process but restore the original settings. Perhaps it's time to take your computer to a shop for the installation or remove the card and exchange it for a plug-and-play PC model.

Configuring Windows for Networking

The next step in creating your network is to configure Windows for networking. This process involves four steps:

- Adding the network client
- Installing the network protocol
- Selecting network services
- Identifying your computer on the network workgroup

Choosing a *network client* determines how users gain access to the network. You can choose whether everyone who uses a networked computer must log on by entering a user name or by selecting the name from a list. In either case, users must enter a password for access to the network.

A *protocol* allows networked computers to send information back and forth and understand what other computers are saying. A protocol is a sort of language, with its own vocabulary and rules of grammar, that all networked computers have to speak to understand each other. If two computers are using different protocols, they're not able to communicate.

Network services are the resources you want to share. For example, you can choose to share your files and to let other network users access your printer.

A *workgroup* is simply a collection of computers that can interact and communicate with each other on a network. Everyone on the network who wants to share resources with others in a particular workgroup must belong to that group and must be identified by a computer name. You must enter the workgroup name for each computer when you set up networking.

The Windows Millennium Edition (Me) Home Networking Wizard

If you have Microsoft Windows Me, you can choose to set up and configure home networking and Internet Connection Sharing by using the Home Networking Wizard. I recommend, however, that you set up your network without using the wizard and instead use the techniques that you'll learn in this chapter. Learning how to use the Network icon in Control Panel and other Windows features gives you the tools to fine-tune and troubleshoot your network beyond the basic steps the wizard provides.

However, if you do decide to run the wizard, perform the following steps:

1. Double-click My Network Places on the Windows Me desktop.

2. Double-click the Home Networking Wizard icon.

3. Follow the directions on the screen.

The wizard will ask you whether you want to set up Internet Connection Sharing to share your modem and Internet account with others on the network, enter your computer name and workgroup, specify the files and printers you want to share, and create a home networking setup disk to use with other Windows Me computers so that they're compatible with yours.

Adding the Network Client

The first step in configuring Windows for networking is to determine how members of your family log on to the network when they start the computer or restart Windows. You do this by installing one of two network clients:

- **Client For Microsoft Windows** lets you start your computer and log on to the network by entering your name and password in a dialog box when Windows starts.

- **Microsoft Family Logon** lets you start your computer and log on to a network by selecting your user name from a list. You can use this option if more than one person uses a single computer. This option isn't available in Windows 2000.

Adding a Network Client in Consumer Windows

Follow these steps to select your network client if you're using Consumer Windows:

> **Note**
>
> You may need to insert your Windows CD later in the process, so have the CD handy.

1. On the Start menu, point to Settings, and then click Control Panel.

2. Double-click the Network icon to open the Network dialog box.

3. Look for either Client For Microsoft Networks or Microsoft Family Logon.

   If one of these clients is already installed and you don't want to change to the other, you can skip the rest of this procedure. If neither is installed or you want to select the other client, continue with the next steps.

4. Click Add.

5. In the Select Network Component Type dialog box, click Client.

6. Click Add.

7. In the Select Network Client dialog box, click Microsoft in the Manufacturers list.

8. From the list of Network Clients in the Select Network Client dialog box, select Client For Microsoft Networks or Microsoft Family Logon.

9. Click OK to close the Select Network Client dialog box.

10. Click OK to close the Network dialog box. You may be asked to insert your Windows CD at this point.

11. Click Yes when you're asked whether you want to restart the computer.

You can have both Client For Microsoft Networks and Microsoft Family Logon installed at the same time. After adding one client, repeat the previous steps but choose the other client. To choose which client to use as the default, follow these steps:

1. On the Start menu, point to Settings, and click Control Panel.

2. Double-click the Network icon to display the Network dialog box.

3. From the Primary Network Logon drop-down list, choose either Client For Microsoft Networks or Microsoft Family Logon.

4. Click OK.

Configuring a Network Client in Windows 2000

If you have Windows 2000, follow these steps to configure the network client:

1. On the Start menu, point to Settings, and then click the Network And Dial-up Connections icon.

2. In the window that appears, right-click Local Area Connection and choose Properties from the shortcut menu to display the Local Area Connection Properties dialog box.

    If Client For Microsoft Networks is listed, you can skip the rest of this procedure. If it isn't installed, continue as follows:

3. Click Install to open the Select Network Component Type dialog box.

4. Select Client, and then click Add to display the Select Network Client box.

5. Select Client For Microsoft Networks and click OK.

6. Click Close to close the Local Area Connection Properties dialog box.

Installing Protocols

Your next step is to install one or more protocols that will allow your computer to communicate with other computers. Three basic protocols are used in home networks:

- **Transmission Control Protocol/Internet Protocol** (TCP/IP) is the protocol used to dial in to an Internet service, so odds are you already have it installed. However, it's not often used in smaller home networks because it requires a few more steps to set up than the other protocols do.

- **Internet Packet Exchange/Sequenced Packet Exchange** (IPX/SPX) was originally developed for an office networking system called Novell NetWare, although it can be used for any type of network.

- **NetBIOS Extended User Interface** (NetBEUI) is a network protocol for smaller networks that's easy to set up.

Note

If you plan to extend your network to shared modems and network printers, consider using TCP/IP because it's often required for connecting devices directly to the network. See "Configuring TCP/IP," later in this chapter.

You can actually have all three protocols installed at the same time for compatibility with any type of network that you connect to. In fact, the manufacturer might already have installed them in Windows. Some NIC installation programs, such as the one from Microsoft, set up and configure all three protocols when they install the network drivers.

With all three protocols installed, your home network will probably work perfectly well by choosing the best protocol when the computers begin communicating. The IPX/SPX and NetBEUI protocols require virtually no special configuration, so once you install them and start the network, your computer should be ready to communicate with other computers on the network.

Installing Protocols in Consumer Windows

To see which protocols are already installed and to add new ones, follow these steps for Consumer Windows:

1. On the Start menu, point to Settings, and then click Control Panel.

2. In Control Panel, double-click the Network icon to display the Network dialog box shown in Figure 8-3. Any network protocols and services already installed are listed.

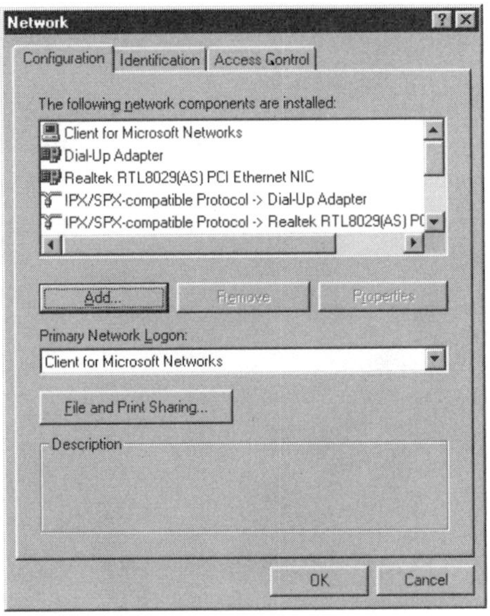

Figure 8-3.
The Network dialog box lists the protocols installed in your system.

3. Click Add.

4. In the Select Network Component Type dialog box, select Protocol and click Add to open the Select Network Protocol dialog box.

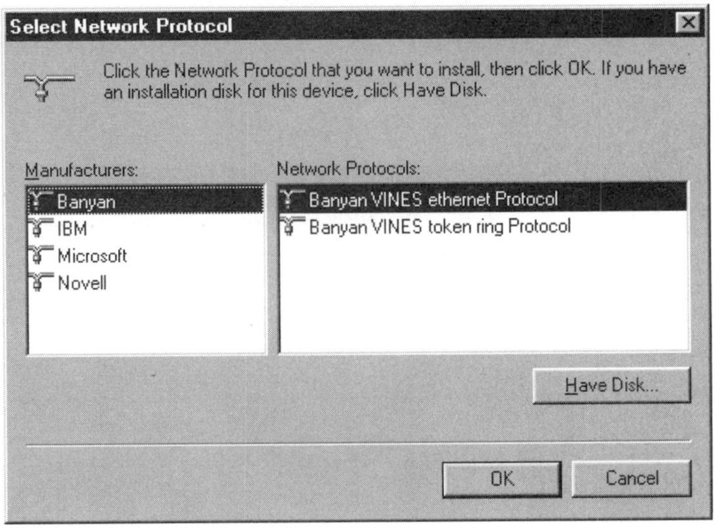

5. Choose Microsoft from the list of manufacturers.

6. Click a protocol in the Network Protocols list—IPX/SPX, NetBEUI, or TCP/IP.

7. Click OK to close the Select Network Protocol dialog box.

8. Click OK to close the Network dialog box. You may be asked to insert your Windows CD at this point.

9. Click Yes when you're asked whether you want to restart your computer.

10. Open the Network dialog box again. You should see a listing for each of the protocols followed by the name of your network card in this form: TCP/IP→NETGEAR PCI Fast Ethernet, for example.

Installing Protocols in Windows 2000

To see which protocols are already installed and to add new ones if you are using Windows 2000, follow these steps:

1. On the Start menu, point to Settings, and then click Network And Dial-up Connections.

2. Right-click Local Area Connection and choose Properties from the shortcut menu to display the Local Area Connection Properties dialog box. Any network protocols and services already installed are listed.

3. Click Install.

4. In the Select Network Component Type dialog box, select Protocol and click Add to open the Select Network Protocol dialog box.

5. Click a protocol in the Network Protocols list—IPX/SPX, NetBEUI, or TCP/IP.

6. Click OK to close the Select Network Protocol dialog box.

7. Click Close to exit from the Local Area Connection Properties dialog box.

8. Click Yes if you are asked to restart your computer.

9. Open the Network dialog box again.

    You should see a listing for each of the protocols. At the top of the box is the name of your NIC. The check mark next to the protocol indicates that the protocol is associated (bound) with your NIC.

Selecting Network Services

Network services allow you to share the resources on your network—primarily files and printers—among all the computers. File sharing lets other network users access your files. If you don't allow file sharing, other users can tell that you're on the network, but they won't be able to use any of your folders or files. Because sharing files is one of the main reasons to set up a network, it makes sense to turn on this feature. You always have the option to specify which folders can be shared and how the files in these folders can be accessed.

Because sharing a printer is another big advantage of networking, you'll want to turn on printer sharing as well. Before you can activate file sharing and printer sharing, however, you have to install the Windows service that allows sharing in the first place.

Selecting Network Services in Consumer Windows

Here's how to add network services in Consumer Windows:

1. On the Start menu, point to Settings, and then click Control Panel.

2. In Control Panel, double-click the Network icon to open the Network dialog box.

3. In the list of network components that are installed, look for File And Printer Sharing For Microsoft Networks.

    If File And Printer Sharing For Microsoft Networks is installed, you can skip the rest of these steps. If not, continue.

4. Click Add.

5. In the Select Network Component Type dialog box, click Service.

6. Click Add.

7. In the Select Network Service dialog box, click File And Printer Sharing For Microsoft Networks.

8. Click OK.

9. Click OK to close the Network dialog box. You may be asked to insert your Windows CD at this point.

10. Click Yes when you're asked whether you want to restart your computer.

After your computer restarts, you're ready to turn on file and printer sharing.

1. On the Start menu, point to Settings, and then click Control Panel.

2. In Control Panel, double-click the Network icon to display the Network dialog box.

3. In the Network dialog box, click the File And Print Sharing button.

4. Select both check boxes in the File And Print Sharing dialog box.

5. Click OK.

6. Click OK to close the Network dialog box.

This doesn't mean that your files and printer are already shared. It means only that the service that allows sharing is now turned on.

Selecting Network Services in Windows 2000

Follow these steps to select services in Windows 2000:

1. On the Start menu, point to Settings, and then click Network And Dial-Up Connections.

2. Right-click Local Area Connection and choose Properties from the shortcut menu.

3. In the list of network components that are installed, look for File And Printer Sharing For Microsoft Networks. If File And Printer Sharing For Microsoft Networks is installed, you can skip the rest of these steps.

4. Click Install to open the Select Network Component Type dialog box.

5. Select Service and then click Add to open the Select Network Service dialog box.

6. Select File And Printer Sharing For Microsoft Networks and then click OK.

7. Click OK to close the Select Network Component Type dialog box.

8. Click Yes if you're asked if you want to restart your computer.

Identifying Your Computer on the Network

The final step in configuring Windows for networking is to make sure that your computer has a name and that you're a member of the same workgroup as the other computers on the network.

Identifying Your Computer in Consumer Windows

If you're using Consumer Windows, identify your workstation by following these steps:

1. On the Start menu, point to Settings, and then click Control Panel.

2. In Control Panel, double-click the Network icon to open the Network dialog box.

3. In the Network dialog box, click the Identification tab to see the options in Figure 8-4.

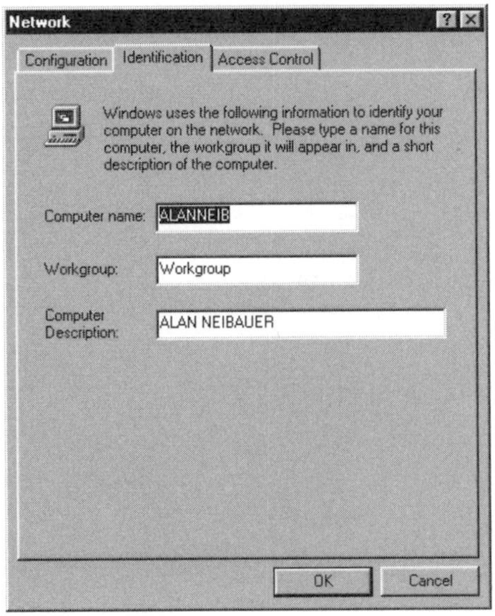

Figure 8-4.
Identify yourself and your workgroup on the Identification tab of the Network dialog box.

4. If you want, change the name of your computer.

5. Make sure the workgroup name is the same one you use for other computers on your network. Windows suggests the name *Workgroup* by default.

6. Enter an optional description that others who browse the network can see.

7. Click OK to close the Network dialog box.

8. Click Yes when you're asked whether you want to restart the computer.

Identifying Your Computer in Windows 2000

If you're using Windows 2000, identify your workstation by following these steps:

1. Right-click My Computer and choose Properties from the shortcut menu to open the System Properties box.

2. Click the Network Identification tab.

3. Click the Properties button in the Network Identification to open the Identification Changes box.

4. If you want, change the name of your computer.

5. Make sure the workgroup name is the same one you use for other computers on your network. Windows suggests the name *Workgroup* by default.

6. Click OK to close the Identification Changes box, and then click OK to close the System Properties box.

7. Click Yes if you're asked if you want to restart the computer.

Configuring TCP/IP

Once installed, the NetBEUI network protocol usually doesn't require any further configuration to get it working. With TCP/IP, however, you must check some settings to make sure that the computers on the network can communicate.

If you have a dial-up Internet account, your computer is probably already using TCP/IP to connect to the Internet. In the Network dialog box, you'll see a listing for TCP/IP→Dial-up Adapter showing that the protocol is installed.

Note

If you get a message stating that file sharing is turned on when you first connect to the Internet, turn it off and restart your computer. This precaution will protect your files from unauthorized use—or even sabotage—by Internet hackers.

TCP/IP requires that each computer on the network have its own IP address—a string of numbers that identifies every computer linked to the Internet and every computer linked to a home TCP/IP network. No two computers on the Internet or two computers on your home network can have the same IP address. If you have a dial-up Internet account, most Internet service providers (ISPs) assign an IP address to your system each time you connect.

For a home network using TCP/IP, you can have Windows automatically assign an IP address to your computer every time your computer is started, or you can assign an IP address to it that will be unique on the network. Letting Windows assign the IP address is called *dynamic addressing* because the address assigned to your computer might change each time you connect to the network depending on which other computers have connected before you. Some Internet sharing software, which you'll learn about in Chapter 13, requires that Windows assign the IP addresses.

You'll need to assign a specific IP address, however, if you plan to use your computer with peripherals, such as a network modem or a printer that requires a certain address. This is called a *static address* because it's the same each time you start your computer.

Note

You should learn both methods of assigning IP addresses. For a home network, I recommend assigning your own addresses, but be prepared to switch to dynamic addressing if the need arises.

An IP address is composed of four sets of numbers, each between 0 and 255, and each set of numbers is separated by a period. When you type an IP address, you must type all four sets of numbers, even if the number is 0, as in 192.168.0.25. Since no two computers on the Internet are allowed to have the same IP address, your ISP will assign you an IP address when you connect. (After you log off, the IP address you just used becomes available for the ISP to assign to another user.) If you have a digital subscriber line (DSL) or cable modem, your ISP has already assigned you an IP address for connecting to the Internet. You have to select a network IP address that's guaranteed not to conflict with your Internet IP address. To make this task easy, the Internet Engineering Task Force (IETF), the organization that determines Internet standards, set aside three ranges of numbers that can't be used as Internet addresses, and you can safely choose any IP address for your network in these ranges:

- 10.0.0.0 through 10.255.255.255
- 172.16.0.0 through 172.31.255.255
- 192.168.0.0 through 192.168.255.255

For your home network, you can use IP addresses starting with 192.168.0.1 and just add 1 to the last number for each computer. (To set up the second computer in your network, for example, enter *192.168.0.2* as the IP address.) Type a period between each number to separate the numbers into the four sections.

You also have to designate a subnet address. To add further flexibility, another set of numbers, called the *subnet mask*, is used to modify how each address is interpreted. The subnet mask determines what portion of the entire IP address is used to specify the network and subnet numbers and what portion specifies an individual computer on the subnet. Since all your computers will be in the same subnet, they must all have the same numbers in the Subnet Mask field.

Note

Conflicts might arise when using TCP/IP. Some computers that use early versions of Windows 95 that have not been updated have difficulties when TCP/IP is used on two devices at the same time, such as your NIC and the modem connecting you to the Internet. One or the other might not work properly. When you connect to a computer on the network, your Web browser might automatically try to connect to your ISP through Dial-Up Networking. Also, communications programs, such as some versions of CompuServe software, might not be able to connect to the ISP when TCP/IP is being used as a network protocol. The easiest way to resolve these conflicts is to use NetBEUI as your network protocol instead.

Setting IP Addresses in Consumer Windows

To set the IP address of a Consumer Windows computer on the network, follow these steps:

1. On the Start menu, point to Settings, and then click Control Panel.

2. In Control Panel, double-click the Network icon to open the Network dialog box.

3. In the list of network components, click the TCP/IP setting for your NIC, and click Properties to see the options in Figure 8-5.

Caution

If you're connected to the Internet through a DSL or cable modem, you might have two TCP/IP settings for Ethernet devices shown in the Network dialog box. One is for your Ethernet connection to the Internet; the other is for your Ethernet connection to the network. In setting up your network, be sure to select the TCP/IP setting for the NIC connected to the network. When you click Properties, if a specific IP address is already shown in the dialog box that appears, you've probably selected the Internet TCP/IP setting. Click Cancel and choose the other TCP/IP setting in the Network dialog box. Check with your ISP if you have any questions.

4. Make sure Obtain An IP Address Automatically is selected if you want Windows to assign an IP address to your computer whenever it's started, and then click OK.

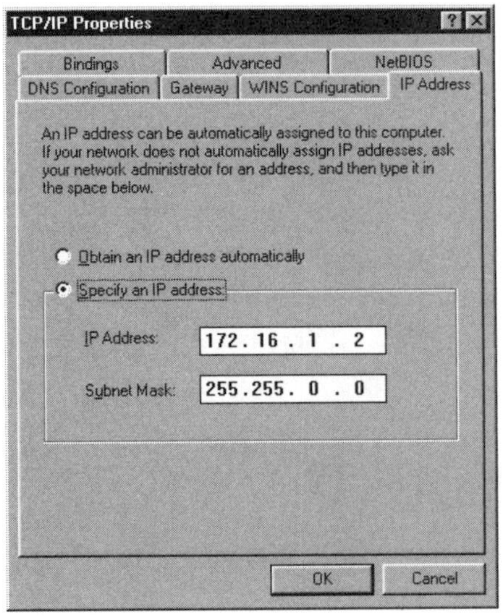

Figure 8-5.
The TCP/IP Properties dialog box displays two TCP/IP settings: IP Address and Subnet Mask.

If you want to assign your own IP address, continue with the following steps:

5. Click Specify An IP Address in the TCP/IP Properties dialog box.

6. Enter an IP address in the text box.

Tip

When you enter an IP address or subnet mask, Windows will move from one set of numbers to the next when you enter the third digit. If you want to put only one or two digits in a set, either type a period to move to the next set, or click in the spot where the next set of numbers is located.

7. Enter *255.255.255.0* as the Subnet Mask for this and every other computer on the network.

8. Click OK to close the Network dialog box.

9. Click Yes when you're asked whether you want to restart your computer.

Configuring TCP/IP in Windows 2000

To configure TCP\IP on a Windows 2000 workstation, follow these steps:

1. On the Start menu, point to Settings, and then click Network And Dial-Up Connections.

2. Right-click Local Area Connection and choose Properties from the shortcut menu to display the Local Area Connection Properties dialog box.

3. In the list of network components, click Internet Protocol (TCP/IP) and click Properties to see the options in Figure 8-6.

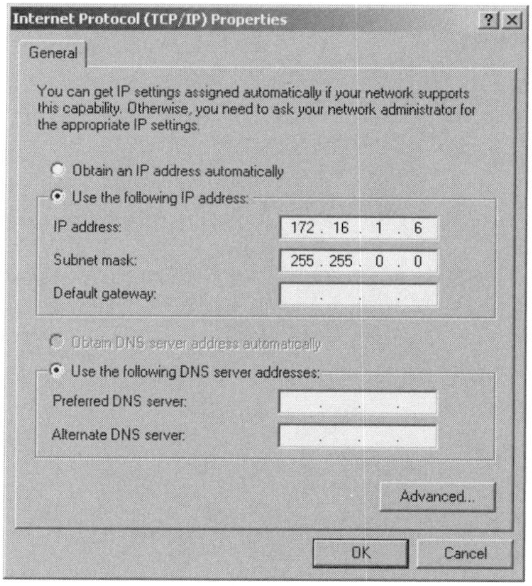

Figure 8-6.

The Internet Protocol (TCP/IP) Properties dialog box displays two TCP/IP settings: IP Address and Subnet Mask.

4. Make sure Obtain An IP Address Automatically is selected if you want Windows to assign an IP address to your computer whenever it's started, and then click OK.

   If you want to assign your own IP address, continue with the following steps:

5. Click Use The Following IP Address.

6. Enter an IP address in the text box.

7. Enter *255.255.255.0* as the Subnet Mask in this and every other computer on the network.

8. Click OK to close the TCP\IP Properties dialog box.

9. Click OK to close the Local Area Connection Properties dialog box.

10. Click Yes when you're asked whether you want to restart your computer.

Welcome to the Neighborhood!

With all your hardware and software properly installed, your network is now complete. All the computers on the network are ready to communicate, and they should be able to "see" each other.

Accessing the Network in Windows 95 and Windows 98

If you're using Windows 95 or Windows 98, double-click the Network Neighborhood icon on your Windows desktop to find other computers on the network. You should see icons for each of the computers on the network, as well as one labeled *Entire Network*, as shown in Figure 8-7.

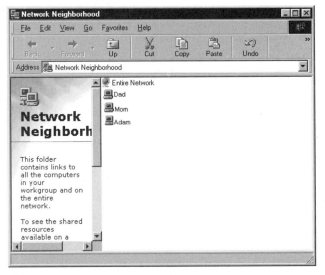

Figure 8-7.
Network Neighborhood displays icons for each of the computers on the network.

Note

Your computer might take a few minutes to "see" the other computers on the network. If no other computers appear in Network Neighborhood, close the Network Neighborhood window and try again in a few minutes.

To access one of the computers on the network, double-click its icon in Network Neighborhood. You should see all the resources listed on that computer that can be shared. Don't worry if nothing appears when you try this now—you'll learn how to share resources in Chapter 10.

If you double-click the Entire Network icon in Network Neighborhood, you'll see an icon representing the workgroup. Open that icon to display the computers in your workgroup.

Network Neighborhood will appear in Windows Explorer and the File Open and File Save As dialog boxes of Windows applications. If you're using Microsoft Word, for example, you can open or save a file on a connected computer by choosing Network Neighborhood in the Look In list that appears in the Open or Save dialog box, as shown here.

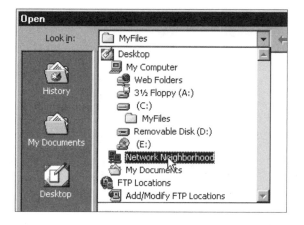

Another way to access a computer on the network in Windows 95 or Windows 98 is by using the Find command. Here's how:

1. On the Start menu, point to Find, and then click Computer.

2. Enter the name of the computer in the Find: Computer dialog box, and click Find Now.

Accessing the Network in Windows Me

If you're using Windows Me, you access the network using My Network Places on the Windows desktop. Here's how to use it:

1. Double-click My Network Places on the Windows desktop.

2. Double-click Entire Network to see an icon for the workgroup.

3. Double-click the workgroup icon to see a list of computers in the workgroup.

4. Double-click a computer to see its shared resources, such as disk drive and shared folders. (Once you perform these steps, by the way, network resources that you accessed will automatically appear in My Network Places.)

See Also

In Chapter 10, you'll learn how to add shortcuts to specific shared drives and how to add folders to the My Network Places window.

Accessing the Network in Windows 2000

To find other computers using Windows 2000, follow these steps:

1. Double-click the My Network Places icon on your Windows desktop to reveal these two options:

   - **Entire Network** includes your workgroup and a server domain.

   - **Computers Near Me** includes computers in your workgroup.

2. Double-click Computers Near Me to see icons for each of the computers on your workgroup. If you double-click Entire Network and click the text to view the entire contents of the network, you can then double-click Microsoft Windows Network to see an icon labeled with your workgroup name. Double-click the icon for the computer you want to locate.

3. To access one of the computers on the network, double-click its icon. You should see all the resources listed on that computer that can be shared.

My Network Places will appear in Windows Explorer and in the File Open and File Save As dialog boxes of Windows applications.

Troubleshooting

Theoretically, every part of your network should be humming along now. But sometimes, even with the best planning, problems can occur. If you can't access the other computers on your network, you'll have to take some time and check out each aspect of the installation.

Exploring the Network Neighborhood

First, give your computers a few minutes to recognize each other before opening Network Neighborhood (or My Network Places). It often takes a minute or so (sometimes longer) for the networking software to find the other computers. If no computers appear, or if you get an error message saying that the network can't be browsed, wait a few minutes and try again.

If you know the name of another computer, try locating it using Find Computer (or Search in Windows Me and Windows 2000) on the Start menu. You can often access a computer this way before it shows up in Network Neighborhood (or My Network Places).

If that fails, check all the cable connections at the computers and at the hub. Make sure the hub is plugged in and turned on and that all of the cables are securely connected.

If you still can't access the network, the problem might be the configuration of the NICs.

Checking Network Settings

The next place to troubleshoot the network is in the Network dialog box. Make sure that you're using the same workgroup name for each computer, with the same spelling and the same combination of uppercase and lowercase characters. If any computer is using a different workgroup name, change it to match the others, restart the computer, and try Network Neighborhood (or My Network Places) again.

Next, make sure that you have all three protocols installed and that the Network dialog box displays a listing for each protocol. The same protocols should be installed on every computer in the network.

If you're using TCP/IP, make sure either that you're assigning IP addresses automatically or that each machine has a different address. Check that the subnet mask is the same for every machine.

Note

The problem may be related to one or more of the different protocols you're using. If all else fails, remove all the protocols except NetBEUI from all of the computers and try again. NetBEUI is the easiest protocol to get started with because it requires no special configuration.

Diagnosing Hardware Conflicts

Finally, if your network still doesn't work, check for conflicts between the NIC and other hardware on your computers. *Return to the section "Checking Hardware Conflicts," earlier in this chapter, to learn how to troubleshoot hardware conflicts.*

Another way to check for conflicts in Windows 98, Windows Me, and Windows 2000 is with the System Information program:

1. On the Start menu, point to Programs, point to Accessories, point to System Tools, and then click System Information.

2. In the Microsoft System Information window, click the plus sign next to Hardware Resources.

3. Under Hardware Resources, click Conflicts/Sharing and see whether any conflicts are listed in the right pane of the window or whether your network card is using the same IRQ as another device. Note that PCI-bus network cards can share an IRQ with other devices without causing a problem, but ISA cards can't.

4. Click Forced Hardware. This folder will show devices that you set up manually using settings other than those chosen by plug-and-play.

5. Click I/O and look for addresses that are shared by two devices.

6. Click IRQs and scan the list for any possible conflicts involving ISA devices.

7. Click the plus sign next to Components.

8. Under Components, click Network.

9. Scroll through the list on the right to confirm that your network card, TCP/IP, and network clients are all listed. If they're not listed, go back to the beginning of this chapter and reinstall the network drivers, protocols, and clients.

Depending on your NIC, setting up your hardware can be either a breeze or a windstorm. Fortunately, almost all NICs that you get these days are plug-and-play or they include software that guides you through the process.

In the next chapter, you'll learn how to create profiles to personalize your computer if you share it with other members of your household.

Chapter 9

Creating Profiles

Even if you have more than one computer in the house, it's likely that more than one person uses each computer. With Microsoft Windows, individual users can have their own personal settings that go into effect whenever they log on to the network. These settings personalize their screen displays, such as their screen saver and desktop theme, and they also maintain other preferences, such as which folders and files to share with other users.

These personal settings are stored in a feature called a *profile*. Each user creates a profile, which is associated with a user name. When each person enters a user name upon starting Windows, the correct profile is used automatically. One set of default settings is reserved for users who don't have their own profiles.

To use profiles, you have to turn them on and create a user name for each person who will be using your computer.

What's in a Profile?

In addition to the user name and password, a personal profile might include the following items:

- Display settings such as the screen saver, desktop theme, and the Windows color scheme

- Icons and other items on the desktop

- Internet cookies and downloaded files

- The files contained in the My Documents folder

- Recently used files on the Documents menu

- Programs on the Start menu

- Favorites in the Favorites folder (if Microsoft Internet Explorer is your Web browser)

- E-mail shown in certain e-mail programs, such as Microsoft Outlook Express

You can probably see just from this list how useful the profiles feature can be. For example, when you have your own user profile, your Web browser saves all of your Internet cookies in a file reserved just for you. A *cookie* is a small file that a site on the Internet saves on your hard disk. When you later revisit that site, your browser reads the information in the cookie file to identify you and any settings or options that you selected on your last visit. Your own personalized settings will show up when you return to many Web sites because your browser retrieves your cookies rather than the cookies stored for other users. Sites that sell books, such as Amazon.com, save your book-buying preferences in a cookie. When you log on to the site, you might see a list of books that matches your interests. If other users of your computer also used your profile, you'd see books of interest to them, as well—but the books would all be listed under your name.

The My Documents folder on the desktop and the Documents list on the Start menu show only your files, so you can quickly open files that you've worked on instead of having to see a multitude of files from other users.

If you share your computer with another avid game player, your profile lets you avoid seeing a long list of somebody else's games on the Start menu. Those games appear only when the other player logs on with a different user name and password.

A personal Favorites list means that only the Web sites you want to visit are listed on the Favorites menu—both on the Start menu and in Internet Explorer. You won't need to scroll through a long list of favorites chosen by other users.

The same notion applies to e-mail messages in programs such as Outlook Express. Each user sees only his or her messages in the Inbox and Sent Items folders; every other user's mail is kept private.

Turning on Profiles

To use the profile feature, you have to specify that you want other users to have their own settings. Otherwise, Windows displays the same desktop and uses the same settings for everyone who uses your computer.

Note

This section discusses profiles with Consumer Windows (Microsoft Windows 95, Microsoft Windows 98, and Microsoft Windows Millennium Edition). For creating and using profiles with Microsoft Windows 2000, see "Windows 2000 Profiles," later in this chapter.

Here's how to turn on the profiles feature:

1. On the Start menu, point to Settings, and then click Control Panel.

2. In Control Panel, double-click the Passwords icon to open the Passwords Properties dialog box, shown in Figure 9-1.

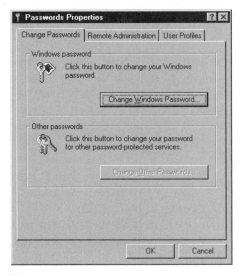

Figure 9-1.
The Passwords Properties dialog box lets you change your Windows password and set up user profiles.

3. Click the User Profiles tab.

4. Click Users Can Customize Their Preferences And Desktop Settings.

5. Click to select the two check boxes in the User Profile Settings section on the User Profiles tab. These settings allow individual users to add icons to the desktop and programs to the Start menu that appear only when they select their profile.

6. Click OK to close the Passwords Properties dialog box.

7. Click Yes when you're asked whether you want to restart your computer.

8. After Windows restarts, enter your user name and password, and then click OK.

9. Click Yes when you're asked whether you want to retain the individual settings in your profile.

You now have your own profile, containing all the settings you created when you were the computer's only user.

Adding Users

The next step is to specify who the users of your computer will be so that each can have a personal profile. You can add as many users as you like, whenever you like, or users can create their own profiles to keep the password confidential.

There are two ways to add a new user. You can simply enter a new name and password when you start Windows, or you can go to Control Panel and select Users.

Note

Adding a new user through Control Panel is possible only if you have Internet Explorer version 4 or later on your computer.

Adding Users When You Log On

It's easy to add a new user when you start Windows, but then you'll have to go to Control Panel to select options. Here's how to do it:

1. When you start Windows or use the Log Off option on the Start menu to log on as another user, enter a new name and type a new password in the Enter Network Password dialog box, and then click OK. (With some versions of Microsoft Windows 95, Log Off is an option in the Shut Down dialog box rather than on the Start menu.) Because you've entered a new user name, the Set Windows Password dialog box appears, asking you to retype your password to confirm it.

Note

A password is optional. If you don't want to use one, just leave the Password text box blank.

2. Enter a password, and then click OK.

3. When a message appears asking if you want to save your own Desktop settings, click Yes.

Adding Users Through Control Panel

If you have Internet Explorer version 4 or later you can add users and select certain profile settings with Control Panel. The first time you add a user this way, Windows runs the Add User Wizard, which takes you through the process step by step.

1. On the Start menu, point to Settings, and then click Control Panel.

2. In Control Panel, double-click the Users icon to open the User Settings dialog box, shown in Figure 9-2.

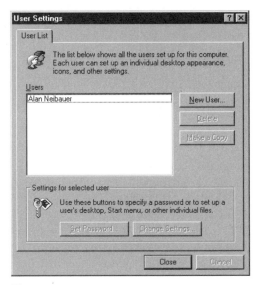

Figure 9-2.
Start the Add User Wizard in the User Settings dialog box.

3. Click New User to start the Add User Wizard.

4. Read the explanation shown on the first page, and then click Next.

5. On the Add User page, enter a new user name, and then click Next.

6. On the Enter New Password page, enter the password in both the Password and Confirm Password text boxes, and then click Next.

7. On the Personalized Items Settings page, shown in Figure 9-3, click to select each of the check boxes for the items that you want in your personal profile. If you leave a check box cleared, you won't have a custom copy of that item.

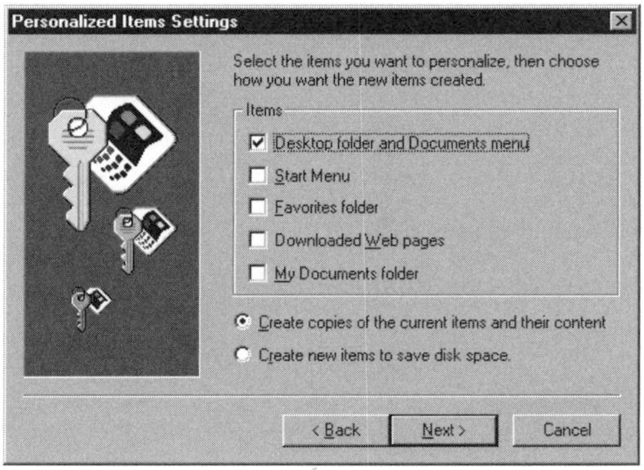

Figure 9-3.
The Personalized Items Settings page allows you to choose the contents of your profile.

8. Select one of the two option buttons near the bottom of the page to determine how you want your personal profile set up.

     If you select the first option button, Windows will make a copy of all of the items in the profile currently being used as the basis for your personal profile. If you choose the second option button, you'll have to create all of the items yourself from scratch.

9. Click Next, and then click Finish. Windows creates your personal desktop and displays the User Settings dialog box.

10. Click Close in the User Settings dialog box.

     If you prefer to use the desktop settings of another user, it's possible to copy those settings to a new personal profile that you can use. Follow these steps to start a new profile using someone else's settings:

1. Double-click the Users icon in Control Panel.

2. Click the user's name whose settings you want to copy.

3. Click Make A Copy to start the Add User Wizard.

4. Follow the steps of the wizard, selecting just the items you want to copy on the wizard's Personalized Items Settings page. For example, you can clear the My Documents Folder check box if you don't want to see the other user's documents displayed in your My Documents folder.

5. Click Finish on the last page of the wizard.

Changing User Settings

Changing your password and profile settings is as easy as adding a new user.

1. Double-click the Users icon in Control Panel.

2. In the User Settings dialog box, click your user name.

3. Click Set Password to change your password. You'll have to enter your current password, and then enter and confirm the new one.

4. Click Change Settings to open the Personalized Items Settings dialog box, and then change your settings.

If you're not using Internet Explorer version 4 or later, see "Changing Passwords," later in this chapter, to learn how to change your password.

You can also delete a user profile, eliminating not only the user name and password, but also all the folders associated with the user name, such as the My Documents and Favorites folders. If you don't want to delete the contents of these folders, be sure to copy the files or favorites you want to save to another location before deleting the user. Then click the user name in the User Settings dialog box and click Delete.

Note

You can't delete a user who is currently logged on.

Logging On as a Different User

You can start Windows on any computer by logging on with your own user name. If you forget your password, you can bypass the logon process and use the default desktop—the desktop that existed when the profile feature was originally enabled.

To log on to any computer, start the computer and enter your user name and password in the Enter Network Password dialog box. Leave the Password text box blank if you didn't enter a password when you created your profile.

If you want to log on using the default desktop, just click Cancel in the Enter Network Password dialog box or press the Esc key. Windows will start using the settings of the default profile. Any files that were in the My Documents and Favorites folders of your personal profile won't be available on the default desktop.

If your computer is already started and you want to switch to another user profile, you have to log off and then log on again using the other profile. You might want to do this if you bypassed the logon when you first started and now want to access your personal profile files. To switch profiles in Windows 98, Microsoft Windows Millennium Edition (Me), and some versions of Windows 95, follow these steps:

1. On the Start menu, click Log Off.

2. Click Yes when asked whether you're sure you want to log off. The Enter Network Password box appears.

3. Enter the user name and password you want to log on with, and then click OK. You can also click Cancel or press Esc to log on using the default profile.

If you're using Windows 95 and Log Off is not an option on the Start menu, follow this procedure to switch profiles:

1. On the Start menu, select Shut Down.

2. In the Shut Down dialog box, click Close All Programs And Log On As A Different User. Windows will restart so that you can enter another user name and password.

The Microsoft Family Logon

If a number of family members are using your computer, you can save them—and yourself—the trouble of typing in user names by choosing the Microsoft Family Logon feature. In Chapter 8, you learned how to install Microsoft Family Logon as a network client when setting up Windows for your network.

When a family member starts a computer on the network, a dialog box lists the profile names of all users. The family member can choose a user name from the list, enter a password, and then click OK to log on using the correct profile.

If you installed Microsoft Family Logon and want to use it, follow these steps to select it as the default logon option:

1. On the Start menu, point to Settings, and then click Control Panel.

2. In Control Panel, double-click the Network icon to open the Network dialog box.

3. In the Primary Network Logon drop-down list, select Microsoft Family Logon, and then click OK.

Note

If you no longer want to use the Microsoft Family Logon feature, select Client For Microsoft Networks instead.

Locating Your Folders

The profiles that are set up on a computer are stored in folders in the Profiles folder, which is in the Windows folder. To locate a profile folder, use either My Computer or Windows Explorer to navigate to the Profiles folder. In the Profiles folder, you'll see folders with profile names.

Double-click the profile name you're looking for to display all of the folders in that user's profile.

Changing Passwords

If you're using Internet Explorer version 4 or later, you can set and change your password in the Users dialog box. But no matter which version of Internet Explorer you're using, you can always change passwords with the Password icon in Control Panel. Here's how:

1. In Control Panel, double-click the Passwords icon to display the Password Properties dialog box.

2. Click the Change Passwords tab.

3. Click Change Windows Password.

4. In the text boxes, enter your current password, and type and confirm your new password.

Note

The Change Other Passwords option, which is not available on all systems, lets you change the passwords you use to log on to a network server. On a family network, you probably won't be using a network server, so you can forget about this option.

See Also

You'll learn how to password-protect individual folders and files in Chapter 10, "Learning to Share."

Surviving Password Forgetfulness

What happens if you forget your password? What you *don't* want to do is log on as a different user and delete your entire profile. This action will delete settings and files that you probably want to retain.

After the initial panic wears off, you can easily delete your password and start over. Passwords are stored in files with a .pwl extension. To locate your password file, follow these steps:

1. On the Start menu, point to Find, and then click Files Or Folders. With Windows Me, point to Search and click For Files Or Folders.

2. In the Find: All Files dialog box, make sure the Look In box is set at C: so you search your entire hard disk.

3. Type *.pwl* in the Named text box and click Find Now. (Click Search Now in Windows Me.) You'll see a list of files with the .pwl extension.

4. Click the file that has your user name, press Delete, and click Yes to confirm the deletion.

Note

After you delete your password file, you'll have to reenter your ISP password when you next log on to the Internet or check your e-mail.

You can now log on using your own user name and no password. You can also create a new password—one that you might not forget so easily. Either enter a new password in the Enter Network Password dialog box or create the new password in the Users or Passwords dialog box from Control Panel.

Deleting All Profiles

If you ever decide that you no longer want to share your computer, you can delete all user profiles from Windows. To do so, however, you need to use the Windows Registry Editor, and this can be tricky. Because the registry is where Windows stores all of its settings, you must be extremely careful not to change a setting you don't want to change.

Warning

Read these steps closely and be sure you are performing each one correctly before going to the next. Making the wrong changes to the Windows registry could cause your computer to stop working and may require you to totally reinstall Windows.

If you do decide to delete all your profiles, follow these steps carefully:

1. Restart your computer and click Cancel when the Enter Network Password or Microsoft Family Logon dialog box appears.

2. Double-click the Password icon in Control Panel.

3. On the User Profiles tab, click All Users Of This PC Use The Same Preferences And Desktop Settings.

4. Click OK and restart your computer.

When the computer restarts, follow these steps:

1. On the Start menu, click Run.

2. In the Run dialog box, type *regedit*, and then click OK. The Registry Editor starts, as shown in Figure 9-4.

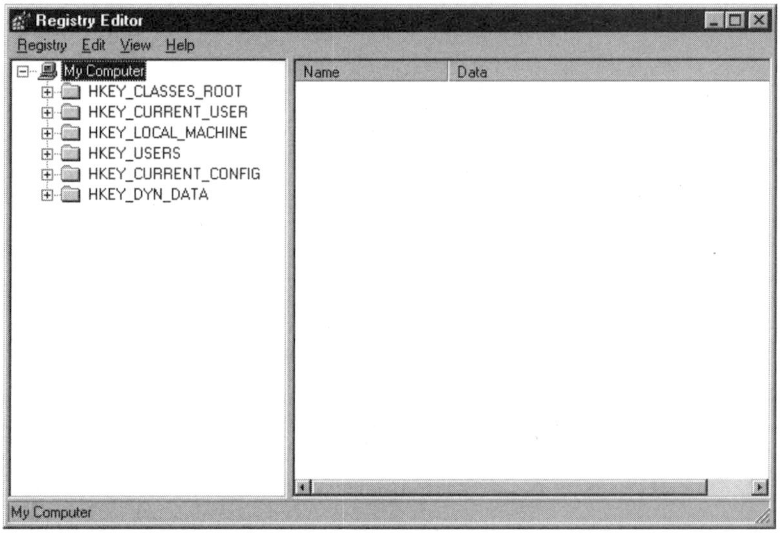

Figure 9-4.
The Registry Editor lets you change settings in the Windows registry.

3. Click the plus sign in front of HKEY_LOCAL_MACHINE to expand this section.

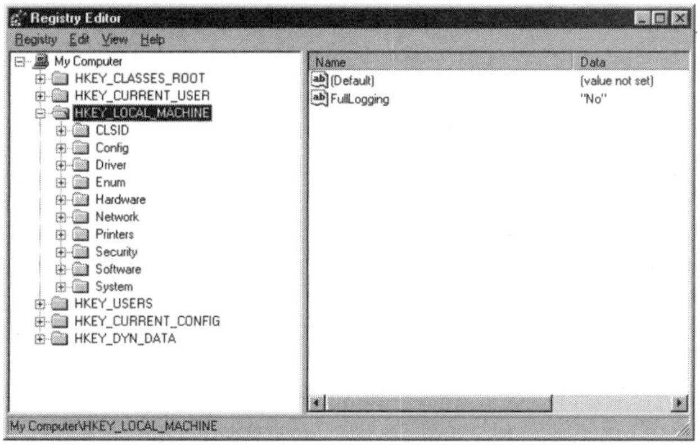

4. Click the plus sign in front of Software.

5. Click the plus sign in front of Microsoft.

6. Click the plus sign in front of Windows.

7. Click the plus sign in front of Current Version.

8. Click ProfileList. The status bar at the bottom of the Registry Editor should look like this.

My Computer\HKEY_LOCAL_MACHINE\Software\Microsoft\Windows\CurrentVersion\ProfileList

9. Press Delete, and then press Enter if you're asked to confirm the deletion.

10. From the Registry menu, choose Exit.

Now that you've edited the registry, follow these steps:

1. Double-click My Computer on the desktop.

2. Double-click the icon for your hard disk.

3. Open the Windows folder. In Windows 95, the contents of the folder are displayed automatically. In Windows 98, click Show Files to display the contents of the folder. In Windows Me, click View The Entire Contents Of This Folder.

4. Click the Profiles folder.

5. Press Delete to delete the folder.

6. Click Yes to confirm that you want to move the folder to the Recycle Bin.

Avoiding Password Forgetfulness

If you share your computer with others in the house but don't want to deal with profiles and passwords, there's a neat little gadget you can use—the U.are.U Fingerprint Recognition System (*http://www.digitalpersona.com*).

U.are.U is a small device that plugs into your computer's USB port and that contains a small scanner just the size of your fingertip. You configure the device to recognize any or all of your fingerprints and then scan your fingertip whenever a password is required.

When you try to log on to the Internet, for example, a message appears telling you to put your finger on the U.are.U sensor. The sensor scans your fingerprint and inserts your ISP password only if the scanned print matches one that you programmed into it.

Some models of U.are.U also include a feature called Private Space—an encrypted folder on your hard disk, network server, floppy drive, or removable drive. The file can be decrypted only by your fingerprint authorization.

Windows 2000 Profiles

If you're using Microsoft Windows 2000, profiles work about the same way as in Consumer Windows. The main difference is that Windows 2000 lets you assign users to groups. A group defines the rights of users who have been assigned to the group, saving you the trouble of specifying permissions for each user individually.

Windows creates six default groups:

- **Administrators** have full access to the computer or network domain.

- **Guests** and **Users** can use the computer and save their documents, but they can't install programs or change system files and settings. The groups are similar, except that Guests can't shut down the system or undock a laptop from a docking station.

- **Backup Operators** can back up files and folders only onto the computer.

- **Power Users** can install programs and change computer settings, but they can't read other users' files.

- **Replicator** can support file replication.

To add a new user, you have to be logged on as the Administrator. When you first set up Windows 2000 and log on, you will automatically be made the Administrator. Once you've logged on to Windows 2000 in this way, follow these steps to add a new user:

1. Open Users And Passwords in Control Panel to see a list of currently defined users, as in Figure 9-5. Windows automatically creates a user called Administrator and an account called Guest for others with whom you want to share the computer. If you set up your computer by entering your own name as the user rather than the default name of Administrator, you'll also see your own user account name.

Note

Depending on the features of Windows 2000 that you installed, you might also see other accounts in the Users and Passwords dialog box that are used for a corporate Web server.

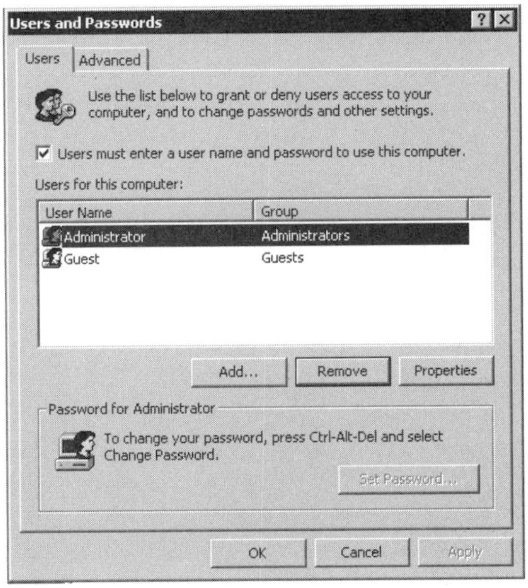

Figure 9-5.
Windows 2000 users and groups.

2. To require that users sign on with their name and password, select the check box labeled Users Must Enter A User Name And Password To Use This Computer.

3. Click Add to see this dialog box:

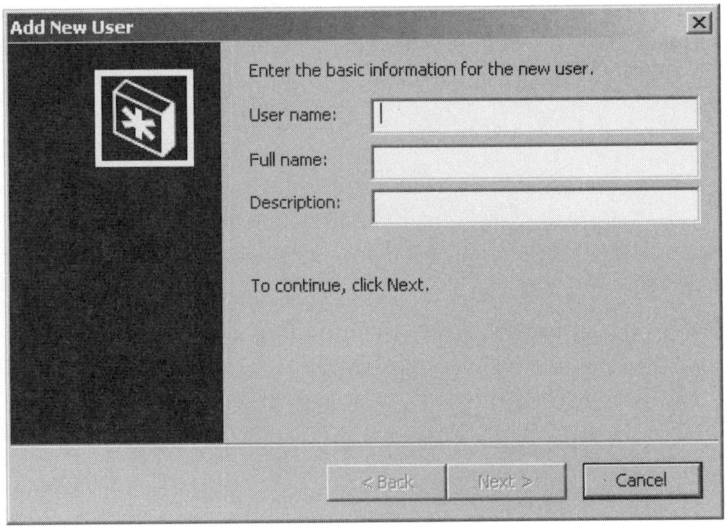

4. Enter the information requested and then click Next.

5. In the box that appears, enter and confirm the password, and then click Next to see the dialog box in Figure 9-6.

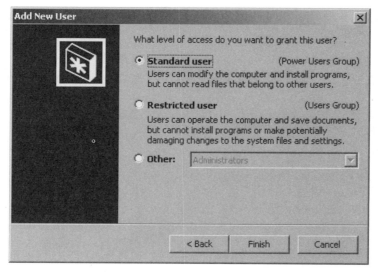

Figure 9-6.

Assigning a user to a group.

6. Select the group to which you want to assign the users; the options are Standard User, Restricted User, and Other. Choose Standard User to add the person to the Power Users Group, or select Restricted User to add the person to the Users Group. Otherwise, click Other and select the group from the list.

7. Click Finish.

The new user will be listed in the Users And Password dialog box and can now log on to the system. If you need to change the user's name or group assignment, select the user's name and then click Properties.

You can create new groups and make other changes to the user's profiles in the Computer Management dialog box shown in Figure 9-7.

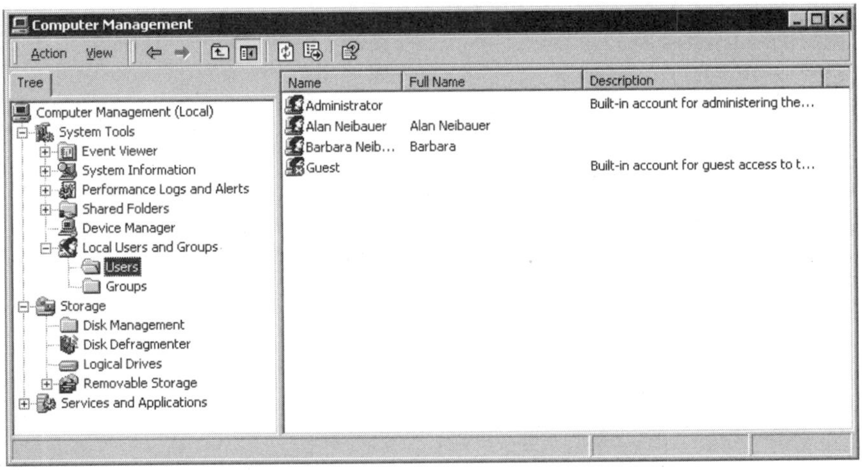

Figure 9-7.

The Computer Management dialog box.

To display the box, open Administrative Tools in Control Panel, and then open Computer Management. To change a profile, click the plus sign next to Local Users And Groups and then click Users to list the users on the right of the window. Select the user whose profile you want to change, and then from the Action menu, select Properties. The user's Properties dialog box appears, as in Figure 9-8.

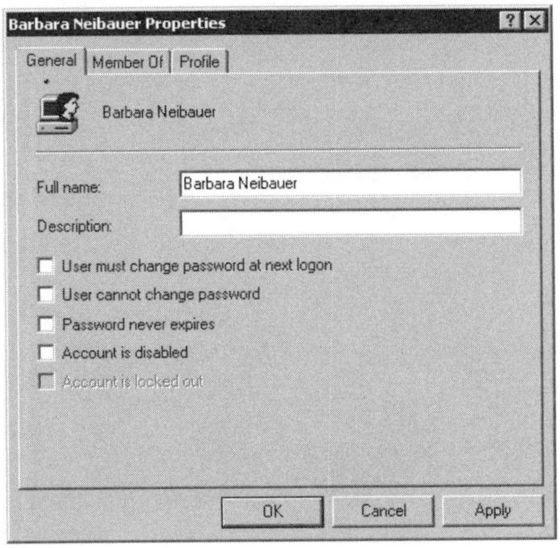

Figure 9-8.

The Properties dialog box for a user's profile.

On the General tab of the dialog box, you can designate whether each user has to change his or her password the first time he or she logs on to the computer, whether the password ever expires, or whether the account is disabled. Use the Member Of tab to change the groups to which the user belongs.

The Profile tab lets you create a roaming or mandatory profile location. A roaming profile allows a user to log on to the computer remotely and download the profile information from the server to the remote computer. A mandatory profile is one that the administrator creates and that the user can't change.

To create a new group in the Computer Management dialog box, click Groups in the Local Users And Groups section, and then choose New Group from the Action menu. In the box that appears, enter the group name and then click Create.

Note

Setting the permissions assigned to a group is more complicated than setting an individual user's permission and is beyond the scope of this book.

User profiles are important when you share a computer with others. Profiles allow individual users to personalize their desktops and have a sense of ownership without changing the settings of other users. In the next chapter, you'll learn how to share files and folders across the network.

Chapter 10

Learning to Share

One of the main advantages of setting up a home network is that it gives you the ability to share files. But sharing doesn't come automatically. You not only have to turn on the file sharing service when you configure your network, but you also have to specify which resources you want to share with other users. In this chapter, you'll learn how to share disks, folders, and files.

Turning On File Sharing

Before you can activate file sharing, you must install the Microsoft Windows service that allows sharing. You probably installed this service along with your network drivers and software, as described in Chapter 8, but just in case you didn't, here's how to do it.

In Consumer Windows (Microsoft Windows 95, Microsoft Windows 98, and Microsoft Windows Millennium Edition), follow these steps. (*To share resources with Microsoft Windows 2000, see the section "Sharing with Windows 2000," later in this chapter.*)

1. On the Start menu, point to Settings, and click Control Panel.

2. Double-click the Network icon to open the Network dialog box.

      In the list of network components that are installed, look for File And Printer Sharing For Microsoft Networks. If it's already listed, you can skip the rest of these steps. If the service isn't installed, continue with these steps.

3. In the Network dialog box, click Add.

4. In the Select Network Component Type dialog box, click Service.

5. Click Add.

6. In the Select Network Service dialog box, click File And Printer Sharing For Microsoft Networks.

7. Click OK.

8. Click OK again to close the Network dialog box. You might be asked to insert your Windows CD.

9. When you're asked whether you want to restart your computer, click Yes.

Now that the service is installed, you're ready to turn on file and printer sharing.

1. On the Start menu, point to Settings, and click Control Panel.

2. Double-click the Network icon to open the Network dialog box.

3. Click the File And Printer Sharing button to open the File And Print Sharing dialog box.

4. Select both check boxes to allow access to your files and your printers.

5. Click OK.

6. Click OK again to close the Network dialog box.

Caution

By default, the TCP/IP protocol is configured to allow file and printer sharing across the network. You do not, however, want to share files over your connection to the Internet using TCP/IP, either through a dial-up connection or a network adapter for a digital subscriber line (DSL) or cable modem. Enabling file and printer sharing over the Internet will make your computer and its contents vulnerable to Internet hackers. See "Turning Off Internet File Sharing," in Chapter 13 on page 319, to learn how to disable file and printer sharing over the Internet.

Sharing and Accessing Network Resources

Installing the hardware and configuring Windows for sharing doesn't make the information on your computer instantly available to everyone. Before someone else can access a folder on your hard disk, you must first specify that the folder is shared.

Note

Resources that can be shared are called *shares*.

Windows organizes disks, folders, and files in a hierarchical manner:

- Disks contain folders.
- Folders contain subfolders (and some files as well).
- Subfolders contain files.

When you share a disk or a folder on a network, everything within it is also shared. For example, if you allow a disk to be shared, all folders and files on that disk are shared as well. If you allow only a folder to be shared rather than the whole disk, all subfolders and files within that folder can be shared but not other folders on that disk. So if you do want everything on your hard disk to be available on the network, turn on sharing for your hard disk.

Once you share the disk, you don't have to turn on sharing for any of the individual folders within that disk—they're automatically shared across the network. You can also share a floppy disk, a CD-ROM, or a Zip disk. When you share a disk, an icon for it appears in the Network Neighborhood or My Network Places of all users on the network when they access your computer.

Note

Throughout this chapter, you'll see references to Network Neighborhood and My Network Places. Windows 95 and Windows 98 users should refer to Network Neighborhood; Windows Millennium Edition (Me) and Windows 2000 users should refer to My Network Places.

Even though a folder on a shared disk is automatically available to network users, it won't appear as a separate icon in Network Neighborhood or My Network Places unless you specifically share that particular folder, and not just the disk on which the folder resides. If you want the folder to be seen on Network Neighborhood or My Network Places so that network users can easily access it, turn on sharing for the folder even if you've already turned on sharing for the disk. It's usually a good idea, for example, to share the Desktop subfolder within the Windows folder so that any user can easily copy files to your Windows desktop.

In addition to turning on sharing, you can also specify how you want the disk or folder to be shared. There are three levels of sharing:

- **Read-Only** sharing means that users can open files in the shared folders and copy them to their own computers, but they can't change, delete, or add files.

- **Full** sharing means that other users can do anything to shared disks or folders that you can do.

- **Depends On Password** sharing means that the password a user enters determines the level of sharing—Full or Read-Only—granted to the user.

If you specify Read-Only access or Full access to a disk or folder, a password is optional. You can do without one and allow all members of your family to access a resource on your computer at whatever level of sharing you've specified for that resource. Or you can create a password and limit access—again, at the level of sharing you've specified—to family members to whom you've given the password.

With the Depends On Password option, you can selectively grant read-only or full access to members of your family. You create two passwords: a read-only password and a full password. Users to whom you give the read-only password can read and copy your files, but they can't change or delete them or add new ones. Users with the full password can do anything they want to your files.

Sharing Drives

To turn on sharing for an entire drive and give only certain people access to it, follow these steps:

1. Double-click My Computer on the Windows desktop.

2. Right-click the drive that you want to share.

3. Select Sharing from the shortcut menu to open the Properties dialog box shown in Figure 10-1.

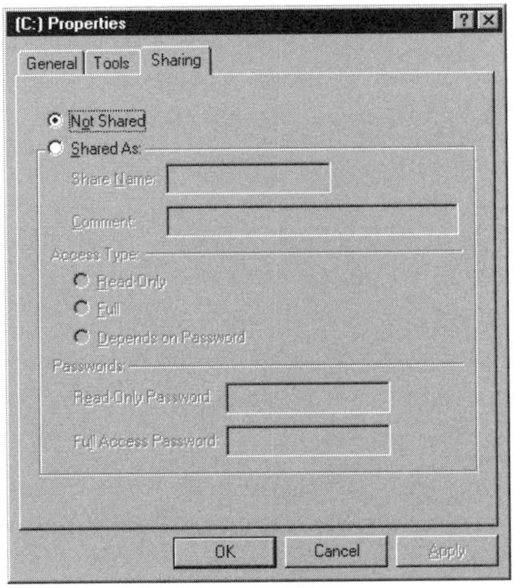

[C:] Properties

| General | Tools | Sharing |

○ **Not Shared**
○ **Shared As:**
  Share Name: [   ]

  Comment: [   ]

  Access Type:
  ○ Read-Only
  ○ Full
  ○ Depends on Password

  Passwords:
  Read-Only Password: [   ]

  Full Access Password: [   ]

  [OK]   [Cancel]   [Apply]

Figure 10-1.
The Properties dialog box allows you to turn on sharing for a resource and limit access to it by password.

4. Click Shared As.

   Windows places a default name in the Share Name text box, usually the same letter as the drive. (The *Share Name* is what appears when network users access your computer.)

5. Leave the Share Name as it is or change it to better identify the drive, as in *Alan's Zip disk*.

6. In the Comment text box, you can enter an optional description.

7. Click one of the three access types—Read-Only, Full, or Depends On Password.

8. Enter an optional password: Read-Only, Full Access, or enter both if you want the level of access to be determined by the password that the person enters.

9. Click OK.

10. If you specified one or two passwords, reenter each in the Confirm Passwords dialog box, and then click OK.

    Now the icon for the drive will show, with a cradling hand, that the drive is shared.

[C:]

When another member of your family is connected to your computer and double-clicks the Network Neighborhood icon on the Windows desktop or on your computer's icon from My Network Places, an icon for your disk appears. If you've granted full access without a password, that family member can access your disk just as if it were a local hard disk rather than a disk in your computer.

If you turn on sharing for a floppy disk or a removable disk, such as a Zip disk, the drive is actually shared rather than a particular disk. Turning on sharing for a floppy disk, for example, means that any floppy in the drive is shared. You might want to think twice about sharing removable drives if some of your disks contain sensitive information.

If you want to make a shared drive or folder available to everyone on a network, you can leave the password for the resource blank. If you do enter a password, however, make sure you remember it. Let's say you're at a computer other than your own and you want to access your own files across the network. Your system won't know that it's you at the computer and will require the same password it does from the computer's primary user.

If you do forget the password that you've assigned to a shared resource, you can easily change it as long as you log on to your own computer. Unlike some passwords, you can change a sharing password without knowing the current one. To change a password, right-click the shared disk or folder, and choose Properties from the shortcut menu. Type the new password in place of the old one and click OK. You'll have to reenter the password to confirm it.

Note

To erase a password so that a shared disk or folder is no longer password-protected, just delete the asterisks in the password text boxes. You'll have to click OK without typing anything in the Confirm box that appears.

Sharing Folders

If you don't want to allow complete access to your disk, you can turn on sharing for only certain folders and not for the entire disk.

To turn on sharing for a folder, follow these steps:

1. Double-click My Computer.

2. Double-click the disk containing the folder you want to share.

3. Right-click the folder that you want to share. You might have to navigate through folders to display the subfolder you want to share.

4. Select Sharing from the shortcut menu to open the Properties dialog box.

5. Click Shared As.

6. Accept the default share name or enter a new one.

7. Enter an optional comment.

8. Choose an access type.

9. Enter an optional password—Read-Only, Full Access, or both.

10. Click OK.

11. If you specified one or two passwords, reenter each to confirm it in the Confirm Passwords dialog box, and then click OK.

You can also turn on sharing from any window that displays the folder, such as Windows Explorer, the Find or Search dialog box, or a Save As or File Open dialog box in an application such as Microsoft Word. To turn on sharing, right-click the folder icon, select Sharing from the shortcut menu, and follow the rest of the steps in the previous procedure.

Note

You can't turn on sharing for the My Documents folder from the Windows desktop. If you want to set sharing for that folder, in My Computer, double-click the disk on which you've installed Windows, right-click the My Documents folder, and choose Sharing from the shortcut menu.

Accessing Shared Disks and Folders

Once disks and folders are shared, network users can access them in much the same way as they access disks and folders on their own computers. The trick is for them to locate the disk or folder on the remote computer.

Note

A *remote computer* is a computer on the network other than the one you're using.

Once you access a shared folder on a remote computer, you can use the files in that folder just as if you were on that computer, but only at the level of sharing you've been granted. If you have read-only access, you'll be able to open or copy files only from the shared folder. You won't be able to change or delete files or add new files to the folder. If you attempt to do so, you'll see the following dialog box.

Windows 95 and Windows 98

With Windows 95 and Windows 98, you can always access remote computers using Network Neighborhood, so let's start from there.

1. Double-click Network Neighborhood on your Windows desktop.

Remember, it might take a few minutes after you turn on your computer for it to recognize the remote computers on the network. You'll see icons representing all the computers on your network, as well as an icon for the Entire Network, such as the one shown in Figure 10-2.

Figure 10-2.

Network Neighborhood displays icons for each computer connected to the network and an icon for the Entire Network.

Note

Clicking the Entire Network icon lets you access other workgroups that are connected to your network.

2. Double-click the icon for the computer you want to access. You'll see icons representing shared drives and printers as well as folders that you've shared.

3. Double-click the disk or folder you want to access. If you see no individual folders at this point, the entire drive is shared.

Windows Me

Windows Me uses My Network Places rather than Network Neighborhood to access shared drives and folders.

1. Double-click My Network Places on the Windows desktop.

2. Double-click Entire Network to see an icon for the workgroup.

3. Double-click the workgroup icon to see a list of computers in the workgroup.

4. Double-click a computer to see its shared resources. Shared resources include shared disk drives, shared folders, and shared printers.

Once you access a shared drive on another computer from My Network Places, Windows Me will insert a shortcut to that resource in the My Network Places window, like this:

You can just double-click the shortcut to access the drive. You can also add a short-cut to a specific folder for quick access to its files. Follow these steps to insert a shortcut to a folder in My Network Places.

1. In My Network Places, double-click Add Network Place to open the Add Network Place Wizard.

2. Click Browse to see the contents of My Network Places, as shown here.

3. If there's a listing for the drive that contains the folder you want to insert as a short-cut, as in *c on Piii* in the previous illustration, click the plus sign to display the folders contained in the drive. Otherwise, click the plus sign next to the workgroup to see a list of networked computers, and then click the plus sign next to the computer to access its resources. Navigate through the directory tree until you see the icon for the folder you want to add to My Network Places, such as the following.

Browse For Folder   ? ☒

Select a shared network folder

```
☐⋯🖳 c
   ⊞⋯🗀 ATI
   ⊞⋯🗀 BJDisk
   ⊞⋯🗀 CN5614CH
   ⊞⋯🗀 COLLWIN
   ⊞⋯🗀 Corel
   ⊞⋯🗁 My Documents
   ⊞⋯🗀 MyFiles
   ⊞⋯🗀 PKWARE
   ⊞⋯🗀 Program Files
```

[OK]   [Cancel]   [New Folder]

4. Click the folder you want to add, and then click OK to return to the Add Network Place Wizard.

5. Click Next.

6. Enter the name for the resource as you want it to appear in My Network Places.

7. Click Finish to open a window with the contents of the folder.

8. Close the window. You'll now see an icon for the folder in My Network Places, as shown here.

Home
Networki...

Entire Network My Documents
                   on Piii

Accessing Resources with Windows Explorer

Another way to access shared disks is from Windows Explorer or any Windows file management dialog box, such as the File Open dialog box in Word. Let's look at Windows Explorer.

1. With Windows 95 or Windows 98, on the Start menu, point to Programs, and click Windows Explorer. With Windows Me, point to Programs, point to Accessories, and then click Windows Explorer.

2. Click the plus sign next to Network Neighborhood or My Network Places in the list of remote computers.

3. Click the plus sign next to the remote computer you want to access.

4. If the disk in the computer is shared, click the plus sign next to the disk to display its contents. You can then access any of the files as if they were on your computer.

Note

The Network Neighborhood or My Network Places icon appears in the Open and Save dialog boxes of most Windows applications that let you access disks and folders. You can always use the icon to access remote computers.

Accessing Resources with the Run and Find Commands

While Network Neighborhood, My Network Places, and Windows Explorer are the most common ways to access a remote computer, Windows offers two other options: the Run command and the Find or Search command on the Start menu.

If you know the name of the remote computer, you can access a shared resource on it by choosing the Run command from the Start menu. The Run dialog box opens.

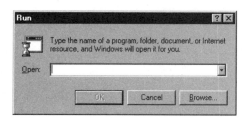

To use a resource on a remote computer, you must enter the path to the resource by typing the *Universal Naming Convention* (UNC). You start the UNC with two backslashes (\\) followed by the name of the computer, as in \\Joe. Press Enter or click OK to open a window showing the shared resources on that computer. If you know the name of the specific disk and folder you're looking for on the remote computer, you can open it directly by adding its resource name to the UNC, as in *\\Joe\C\Budget*.

You can also search for a computer on the network. With Windows 95 and Windows 98, use the Find command on the Start menu. Just follow these steps:

1. On the Start menu, point to Find, and click Computer.

2. In the Find: Computer dialog box, enter the remote computer's name, and press Enter or click Find Now.

3. When the computer is located and listed in the Find dialog box, double-click its icon to access its shared resources.

With Windows Me, use the Search command on the Start menu by following these steps:

1. On the Start menu, point to Search, and click For Files And Folders.

2. In the Search For Other Items section of the Search Results window, click Computers.

3. In the Computer Name box that appears, enter the remote computer's name, and press Enter or click Search Now.

4. When the computer is located and listed in the Search Results window, double-click its icon to access its shared resources.

Accessing Resources with Passwords

When a resource requires a password in order to be shared, you must enter the password before you can open the disk or folder—or at least you must enter it the first time you try to access the resource. As you'll see, there's a way to save the password so that you don't have to enter it each time you open a password-protected disk or folder.

When you first try to access a resource, you'll see the Enter Network Password dialog box.

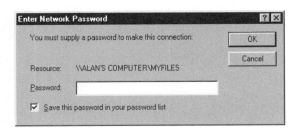

Before you enter the password and click OK, you can select the check box labeled Save This Password In Your Password List. Windows maintains this password list in a file whose name is your user name plus the extension .pwl, as in alan.pwl. If you select this check box, the name of the shared resource and the password will be saved in your .pwl file. The next time you access the same disk or folder, Windows automatically locates the password so that you don't have to enter it again.

Note

Don't select the Save This Password In Your Password List check box if you want to prevent other network users from accessing shared resources with your password.

When the Enter Network Password dialog box opens, type in your password, and then click OK. If the password you've typed is incorrect, a message appears telling you so. Click OK to clear the message, and then reenter the correct password.

Making Sharing Easier

Navigating through Network Neighborhood or My Network Places to locate a folder or file can be time-consuming. Fortunately, Windows offers a number of ways to simplify network life.

Creating a Desktop Shortcut

The easiest way to access a remote disk, folder, or file is to add an icon for it to your Windows desktop.

1. Use Network Neighborhood or My Network Places to locate the disk, folder, or file on the remote computer.

2. Click the disk, folder, or file with the right mouse button, and then hold down the button while you drag the icon to your desktop.

Note

To create a shortcut to the remote computer itself, right-drag the remote computer icon to your desktop.

3. Release the mouse button and select Create Shortcut(s) Here from the shortcut menu.

Windows 98 and Windows Me also allow you to drag the shortcut icon you placed on your desktop to the taskbar so that you can access it with a single click.

Adding Shared Resources to Favorites

If you're using Windows 98 or Windows Me (or Windows 95 with version 4 or later of Microsoft Internet Explorer), you can store frequently used folders and files in a Favorites folder, which is quickly accessible from the Start menu.

You'll also find a Favorites menu item in Windows Explorer, My Computer, Network Neighborhood, My Network Places, and other dialog boxes in Windows that let you manage files. After you've added a shortcut to a folder or file to your Favorites list, you can open Favorites and click the shortcut to open the folder or file.

To add a resource to the Favorites list, follow these steps:

1. Use Network Neighborhood or My Network Places to locate the folder or file.

2. Double-click the folder or file so that its path appears in the Address field in the Address toolbar.

3. From the Favorites menu, choose Add To Favorites to open the Add Favorite dialog box.

4. Click OK. You can also click the Create In button if you want to add the item to a folder within Favorites or to create a new subfolder of Favorites.

Mapping Network Drives and Folders

Another way to gain easy access to a disk on a remote computer is to assign it a drive letter on your own machine. This technique is called *mapping* the disk. For example, suppose you have the following disks in your computer:

- A floppy disk drive, designated as A
- The hard disk, designated as C
- A CD-ROM or DVD disk drive, designated as D

If you frequently access a hard disk, CD-ROM, or other drive on a remote computer, you can map it so that it appears as drive E or F on your computer. Even better, you can map to a specific folder on a remote computer, giving it a drive letter, as long as the folder has been enabled for sharing. Let's say you often access a folder named Budget on a remote computer. You can map to the folder so that it shows up in My Computer as drive F on your computer.

Myfiles on
'Alan's
computer' (F:)

To map a shared disk or folder in Windows 95 and Windows 98, follow these steps:

1. Use Network Neighborhood to display the icons for each of the disks and folders on the remote computer that have been shared.

2. Right-click the icon for the resource you want to map to, and then choose Map Network Drive from the shortcut menu to see the Map Network Drive dialog box.

Map Network Drive	? X
Drive: ☐ F: ▼	OK
Path: \\Alan's computer\myfiles	Cancel
☐ Reconnect at logon	

3. In the Map Network Drive dialog box, select the Reconnect At Logon check box if you want Windows to map to this resource every time you start your computer.

4. Click OK. A window opens showing the contents of the drive or folder; the address box in the Address toolbar shows that the resource is now mapped to a drive on your computer.

To map a shared disk or folder in Windows Me and Windows 2000, follow these steps:

1. Double-click My Network Places.

2. In Windows Me, double-click Entire Network and then the icon for your workgroup. In Windows 2000, double-click Computers Near Me. You will see icons for each of the computers on the network.

3. Double-click the icon for the computer having the resource you want to map.

4. Right-click the icon for the resource you want to map to, and then choose Map Network Drive from the shortcut menu to see the Map Network Drive dialog box. If Map Network Drive is not on the shortcut menu, you can select it from the Tools menu.

5. In the Map Network Drive dialog box, select the Reconnect At Logon check box if you want Windows to map to this resource every time you start your computer.

6. Click OK in Windows Me; click Finish in Windows 2000.

If you close the window and open My Computer, you'll see the shared resource listed as a drive. Just double-click the icon as you would any actual disk drive to access its contents on the remote computer.

When you turn on Reconnect At Logon, Windows browses the network looking for the mapped disk or folder each time you start your computer. If the remote computer isn't turned on, Windows starts normally but doesn't map to the shared resource. You'll have to remap to it after the remote computer joins the network.

If you don't select Reconnect At Logon, the drive you mapped to is disconnected when you turn off your computer or restart Windows. You'll have to repeat the previous procedure to map to the drive again.

Browsing for mapped resources takes some time, and it will slow down the logon process, so if you don't need to map to the resource every time you use your computer, don't select the Reconnect At Logon option.

To speed up the process of mapping resources, an alternative is to tell Windows not to browse the network automatically when your computer starts. With the Quick Logon feature, Windows displays the icons for mapped resources in Network Neighborhood or My Network Places, My Computer, and Windows Explorer without checking to see whether the resource is really available. Windows waits until you first try to use the resource before actually connecting to it. To turn on the Quick Logon feature, follow these steps:

1. On the Start menu, point to Settings, and click Control Panel.

2. In Control Panel, double-click the Network icon to open the Network dialog box.

3. In the list of installed network components, select Client For Microsoft Networks.

4. Click Properties to open the Client For Microsoft Networks Properties dialog box shown in Figure 10-3.

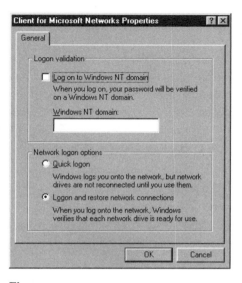

Figure 10-3.
You can change logon options in the Client For Microsoft Networks Properties dialog box.

5. Click Quick Logon. The other option, Logon And Restore Network Connections, maps and connects to shared resources you've mapped every time Windows starts.

6. Click OK to close the Client For Microsoft Networks Properties dialog box.

7. Click OK to close the Network dialog box. You might be asked to insert your Windows CD at this point.

8. Click OK if you're asked whether to restart your computer.

Working with Remote Files

After you've accessed a disk or folder on a remote computer, you can start working with its files in Network Neighborhood or My Network Places, My Computer, or Windows Explorer. Here's how to access a file with Network Neighborhood, My Network Places, or My Computer:

1. Open Network Neighborhood or My Network Places, or double-click My Computer if the disk on the remote computer has been mapped.

2. Double-click the icon for the computer you want to access.

3. Double-click the disk or folder you want to open.

4. Select the file you want to work with.

To access the file with Windows Explorer, follow these steps:

1. On the Start menu, point to Programs, and click Windows Explorer. With Windows Me, point to Programs, point to Accessories, and then click Windows Explorer.

2. Click the plus sign next to Network Neighborhood or My Network Places in the Folders list on the left.

3. Click the plus sign next to the remote computer you want to access.

4. Click the plus sign next to the disk you want to open on the remote computer.

5. Click the folder containing the file you're looking for. If the folder contains subfolders, click the plus sign next to the folder to display its contents, and then select the subfolder containing the file.

After you've accessed a file, you can do anything with it that your level of sharing allows. If you have read-only access to the folder, you can open the file or copy it to another location, but you can't do anything else to it. If you have full access, you can also change, delete, or move the file.

Let's take a closer look at how to work with files on remote computers.

Opening Remote Files from Within Applications

On the network, you can open a file on a remote computer just as you would open it on your own computer. In Consumer Windows, you can locate the file in My Computer, Network Neighborhood or My Network Places, or Windows Explorer, and open it by double-clicking its icon.

You can also open files from within Windows applications, such as the programs in Microsoft Office. Because Network Neighborhood and My Network Places are integrated parts of the Windows file system, one or the other (depending on your version of Windows) shows up in all the lists you see whenever you try to access files. Consequently, you can treat a remote computer as you would any disk drive—locate it in the application's Open dialog box, choose the drive, choose the folder, and then choose the document you want to access.

For example, suppose you're working in Word and need to open a file in the My Documents folder of a remote computer. Here's how you'd do it:

1. From the File menu, choose Open to display the Open dialog box.

2. In the Look In drop-down list, select Network Neighborhood or My Network Places. A list of computers on the network appears in the Open dialog box.

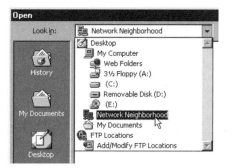

3. Double-click the icon for the computer whose disk contains the file you want. A list of shared resources on the remote computer appears in the Open dialog box.

4. Double-click the hard disk that contains Windows on the remote computer. It's usually the C: drive.

5. Double-click My Documents.

6. Double-click the file you want to open.

Saving Remote Files from Within Applications

Saving a remote file from within a Windows application is even easier than opening it, as long as you have full access privileges. If you've made changes to an existing remote file, you save it just as you would any other document by clicking the Save button on the application's Standard toolbar or by choosing Save from the application's File menu.

You can also use the Save As command on the application's File menu to save the document to another location or with a new filename. When the Save As dialog box opens, it shows the folder from which you opened the document. Choose another location from the Save In list in the Save As dialog box, a folder either on your own computer or on any other computer on the network.

If you're working on a new document and want to save it on a remote computer, use the Save In list in the Save As dialog box to select Network Neighborhood or My Network Places, choose the remote computer, and then select the destination folder.

Saving a Read-Only File

If you've made changes to a file that you opened from a read-only folder, you can't save it to the same location. If you try to do so, you'll see a warning message.

However, you can still make changes to the file; you just can't replace the existing version in the shared folder with your edited version. (Remember that when a folder has been designated as read-only, you can't change its contents.) To save your changes, you must use the Save As command and save the file as a new document in a folder to which you have full access. The folder can be on your own hard disk or on a disk in a remote computer.

To save a file to a remote computer, navigate to the computer using Network Neighborhood in the application's Save As dialog box, using these steps:

1. From the application's File menu, choose Save As to display the Save As dialog box.

   Note

   In some Windows programs, clicking Save when a file is read-only automatically opens the Save As dialog box.

2. In the Save In drop-down list, choose Network Neighborhood or My Network Places. A list of computers on the network appears in the Save As dialog box.

3. Double-click the icon for the remote computer to which you want to save the file to see a list of its shared resources.

4. Double-click the disk drive.

5. Double-click the folder in which you want to save the file.

6. Click Save.

Avoiding Double Trouble

It doesn't make sense for two people to try to work on the same file at the same time. The result can be lost work and confusion.

Suppose, for example, that you and your spouse want to work on the family budget using two different computers. Here's what might happen:

1. You and your spouse both open the document and see that Entertainment is set at $100 per month.

2. You change Entertainment to $200.

3. Your spouse changes it to $50.

4. You save the document. The $200 amount for Entertainment is recorded on the disk.

5. Your spouse saves the document after you do. The $50 figure is recorded on the disk, and your changes to the budget are lost! If your spouse had saved the document before you did, your $200 choice would have prevailed.

To avoid such situations, only one person at a time should work on a document in a folder to which full access has been granted. What happens, however, when one person opens a document that's already being used by another person depends on the version of Windows and the application you're both using.

For example, you might receive a message that the document you're trying to open is already in use and you might get the option to open it in read-only mode. Although this option will allow you to make changes to the document, you won't be able to save it back to the same location, using the same name.

Note

There are exceptions to the one-person-at-a-time rule. With a program such as Microsoft NetMeeting, two people can collaborate on a document at the same time and see each other's changes as they're made. You'll learn more about this type of simultaneous file sharing in Chapter 12 and Chapter 17.

Some applications provide safeguards against opening a document in use. Microsoft Word 2000, for example, displays this message if you try to open a file that's being used.

In the File In Use message box, click Read Only to open the document in read-only mode. Clicking Notify opens the document in read-only mode too, but you'll also see a message such as this when the other user closes the file.

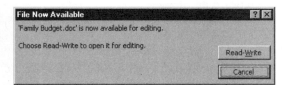

Click Read-Write to reopen the latest version of the document with the other user's changes. If you made any changes to the document, you'll see a message that tells you so.

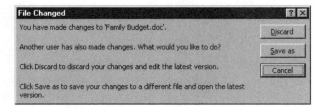

- Click Discard to ignore your changes and to reopen the latest version of the document.
- Click Save As to save your document under a new name and to open the latest version of the original file.

Copying and Moving Remote Files

You move or copy a file between computers on a network the same way you move or copy a file between folders on your own hard disk.

When you copy a file, you leave the original in its location and place a duplicate on another computer. Copying a file is smart when you want to make changes to a document without deleting the original version. Just remember that if someone changes one of the copies, two different versions of the same file will exist on the network.

When you move a file, you delete the original from its location and place it on another computer. If you move a file that someone else might want to work with, let the other user know where you're placing it. You can't move a file from a read-only folder because moving it would be the same as deleting it from that folder, and read-only access doesn't permit deletion of files. If you try to move such a file, you'll get an error message.

You can move and copy files between a remote computer and your own, using either Windows Explorer, Network Neighborhood, or My Network Places.

Copying Files Between Computers

Whether you're copying a file between your folders on your own hard disk or between computers on the network, you can use two basic methods. You can drag the file from one location to another, or you can use the copy-and-paste method.

Dragging Files   To copy a file by dragging it, you need to have open both the folder that contains the file and the folder to which you want to copy it. This process is easiest with Windows Explorer, so let's start there.

Let's assume that you want to copy a file from a remote computer to your own computer.

1. On the Start menu, point to Programs, and click Windows Explorer. With Windows Me, point to Programs, point to Accessories, and then click Windows Explorer.

2. In the Folders list on the left, locate the folder in which you want to place the file.

    For example, if you want to place the file in the My Documents folder, make sure you see the folder in the list. If necessary, click the plus sign next to the C: drive.

3. To locate the file you want to copy, click the plus sign next to Network Neighborhood or My Network Places in the list on the left.

4. Click the plus sign next to the remote computer you want to access.

5. Click the plus sign next to the disk drive on the remote computer that contains the file.

6. Click the folder containing the file you're looking for.

    If the folder contains subfolders, click the plus sign next to the folder to display its contents, and then select the subfolder containing the file. You should see the file you want to copy in the list on the right.

7. Now scroll through the list on the left until you see the folder to which you want to copy the file, *but do not click it.*

    Being able to see the icon for the folder is enough for now. You should still see the file you want to copy on the right.

8. Drag the icon of the file you want to copy from the list at the right to the destination folder in the Folders list on the left. As you drag, a small plus sign appears next to the mouse pointer indicating that you are copying, rather than moving, the file.

    In Figure 10-4, the file named Budget from the Microsoft Excel book folder on a remote computer is being copied to the My Files folder on the local computer.

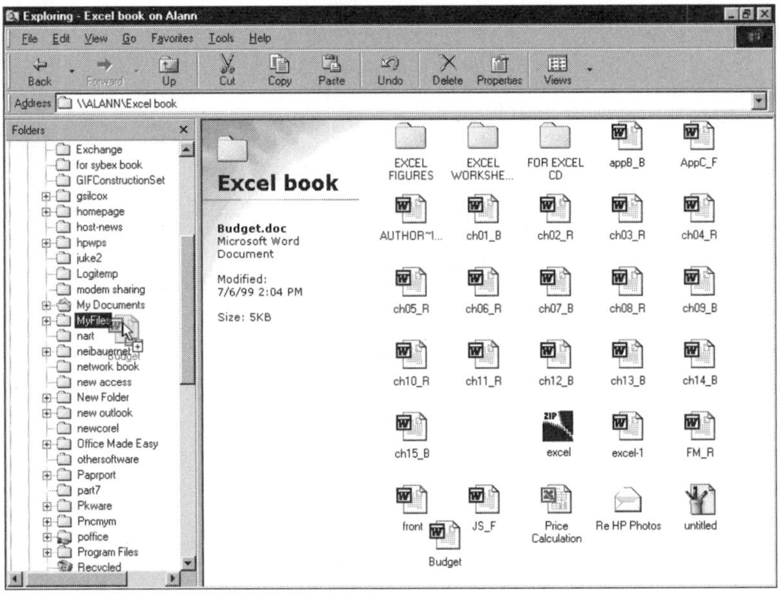

Figure 10-4.
To copy a remote file, drag it from its current location to the proper folder in the Folders list.

Note

You can also drag a file by holding down the right mouse button as you drag rather than the left. Using the right mouse button causes a shortcut menu to appear, from which you can choose Copy Here when you release the mouse button.

In addition, you can copy a file using a combination of My Computer and Network Neighborhood or My Network Places. With this approach, you drag the file to be copied between two windows on your screen: one that shows the file's original location, and another that shows its destination. This time, you'll copy a file from your computer to a remote one.

1. Double-click My Computer on the desktop and double-click the drive containing the file.

2. Double-click the folder containing the file.

3. If the folder window fills the screen, click the Restore button to make the window smaller.

4. Drag the window to the left side of the screen.

5. Double-click Network Neighborhood on the Windows desktop or open My Network Places.

Network Neighborhood or My Network Places appears in a new window. If the two windows overlap, drag the Network Neighborhood window to the right.

6. In the Network Neighborhood or My Network Places window, double-click the icon for the computer you want to access.

7. In the Network Neighborhood or My Network Places window, double-click the disk, and then double-click the folder in which you want to place the file. The Network Neighborhood screen should look similar to the one shown in Figure 10-5.

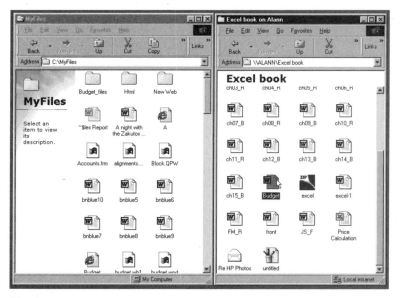

Figure 10-5.
Copy a file by dragging it between the My Computer and Network Neighborhood windows.

8. Drag the file from the Network Neighborhood or My Network Places window on the left to the My Computer window on the right.

Copying and Pasting   If copying a file by dragging seems too time-consuming, you can always do it the old-fashioned Windows way, by using the Copy and Paste commands. You'll still need to open both a window showing the file in its original location and a window showing the new location, but you don't need to have both open at the same time.

You can copy and paste using Windows Explorer, Network Neighborhood, My Network Places, or My Computer. Here's how:

1. Open the folder containing the file you want to copy and select the file.

2. Right-click the file and choose Copy from the Shortcut menu. You can also click Copy on the Windows Explorer toolbar.

3. Open the folder to which you want to copy the file.

4. Right-click and choose Paste from the Shortcut menu. You can also choose Paste from the Edit menu or from the toolbar.

Note

If you periodically access a file on a remote computer, you can create a shortcut to it on your machine by dragging it to your desktop while holding down the right mouse button and choosing Create Shortcut(s) Here from the shortcut menu that appears.

Sending Files to Remote Drives   One handy feature of Windows is the Send To list. If you need to save a file on a floppy disk, for example, you can right-click its icon on the desktop or in any folder, and then point to Send To to see a list of possible destinations. Click 3½ Floppy (A) at the top of the list to copy the file to the floppy disk drive, for example.

It's possible to add your own destinations to the Send To list so that you can copy files quickly to a remote computer of your choice. To do so, you first have to create a desktop shortcut to the disk or shared folder on the remote computer that you want to add to the Send To list. (*See "Creating a Desktop Shortcut," earlier in this chapter.*) Next, right-click the shortcut you've created to the remote computer and choose Rename from the shortcut menu. Type a name that you'd want to see in the Send To list and press Enter. Finally, drag the icon to the C:\Windows\SendTo folder.

Now, whenever you want to copy a file to the remote location, right-click the file, point to Send To, and click the listing for the remote location.

Moving Remote Files

You move a file between computers almost exactly the same way you copy a file. To move a file by dragging, follow the steps for copying, but hold down the Shift key when you release the mouse button. While you hold down the Shift key, the small plus sign next to the pointer disappears, indicating that you're moving, rather than copying, the file. You don't have to hold down the Shift key while you're dragging the mouse, only when you release it.

If you prefer not to move a file by dragging it, you can move the file by using the Cut and Paste, rather than the Copy and Paste, method. Right-click the file and choose Cut from the shortcut menu instead of Copy. Open the folder to which you want to move the file, right-click again, and choose Paste from the shortcut menu. When you paste the file into its new location, it's removed from its original folder.

Note

As with copying, it's also possible to drag the file by holding down the right mouse button instead of the left. In this case, choose Move Here from the shortcut menu that appears when you release the mouse.

Deleting Remote Files

When you have full access to a remote folder, you can delete it or delete the files within it. But before you delete anything, you should be aware that the Recycle Bin doesn't work across the network.

The Recycle Bin, on the Windows desktop, is a holding tank for files or folders that you delete from your hard disk. If you change your mind about deleting an item, you can open the Recycle Bin, select the deleted file or folder in the Recycle Bin window, and choose Restore from the File menu. If you're sure you don't need the files in the Recycle Bin anymore, you can open the Recycle Bin and choose Empty Recycle Bin from the File menu.

When you delete a file that's on another computer on the network, however, it's immediately deleted from the disk without making a protective stop at the Recycle Bin of either computer. Even dragging the file to the Recycle Bin of your computer erases it automatically.

Note

The Recycle Bin also doesn't work for files and folders deleted from floppy disks or removable drive disks, such as Zip disks.

With these caveats in mind, if you're sure you want to delete a remote file, just lo-cate the file by using Network Neighborhood, My Network Places, Windows Explorer, or any other method. Select the file and press the Delete key, or right-click the file and choose Delete from the shortcut menu. When you're asked whether you really want to delete the file, click Yes if you do or click No if you've changed your mind.

Note

You can delete an entire folder from a remote computer with this same procedure.

Sharing with Windows 2000

The general concept of file sharing and accessing shared files is the same for Windows 2000 as it is in Consumer Windows. However, Windows 2000 has inherited the file-sharing capabilities of Microsoft Windows NT. With Windows 2000, you can set permissions for specific users and encrypt folders and files for added security.

In Consumer Windows, for example, you could limit access to a folder by assigning it a password. Anyone who had the password could then access the folder. If an unautho-rized user learned the password, he or she could access the folder from any computer on the network.

Windows 2000 doesn't use passwords because it offers user-level access, which means you can assign specific permissions to each user individually or in groups. To as-sign permission to an individual, you would use the Users and Passwords icon on the Control Panel to create a user account for the individual and then set his or her permis-sions. The user needs to log on to the network with his or her name and password to ac-cess the folders you've allowed.

The level of security that you choose depends on your network and office re-quirements.

Turning On File Sharing

Before you can activate file sharing, you must install the Windows service that allows sharing. You probably installed this service along with your network drivers and software, as described in Chapter 8, but just in case you didn't, here's how to do it.

Follow these steps to select services in Windows 2000:

1. On the Start menu, point to Settings, and then click the Network And Dial-up Connections icon.

2. Right-click Local Area Connection and choose Properties from the shortcut menu.

3. In the list of network components that are installed, look for File And Printer Sharing For Microsoft Networks. If it's installed, you can skip the rest of these steps.

4. Click Install to open the Select Network Component Type dialog box.

5. Select Service and then click Add to open the Select Network Service dialog box.

6. Select File And Printer Sharing For Microsoft Networks and then click OK.

7. Click OK to close the Select Network Component Type dialog box.

8. Click Yes when you're asked whether to restart your computer.

Sharing Drives

To turn on sharing for an entire drive and give only certain people access to it, follow these steps:

1. Double-click My Computer on the Windows desktop.

2. Right-click the drive that you want to share and select Sharing from the shortcut menu to see the dialog box shown in Figure 10-6.

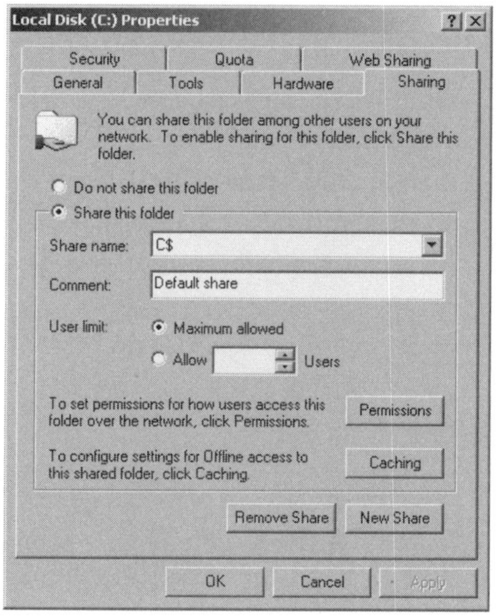

Figure 10-6.

The Properties dialog box allows you to turn on sharing for a resource.

The Share This Folder check box might already be enabled and an entry with a dollar ($) sign, such as C$, may appear in the Share Name box. The $ sign indicates a special shared resources that Windows needs for administrative purposes. You can't remove this type of sharing, but network users won't be able to see it when they browse the network to access your computer.

1. If the drive is already assigned for sharing, click New Share, type the share name, and click OK. If no default name exists for the drive already, click Share This Folder. Windows places a default name in the Share Name text box, usually the same letter as the drive.

2. In the User Limit section, choose either Maximum Allowed, or Allow, and enter the number of users allowed to access the drive at one time. The maximum is 10.

3. Click Permissions to see the box shown in Figure 10-7.

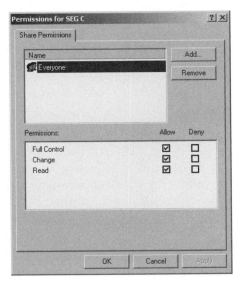

Figure 10-7.
Setting permissions for sharing.

4. The default is set to Everyone, meaning that permissions are granted to every network user accessing your computer. In the Permissions section, choose Allow or Deny for the specific permissions you want to allow to everyone: Full Control, Change, and Read.

If you want to limit access to certain groups or users, you can remove Everyone (the default) from the access list and add specific users or groups. Create a user account for network users you want to access the system. Click Add to open the box shown in Figure 10-8. Double-click the user or group, and click OK. Then set the permissions for the individual or group.

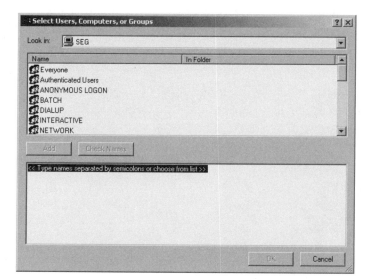

Figure 10-8.
Setting permissions for sharing.

For even more control over permissions, click the Security tab to set permission options.

Note

If you want to change permissions, display the Share Name list by selecting the down arrow to the right of the selected name, and choose the new share you created. You can't set or change permissions for shares whose names include the $ sign.

Sharing Folders

If you don't want to allow complete access to your disk, you can turn on sharing only for certain folders and not for the entire disk.

In fact, each user of the computer has a folder assigned with his or her name in the Documents And Settings folder of the hard disk. Granting access to the disk doesn't automatically grant access to these personal folders. If you want to grant access to this folder, you have to turn on sharing for it specifically.

To turn on sharing for a folder, follow these steps:

1. Double-click My Computer on the Windows desktop.

2. Double-click the disk containing the folder you want to share.

3. Right-click the folder you want to share. You might have to navigate through folders to display the subfolder you want to share.

4. Select Sharing from the shortcut menu to open the Properties dialog box.

5. Click Share This Folder.

6. Click Permissions if you want to specify the rights and users, as you learned for disks.

Sharing Programs

So far, we've been looking rather generically at sharing files, primarily documents, graphics, sounds, and other files that aren't programs. Sharing a program on a network is a slightly different matter.

What Can Be Shared?

Sharing programs on a network might have legal ramifications:

- It's not always legal to purchase one copy of a program and install it on each of the computers on your network.

- It's not always legal to purchase one copy of a program, install it on one computer, and then let more than one person on the network run the program at the same time.

Remember that software is usually licensed, and many software companies prohibit program sharing as part of their licensing agreement. This limitation means that all you're really purchasing is a license to use the software and, according to the rules, you don't own the software itself. By opening and using a piece of software, you're agreeing to abide by the terms of your software license agreement.

Many licensing agreements require you to purchase a separate copy or license for every computer on which you want to run the software, even if you're using the software on just one computer at a time.

Some programs can't be shared at all. Many older versions of programs, particularly those that run on MS-DOS rather than Windows, can be run only on the computer on which they're installed. These programs are designed to access additional files within the same computer. When you try to run such programs remotely, they can't find the files they need and either display an error message or don't work at all.

Running a Program Remotely

Running a program on a remote computer is essentially the same as opening it on your own computer. You locate the program file and then open it by double-clicking it. When you run a program that's on a remote computer, the program runs in your computer, but its files remain on the remote computer.

See Also

In Chapter 14, you'll learn how to share and play games across a network.

Because some programs frequently draw information from the disk as they run, you might find that running a remote program uses up quite a bit of your network resources. You might also encounter problems with programs that won't run properly across a network. If you get error messages when you start the program or while you're using it, you won't be able to run it remotely. You'll have to either install the program on your computer (if the licensing agreement allows), or go to the computer on which it's installed and run it from there.

Sharing a Data File

Sometimes you must share access to certain files, such as calendars and databases, on other computers. The shared data file might be a calendar, for example, that each member of the family accesses to check for appointments and special events. You want only one copy of this calendar on the network so that everyone sees the same information and so that changes made to it are available to everyone.

You can open a data file by simply navigating to it and opening it, as you've learned in this chapter, or you can set up your application program to access the file on a remote computer automatically.

If you want to share a document or data file with other network users, think about the best location in which to keep the file. For example, storing it on the computer that's turned on most often increases the odds that the file will be available when someone needs to access it.

Security is another issue to consider. If you want to use a password to limit access to a file, you'll need to store the file in a folder that is password-protected, which might limit your placement options. The computer in your child's room might be on almost all the time, for example, for game-playing, doing homework, and chatting online, but you wouldn't want to store a personal or parent-only file there. The tradeoff for security might be to store the file on a computer that's used less frequently, but mainly by adults.

Another factor to consider when sharing files on different computers is that many programs expect to see files in specific places. They're set up to look in a default folder for the files they need to open. When you need to use this type of program, you have two choices: place the files where the program expects to see them, or tell the program where you've chosen to keep the files.

Microsoft Money, for example, which lets you keep track of your bank accounts and even transfer funds and pay bills online, uses a data file named Mymoney.mny. The program stores this file in a reserved folder on the hard disk.

To change where Money should look for Mymoney.mny, just copy the file to wherever you want to store it, and then double-click Mymoney.mny to start the program. Because Money always uses the last data file you opened, the new data file in its new location becomes the default.

You can share a Money file between computers on the network so that anyone who runs the program can have access to the most current bank accounts. Just copy the Mymoney.mny file to the computer where you want the shared file to be located and then have all network users start their copy of Money by navigating to the remote computer and opening the Mymoney.mny file.

Other applications let you set the default location for documents in a dialog box, such as Word's Options dialog box, shown in Figure 10-9.

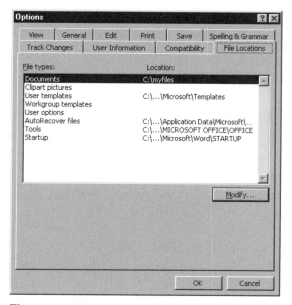

Figure 10-9.
In Word, the default location for documents is set in the Options dialog box.

If you want Word to automatically look for new documents on a remote computer or to save new documents to a remote computer, enter the UNC path as the document's location. Here's how to do it:

1. Start Word and, from the Tools menu, choose Options.

2. In the Options dialog box, click the File Locations tab.

3. Click Documents in the File types list, and then click Modify.

4. In the Modify Location dialog box, type the full path for the folder on the remote computer, such as *\\Barbara\C\Myfiles*. You can also browse for the location by choosing Network Neighborhood or My Network Places in the dialog box's Look In list.

5. Click OK to close the Modify Location dialog box.

6. Click OK to close the Options dialog box.

Backing Up Important Files

When it comes to backing up, the best rule of thumb is, "Back up what you don't want to lose." Unfortunately, backing up is one of those tasks we all know we should do but too often don't.

Backing up means making a copy of important files in some location other than your hard disk. That way, if your hard disk decides it's had enough of your interference and departs to never-never-land, your important files are safe and sound somewhere else. Sounds logical, only many of us forget to back up important files or we just get too lazy to do it.

When you're sharing files on a network, backing up is even more important for two reasons:

- The more people who access your disk, the greater the chance an important file will be deleted or corrupted. This possibility is especially true if you allow full access to your network's resources.

- More people depend on being able to use a given file and will be affected by its loss. It's not just you anymore.

It's really up to all network users to take some precautions to safeguard important files that would be difficult or impossible to re-create. Backing up programs isn't as critical because you can always reinstall them from their original disks. But your documents, database files, spreadsheets, banking files, and other data files might be unique and difficult to replace.

Some programs, such as MECA's Managing Your Money and Microsoft Money, automatically create a backup file each time you exit them. Although the setup procedure varies, in most cases, the backup option is available as a menu choice or in a dialog box that opens when you choose to exit the program. You can usually specify the backup location, including a disk on a remote computer.

Using Removable Disks

The best choice for quick and easy backup of files and folders is a Zip, Jaz, or other type of removable disk anywhere on your network. Removable disks hold at least 100 MB of information, the equivalent of about 70 floppy disks. That's not as much storage as you have on a hard disk or tape drive, but it can certainly accommodate a lot of files. Because the disk is removable, you can use multiple disks to store as much information as you like.

If the drive is attached to your computer, it will appear as a drive icon in My Computer. Just drag the files or folders you want to back up to this icon. If your computer has a built-in removable disk or tape drive, it might appear automatically in your Send To list. If it doesn't, create a shortcut to the drive on the desktop and add it to the SendTo folder yourself. *(See "Sending Files to Remote Drives," earlier in this chapter.)*

When the drive is attached to a remote computer, consider mapping to the drive so that you can access it from My Computer, or creating a shortcut to it in the SendTo folder.

Storing Files Remotely

Another option worth considering is backing up your files to the hard disk of a remote computer. One of the computers on the network might be newer and have a much larger hard disk than the disk in your own computer. Or it might not be used quite as much as other computers in the house, so it has extra hard disk space that can be shared among the family.

Create a folder on that computer with your name so that you can easily identify it. Create a shortcut to the folder on your desktop, and then add the shortcut to the SendTo folder. You'll now be able to back up folders and files to that remote disk quickly and easily.

Using Microsoft Backup

As an alternative to backing up individual files and folders, you can automate the backup process with Microsoft Backup. The program comes with Windows, so you can't beat the price, and it works with floppy disks, tape backup drives, and most removable disks. It's great for a network because you can use it to back up files from your own or any other computer on the network and store the backup on a remote computer.

Note

Backup is supplied with Windows 95 and Windows 98, but it isn't included with Windows Me.

Backup isn't usually installed in Windows 95 or Windows 98, so you'll have to do it yourself. But don't worry, it's easy. Just follow these steps:

1. Insert your Windows CD in the CD-ROM drive.

2. On the Start menu, point to Settings, and click Control Panel.

3. In Control Panel, double-click Add/Remove Programs.

4. In the Add/Remove Programs Properties dialog box, click the Windows Setup tab. After a moment or two, you'll see a list of Windows components.

5. Scroll through the list and click System Tools. Make sure you don't remove the check mark from the check box to the left.

6. Click Details to see a list of items in the System Tools category.

7. In the System Tools dialog box, select the Backup check box to enable it.

8. Click OK to close the System Tools dialog box.

9. Click OK again to close the Add/Remove Programs Properties dialog box.

10. Click Yes when you're asked whether you want to restart your computer.

After your computer restarts, you're ready to configure and run Backup. The process varies slightly, depending on the type of drive you're using for backup—tape, removable disk, or floppy disk.

Windows 2000 Backup

The Backup program included with Windows 2000 is similar to the version for Windows 95 and Windows 98 discussed here, but it has a different look. To start the program, click Start, point to Programs, point to Accessories, point to System Tools, and then click Backup. The Welcome menu appears with three choices, as shown here.

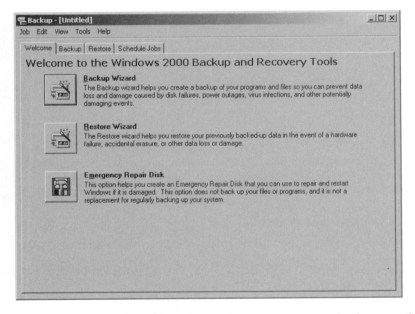

You can use the Backup Wizard to automate your backup, or click the Backup tab to specify the files you want to back up and their destination. Use the Restore Wizard or the Restore tab to restore files. The Emergency Repair Disk option creates a floppy disk that you can use to start your computer if Windows is damaged on your hard disk.

The Schedule Jobs tab lets you schedule backup operations for specific dates and times.

Note

If you don't have a tape backup drive or another device automatically recognized by Backup as a backup device, you might be asked the first time you run the program whether you want it to search for a backup device. Click No.

Microsoft Backup lets you create a *backup job* that defines which files you want to back up and where you want them stored. It's possible to have any number of backup jobs defined, and you can easily repeat a backup to save updated files.

To start the program, follow these steps:

1. On the Start menu, point to Programs, point to Accessories, point to System Tools, and then click Backup. The Microsoft Backup dialog box appears, as shown in Figure 10-10.

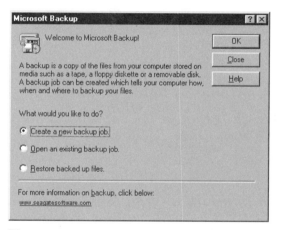

Figure 10-10.
The Microsoft Backup dialog box prompts you to create a new backup job, which starts the Backup Wizard.

2. Choose Create A New Backup Job to define a backup job, and then click OK to start the Backup Wizard.

The wizard takes you step by step through the process of defining a backup job and performing the backup itself. You can choose options such as these:

- The name of the backup job
- Whether to back up your entire computer or only selected files
- The storage location for backup files

- Whether backups and originals are compared to verify their accuracy
- Whether backup files are compressed to save space

The Backup Wizard isn't the only way to define a backup job. You can also use the main Backup window, shown in Figure 10-11. This window allows you to specify what to back up, where to store it, and how to save it. Then you just click the Start button. To back up important files from a remote computer, for example, you just scroll through the What To Back Up list and click the plus sign next to Networks to access remote computers.

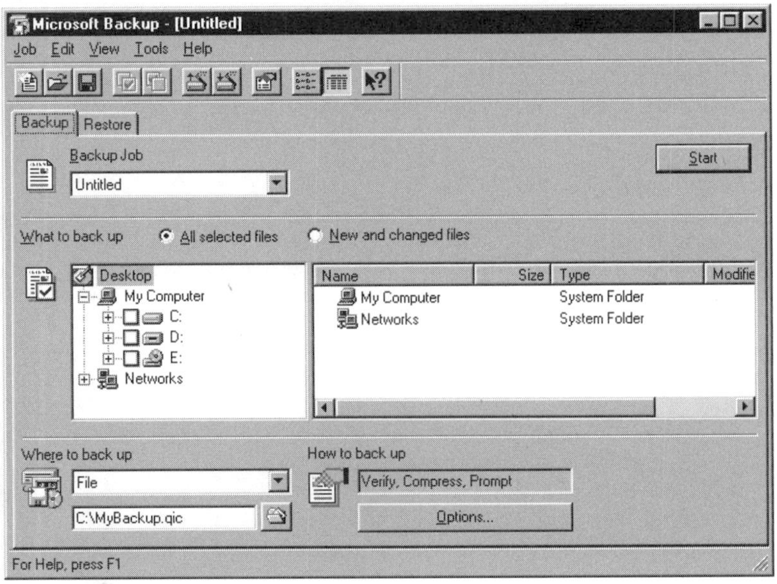

Figure 10-11.
Using the controls in the Microsoft Backup window is an alternative to using the Backup Wizard.

Microsoft Backup doesn't store files individually. Instead, it combines them in one large file or a series of large files spread over several disks. Therefore, you can't use standard Windows or MS-DOS techniques to access individual files in a backup. If you want to retrieve files from the backup, you have to perform a *restore* operation.

To restore files, choose the Restore Backed Up Files option when you start Backup. The Restore Wizard opens. You can also click Close in the Microsoft Backup dialog box after you start Backup and use the controls on the Restore tab to specify restore options. If you choose to restore selected files, you'll see a list of the individual files in the backup from which to choose.

Summary

In this chapter, you've learned to share disks, folders, files, and programs among computers on the network so that everyone can use them. You've also learned how to back up important files to a different computer. In the next chapter, you'll learn how to share another important resource on a network—the printers connected to the computers.

Part 4

Running the Network

Chapter 11
Printing Across the Network   231

Chapter 12
Communicating Over the Network   251

Chapter 13
Going Online Through the Network   291

Chapter 14
Playing Games   323

Chapter 11

Printing Across the Network

Sharing files and folders is one great advantage of connecting computers on a network; sharing printers is another. When you share printers, everyone on the network can access them. You might need to walk to the printer in another room to retrieve your printed copies, but the pages will be there, ready and waiting for you.

Here are a couple of scenarios in which sharing printers can be a great benefit:

- You don't have a printer for each computer.

- You want to use a feature of a printer that's connected to a remote computer.

Let's say you purchased printers for some but not all the computers in your home. If your computers aren't connected to a network, you'll need to perform one of two actions to get a printout from a computer that doesn't have a printer:

- Save your documents on a disk and take the disk to a computer that's connected to a printer.

- Disconnect the printer from one computer and hook it up to the computer from which you want to print (and load the appropriate printer driver on that computer, if necessary).

If you've set up a home network, it doesn't matter whether all your computers are linked to printers. You can send a document to printers connected to other computers on the network.

Even if you do have a printer for each computer, the printers might not all be of the same type. For example, you might have a laser printer connected to your computer for printing business documents, while your children have a color printer for school reports and kids' stuff. If your computers are connected on a network, you can get to your kids' color printer whenever you want, and the kids will be able to print with your laser printer.

See Also

Chapter 2, "Getting Connected Without a Network," covered ways to share printers without a network.

You can link a printer to a network in two basic ways. The cheaper and easier method is simply to connect the printer to the parallel or universal serial bus (USB) port of one of the computers on the network. The other way is to connect the printer directly to the network. Although this second option is more expensive, connecting a printer directly has many advantages, as you'll learn in "Connecting Printers Directly to the Network," later in this chapter.

Sharing Printers

When you print to a printer connected to a remote computer, your print job travels over the network, through the remote computer, and then to the printer attached to it. The remote computer, rather than your own, causes the printer to print.

Let the Printer Beware!

Sharing printers attached to computers connected on a network is a great time-saver, but there's one big gotcha: both the printer and the computer it's attached to must be turned on, and the printer must be online, stocked with paper, and ready to go. Otherwise, it's no go!

So before you print to a printer on the network, you have to check to make sure it's ready. If no one is using the computer that's attached to the printer, you might have to go to the computer, turn on both the computer and the printer, and set up the printer for printing.

Even if the computer and printer are turned on and ready, they might be busy with someone else's print job. When the printer completes the job, it will start printing your document and others that are waiting on a first in, first out (FIFO) basis, which means the first in line gets printed first. Another problem can occur if the person using the computer attached to the printer shuts down the computer before the printer starts printing your work. A little coordination among the family is clearly needed here.

You might suggest to everyone on the network that anyone who wants to print to someone else's shared printer should first send a short message to make sure the printer is on and ready. You could also try yelling from room to room, but that's not always the best approach.

See Also

In Chapter 12, you'll learn how to send messages to other people on your network.

Setting Up Printer Sharing

Before you can share the printer connected to your computer on the network, you must have installed the File And Printer Sharing For Microsoft Networks service. Chances are, you already installed the service when you set up file sharing. But you should make sure that you've enabled the printer sharing part of the service.

See Also

For more information about installing the File And Printer Sharing For Microsoft Networks service on your system, see "Turning on File Sharing," in Chapter 10, on page 187.

If you're using Consumer Windows (Microsoft Windows 95, Microsoft Windows 98, and Microsoft Windows Millennium Edition), follow these steps to enable printer sharing:

1. On the Start menu, point to Settings, and then click Control Panel.

2. In Control Panel, double-click the Network icon to open the Network dialog box.

3. Click the File And Print Sharing button to open the File And Print Sharing dialog box.

4. Make sure the I Want To Be Able To Allow Others To Print To My Printer(s) check box is selected.

5. Click OK to close the File And Print Sharing dialog box.

6. Click OK to close the Network dialog box. Depending on how Windows is set up on your computer, you might be asked to insert your Windows CD so the files necessary for sharing are installed.

If you're using Microsoft Windows 2000, follow these steps to enable printer sharing:

1. On the Start menu, point to Settings, and then click Network And Dial-up Connections.

2. In the Network And Dial-up Connections dialog box, right-click a connection and choose Properties from the context menu to open the Properties sheet for the connection.

3. On the General tab, in Components Checked Are Used By This Connection, check File And Printer Sharing For Microsoft Networks.

4. Click OK and close the Network And Dial-up Connections dialog box.

Installing a Printer

The next step in setting up a printer is to check that it's actually installed on your computer and working properly. If you can't use the printer directly attached to your computer, no one else will be able to use it over the network.

To make sure that your printer is installed in all versions of Windows, point to Settings on the Start menu, and then click Printers. If you see a listing for your printer, it's already installed and you can close the Printers window. If your printer isn't listed in the Printers window, you'll have to add the printer now.

If your printer came with a floppy disk or CD, it might have its own special printer drivers and installation program. Take a quick look at the documentation that came with the printer, and if the printer came with a CD, take a look at the CD too—sometimes you'll see instructions printed right on the CD.

Depending on the type of printer, running its special installation program can be as simple as inserting the CD in the computer and waiting for the installation program to start by itself. If nothing happens when you insert the CD, go to My Computer and double-click the icon for the CD. If that doesn't start the installation program, you might have to run the Setup or Install program on the CD. When the installation program starts, just follow the instructions that appear on the screen.

In many cases, however, setting up your printer doesn't require running a special installation program. Instead, you can set up the printer using the Add Printer Wizard in Windows. Here's how:

1. Insert your Windows CD into the CD-ROM drive. (Depending on how your computer was set up, this step might not be necessary, but it can't hurt.)

2. On the Start menu, point to Settings, and then click Printers.

3. Double-click the Add Printer icon to start the Add Printer Wizard.

4. Click Next. Now the Add Printer Wizard will take you through the steps of installing the printer.

Installing a Printer in Consumer Windows

If you're using Consumer Windows, follow these steps to complete the installation with the Add Printer Wizard:

1. When the wizard asks whether you want to install a local printer or a network printer, select Local Printer, and then click Next.

   Windows 2000 now asks you to select the port to which your printer is attached. (This step comes later if your computer is running Consumer Windows.) Select the port, and click Next. You'll now see a dialog box similar to the one shown in Figure 11-1, which contains lists of printer manufacturers and printer models. *If your printer model isn't listed, see the next section, "Handling Problem Printers."*

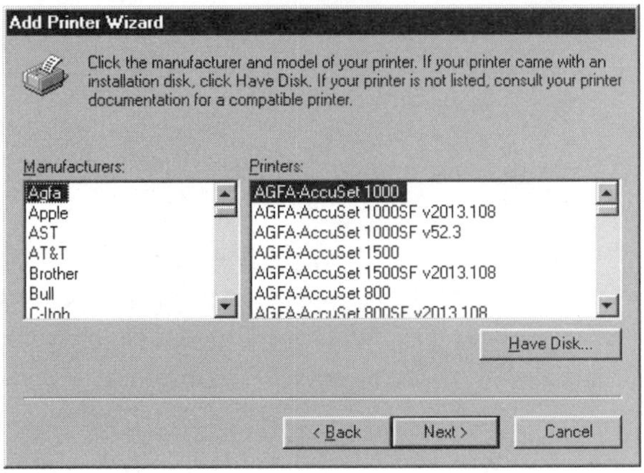

Figure 11-1.
Select your printer's make and model in the Add Printer Wizard in Consumer Windows.

2. Click the manufacturer of the printer on the left, click the model of the printer on the right, and click Next.

3. If your computer already has a driver for your printer, Windows will ask you whether it should keep the existing driver or replace it. You should keep the existing driver unless you're sure that you need to replace it. Click Next.

4. If your computer is running Consumer Windows, you'll now be asked to select the port to which the printer is attached. In most cases, your printer is attached to the LPT1 port, the standard parallel printing port on most PCs. If your computer has more than one printer port, the ports will be labeled LPT1, LPT2, and so on. If you

have a USB or serial printer, it might be connected to the USB or a serial (COM) port instead. Click the port that your printer is attached to, and click Next.

5. Type in a new name for the printer if you want, such as *Dad's laser printer*, or leave the default name.

6. If you're installing the first printer on your computer, the printer will automatically be the default. If there are other printers installed on the computer, Windows asks whether you want the new printer to be the default. Click Yes if you want the printer to be the default printer in all Windows programs. Click No if you want to leave another printer as the default. If you click No, you can still select the printer when you're ready to print. *See "Selecting a Different Printer on the Network," later in this chapter for more information.* Click Next.

   In Windows 2000, the wizard now asks whether you want to share the printer on the network. Type in a name for the shared printer, and click Next.

7. In Windows 2000, you can now type in a location and a comment for the printer. This information can help other users determine the printer location and its capabilities.

   The wizard now asks whether you want to print a test page. Make sure your printer is turned on and loaded with paper, and then click Yes to print a test page. Printing a test page isn't really necessary, but it's a good idea to confirm that everything is working properly rather than waiting until you have an important document to print.

8. In Consumer Windows, click Finish. In Windows 2000, click Next and then click Finish.

   Windows loads the appropriate printer drivers and prints the test page. A dialog box opens to ask whether the page printed correctly.

9. Click Yes if the page printed without a problem. If the page didn't print correctly, click No to start the Print Troubleshooter. Follow the dialog boxes that appear, selecting the answers that best explain the problem you're having.

Handling Problem Printers

If you run the Add Printer Wizard and your printer's model doesn't appear on the list, don't give up hope. Many new printer models and many old ones might not be listed.

   If your printer is new, insert the floppy disk or CD that came with it in the appropriate drive before you start the Add Printer Wizard. When you see the dialog box in the

Add Printer Wizard that prompts you to select the printer's manufacturer and model, click the Have Disk button. In the dialog box that appears next, specify the location of the disk and then continue following the prompts. You might have to specify a subfolder on the disk that contains the proper drivers for your printer or browse the disk to locate the drivers.

If your printer is older, it might not be listed in the Add Printer Wizard, and you might no longer have its installation disk. If so, try selecting the same manufacturer as your printer's and choosing one of the older models listed for that manufacturer. If that doesn't work, look for information in the printer's manual about other printers that yours can emulate. Many laser printers, for example, use the same drivers as some Hewlett-Packard (HP) printers. If you have an older laser printer with no documentation or software, try selecting the LaserJet Plus, LaserJet II, or LaserJet III models from the HP list.

If you still can't get the printer to work, try searching the Internet. You might be able to download the drivers you need to install the printer from a Web site. On the Web, look for the printer manufacturer's home page. If the manufacturer is out of business, search the Microsoft Web site, *http://www.microsoft.com/downloads/search.asp*, for driver information (select Keyword Search and enter *printer driver* for keywords). You also can perform general Web searches using your printer's make and model as keywords.

Sharing a Printer

Sharing a printer is similar to turning on sharing for a disk drive or folder. In this section, we'll look at printer sharing in Consumer Windows. *For information about how to share printers in Windows 2000, see "Sharing Printers in Windows 2000," later in this chapter.*

1. On the Start menu, point to Settings, and then click Printers.

2. In the Printers window, right-click the printer you want to share.

3. Choose Sharing from the shortcut menu.

4. On the Sharing tab of the Properties dialog box, click Shared As.

5. In the Share Name text box, enter a name for the printer that will identify it to other network users.

   You also have the option of entering an identifying description of the printer in the Comment text box. To make it easier for other users to select the printer, include its type, such as Canon Color InkJet or HP LaserJet Printer, in the description.

6. If you want to allow sharing only for users with a password, enter a password.

7. Click OK.

8. If you entered a password, type it again to confirm it, and then click OK. The printer's icon now shows that it's a shared resource.

HP DeskJet
895C Seri...

The check mark next to a printer icon in the Printers window indicates that the printer is the default in all Windows applications. To make a different printer the default, right-click its icon and choose Set As Default from the shortcut menu.

Separating Print Jobs

Once other folks start using your printer, don't be surprised if it starts churning out pages that you're not expecting. Windows will print documents in the order in which they are received, so if another network user starts a job before you do, you'll have to wait a bit for your document to print.

If you're not careful, you might wind up with several documents in the printer's output tray at one time. And you certainly wouldn't want to grab your quarterly report and your kid's homework and distribute both to the board members later in the morning. You also wouldn't want your document to disappear with someone else's job.

To help prevent this problem, you can have Windows automatically print a separator page between documents. The page prints at the start of each job and shows the name of the person who printed it.

Here's how to turn on the Separator page feature:

1. On the computer to which the printer is attached, click Start, point to Settings, and then click Printers.

2. Right-click the printer that is being shared, and choose Properties from the shortcut menu. The General tab of the printer's Properties dialog box appears, as shown in Figure 11-2.

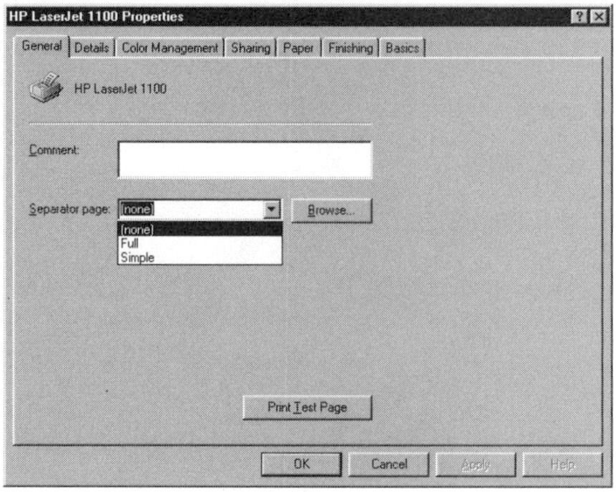

Figure 11-2.
You can turn on separator pages on the General tab of the printer's Properties dialog box.

3. Choose either Full or Simple from the Separator Page drop-down list. Both options print the user's name, document name, and current date and time. The Full option just prints it larger.

Note

Choose None from the Separator Page list if you no longer want to print separator pages.

4. Click OK.

Sharing Printers in Windows 2000

The concepts you learned for sharing printers in Consumer Windows also apply to Windows 2000, although there are some differences in the dialog boxes to allow sharing.

The Sharing tab in Windows 2000, for example, is shown in Figure 11-3. If Windows 2000 is sharing your printer with computers that run another version of Windows, click Additional Drivers to select and install the drivers for their systems.

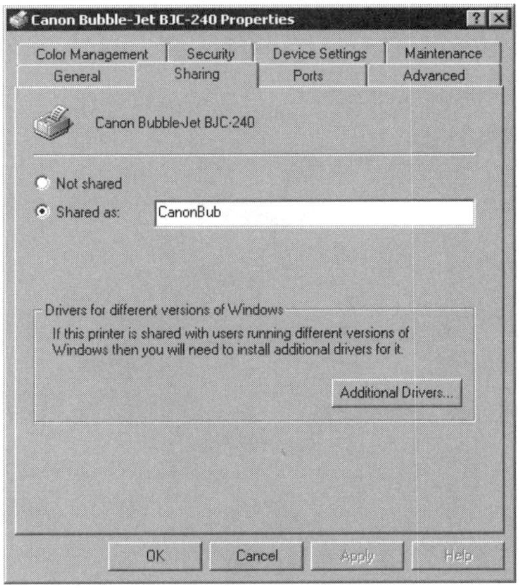

Figure 11-3.

Sharing printers in Windows 2000.

After enabling sharing, you have to set the permissions. Click the Security tab to display the options shown in Figure 11-4. As with sharing files, you can choose the users or groups to which you want to assign permissions. Three levels of permissions are possible:

- **Print** allows users to print documents.

- **Manage Printers** allows users to change printer properties.

- **Manage Documents** lets users delete print jobs and manage the printer queue.

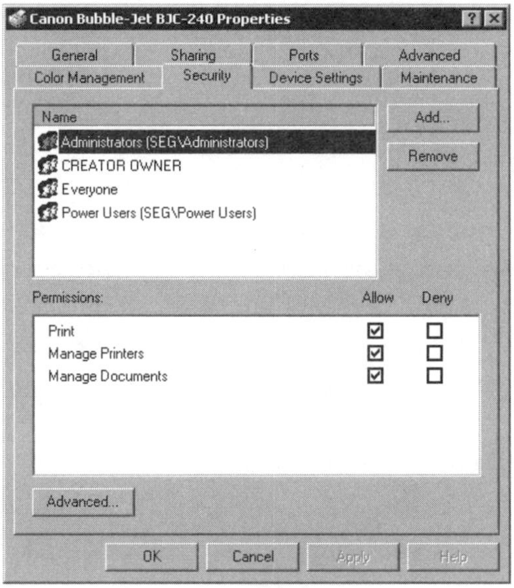

Figure 11-4.
Setting permissions for printer sharing.

Accessing a Shared Printer

The printer you've set up for sharing is now available to all the computers on the network. But before the other computers can access it, you must first install the printer on the other computers as a remote network printer rather than as a directly connected local printer. The procedure for installing a network printer is similar to that for a local printer, but with a few twists along the way. And you must be sure that everyone who wants to add the network printer to a computer has access to the printer drivers.

To install a network printer on a computer, you must follow these steps:

1. Insert the Windows CD in the CD-ROM drive. (This step might not be necessary because the drivers might already be on the computer's hard disk, but it can't hurt.)

2. Double-click Network Neighborhood and then double-click the computer connected to the shared printer. Use My Network Places to access the network computer in Windows Millennium Edition (Me) and Windows 2000.

3. Right-click the icon for the shared printer and choose Install from the shortcut menu to start the Add Printer Wizard. If your computer is running Windows Me or Windows 2000, choose Connect from the shortcut menu. (Windows 2000 is very smart about adding network printers; it will probably install the correct drivers for the printer without any further intervention on your part.)

If your computer is running Consumer Windows, you now have to specify whether you want MS-DOS programs, such as an older version of WordPerfect or dBase, to be able to print to the network printer. Normally, MS-DOS programs can't print to printers across the network. They can print only to local printers. But when you tell Windows to provide network printing capability to MS-DOS programs, Windows captures the information the MS-DOS program is trying to print and then channels it to the network printer.

4. If you want to be able to print from MS-DOS programs to network printers, click Yes. If you don't use MS-DOS programs or you want to print with them only to a local printer, click No.

5. Click Next.

6. If you chose to capture MS-DOS printing, you'll be asked to select a port. Click the Capture Printer Port button, select LPT1, click OK, and then click Next.

7. If your computer is running Windows 95, click the manufacturer of the printer on the left, click the model of the printer on the right, and then click Next.

8. Enter a name for the printer if you want, such as *Mom's color printer*, or leave the default name, which is usually the printer's model name.

9. If you're installing the first printer on your computer, the printer will automatically be the default. If there are other printers installed on the computer, Windows asks whether you want the new printer to be the default. Click Yes if you want the printer to be the default printer in all Windows programs. Click No if you want to have another printer as the default. You can still select the printer when you're ready to print. *See "Selecting a Different Printer on the Network," later in this chapter.*

10. Click Next.

11. When you're asked whether you want to print a test page, make sure the printer is turned on and loaded with paper, and then click Yes. (Click Finish in Consumer Windows.)

12. Click Finish. A dialog box then asks whether the page printed correctly.

13. Click Yes if the page printed without a problem. If the page didn't print correctly, click No to start the Print Troubleshooter. Follow the dialog boxes that appear, selecting the answers that best describe the problem you're having.

Selecting a Different Printer on the Network

Whenever you set a printer as the default—either your local printer or one of the printers on the network—all your documents are directed to that printer unless you choose a different printer. To change which printer is the Windows default, click Start, point to Settings, and then click Printers to open the Printers window, right-click the printer you want as the default, and then choose Set As Default from the shortcut menu.

You can also choose to print a particular document at a printer other than the default printer. How you perform this task depends on the application you're using. In many programs, such as Microsoft Word, clicking the Print button on the toolbar automatically prints the document to the default printer. If you want to choose a different printer, you must select the printer in the Print dialog box.

For example, suppose your own laser printer is the current default, but you want to print a document in color. Your kids have a color printer that's been set up as a network printer. Here's how you'd print a document on your kids' printer:

1. Choose Print from your application's File menu.

2. Click the drop-down arrow next to the Name box, which shows the default printer, and choose the printer in your kids' room from the drop-down list.

3. Click OK.

4. Go and get your document before the kids turn it in as homework!

Using Printer Shortcuts

Normally, you start an application and then print a document. But with all versions of Windows, you can use several shortcuts for printing documents.

In My Computer or Windows Explorer, you can right-click a document's icon and choose Print from the shortcut menu. Windows opens the application that was used to create the document, sends the document to the printer, and then closes the application.

You can also drag a document onto a printer icon that you've placed on the Windows desktop. To place a printer icon on the desktop, follow these steps in all versions of Windows:

1. On the Start menu, point to Settings, and then click Printers.

2. In the Printers window, right-click a printer and choose Create Shortcut from the shortcut menu.

3. When a message tells you that you can't place a shortcut in the Printers folder and asks whether you want to place the shortcut on the desktop instead, click Yes.

Connecting Printers Directly to the Network

Because a printer that's connected to a computer on the network works only when the computer is on, you might want to use an alternative: connecting the printer directly to the network. Connecting a printer directly to the network also frees up a computer's printer port so that you can hook up an external Zip drive, scanner, or other parallel device without a conflict.

In a twisted-pair network, you use twisted-pair cable to connect a printer to the hub. In a thin Ethernet network, you use coaxial cable to connect the printer to the network interface card (NIC) of the nearest networked device. Because the printer isn't connected to the printer port of a computer, anyone on the network can access it directly as long as the printer is turned on.

The disadvantage of connecting printers directly to the network is expense. Most printers are designed only for standard parallel connections. To connect them directly to the network, you'll need to purchase either a network-ready printer or a *print server*, a device that makes your printer network-ready.

Network-ready printers have a NIC built in. They cost more than standard printers and can be a little harder to find. The print server is equipped with an Ethernet connection on one side and a parallel, or possibly serial, connection on the other.

The least expensive print servers are called *pocket servers*. About the size of a pack of cigarettes, a pocket server plugs directly into a printer's parallel port. The twisted-pair cable from the network hub or the coaxial cable from another networked device plugs into the other end of the server.

Another type of print server connects to a printer with a cable. These external servers are usually more expensive than pocket servers, but they might include additional features. Some models, for example, have more than one parallel port, allowing them to connect several printers to the network at the same time.

Note

For some HP LaserJet printers, you can purchase an internal print server that fits inside the printer, much the way some NICs fit inside a computer.

When selecting a print server, make sure it matches your cable type—either twisted pair or coaxial. Some print servers, but not all, can accommodate both types.

The print server must also support the protocol you're using on your network. Some print servers support only IPX/SPX; others require either TCP/IP or NetBEUI.

Finally, while most printers have a standard-sized parallel port, called a *Centronics* port, some models, such as the LaserJet 1100, have a smaller mini-Centronics port. The standard-sized connection on a pocket print server won't fit a mini-Centronics port. If you're using such a printer, you'll need an adapter for the print server.

Note

To install an external print server, just connect the cable that came with the printer to the server's parallel connection. Connect the network cable to the server's network connection.

Setting Up a Pocket Print Server

Many different models of pocket print servers exist. Although they all operate in about the same way, their setup procedures vary. Most servers are sold with software that helps them connect to the network, but the process really depends on the type of protocol the server supports.

A TCP/IP server needs to be assigned an IP address. With a Windows peer-to-peer network, you'll probably have to assign the server a static IP address that isn't used by any computer on the network. Consequently, you might have to assign static IP addresses to every computer on the network as well, rather than have Windows assign them for you. Check the literature that came with your server for step-by-step directions for assigning it an IP address.

Most manufacturers provide programs to help you through the process. The Microplex Ethernet Pocket Print Server, for example, offers two programs for configuring the print server—IPAssign and Waldo. The IPAssign program, whose main dialog box is shown in Figure 11-5, accesses the print server through the Ethernet address and assigns it an IP address of your choosing.

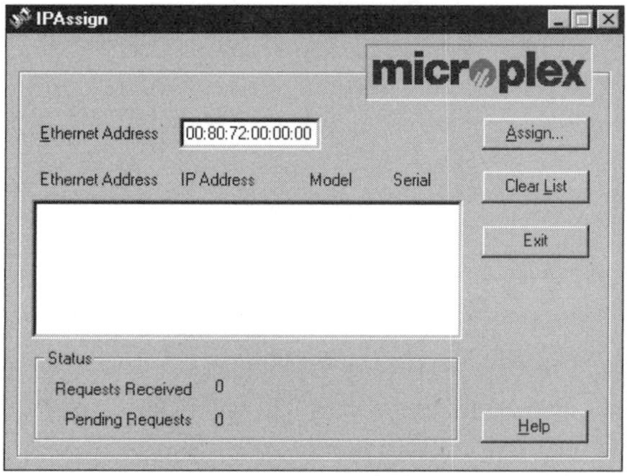

Figure 11-5.

The IPAssign program for a Microplex print server assigns an IP address to the server.

The Waldo program is Java based, so you must have the Java runtime files installed on your computer. When you run Waldo, it searches for a Microplex print server on the network and displays its Ethernet address.

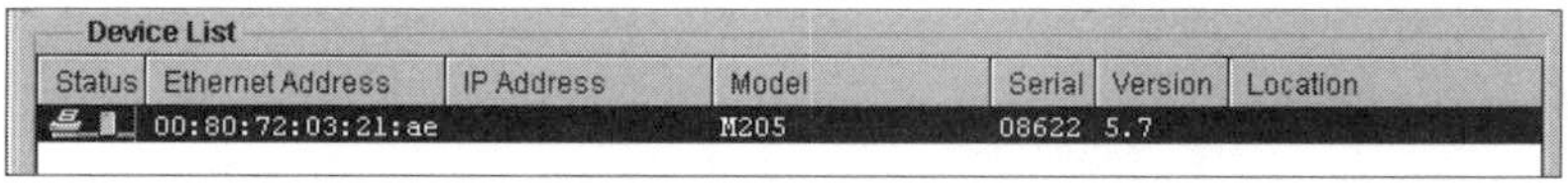

You can then click the Assign button in the Waldo window to associate an IP address and subnet to the Ethernet address.

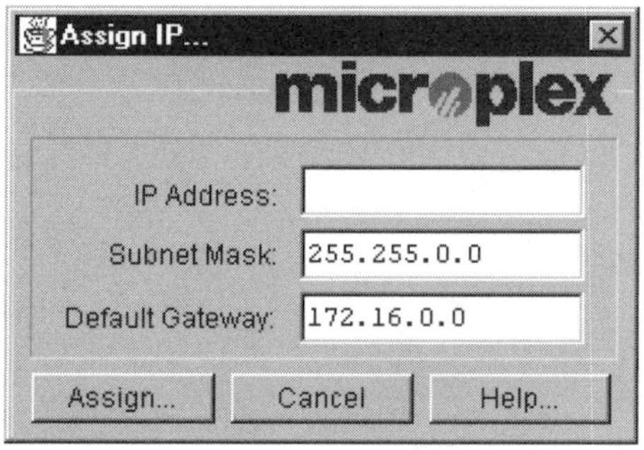

Once you assign an IP address to your server, you configure Windows to communicate with the printer. You first have to associate the server with a printer port. The default port most printers use is called LPT1, the parallel connector that the printer cable plugs into. When you configured your printer, as you learned in "Installing a Printer" earlier in this chapter, you associated the printer with the port so Windows knows where to send the information to be printed—to the LPT1 port and then out to the printer.

When you connect a print server to the network, you need to create a port with which the IP address is linked. When you associate a printer to that port, Windows sends the information to be printed through the network and the Ethernet address of the print server.

How you associate a printer port to the print server depends on the print server itself. With Microplex servers, for example, the server appears as a device in Network Neighborhood or My Network Places and has four ports associated with it. When you configure the printer, you browse to the port you want to use in the same way you would browse to a workstation, as explained in the section "Accessing a Shared Printer," earlier in this chapter.

Other manufacturers handle port assignments differently. The pocket print servers from Axis Communications, for instance, don't appear in Network Neighborhood or My Network Places. Instead, you use the NetPilot program to associate the server with a port, and then you use a program called Axis Print System to add the printer to Windows.

Microplex and Axis certainly aren't the only makers of pocket print servers. Table 11-1, later in this chapter, lists other print server makes and models.

Setting Up an External Print Server

External print servers, an alternative to pocket print servers, connect to a printer by cable rather than plug directly into the printer itself. External servers work in the same way and are set up the same way as pocket print servers, although they're more expensive than pocket print servers. Many models also come with two or more parallel connections that allow you to place multiple printers on the network so that you can use different printers for different documents.

Hewlett-Packard's JetDirect print servers, for example, work with virtually any printer equipped with a parallel port—not just HP's own brand. The line includes two models that have three parallel connections and a one-printer model, the 170X, that's more suitable for home networks.

Setting up an HP print server is easy. After you connect the server both to the printer and to your network hub, you press a small button on the back of the server to print out a page of configuration information, including the electronic hardware address that is built into the device.

You then install the JetAdmin program supplied with the server and use the HP JetDirect Printer Wizard to configure the device. Figure 11-6 shows the wizard page in which you select a protocol and enter the unit's hardware address.

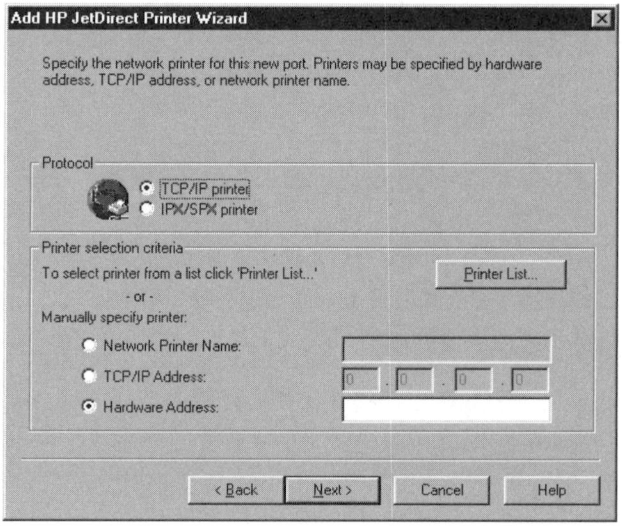

Figure 11-6.

The HP JetDirect Printer Wizard prompts you to select a protocol and enter the server's hardware address.

Using the address, JetAdmin locates the printer and displays a dialog box in which you can specify an IP address if you're using the TCP/IP protocol. After a few additional steps, JetAdmin starts the Add Printer Wizard in Windows, which opens a dialog box that prompts you to assign an IP address.

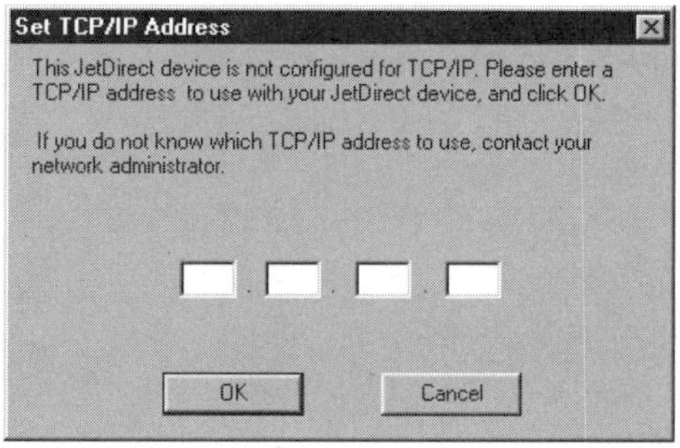

After the JetAdmin setup, you can send documents to the printer from your computer, and other network users can select the printer as their network printer and print documents even when your computer isn't on.

Many manufacturers of print servers exist, so you have plenty of choices. Table 11-1 lists print server makes and models and each manufacturer's Web address.

Table 11-1. Print Server Manufacturers and Models

Manufacturer	Models	Web site
Axis Communications	Pocket, and one-port and two-port models, some with both parallel and serial ports	*http://www.axis.com/*
NETGEAR	One- and two-port models, some with built-in four-port hub	*http://www.netgear.com/*
Emulex	Pocket, and two-port and three-port models	*http://www.emulex.com/*
Extended Systems	Pocket, and one-port and two-port models, some with both parallel and serial ports	*http://www.extendedsystems.com/*
Hewlett-Packard JetDirect	One-port and three-port models, external and internal, and one model for sharing over home telephone lines	*http://www.hp.com/*
Intel NetPort Express	One-port and three-port models	*http://www.intel.com/*
Lantronix	Pocket and external print servers, up to six-port models (four parallel and two serial)	*http://www.lantronix.com/*
Linksys EtherFast	One-port and three-port models	*http://www.linksys.com/*
MicroPlex	Pocket, and a four-port model (two parallel and two serial)	*http://www.microplex.com/*

Sharing printers on a network can be a great time-saver and step-saver. You'll no longer need to carry a disk to another computer to print a document or carry a printer to another computer. With Windows, you don't have to purchase any additional software or hardware unless you want to connect your printer directly to the network.

Sharing files and printers isn't the only benefit of connecting computers on a network, however. You'll learn in the next chapter that you can use your network to create a family e-mail system for sending and receiving messages between family members.

Chapter 12

Communicating Over the Network

You've seen how a home network is great for sharing files and printers, but it's also a convenient way to communicate with other members of your family. Why yell across the house or leave scribbled notes when you can transmit messages over your network?

In this chapter, you'll learn three ways to communicate via the network, ranging from the easiest to the most advanced. You'll learn how to do the following:

- Send and receive short messages that pop up on the recipient's screen

- Send and receive e-mail messages just as you can over the Internet

- Set up Microsoft Outlook to communicate over your network

Note

You can also communicate over the network with the program Microsoft NetMeeting, which is described in Chapter 17. You can use NetMeeting like an intercom system to speak with other family members and even to see them (if your computers are equipped with cameras).

Sending and Receiving Pop-up Messages

The easiest and least formal way to communicate over the network is to send and receive pop-up messages. You can send a message to a specific family member or "broadcast" it to everyone on the network.

With a program named WinPopup, which comes with Consumer Windows (Microsoft Windows 95, Microsoft Windows 98, and Microsoft Windows Millennium Edition), you can announce that dinner is ready, tell your daughter that the phone call is for her, or send out a quick reminder or word of wisdom to your loved ones. Your message simply pops up in a window on the recipient's screen. Keep in mind that WinPopup doesn't save your messages after you close it or after you shut down your computer.

Note

Although WinPopup isn't included with Microsoft Windows 2000, you can download programs over the Internet that let Windows 2000 send and receive pop-up messages. One example is Net Hail at *http://www.nethail.com.*

Starting WinPopup

WinPopup is usually installed when you set up Windows, but it's not listed with other programs on the Start menu. If you plan to use WinPopup regularly, you can add it to the Start menu, to your desktop, or to your Windows taskbar.

To locate WinPopup and add it as a shortcut on your Windows desktop, follow these steps:

1. On the Start menu, point to Find, and click Files Or Folders. With Windows Millennium Edition (Me), point to Search on the Start menu and click For Files Or Folders.

2. Make sure the Look In box is set at C: (or Local Hard Drives in Windows Me) so your entire drive is searched.

3. In the Named text box (or the Search For Files Or Folders Named text box in Windows Me), type *winpopup.* In the Look In drop-down list, choose the drive on which Windows is installed (usually the C: drive) and then click Find Now (click Search Now in Windows Me).

   Windows searches your disk and locates the WinPopup program. If Windows doesn't locate the program, see the next section, "Installing WinPopup."

Name	In Folder
Winpopup	C:\WINDOWS
Winpopup	C:\WINDOWS\INF
winpopup	C:\WINDOWS\INF\INFBACK

9 file(s) found

4. In the list of files, right-click WinPopup and choose Create Shortcut from the short-cut menu.

5. Click Yes when a message appears reporting that you can't add the shortcut to the current location and asking whether you want to add the shortcut to your desktop.

6. Close the Find window (the Search Results window in Windows Me). You now have a shortcut to the program on your desktop.

Shortcut to Winpopup

If you're using Windows 98, Windows Me, or Windows 95 with Microsoft Internet Explorer 4.0 or above installed, you can add the shortcut to your Quick Launch toolbar on the taskbar so that you can access it from within any application. To perform this task, drag the shortcut icon to the Quick Launch toolbar, which is just to the right of the Start button. You can now delete the shortcut from the desktop if you want, by right-clicking it and choosing Delete from the shortcut menu.

Note

If the Quick Launch toolbar is now too narrow to fit all the icons it needs to display, you can bring them all back into view by dragging the vertical line to the right of the last icon farther to the right.

Because WinPopup must be running for someone to send or receive messages, you should have everyone on the network copy the WinPopup shortcut to the Startup folder, usually located at C:\Windows\Start Menu\Programs\StartUp. When the shortcut is in that folder, it automatically starts whenever Windows is started.

Installing WinPopup

If the WinPopup program isn't already installed on your computer, you'll have to install it yourself. Insert the Windows CD into your CD-ROM drive just in case you need it, and then follow these steps:

1. On the Start menu, point to Settings, and click Control Panel.

   Note

   If you don't have a Windows CD, the installation program might already be on your hard disk.

2. In Control Panel, double-click Add/Remove Programs.

3. In the Add/Remove Programs Properties dialog box, click the Windows Setup tab.

4. In the list of components, click System Tools (in Windows 95, click Accessories), but be careful not to remove the check mark in the check box to its left.

5. Click Details.

6. In the System Tools dialog box (the Accessories dialog box in Windows 95), scroll through the components list and select the check box next to WinPopup.

Components:	
☐ Group Policies	0.0 MB
☐ Net Watcher	0.0 MB
☐ System Monitor	0.0 MB
☐ System Resource Meter	0.0 MB
☑ WinPopup	0.1 MB

7. Click OK to close the System Tools or Accessories dialog box.

8. Click OK again to close the Add/Remove Programs Properties dialog box.

Using WinPopup

WinPopup must be running in order for you to send or receive a message. If the WinPopup shortcut isn't in the Startup folder on your machine, which starts WinPopup automatically when you start Windows, you must run WinPopup by double-clicking the icon you placed on the desktop or on your Quick Launch toolbar.

When WinPopup starts, you see the dialog box shown in Figure 12-1. If you're not ready to send a message, just minimize the window so that WinPopup appears on the taskbar.

Figure 12-1.

The WinPopup dialog box allows you to send or receive messages on the network.

Here's how to send a message:

1. Click the WinPopup button on the taskbar to open the WinPopup window.

2. Click the Send button on the toolbar, which shows a picture of an envelope, or choose Send from the Messages menu to open the Send Message dialog box.

3. To send a message to everyone on the network, click Workgroup. To send a message to a specific person on the network, click User Or Computer.

4. If you want to send a message to everyone and the workgroup name doesn't appear automatically, enter the name of the workgroup in the text box in the To area of the Send Message dialog box. If you want to send a message to one person, enter that person's user name or computer name.

5. Type the message (which can be up to 127 characters if you are sending the message to a workgroup, or 500 characters if you are sending the message to an individual) in the Message box, and then click OK. A complete message might look like this.

Note

To paste text into the message from the clipboard, right-click the Message text box and choose Paste from the shortcut menu.

6. A message box reports that the message was sent successfully.

7. Click OK.

When you receive a message from another computer on the network, you'll hear a beep. If the WinPopup window is open, the message appears in the window, as shown in Figure 12-2.

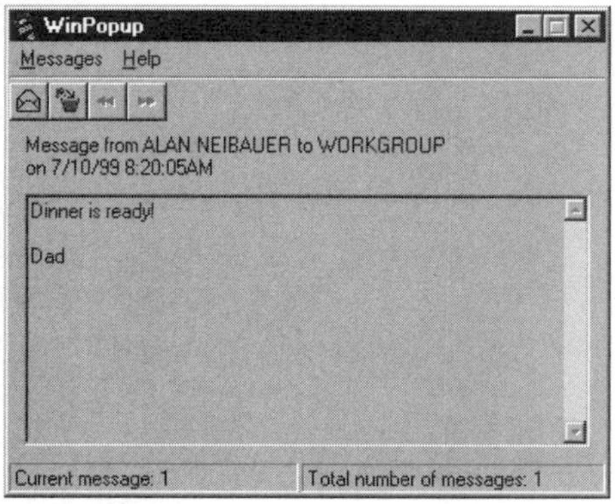

Figure 12-2.

A received message appears in the WinPopup window.

If the window is minimized, click its button on the taskbar to display the message. The WinPopup icon on the taskbar, by the way, indicates whether you have pop-up messages to read. When you have no messages, the icon looks like this.

As you receive messages, the icon indicates how many you have. Here's what the icon looks like when you've received a message.

If you want the WinPopup window to open automatically when a message arrives, choose Options from the Messages menu and select the check box Pop Up Dialog On Message Receipt. Other options allow you to turn off the beep that sounds when a message arrives and to keep the WinPopup window in the foreground above other program windows.

When you have more than one message, click the Previous and Next buttons on the WinPopup toolbar to switch from one message to the next. Click the Delete button on the toolbar to delete a displayed message.

When you close the WinPopup window, a message reminds you that you can't send or receive any more messages. If you still have undeleted messages, the message box also reminds you that all of them will be discarded when you close WinPopup because the program doesn't save messages from session to session. If you decide you still want to exit the program, click OK to close the WinPopup window.

Creating Your Own Post Office

Although WinPopup is free (with Consumer Windows), quick, and convenient, it does have its limitations. A pop-up message can have only a relatively small number of characters and it's available only while WinPopup is open. When you exit WinPopup, all messages you've received are erased. It certainly would be better if you could send and receive e-mail over the network, just as you can over the Internet. Well, as it happens, Windows allows you to do just that.

To send and receive e-mail on your network, you must set up a network mail server. The mail server lets you create mailboxes in which messages are stored until the recipient reads them.

Windows 95 and Windows 98 include a mail server program named Microsoft Mail Postoffice. You can also find shareware mail server programs that you can download from the Internet. We'll look at both Microsoft Mail Postoffice and a shareware server program, VPOP3, in this chapter.

Note

Windows Me and Windows 2000 don't include Microsoft Mail Postoffice. To create a home network e-mail system with computers running these operating systems, you'll need to use another mail server such as VPOP3. See "Using a Shareware Mail Server" later in this chapter for information on setting up a home network e-mail system with Windows Me or Windows 2000.

Mail Servers and E-Mail Clients

To understand how e-mail works, you should understand the different roles played by the mail server and an e-mail program, such as Microsoft Outlook Express.

A mail server, such as the mail server at your Internet service provider (ISP), or the mail server you set up on your network, receives incoming e-mail, transmits outgoing messages, and organizes and stores in mailboxes messages that have been received. Your ISP's mail server, for example, maintains a mailbox for each member and stores incoming messages until you retrieve them. Similarly, programs for creating a post office on your network let you create a mailbox for each user, and they handle the transfer of messages between the sender and the recipient.

An e-mail program, called the *e-mail client,* is the software that you run on your computer to read and write messages. It also transfers the messages you send to the mail server and picks up from the mail server messages that are waiting for you.

Most ISP mail servers on the Internet use the Post Office Protocol (POP), which means that you can communicate with them using any e-mail program that can handle POP e-mail. Outlook Express, Outlook, Eudora, and Netscape Messenger are all POP e-mail programs. The abbreviation POP3 that you'll often see indicates version 3 of the Post Office Protocol.

Note

Some mail servers, such as the one used by America Online (AOL), are designed to communicate only with the e-mail programs built into their own software.

When you install Microsoft Mail Postoffice to add e-mail capabilities to your network, an e-mail program called Windows Messaging is installed at the same time. Windows Messaging works with Microsoft Mail Postoffice as well as Internet e-mail.

Note

Outlook Express, the e-mail program that comes with Internet Explorer versions 4 and 5 and Windows 98, works with Internet e-mail servers, but it doesn't work with Microsoft Mail Postoffice. To use Outlook Express for network e-mail, you'll need a program such as VPOP3 or another mail server.

You can also use Outlook as your e-mail program because it can communicate both with Internet POP e-mail servers and Microsoft Mail Postoffice. Outlook has more features than Windows Messaging, but you must purchase it separately because it doesn't come free with Windows. *See "Communicating Using Outlook," later in this chapter, if you want to use Outlook for your network e-mail.*

Microsoft Exchange

Windows 95 includes a program named Microsoft Exchange. Exchange was an e-mail client for sending and receiving mail through Microsoft Mail Postoffice on a network, but it didn't support Internet mail.

To use Exchange for Internet mail, you had to install Microsoft Internet Mail Services, which were available in a product named Microsoft Plus! and was included with versions of Internet Explorer starting with version 2 or as a separate update available from Microsoft.

The name of the product was later changed from Microsoft Exchange to Windows Messaging to distinguish it from Microsoft Exchange Server, the client/server network e-mail and messaging system.

Another alternative, covered in the section "Using a Shareware Mail Server" later in this chapter, is to set up a POP mail server on your network rather than Microsoft Mail Postoffice. The shareware program VPOP3, for example, lets you handle e-mail both over the Internet and on your network using a regular e-mail program such as Outlook Express.

Using Microsoft Mail Postoffice

Just like an Internet e-mail server, your network post office can handle messages of any length, including attachments. Messages you send are stored in your own Sent Items folder, so you can keep a record of your communications. Messages you receive are stored in an Inbox until you decide to delete them. You can reply to messages and forward them to others on the network with a single click.

You perform all these tasks by creating a post office on one of the computers on the network. The post office acts as a central station for channeling mail from senders to receivers. If you send a message to someone whose computer isn't turned on and ready to receive the message, the post office stores it until it can be received.

The person who sets up the post office has to specify who will be using it. Each user gets a post office mailbox in which messages are stored and a password for accessing the messages. To work with the post office, each computer on the network must have Microsoft Mail Postoffice installed.

If you create a message and the post office is closed—the computer storing the post office is turned off or disconnected from the network—your message is held in the Outbox on your own computer until it can be sent. To ensure that messages won't sit in a sender's Outbox for too long, you should set up the post office on the computer that's turned on most often.

Installing Microsoft Mail Postoffice

The first step in creating your postal system is to make sure the Microsoft Mail Postoffice program that comes with Windows is installed on each computer on the network. To install the program, open each computer's Control Panel and look for two icons, labeled Mail (or Mail And Fax on some systems) and Microsoft Mail Postoffice.

Mail   Microsoft Mail
            Postoffice

If you're running the original version of Windows 95, Microsoft Mail Postoffice was installed automatically with the program Exchange. If your computer came with one of the updates to Windows 95, Microsoft Mail Postoffice was installed along with Windows Messaging. *To create a home network e-mail system with Windows Me and Windows 2000, see "Using a Shareware Mail Server," later in this chapter.*

If you don't see the Microsoft Mail Postoffice icon in Control Panel, use the Windows Setup tab on the Add/Remove Programs icon in Control Panel to install either Exchange or Windows Messaging. When you look in the list of components that you can install, one or the other program will be available.

Setting up Windows 98 or Windows 98 Second Edition doesn't install Microsoft Mail Postoffice. If you installed either version of Windows 98 over Windows 95, Windows 98 will leave the existing version of Microsoft Mail Postoffice on your computer, though.

Fixing Microsoft Office 2000

If you have Office 2000 installed at the time you install Microsoft Mail Postoffice, the Microsoft Windows Messaging System (WMS) program might replace some Office 2000 files on the hard disk, making Office 2000 unstable or unusable. If you run WMS after installing Office 2000, you should then repair the Office installation by following these steps:

1. Insert the Office CD into your CD-ROM drive.

2. Double-click My Computer.

3. In the My Computer window, double-click Control Panel.

4. In Control Panel, double-click the Add/Remove Programs icon.

5. In the list of installed software, click Microsoft Office 2000, and then click Add/Remove.

6. In the Microsoft Office 2000 Maintenance Mode window, click the large Repair Office button.

7. In the Reinstall/Repair Microsoft Office 2000 window, choose Repair Errors In My Office Installation.

8. Click Finish, and then wait until the process is completed. This might take some time.

Repairing Office won't cause any harm to the files installed by WMS.

To install Microsoft Mail Postoffice in either version of Windows 98, run the WMS program, which you'll find on your Windows CD in the \tools\oldwin95\message\us folder. If you have an international installation, choose the \tools\oldwin95\message\intl folder instead of \tools\oldwin95\message\us.

Restart your computer after running the program, even if you aren't prompted to do so.

Creating the Post Office

Now that each computer on the network has Microsoft Mail Postoffice installed, you're ready to create the post office itself on one of them. Be sure to pick a computer that will be on frequently and then create and share a folder on that computer's hard disk, on which you'll store the post office files. Here's how you do it:

1. On the Windows desktop, double-click My Computer.

2. Double-click the C: drive icon.

3. Right-click in the C: window, point to New, and click Folder. The new folder is created and its default name is highlighted.

4. Type *poffice* to replace the default name of the folder and press Enter.

5. Right-click the poffice folder, and choose Sharing from the shortcut menu.

6. In the Properties dialog box, click Shared As.

7. Click Full.

8. Click OK.

   You now have to create the post office itself, along with your own mailbox.

1. In Control Panel, double-click the Microsoft Mail Postoffice icon.

2. In the Microsoft Workgroup Postoffice Admin window, click Create A New Workgroup Postoffice, and then click Next to see the dialog box shown in Figure 12-3.

3. Type the path of the folder you created to store the post office (*c:\poffice*), and then click Next.

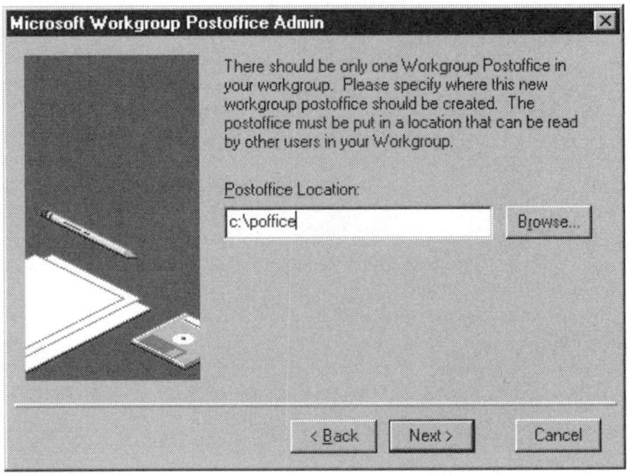

Figure 12-3.

Type the path in the Microsoft Workgroup Postoffice Admin dialog box.

4. The Microsoft Mail Postoffice program creates a folder within the C:\poffice folder named Wgpo0000 that contains numerous files and subfolders, and it asks you to confirm its location.

5. Click Next.

6. In the Enter Your Administrator Account Details dialog box, type your name in the Name text box.

7. Make a note of the mailbox name in the Mailbox text box. You'll need to know it later.

8. Press Tab twice and type a replacement password in the Password text box.

9. Click OK.

10. Click OK in the Mail dialog box.

Adding Post Office Users

When you set up Microsoft Mail Postoffice, a mailbox is created for you. For other post office users, you'll need to create additional mailboxes. To add a user and automatically create a mailbox, follow these steps:

1. In Control Panel, double-click the Microsoft Mail Postoffice icon.

2. In the Microsoft Workgroup Postoffice Admin dialog box, click Administer An Existing Workgroup Postoffice, and then click Next.

3. Click Next to accept the path to your post office.

4. Enter your mailbox name as the post office administrator.

5. Enter the password you entered earlier.

6. Click Next to open the Postoffice Manager dialog box, which lists all current users.

7. Click Add User to see the dialog box shown in Figure 12-4.

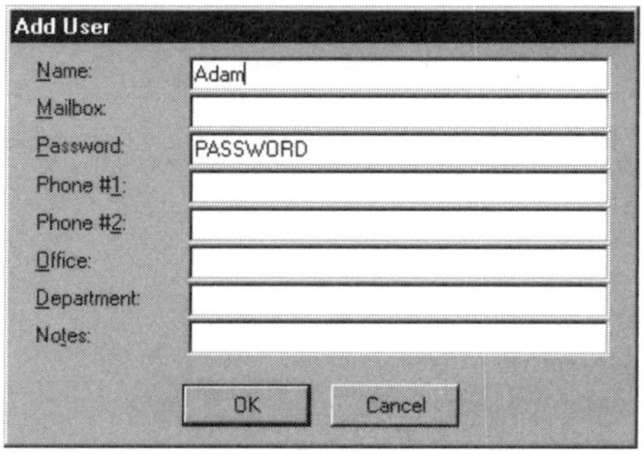

Figure 12-4.
The Add User dialog box allows you to add new users to your post office.

8. Enter the user's name.

9. Enter the name for the user's mailbox and change the default password, replacing it with one of your own.

10. Click OK.

11. Give to the user the path and name of the post office, the name of the mailbox, and the password.

12. Repeat steps 7 through 11 for each additional user, and then click Close.

Setting Up Windows Messaging

Each user must set up an e-mail program to be able to send and receive files through Microsoft Mail Postoffice. All users should now have an Inbox icon on their desktops.

Double-clicking this icon starts an e-mail program called Windows Messaging or Exchange, depending on the version of Windows you use, through which you can send and receive information over the network. You can also use Outlook to send and receive mail through the network. Because either Windows Messaging or Exchange is included with Windows 95 and Windows 98, we'll look at this program in some detail. You'll learn how to set up Outlook for network e-mail later in this chapter.

The first time you open the Inbox, you must create a profile. A *profile* lists the mail services that Windows Messaging can use. To create a profile, follow these steps:

1. Double-click the Inbox icon on the desktop to see the Inbox Setup Wizard dialog box shown in Figure 12-5.

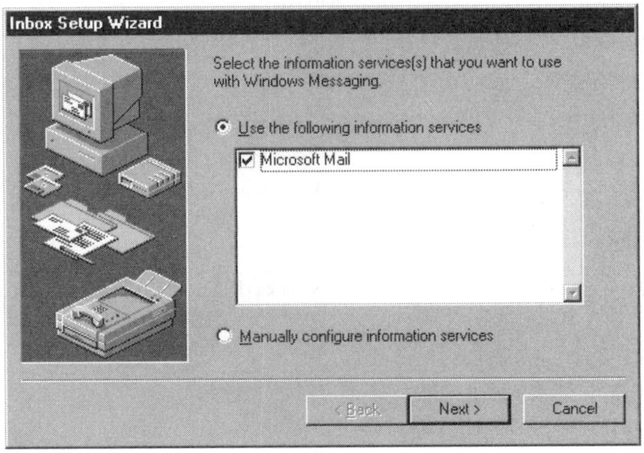

Figure 12-5.
In the Inbox Setup Wizard dialog box, you can select the information services that you want to use with Windows Messaging.

2. Make sure the Use The Following Information Services option button is selected and the Microsoft Mail check box is selected, and then click Next. You'll be asked to provide the path to the post office folder.

3. Click Browse to open the Browse For Postoffice dialog box.

4. Double-click Network Neighborhood and locate the post office folder you created earlier.

5. Click OK to return to the Inbox Setup Wizard, and then click Next. The wizard displays a list of mailboxes in the post office.

6. Click your mailbox, and then click Next.

7. In the box that appears, enter your mailbox password, and then click Next. The wizard now shows you the default location of your personal address book, which is where you can store e-mail addresses.

8. Click Next to accept the default location. The wizard now shows you the default location of your personal folder, in which your messages are stored.

9. Click Next to accept the default location and to see a summary of your profile.

10. Click Finish.

Fixing Windows 98 Second Edition

If you have Windows 98 Second Edition, you might get the following error message when starting Windows Messaging:

MAPISP32 caused an invalid page fault in module KERNEL32.DLL.

If this message appears, you'll need to take a few extra steps to get Windows Messaging working. Here's how to fix the problem:

1. Restart your computer.

2. Locate the file mapi32.dll file in your Windows\System folder.

3. Rename the file to mapi32.lld.

4. Reinstall Windows Messaging from your Windows 98 Second Edition CD.

5. Restart your computer.

Adding Microsoft Mail to Your Profile

If you're already using Windows Messaging or Exchange for your Internet e-mail, you can add Mail to your profile to send and receive mail over the network. Here's how:

1. In Control Panel, double-click Mail (the icon might be labeled Mail And Fax on some systems).

2. If the profile to which you want to add Mail isn't displayed, click the Show Profiles button to display the Mail dialog box, select the profile you want to change, and then click Properties.

3. In the Properties dialog box, click Add to display a list of services that can be installed in Windows Messaging.

4. Click Microsoft Mail in the list of information services.

5. Click OK to open the Microsoft Mail dialog box.

6. On the Connection tab of the Microsoft Mail dialog box, shown in Figure 12-6, enter the name of the post office folder or browse for it. The name contains the path to the computer on the network. If the post office is on your computer, it might appear as C:\poffice\wgpo0000. If the post office is on another network computer, the path might be something like \\JoesComputer\C\poffice\wpgo0000.

Figure 12-6.
Enter the path to your post office in the Microsoft Mail dialog box.

7. Click the Logon tab and enter your mailbox name and password.

8. Click OK twice.

Note

To set up Windows Messaging for Internet e-mail, you have to add Internet Mail to the profile. See "Working with Profiles," later in this chapter.

Sending and Receiving E-Mail

After you create a profile, opening the Inbox opens the Windows Messaging window shown in Figure 12-7. The window shows the Inbox, which displays the messages you've received. An initial welcoming message from Microsoft appears in the Inbox the first time you use Windows Messaging.

Figure 12-7.

The Windows Messaging Inbox displays your incoming messages.

Note

You can use the Columns command to determine how received messages are displayed. This command lets you add or remove various columns that display additional information about your mail, including whether it was sent, the recipient, the message's sensitivity, and other options. To use it, select Columns on the View menu of the Inbox. In the dialog box that appears, select the options that you want to be listed with each message and click the Add button. You can then use the Move Up and Move Down buttons to change the order in which items appear.

Creating and Addressing a Message

To create a message, click the New Message button on the toolbar. A new message window opens, as shown in Figure 12-8. Click the To box to view a list of post office mailboxes. In the list of mailboxes, click each person to whom you want to send a message, and then click the To button. When you've selected all the intended recipients, click OK.

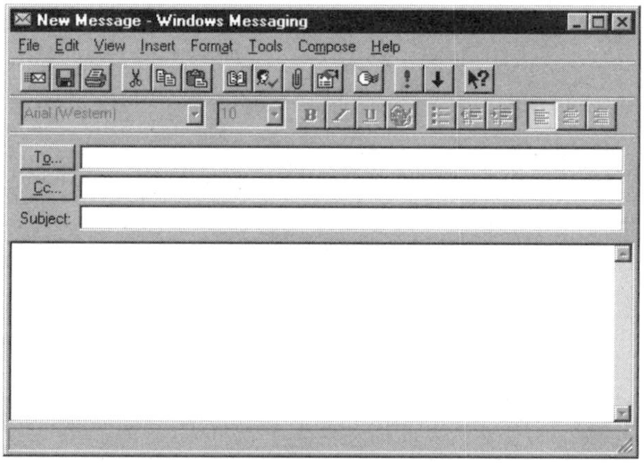

Figure 12-8.

A new message window opens when you click the New Message button on the toolbar.

Instead of clicking the To button to select recipients' names, for example, you can just type a recipient's user name in the To text box rather than look up the recipient in the address book. But if you type a name, click the Check Names button on the toolbar before you send the message. This feature makes sure that each name you've entered belongs to a person who actually has a mailbox in the post office and warns you if that's not the case.

Next, enter the subject of the message and press Tab to move the cursor to the main message area, in which you type the message.

Attaching a File

To send a file along with your message, click the Attach button, select the file you want to send, and then click OK. The file becomes an attachment that is transmitted along with the message.

Using Special Message Options

If you click the Read Receipt button before sending a message, Microsoft Mail Postoffice will send you an e-mail message when the recipient opens the message. This e-mail message confirms that the message was at least opened, if not necessarily read.

Note

In addition to a read receipt, you can also request a *delivery receipt*—an e-mail message that Windows Messaging sends you when your message is delivered. To request a delivery receipt, click the Read Receipt button on the toolbar.

The two Importance buttons allow you to assign a level of importance to your message. By clicking either button, the message will be flagged in the recipient's Inbox with an icon indicating its level of importance—High or Low.

Clicking the Properties button on the toolbar displays information about the selected message and offers you additional delivery options, as shown in Figure 12-9. It also allows you to assign your message one of four sensitivity levels—Normal, Personal, Private, or Confidential. When you designate a message as Private, for example, the recipient can't modify it when replying or when forwarding it to someone else. The other options merely display an icon next to the message in the Inbox showing the message's sensitivity level.

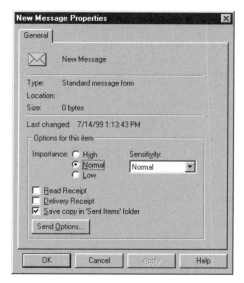

Figure 12-9.

Message properties include several useful delivery options.

Sending the Message

When your message is ready to go, click the Send button on the toolbar to move the message to the Outbox, where it's temporarily stored until it's sent to the post office. To make sure that all your messages are actually sent to and received from the post office, choose Deliver Now from the Tools menu, which sends and also collects all e-mail.

Reading Messages from Others

When you receive mail through the post office, its header appears in your Inbox. The header shows the sender, subject, and the date and time the message was received. Double-click a message header to read the message.

If the message has an attachment, you'll see a paper clip icon to the left of its header. Open the message and then double-click the icon representing the attachment that appears in the body of the message. Depending on the format of the attachment, its contents might appear immediately or you might be prompted to save the attachment to your hard disk.

After you read a message, you can close it (which leaves it in your Inbox), or you can delete it. The headers of messages you haven't read appear in bold text. To reply to a message, click the Reply To Sender button. You'll see a message window addressed to the sender and containing the text of the original message. If the sender sent the message to more than one person, you can click Reply To All to send your reply to all recipients of the original message.

Click the Forward button to send a copy of the message on to someone else without responding to the original sender.

Filing Messages in Folders

In addition to an Inbox, Windows Messaging has an Outbox, a Sent Items folder, and a Deleted Items folder. To display the entire list of folders when you have one of the folders open, click the Up One Level button.

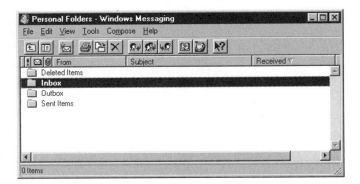

Double-click the folder you want to open. You can also display the list of folders by clicking the Show/Hide Folder List button on the toolbar. Click a folder in the folder list to display its contents.

The Deleted Items folder stores the messages that you delete from the other folders, just in case you change your mind. These messages might be permanently deleted when you exit Windows Messaging. To keep the messages in the Deleted Items folder, choose Options from the Tools menu and clear the Empty The Deleted Items Folder Upon Exiting option. Then if you really want to erase the messages, you can always open the Deleted Items folder and delete the messages you find there.

Communicating Using Outlook

Outlook is an e-mail program that is a component of Office. If you're using Office and Outlook is installed on your computer, you can use Outlook to send and receive mail through your network as well as through the Internet.

Note

Outlook Express, which comes with Internet Explorer version 4 or later, is designed for Internet e-mail. Only Outlook, not Outlook Express, however, can use Microsoft Mail Postoffice to send and receive mail over a network. If you want to use Outlook Express for both Internet e-mail and e-mail on your network, you'll need a mail server other than Microsoft Mail Postoffice, such as the shareware program VPOP3, which is available for download on the Internet.

To use Outlook for your network e-mail, you have to install the Microsoft Mail Postoffice program, as described earlier in this chapter. You can then install Outlook in its Corporate Or Workgroup configuration and create or choose a profile. A profile tells Outlook how to connect to your e-mail server, your network, or the Internet.

Note

This chapter discusses Microsoft Outlook 2000, although Microsoft Outlook 98 offers the same basic features and mail service options.

Selecting the Mail Service

When you first start Outlook, you'll be given three options: Corporate Or Workgroup, Internet Only, and No E-Mail.

- **Corporate Or Workgroup** lets you send and receive e-mail messages either through the network or over the Internet.

- **Internet Only** lets you exchange e-mail only through the Internet. When you choose Internet Only, you won't be able to use Outlook on a network to send and receive e-mail. But you will be able to send and receive e-mail, check schedules, assign tasks, and perform other Outlook functions through the Internet.

- **No E-Mail** lets you use Outlook's record-keeping and time-management tools but not its communications capabilities. You won't be able to use Outlook to send or receive e-mail through your network or the Internet.

If you've already set up a profile, such as the one that was set up for a previous version of Outlook, Outlook will use that profile. If you haven't yet set up a profile when you choose the Corporate Or Workgroup installation, Outlook begins the Inbox Setup Wizard that guides you through the process. You set up Outlook to use Microsoft Mail Postoffice for network e-mail by using the Inbox Setup Wizard as described in "Setting Up Windows Messaging," earlier in this chapter. If you already have a profile, you can add Microsoft Mail to your Outlook profile to access your post office, as described in "Adding Microsoft Mail to Your Profile," later in this chapter.

Note

If you've already installed Outlook 2000 in its Internet Only or No E-Mail configuration, you can change it to Corporate Or Workgroup without reinstalling the entire program. Start Outlook, choose Options from the Tools menu, and click the Mail Services tab. Click the Reconfigure Mail Support button and choose the Corporate Or Workgroup option in the dialog box that appears. To reconfigure previous versions of Outlook, you must reinstall the program.

Working with Profiles

After you create a profile, it's not too late to create a new profile, or to add, remove, or modify the properties of the services within a profile. If you use your computer at more than one location, for example, you might need a separate profile for each location. You might also want a separate profile to send faxes from your computer over a telephone line that you also use for connecting to an Internet e-mail server. Just be cautious when you make changes. An incorrect profile could prevent Outlook from starting or connecting to your network or ISP, or you could potentially lose the information you've stored in Outlook.

Creating a Profile

You can set up, change, and remove a profile with the Mail icon in Control Panel. After you've set up Outlook, you can add services to a profile or remove them from within Outlook.

To create a new profile, follow these steps:

1. Double-click the Mail icon in Control Panel.

2. If one or more profiles have been set up, click the Show Profiles button in the Properties dialog box for the currently active profile.

    The Mail dialog box opens. If no profiles have been set up on your system, the Mail dialog box opens automatically.

3. Click the Add button in the Mail dialog box to start creating a new profile using the Inbox Setup Wizard.

4. After completing all the steps of the wizard, click Finish to return to the Mail dialog box.

5. In the Mail dialog box, you choose a default profile in the box labeled When Starting Microsoft Outlook, Use This Profile.

6. Click Close.

You can use the Inbox Setup Wizard to create profiles specific to each location from which you use Outlook: office, home, and on the road.

Adding Microsoft Mail to Your Profile

Suppose you signed up for a new online service. At the same time, you also bailed out of an online service that wasn't giving you what you wanted. Your profile is now out of date, so you want to update the online service information. Here's how you do it.

1. Double-click the Mail icon in Control Panel to open the Properties dialog box.

2. If the profile you want to change isn't displayed, click the Show Profiles button to display the Mail dialog box, select the profile you want to change, and then click Properties. The Services tab of the Properties dialog box lists all the services in the profile you've selected.

3. On the Services tab of the Properties dialog box, take the following steps:

   - Click Add to install a new service to the current profile. Fill in the text boxes in the dialog boxes that appear to help you configure the service.

   - Click Copy to copy the selected service to another profile.

   - Select a service and click Properties to view or edit its settings.

   - Select a service and click Remove to delete the service from the profile.

   Click OK when you're finished modifying the profile. If you want to make changes to another profile, click Show Profiles and repeat the process. Click the Close button in the Mail dialog box when you've finished.

Using a Different Profile

If you have more than one profile set up, you can select which profile to use when you start Outlook.

1. Double-click the Mail icon in Control Panel.

2. Click Show Profiles, and then choose the profile you want to use by default from the When Starting Microsoft Outlook, Use This Profile drop-down list.

3. Click Close.

   You can set Outlook to always use a particular profile or to let you choose a profile each time you start the program.

   To use the same profile every time, do this:

1. In Outlook, choose Options from the Tools menu, and then click the Mail Services tab, if it isn't already displayed.

2. Enable the Always Use This Profile option, and then select the profile you want to use from the drop-down list.

3. Click OK.

If you prefer, you can choose a profile at the start of each Outlook session. To do so, follow these steps:

1. In Outlook, choose Options from the Tools menu, and then click the Mail Services tab, if it isn't already displayed.

2. Click the Prompt For A Profile To Be Used option.

3. Click OK.

Once the Prompt For A Profile To Be Used option is selected, you'll need to select a profile in the Choose Profile dialog box each time you start Outlook.

Removing a Profile

Now suppose that your situation changes and you no longer need all the profiles that you created. For example, suppose you created one profile for your home network and another for when you take your laptop to your office. Perhaps you no longer have access to your office network and you want to delete that profile from your laptop. To simplify your Outlook life, you can remove the unwanted or unnecessary profiles.

To remove a profile from Control Panel, follow these steps:

1. Double-click the Mail icon in Control Panel.

2. In the Properties dialog box, click the Show Profiles button.

3. Select the profile you want to remove.

4. Click the Remove button, and then click Yes when asked whether you want to remove this profile.

5. Click the Close button.

Using the Outlook Address Book

Outlook maintains its own address book, separate from addresses you might have in Windows Messaging, Outlook Express, and other mail programs.

Network users will have more than one address list within the address book. On a peer-to-peer network using Microsoft Mail Postoffice, you have the post office address list of other network users. You'll also have a personal address book for e-mail addresses of people not on the network, and maybe an offline address book so that you can address messages when you aren't connected to the network. You'll also probably have an Outlook address book, which is created automatically from entries in your Contacts folder. And finally, you can have separate address lists for each online service you use to send and receive e-mail.

When you open the Outlook Address Book, you have to select the address list that contains the names to which you want to send your e-mail.

Opening the Address Book

To open Address Book, choose Address Book from the Tools menu. (If you're creating an e-mail message, click To in the new e-mail message to see the address list.) Address Book opens and displays the names from the address list that is set up as the default, as shown in Figure 12-10.

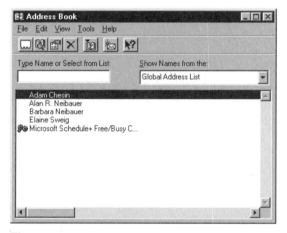

Figure 12-10.

Choose a name from the Outlook Address Book.

Note

You can change the default address list by using the Services dialog box. To open this dialog box, choose Services from the Tools menu. Click the Addressing tab and select the list you want to see first from the Show This Address List First drop-down list.

If the list of names that appears in Address Book isn't the one with the information you need, do the following:

1. Click the arrow next to the Show Names From The drop-down list to display the available address lists.

2. Select the list you want to open, such as Postoffice Address List for addresses on your peer-to-peer network.

Adding a Personal Address Book to Your Profile

You can't add names to the Postoffice Address List of Address Book. The names in this list are taken directly from the Microsoft Mail Postoffice mailbox names that you've set up as the Postoffice administrator.

If you want to use Address Book for Internet e-mail as well, you can add a personal address list to the address book by putting it in your profile. To add a personal address list, follow these steps:

1. Start Outlook and choose Services from the Tools menu.

2. On the Services tab, click the Add button.

3. In the Add Service To Profile dialog box, select Personal Address Book, and then click OK.

4. In the Personal Address Book dialog box, enter a name for the personal address book in the Name box.

5. In the Path text box, enter the path of the personal address book file, or click the Browse button to locate a personal address book file that already exists. Personal address books are maintained in files with a .pab extension.

6. Click OK in the Personal Address Book dialog box, and then click OK again in the message box that appears.

7. Click OK in the Services dialog box, and then exit and restart Outlook.

To add a personal address book to a profile other than the one you're currently using, double-click the Mail icon in Control Panel. On the Services tab, click Show Profiles. On the General tab, click the profile you want in the Profile box, click Properties, and then follow steps 2 through 7 in the previous procedure.

To add a name and address to your personal address book, do the following:

1. Choose Address Book from the Tools menu.

2. Click the New Entry button on the Address Book toolbar to open the New Entry dialog box, shown in Figure 12-11.

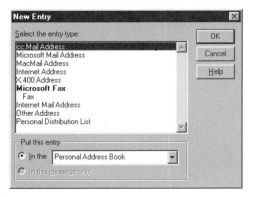

Figure 12-11.

You can choose a new entry type and destination in the New Entry dialog box.

3. Click the arrow next to the Put This Entry In The drop-down list and choose Personal Address Book in the list.

4. In the Select The Entry Type list, select the type of address you want to enter and click OK.

   The next dialog box you see varies according to the type of entry you've selected. For most new entries, you'll enter information to display in the address book and the e-mail address. The example in Figure 12-12 is based on selecting Other Address in the Entry Type list.

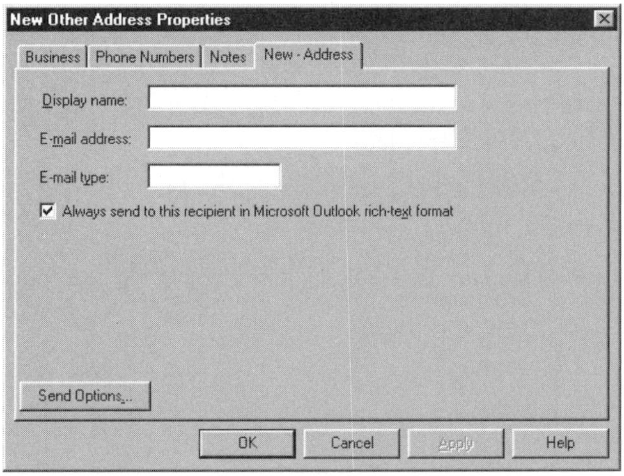

Figure 12-12.

You enter contact information in the New Other Address Properties dialog box.

5. In the Display Name text box, type the name as you want it to appear in the address book.

6. In the E-Mail Address text box, type the e-mail address, such as *alan@neibauer.net.*

7. In the E-Mail Type text box, enter the designation for the recipient's e-mail system, such as Simple Mail Transfer Protocol (SMTP), a common format for Internet e-mail.

8. Select the check box labeled Always Send To This Recipient In Microsoft Outlook Rich-Text Format if you want to send meeting and tasks requests to other Outlook users.

9. Fill in the text boxes on the other tabs with as much information as you want. For example, the Business tab provides text boxes for a mailing address and phone number. The Phone Numbers tab contains text boxes for multiple phone numbers, including a text box for a fax number. If you want to send a fax to this person, be sure to enter the fax telephone number.

   When you add a name and address, Outlook requires that you fill in the text boxes only on the New Address tab. You can leave the other tabs blank and fill them in later by double-clicking the name in the Address Book window or by using the Properties button on the Address Book toolbar.

10. Click OK.

Note

If you communicate with other Outlook users over the Internet, make sure you select the Always Send To This Recipient In Microsoft Outlook Rich-Text Format check box. Then you can send Outlook items, such as meeting and tasks requests, which will be properly formatted when opened by others in their Calendar or Tasks folders.

Sending a Message

The fastest and easiest way to send a message is simply to type the text and click Send. To send a simple message from a mail folder, do the following:

1. Click the New Mail Message button at the left end of the Standard toolbar to open a message window, as shown in Figure 12-13. Depending on how you set up Outlook, the window might look a little different on your screen.

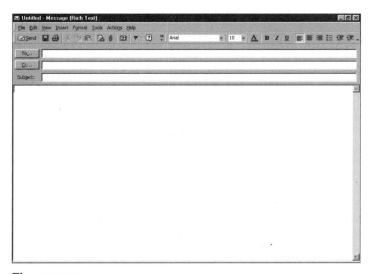

Figure 12-13.

Enter a new e-mail message in a new message window.

Note

You can create a new message from any folder in Outlook. From the Inbox, Outbox, or Drafts folder, click the New Mail Message button. From another folder, click the down arrow on the Standard toolbar's New button and select Mail Message.

2. In the new message window, click the To button to display the Select Names dialog box, as shown in Figure 12-14.

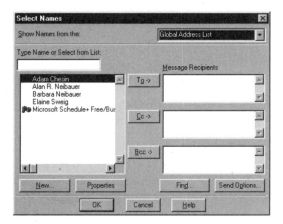

Figure 12-14.

Choose addressees in the Select Names dialog box.

3. Select the address book you want to use from the Show Names From The drop-down list box.

4. In the Type Name Or Select From List text box, type part of the name of a recipient, type the full name, or select a name from the list below the list box.

   When you type the beginning of a name in the Type Name Or Select From List text box, Outlook scrolls through the list of addresses to the first name that matches the letters you've typed. You can then scroll further, if you need to, to find the name you want.

   You can also select a distribution list from either the personal address book or from the Contacts list to send the message to a group of people. To select more than one addressee, hold down the Ctrl key and click each name.

5. Click the To button to enter the main addressees, and click the Cc box to send copies to others. The name or names you've selected appear in the boxes to the right of each button.

6. Click OK when you've chosen all the addressees.

7. In the message window, click in the Subject box and type a brief description of the subject of your message.

8. Click the message text area or press the Tab key to move to the message text area, and then type your message.

9. When your message is ready to send, click the Send button.

Note

If you don't complete your message and aren't ready to send it, choose Save from the File menu. Outlook stores the message in the Drafts folder. To complete the message, open the Drafts folder, and then double-click the message in the message list. Click Send when you're ready to send the message.

What happens when you click the Send button depends on how your system is set up and to whom the mail is addressed. E-mail messages that you've sent to recipients on your network (those people who have mailboxes in your Microsoft Mail Postoffice program) are transmitted immediately. E-mail messages to Internet recipients, however, are stored in the Outbox until you're ready to dial in and connect. To actually send the messages, click the Send And Receive button on the Standard toolbar. Outlook sends any messages in the Outbox and checks for new messages waiting for you.

When you send a message, Outlook automatically saves a copy of it in the Sent Items folder. To check your sent messages, click the Sent Items folder.

Reading a Message

When e-mail arrives in your Inbox, you can read it, respond to it, and forward it to others. You can read a message in the preview pane or in a separate window. The preview pane is an area at the lower right of the Inbox that displays the contents of the selected message. If the preview pane isn't displayed, choose Preview Pane from the View menu.

To quickly read e-mail text when the preview pane is displayed, click the message in the Inbox message list. If part of a long message falls below the bottom of the preview pane, scroll through the message window to read the rest of the message. To see the first three lines of messages directly in the message list, choose AutoPreview from the View menu.

To read the message in its own window, simply double-click the message line in your Inbox's message list. If you want to add the sender's name to your address book, right-click the person's name in the open message (even though it appears dimmed), and then choose Add To Contacts. Choose Properties from the shortcut menu if you just want to see the sender's e-mail address.

Once you've opened a message in its own window, you can use the Previous Item and Next Item buttons on the Standard toolbar in the message window to move from message to message (the buttons with the large up and down arrows). Next to each of these buttons is a small down arrow that you can click to see a list of commands that let you move more quickly to the messages you want to read. For example, you can move to the next or previous message from the same sender or to the next or previous unread message.

See Also

For more information on using Microsoft Outlook for network and Internet e-mail, see *Running Microsoft Outlook 2000*, from Microsoft Press.

Using a Shareware Mail Server

Although using Microsoft Outlook for all your e-mail needs is a good solution, you might want to use Outlook Express or some other e-mail program for both Internet e-mail and e-mail on your home network. If so, you'll need a mail server other than Microsoft Mail Postoffice.

The shareware program VPOP3 (for Virtual POP3 server) is one example of such a mail server. You can download an evaluation version of the program at this address: *http://www.pscs.co.uk/products/vpop3/index.html.*

VPOP3 installs a mail server that monitors incoming and outgoing mail. It collects mail coming from your ISP and channels it to your e-mail program. It also sets up its own network post office for collecting mail to and from network users. You can then use an Internet e-mail program, such as Outlook Express, to send e-mail to other family members on the network. This e-mail is stored in a mailbox until the recipient checks the VPOP3 server for mail with an e-mail program.

VPOP3 is a robust mail program with a great many features. I'll just summarize here how the program works.

You need to install and run VPOP3 only on the computer you plan to use as your mail server. When you first run the program, the VPOP3 Configuration Wizard lets you specify how it should connect to your Internet mail server. You can select from several popular ISPs, or if your ISP isn't listed, specify how to connect as shown in Figure 12-15.

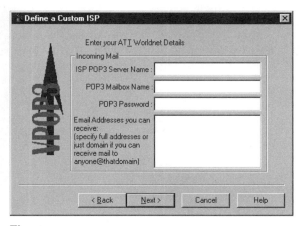

Figure 12-15.
Configuring VPOP3 for your ISP.

When you start VPOP3 for the first time, you'll be asked to designate yourself as the post office administrator so that you can create and manage mailboxes.

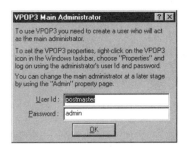

You can then log on as the administrator when you start VPOP3.

You create mailboxes by adding users, and you make other changes to VPOP3 settings by using the VPOP3 Settings dialog box, shown in Figure 12-16, which appears when you start the program and log on.

Figure 12-16.

VPOP3 settings.

On the Users tab, for example, you can create a VPOP3 mailbox by clicking Add User and then entering a user name and password, as shown in Figure 12-17.

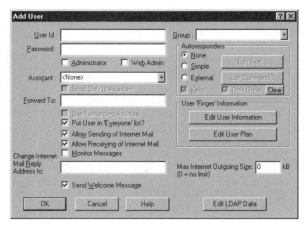

Figure 12-17.
Adding a VPOP3 user.

On the Local Mail tab of the VPOP3 Settings dialog box, you enter the local do-main of your network users. The local domain is the part of your Internet e-mail address after the @ symbol. If you access the Internet and get e-mail through AT&T Worldnet, for example, your local domain is att.net. After you set up your e-mail program to work with VPOP3, you can send mail to someone with that domain. For example, if you create a VPOP3 post office for a user named Barb, you can then use Outlook Express to send mail to barb@att.net through VPOP3 to the user on the network.

After you configure VPOP3 and add users, however, you must adjust your e-mail program to send and receive mail locally through the network. As an example of this, here are the steps you'd follow in Outlook Express to create an account for a VPOP3 post of-fice user. Outlook Express allows you to create and use more than one mail account so that you can use it to check for e-mail sent to more than one member of the family over your ISP, or to check multiple ISPs or free Web-based e-mail services.

Before you start, however, you'll need to get the Internet Protocol (IP) address of the computer on which VPOP3 is installed. The IP address identifies the server computer to the other computers on the network. Outlook Express uses the IP address to connect to the VPOP3 server through the network.

If you're using Consumer Windows, follow these steps to get the server's IP address:

1. Open Network in Control Panel of the computer you are using as the VPOP3 server.

2. On the Configuration tab of the Network box, click the TCP/IP setting that is followed by the name of your network card.

3. Click Properties to open the TCP/IP Properties dialog box.

4. The setting is displayed in the IP Address box on the IP tab. Make a note of the address.

5. Click Cancel twice.

If you're using Windows 2000, follow these steps to get the server's IP address:

1. Double-click My Network Places on the Windows desktop of the computer you are using as the VPOP3 server.

2. Click Network And Dial-up Connections.

3. Right-click on the Local Area Connection icon and choose Properties.

4. Click Internet Protocol (TCP/IP).

5. Click Properties.

6. Make a note of the setting in the IP Address box.

7. Click Cancel twice.

Once you have the server's IP address, just follow these steps to set up Outlook Express for VPOP3:

1. Start Outlook Express.

2. Select Accounts from the Tools menu.

3. Click Add and then click Mail to start the Internet Connection Wizard.

4. Type your name, and then click Next.

5. Enter your e-mail address, consisting of your VPOP3 user name and the default domain, and then click Next. You can now enter the server names.

6. In both the Incoming Mail Server and Outgoing Mail Server text boxes, enter the IP address of the VPOP3 server, as shown in Figure 12-18.

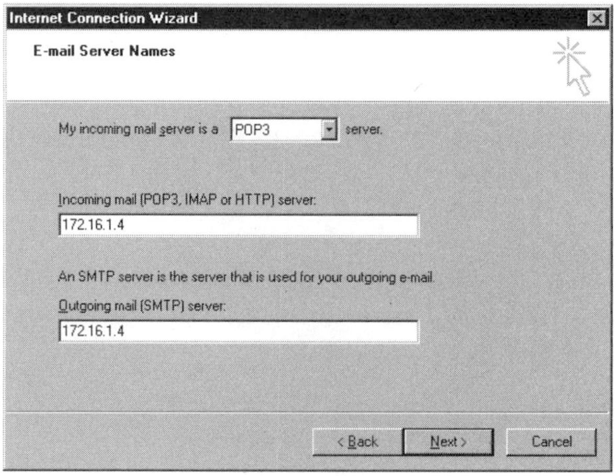

Figure 12-18.
The VPOP3 server IP address.

7. Click Next, enter your VPOP3 user name and password, and then click Next again.

8. Click Finish. You now see the IP address listed as the mail account in the Internet Accounts dialog box.

9. Click the IP address and then click Properties to open the dialog box shown in Figure 12-19. Replace the IP address in the top box of the General tab with VPOP3.

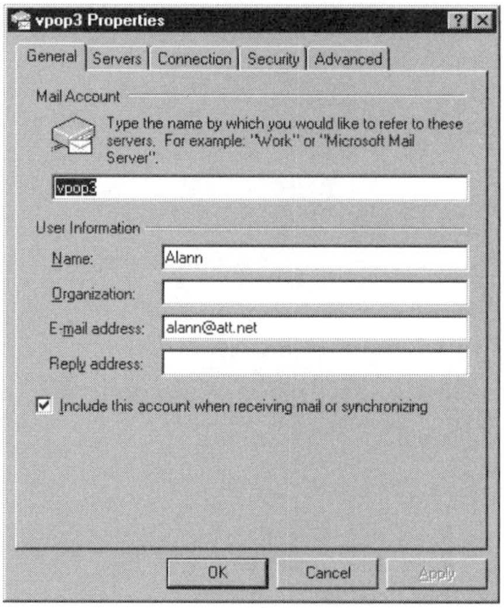

Figure 12-19.
Configuring the e-mail account.

10. Click the Connection tab.

11. Select the check box labeled Always Connect To This Account Using.

12. Click the down arrow next to the drop-down list below the check box and choose Local Area Network from the list.

13. Click OK.

Now when you want to send an e-mail message to a network user with Outlook Express, click the New Mail button on the toolbar to open a new message window, and choose your VPOP3 account from the From drop-down list.

Complete the message as you would normally and click Send.

You can then click Send/Recv on the Outlook Express toolbar to send and receive mail from all your accounts, or choose the VPOP3 account to send and receive mail just over the network from the Send/Recv button's drop-down list.

VPOP3 isn't the only alternative for sending and receiving both Internet and network mail. For example, the program @MailGate, which you can download from many shareware collections on the Internet, gets mail from your ISP and channels it to your Postoffice mailbox. The @MailGate program is shown in Figure 12-20 being configured to copy Internet e-mail to Adam's Post Office mailbox.

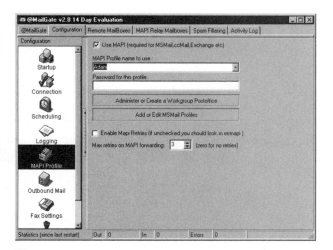

Figure 12-20.
Configuring @MailGate.

Sending e-mail, whether over your network or the Internet, is a great way to communicate. When the computers in your home are connected by a network, you can use Postoffice or another mail server to send messages and files and share information with all members of the family. Sending e-mail over the Internet lets you connect to family and friends all over the world. If you have only one phone line and one Internet account, however, you might think that your family can use the Internet only one at a time. But you would be mistaken. In the next chapter, you'll learn how to share Internet accounts over your network.

Chapter 13

Going Online Through the Network

Chances are, if you have more than one computer in your household, you have more than one modem. But if you have only one phone line, only one family member at a time can be online. Even if you have two phone lines at home, most Internet service providers (ISPs) won't allow more than one person at a time to access the Internet using the same account. If you try, you'll get a message telling you that the account is already in use. Most ISPs prefer that you sign up for multiple accounts.

Another great advantage to connecting your home computers through a network is that it allows you to share one phone line and one Internet account with everyone in the household. You could look up stock quotes, for example, while someone else is downloading software or just surfing the Net for fun or profit.

Note

With modem sharing now so easy and popular, many ISPs have fine-tuned the small print in their customer agreements to discourage simultaneous sharing of an account. You shouldn't share an ISP account if the membership agreement forbids it.

Sharing a phone line is especially useful when one computer on the network has a modem that's faster than the others, such as a 56 Kbps modem or an ultra-fast digital subscriber line (DSL) or cable modem. In fact, when you're connected on a network, you don't even need a modem on more than one machine. All the computers on the network can share the high-speed modem that's connected to a single computer.

When a modem is shared on a network, only one user—the first to dial in to the ISP—is actually logged on, and that user can be anyone on the network. Other users who want to access the Internet just piggyback onto the existing connection through the network. Their modems don't need to dial in because the first computer has already made the connection. As far as the ISP is concerned, only one person is logged on.

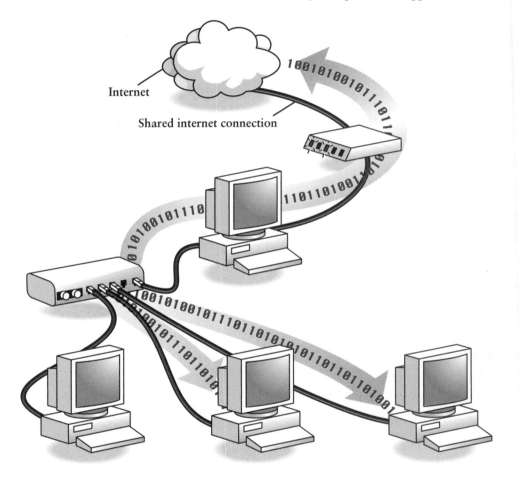

Internet Sharing Alternatives

You can share a modem and an Internet account in two basic ways—by using software or by using hardware.

When you use software to share a modem, you have to designate one computer on the network as the *host*. The other computers on the network, called the *clients*, will then share the host computer's modem. A modem-sharing program, such as Microsoft Windows Internet Connection Sharing or one of the others described in this chapter, reconfigures the network to accept Internet requests from the client computers and channels them to the shared modem on the host computer. The host computer's modem dials the ISP directly; the client computers are reconfigured to connect to the ISP through the network rather than through their own dial-up connections and modems.

If the host computer is already online, a client computer can go online without dialing. If the host computer is turned on but isn't online, the client computer requests that the host computer make the connection so the client can access the Internet through the host's modem.

The shared modem can be any of the following types:

- A standard modem

- An Integrated Services Digital Network (ISDN) modem

- A DSL modem

- A cable modem

Table 13-1 summarizes the advantages and disadvantages of each type of shared modem. Whatever type of modem you have in your home, just select the one that's fastest or most reliable and designate the computer connected to it as the host.

Table 13-1. Sharing Different Modem Types: Advantages and Disadvantages

Modem Type	Advantages	Disadvantages
Standard modem	Connects to a standard telephone line. Usually included with PCs or inexpensive to purchase and upgrade.	Connects at the slowest speeds, with a maximum of 56 Kbps.
ISDN	Connects at a high speed, up to 128 Kbps. Uses a dedicated connection so you can use your regular phone line at the same time.	Costs more than a standard modem and requires special telephone service that costs more than a regular phone line. Most ISPs charge more for ISDN service.
DSL	Connects at an ultra-high speed, up to 1.5 Mbps. Uses a dedicated connection so you can use your regular phone line at the same time. Always connected to the Internet for instant access.	Costs more than a standard modem and requires special telephone service that costs more than a regular phone line. DSL service might not be available everywhere, and your ISP might not support it.
Cable	Connects at an ultra-high speed, up to 10 Mbps. Uses cable TV service instead of your phone line. Always connected to the Internet so you can have instant access.	Costs more than a standard modem because you'll have to pay a setup and installation fee, as well as monthly ISP charges that are usually higher than regular dial-up ISP charges. Not all cable companies offer modem service.

The main disadvantage of using software to share a modem is that the host computer must be turned on for its modem to be shared. If the computer is turned off, a client computer will get an error message when it tries to connect to the Internet through the host on the network.

There are ways around this problem, however. The fastest solution is just to go to the room with the shared modem and turn on the computer. An alternative to sharing a modem with software is to buy and install special hardware. You can purchase a local area network (LAN) modem that shares a 56 Kbps dial-up modem to everyone on the network, or a router that shares a DSL, cable, or ISDN modem.

Both the LAN modem and router connect directly to the network in much the same way a printer can be connected to a network, as you learned in Chapter 11. As long as the modem or router and network hub are turned on, anyone on the network can access the Internet at any time.

The downside to LAN modems and routers is cost. Both are more expensive than standard modems and they can be difficult to set up.

Getting Ready to Share a Modem

If you're considering using software to share an Internet connection, make sure that the modem on the host computer works and that you can use the host computer to connect to the Internet.

The network connections between computers must also be working properly. Each computer should be able to see the others in Network Neighborhood (or My Network Places) and communicate with them.

Making Sure TCP/IP Is Installed in Consumer Windows

Almost all Internet connection sharing requires that you have the TCP/IP installed on each computer connected to the network. You'll need TCP/IP installed even if it's not the primary protocol you use for the network.

To determine whether TCP/IP drivers are installed on computers running Consumer Windows (Microsoft Windows 95, Microsoft Windows 98, and Microsoft Windows Millennium Edition), follow these steps:

Note

For information on checking the TCP/IP drivers on computers running Microsoft Windows 2000, see "Making Sure TCP/IP Is Installed in Windows 2000," later in this chapter.

1. On the Start menu, point to Settings, and then click Control Panel.

2. In Control Panel, double-click the Network icon.

3. On the Configuration tab of the Network dialog box, look for an entry in the installed network components list showing TCP/IP followed by your network card.

If the listing isn't present, you'll need to install TCP/IP. You'll find complete instructions for setting up a network protocol in "Installing Protocols," in Chapter 8, on page 152. But here's a quick recap of the steps:

1. In the Network dialog box, click Add.

2. In the Select Network Component Type dialog box, click Protocol, and then click Add.

3. In the Select Network Protocol dialog box, choose Microsoft from the list of manufacturers.

4. Select TCP/IP from the Network Protocols list.

5. Click OK to close the Select Network Protocol dialog box.

6. Click OK to close the Network dialog box. You may need to insert your Windows CD at this point so Windows can install the necessary files.

7. Click Yes when you're asked whether to restart your computer.

You'll have to configure TCP/IP, but how you do it depends on the particular software you're using for sharing an Internet connection and on whether you're also using TCP/IP as your network protocol. *For more information, see "Configuring TCP/IP," in Chapter 8, on page 158.*

Making Sure TCP/IP Is Installed in Windows 2000

To see which protocols are already installed in Windows 2000, follow these steps:

1. On the Start menu, point to Settings, and then click Network And Dial-up Connections.

2. Right-click Local Area Connection, and choose Properties from the shortcut menu to display the Local Area Connection Properties dialog box. Any network protocols and services already installed will be listed.

If TCP/IP is not installed, you will have to install it. *You'll find complete instructions for setting up a network protocol in "Installing Protocols in Windows 2000," in Chapter 8, on page 154.* But here's a brief recap of the steps:

1. On the Start menu, point to Settings, and then click Network And Dial-up Connections.

2. Right-click Local Area Connection and choose Properties from the shortcut menu to display the Local Area Connection Properties dialog box. Any network protocols and services already installed are listed.

3. Click Install.

4. In the Select Network Component Type dialog box, select Protocol and click Add to open the Select Network Protocol dialog box.

5. Select TCP/IP from the Network Protocols list.

6. Click OK to close the Select Network Protocol dialog box.

7. Click Close to exit from the Local Area Connection Properties dialog box.

8. Click Yes if you are asked to restart your computer.

Using Modem-Sharing Software

Many programs let you share a modem and an Internet connection (subject to the terms of your ISP agreement) over a network. One such modem-sharing program is built into Microsoft Windows 98 Second Edition and Microsoft Windows Millennium Edition (Me). If you have that version of Windows, you don't need to download or purchase any additional modem-sharing software. You'll also find modem-sharing software in most network starter kits, although the programs vary in the way they are set up. Internet Connection Sharing is automatically installed when you install Windows 2000. *See "Internet Connection Sharing with Windows 2000," later in this chapter, for more information.*

Some modem-sharing programs are also available as *shareware*, which means that you can download them from the Internet and try them out for free during a trial period. If you like the program, you can then register it for a fee. When you register, you'll get a password or serial number that enables the program to work beyond the trial period.

Installing Windows Internet Connection Sharing

Internet Connection Sharing is a feature that comes with Windows 98 Second Edition, Windows Me, and Windows 2000. But it isn't installed automatically when you install or upgrade to Windows 98 Second Edition or Windows Me, so you'll need to add it as an additional component to the Windows installation on the computer you plan to use as the host. Here's how to do it:

1. Make sure the Windows 98 Second Edition or Windows Me CD is in your CD-ROM drive.

2. On the Start menu, point to Settings, and then click Control Panel.

3. In Control Panel, double-click the Add/Remove Programs icon.

4. In the list of components on the Windows Setup tab, click Internet Tools (or Communications in Windows Me) to select it. Don't clear the check box to the left of Internet Tools or Communications.

5. Click the Details button to see a list of the items in the Internet Tools or Communications category, as shown in Figure 13-1.

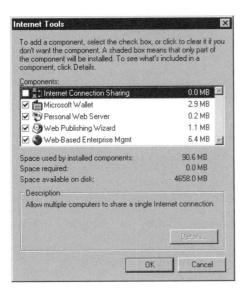

Figure 13-1.

Select Internet Connection Sharing from the list of components in the Internet Tools dialog box in Windows 98 Second Edition.

6. In the list of components, select the Internet Connection Sharing check box.

7. Click OK to close the Internet Tools or Communications dialog box.

8. Click OK in the Add/Remove Programs Properties dialog box. Windows installs the Internet Connection Sharing feature and then starts a wizard that takes you step-by-step through the rest of the process.

The wizard will change the IP address of the computer being used as the server to 192.168.0.1 and will assume that your client computers use dynamic IP addresses assigned by the Dynamic Host Configuration Protocol (DHCP) rather than static IP addresses that you assign. If you set up your network so that computers obtain their TCP/IP addresses automatically, they'll all be able to communicate after you install Internet Connection Sharing.

If you're using static TCP/IP addresses that you entered yourself, however, the Internet connection server might no longer be able to communicate with the other computers on the network. When you configure the client computers, as explained in "Setting Up the Client Computers," later in this chapter, they'll be set to automatic IP addresses so your network will work again.

Note

If you want to use static network addresses with Internet Connection Sharing using Windows 98 Second Edition or Windows Me, see "Static Networking Addresses," later in this chapter.

The Windows 98 Second Edition and Windows Me wizards are different, so we'll look at each individually.

Windows 98 Second Edition

Installing Internet Connection Sharing in Windows 98 Second Edition displays the Internet Connection Sharing Wizard page, which starts the process of setting up connection sharing.

1. Read the information and then click Next.

2. Make sure the adapter you want to use for the connection is selected. Click Next on the next page. The wizard explains that it will create a floppy disk to set up the client computers for Internet sharing through the host computer.

3. Click Next.

4. Insert a formatted floppy disk that has at least 200 KB of space into your floppy disk drive, and then click OK.

5. When the wizard tells you to do so, remove the disk, and then click OK.

6. Click Finish.

7. Click Yes when you're asked whether to restart the computer.

Windows Me

Installing Internet Connection Sharing on Windows Me starts the Home Networking Wizard, shown in Figure 13-2.

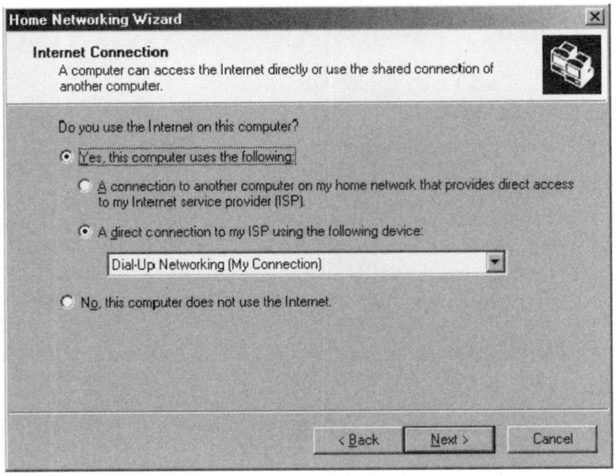

Figure 13-2.

Configuring your computer as the host.

1. Click Next on the first page of the wizard.

2. Because you'll be using this computer as the sharing host, select the option A Direct Connection To My ISP Using The Following Device.

3. Display the device list and select your Internet dial-up networking account.

4. Click Next.

5. You'll be asked whether you want other computers on the network to share this computer's Internet connection. Click Yes and then choose your network interface from the list box.

6. Click Next.

7. You'll be asked whether you want to create a home networking setup disk. You need to create this disk only if you want to share the connection with a computer running Windows 95 or Windows 98. If you do want to share the connection, click Yes, click Next, and continue with the next steps. Otherwise, click No to complete the wizard.

8. Insert a formatted floppy disk into your floppy disk drive, and then click Next.

9. Click OK in the message box that appears.

Windows will now create the setup disk for other computers on your network. *You'll learn how to use the disk in "Setting Up the Client Computers," later in this chapter.*

Adjusting Internet Connection Sharing

After you install Internet Connection Sharing, you can make the following adjustments to its settings:

- Turn Internet Sharing on or off.

- Place an icon for changing Internet Sharing in the system tray.

- Select which connection the host will use to access the Internet if you have more than one Internet account.

- Choose which network interface card (NIC) to use for the network if you have more than one.

    To change any of these settings, follow these steps:

1. On the Start menu, point to Settings, and then click Control Panel.

2. In Control Panel, double-click the Internet Options icon.

3. In the Internet Properties dialog box, click the Connections tab.

4. Click Sharing in the Local Area Network (LAN) Settings section of the dialog box.

5. Change options in the Internet Connection Sharing dialog box, and then click OK. If you choose to show the icon on the taskbar, you can right-click the taskbar icon to see a shortcut menu.

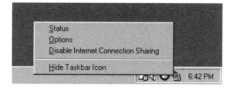

You can then choose Status to see which computers are sharing the Internet connection, or choose Options to change your connection and network interface card (NIC). If you find that sharing your connection slows down Web surfing or program downloading significantly, you might want to turn off Internet Connection Sharing. To do so, you can select the Disable Internet Connection Sharing option.

Setting Up the Client Computers

After you've installed Internet sharing on the host computer, the next step is to configure each client computer to access the Internet through the network rather than through its own dial-up connection and modem. But first, you need to set up each client computer so that its TCP/IP gets an IP address automatically. Here's how:

1. On the Start menu of each client computer, point to Settings, and then click Control Panel.

2. In Control Panel, double-click the Network icon.

3. On the Configuration tab of the Network dialog box, select the TCP/IP listing for your NIC.

4. Click Properties.

5. On the IP Address tab of the TCP/IP Properties dialog box, select Obtain An IP Address Automatically.

6. Click the WINS Configuration tab, shown in Figure 13-3.

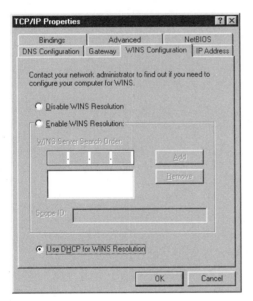

Figure 13-3.
The WINS Configuration tab of the TCP/IP Properties dialog box.

7. Make sure the Use DHCP For WINS Resolution option is selected. (The Disable WINS Resolution option must be selected before you can choose this option.)

8. Click the Gateway tab.

9. Make sure the Installed Gateways list is empty. If you see entries in the Installed Gateways list, select each entry and then click Remove.

10. Click the DNS Configuration tab.

11. Make sure the Disable DNS option is selected.

12. Click OK.

13. Click OK to close the Network dialog box.

14. Click Yes when you're asked whether to restart your computer.

Running the Internet Connection Setup Wizard

When you installed Internet Connection Sharing on the host computer, you created a floppy disk containing a program that configures client computers. You now need to use this disk to configure each of the client computers so that they access the Internet through the network.

Note

If the host and client computer are running Windows Me, you don't need to use the floppy disk. Start the Home Networking Wizard by double-clicking My Network Places on the Windows Me desktop and then double-clicking Home Networking Wizard. Choose the first option under Yes in the initial dialog box: A Connection To Another Computer On My Home Network That Provides Direct Access To My Internet Service Provider. Click Next and complete the wizard.

1. Start the host computer and use it to connect to the Internet.

2. Insert the disk into the floppy drive of a client computer.

3. On the Start menu, click Run.

4. In the Run dialog box, type *A:\Icsclset.exe* if you used Windows 98 Second Edition; type *A:\Setup.exe* if you used Windows Me. Click OK.

5. Click Next until the last wizard page appears, and then click Finish.

6. Repeat the process on each client computer.

Once you've configured the client computers, you'll be able to access the Internet from any of them through the host computer's modem. If, however, you try to connect to the Internet from a client computer and receive an error message, the host computer might be turned off. In this case, you can change the client computer's settings to connect through its own modem rather than through the host's. How you perform this task depends on your browser. With Microsoft Internet Explorer, follow these steps:

1. Right-click the Internet Explorer icon on the client's desktop and choose Properties from the shortcut menu. If there's no icon, double-click the Internet Options icon in Control Panel.

2. Click the Connections tab.

3. With Internet Explorer 5, select Always Dial My Default Connection. You can also click Setup and use the Internet Connection Wizard to select your dial-up connection. With Internet Explorer 4, select Connect To The Internet Using A Modem on the Connections tab, or click Connect to start the wizard.

The Browser Connection Setup Wizard doesn't change the settings of other programs that access your ISP, including e-mail programs such as Outlook Express. If you want these programs to connect through the network as well, you have to change their setup yourself. Most of these programs have a dialog box or menu option that allows you to specify a type of connection. As an example, let's run through the process for Microsoft's Outlook Express program.

Click the Outlook Express icon on the taskbar, or start the program as you would normally, and then follow these steps:

1. From the Tools menu, choose Accounts.

2. In the Internet Accounts dialog box, click your account, and then click Properties.

3. On the Connection tab of the Properties dialog box, click Always Connect To This Account Using.

4. Click the down arrow next to the drop-down list and choose Local Area Network.

5. Click OK.

6. Repeat the process for each account and then click Close to close the Internet Accounts dialog box.

Note

Versions of Outlook Express earlier than 5 have an option button on the Connection tab that you can click to connect through the network.

Static Network Addresses

Internet Connection Sharing is set by default to use dynamic IP addresses. If you want to specify IP addresses on the client computers yourself, you'll need to assign them addresses in the range 192.168.0.2 to 192.168.0.253 and with the subnet address of 255.255.255.00, as explained in the section "Configuring TCP/IP," in Chapter 8, on page 158.

First, however, you'll need to know the DNS server address that your ISP uses. If you don't know this number, follow these steps:

1. Connect to the Internet on the computer serving as the Internet Connection Sharing host.

2. Click Start and then click Run on the taskbar.

3. Type *winipcfg* and click OK to see the box shown here.

4. From the drop-down list at the top of the box, select ICShare Adapter.

5. Click More Info>> and write down the DNS server address that appears.

6. Click OK, and then disconnect from the Internet.

You can now configure the client computers to connect to the Internet through the ICS host. On each client computer, follow these steps:

1. Open Control Panel and double-click Network.

2. Click the Identification tab.

3. Write down the name in the Computer Name box. Names are case sensitive, so be sure to copy down the name exactly.

4. Click the Configuration tab.

5. Double-click the TCP/IP setting that's followed by the name of your NIC.

6. On the IP Address tab, select Specify An IP Address.

7. Enter an IP address in the range between 192.168.0.2 through 192.168.0.253—making sure that no other computer on the network is using the address you've chosen.

8. Enter the subnet mask 255.255.255.0.

9. Click the DNS Configuration tab.

10. Click Enable DNS.

11. In the Host box, enter the name of the computer that you copied down in step 3.

12. In the DNS Search Order box, type your ISP's DNS server address, and click Add.

13. Click the Gateway tab.

14. In the New Gateway box, enter *192.168.0.1* and click Add.

15. Click OK twice and then click Yes to restart your computer.

Disabling DHCP

If Internet Connection Sharing doesn't seem to work in Windows 98 Second Edition after you assign static addresses, you should disable the dynamic addressing feature. Follow these steps to perform this task in Windows 98 Second Edition:

1. Using the computer that will be the Internet Connection Sharing server, insert the Windows 98 Second Edition CD into the CD-ROM drive.

2. Double-click My Computer, right-click the Windows 98 CD, and choose Open from the shortcut menu.

3. Go to the \Tools\Mtsutil\Ics folder.

4. Right-click the file Dhcp_off.inf and click Install on the shortcut menu.

5. Restart your computer.

Connecting to the Internet Through Internet Connection Sharing

When you're ready to connect to the Internet, just start your browser as you would normally. If you're on a client computer, it will connect through the network, dialing the modem on the host computer if the host isn't already connected.

Note

If you get an error saying that the site can't be found on your browser when it first connects through the server, just enter the address of a site you want to access in the browser's
address box and press Enter.

If you're on the host computer, don't disconnect from the Internet unless you're certain no one else is connected through the network.

To check whether anyone is online, use the Sharing option to place the icon in the
system tray, the area of the taskbar adjacent to the clock. Then right-click the Internet
Connection Sharing icon in the system tray, and choose Status. A box appears reporting
the number of computers using the connection. The number includes your own computer even if you aren't connected, so don't disconnect if the number is greater than 1. If
you do, you'll disconnect the other members of your family who are connected.

If no one else is connected to the Internet, you can disconnect. If you're used to seeing a message asking whether you want to disconnect when you close your browser, don't
be surprised if it no longer appears. The message is turned off to avoid disconnecting
when someone else is using the modem.

Internet Connection Sharing with Windows 2000

Internet Connection Sharing is installed automatically when you install Windows 2000
on your computer. You have to enable sharing, however, before other network users can
access the modem and Internet account.

To use Internet Connection Sharing, your network can't use static IP addresses.
When you enable the Internet Connection Sharing feature, your computer is assigned an
address. If other computers are set for static addressing, they might not be able to connect
to your computer any longer. To enable Internet Connection Sharing on your computer,
you must be logged on as a member of the Administrators group.

To enable Internet Connection Sharing, follow these steps:

1. Open Control Panel and double-click Network And Dial-up Connections.

2. Right-click your dial-up connection and choose Properties from the shortcut menu.

3. Click the Sharing tab and select the check box labeled Enable Internet Connection
   Sharing For This Connection, as shown in Figure 13-4.

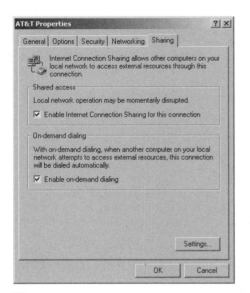

Figure 13-4.
Enabling Internet Connection Sharing in Windows 2000.

4. Select the check box labeled Enable On-Demand Dialing if you want network computers to use this connection for all their dial-up needs.

    You then have to set the Internet browsers in the other workstations to access the Internet through your LAN. You perform this task by configuring your Internet browser to connect to the Internet through the computer acting as the server.

Other Software Solutions for Internet Connection Sharing

Other software solutions for sharing an Internet connection are similar in concept to Internet Connection Sharing in Windows, but they're set up differently. Table 13-2 lists some of the Internet Connection Sharing programs you can download from the Internet.

Table 13-2. Other Internet Connection Sharing Software

Software	Internet Address
aVirt Soho Server	*http://www.avirt.com*
Internet Gate	*http://www.maccasoft.com*
LanBridge	*http://www.virtualmotion.com*
MidPoint	*http://www.midcore.com*
PPPShar	*http://www.pppindia.com*
RideWay	*http://www.itserv.com*
ShareTheNet	*http://www.sharethenet.com*
SyGate	*http://www.sygate.com*
Wingate	*http://www.wingate.com*

All these programs require that TCP/IP be installed on the computers on the network and that you install their Internet sharing software on the host computer. The main difference among the programs is how the client computers are configured to access the shared modem.

With aVirt Soho Server software, for example, each client must be set to access the Internet through a proxy server. A *proxy server* is a computer that handles the flow of information between the Internet and other computers sharing the modem. Although you can manually set up a client computer to access the proxy server in your browser by designating the IP address of the computer with the shared modem, aVirt provides a client wizard to set up all the Internet applications automatically.

The RideWay program works similarly, except that you must manually enter the host computer's IP address to use as the proxy server.

With Wingate, you install the program on all the computers on the network. The initial dialog box of the installation program asks whether you're setting up a Wingate Server or a Wingate Internet Client. If you choose the client option, the program configures your computer to access the modem connected to the server.

With SyGate, you need to install the program only on the host computer and set up the browser on each client computer to access the Internet through the network. If you have Internet Explorer, for example, you can run the Internet Connection Wizard and select I Connect Through A Local Area Network (LAN), as shown in Figure 13-5.

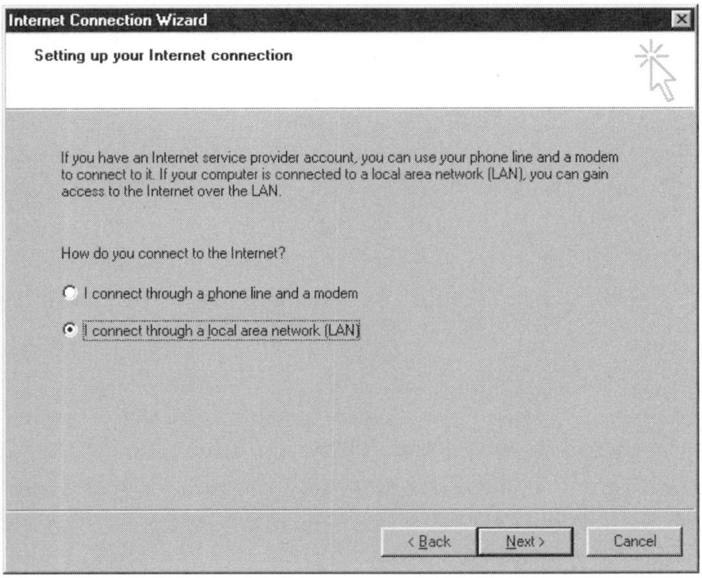

Figure 13-5.
Choose to connect to the Internet through a local area network in the Internet Connection Wizard.

Using Internet Sharing Hardware

As an alternative to using software to share an Internet connection, you can purchase hardware that provides a modem-sharing solution.

Some routers have built-in modems and hubs that connect directly to the phone line and network computers, while other routers must be connected to an external analog (56 Kbps), ISDN, DSL, or cable modem. Some routers even have one or more internal modems and a connection for an external modem as well.

When you use a router, you set up your hardware so that the router is turned on whenever your network hub or switch is turned on. That way, the modem will be available to everyone on the network all the time regardless of which computers on the network are turned on.

In addition, many routers let you create a firewall between your network and the Internet. The router can prevent unauthorized access into your network by hackers, and it can control the type of access allowed to each family member. As you can with some of the Internet connection sharing software, you can limit a family member to just sending and receiving e-mail, for example, without allowing them to surf the Internet. Some models also let you use Web content filtering to control the type of sites your family members can access. These models are ideal if you'd like to limit access to gaming, auction, and other sites that you feel aren't appropriate for younger members of the family.

If you connect to the Internet over the telephone through a dial-up account, consider a LAN modem. A *LAN modem* is a router with a 56 Kbps modem built into it. The OfficeConnect LAN modem from 3Com, for example, even includes its own four-port hub, which allows it to serve as the network's modem and hub at the same time. After connecting the device, you can set it up just by starting your browser and connecting to a configuration Web page that's stored within the modem. Use the information on the Web page to set up the modem for your ISP. The 56 Kbps version of the LAN modem costs under $300; the ISDN version was just under $400.

The WebRamp series of LAN modems has seven models, ranging from just under $300 to almost $1,200. Some models have built-in 56 Kbps modems; others have ISDN modems with enhanced features for business users. For home users, the model 2001, available for under $300, contains a built-in 56 Kbps modem and four-port hub, and you can connect to it another external 56 Kbps or ISDN modem.

Other companies that manufacture LAN modems include Netopia, Adtran, and Intel.

If you already have an external modem, you can purchase a device called a *modem server* that, in effect, turns your external modem into a LAN modem. In that setup, the server connects to the network and your modem connects to the server. A modem server doesn't usually have its own modem built in, but some models do give you that option.

Companies such as Atronics, Lantronix, Netgear, and others make a variety of models. A modem server, however, is more expensive than a LAN modem, and you still need to connect it to an external modem. Prices start at about $500 and go into the thousands.

Sharing Broadband Internet

Both DSL and cable modems offer speed that makes the Internet a great experience. You can download files in just minutes and watch videos online as if you were watching television. If you're networked, you can share the high-speed DSL or cable modem with everyone, but there are several ways to do it.

The easiest way to share a high-speed modem is to connect the modem to one computer and use Internet Connection Sharing software, as explained earlier in this chapter.

The computer the modem is attached to becomes the host; the other computers are the clients. The host computer must have two Ethernet connections: one for the network, and another for the modem. The disadvantage is that the computer the modem is attached to must be running for anyone else on the network to access the modem.

As an alternative, you can connect the modem directly to the network. How you connect it, however, depends on the number of IP accounts you purchase from your ISP.

DSL and cable modems communicate on the Internet through an IP address. When the ISP connects the modem to your computer, it assigns the computer a unique IP address. This IP address identifies your computer on the Internet. Depending on your ISP, the address can be static (fixed at the time of installation), or it can be dynamically assigned each time you access the Internet.

Most DSL and cable ISPs will let you connect the modem directly to a network hub or switch, as shown in Figure 13-6. However, you'll need to pay for an IP address for each computer that you want to access the Internet. The monthly fees for extra IP addresses vary but can be as much as $10 per month for each additional address.

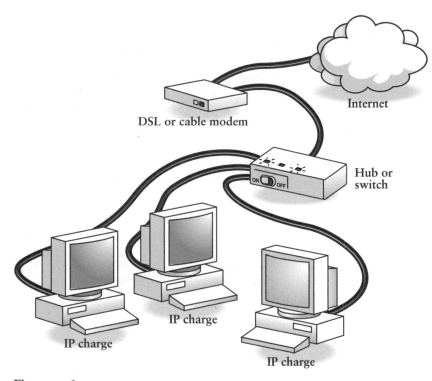

Figure 13-6.
Connecting a broadband modem to the hub requires multiple IP addresses.

If you want to connect your modem to the network but not pay for additional IP addresses, you'll need a *broadband router*, a device that lets everyone on a network access the same DSL or cable modem. You connect the router to the network hub or switch, and then connect the modem to the router, as illustrated in Figure 13-7. You have to pay for only one IP address, just as if the modem were connected directly to a computer.

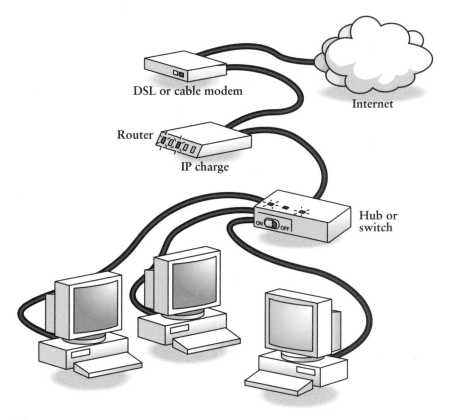

Figure 13-7.
Using a broadband router avoids extra IP charges.

Routers work using a system called *network address translation* (NAT). When a computer makes a request to display an Internet site, the router replaces the IP address of the network computer with the IP address assigned by the ISP and retrieves the site from the Internet. As far as the ISP is concerned, the IP address of the computer making the request is always the same regardless of which computer on the network is accessing it.

A number of companies manufacture routers, and the setup and configuration of the different routers vary. In general, you set up a router in four steps:

1. Install the router on your hub or switch.

2. Connect the modem to the router.

3. If your ISP assigns you an IP address dynamically, you set the router for dynamic addressing. If the ISP assigns you a static IP address, you configure the router with the same address that your ISP assigned to your computer during installation.

4. You use the DHCP service provided with the router to assign IP addresses to all your computers on the network, or you manually assign IP addresses in the proper range to each of your computers.

We'll look at several broadband routers that work with both DSL and cable modems to illustrate their various features. After installing and configuring either router, everyone on your network can share the high-speed connection.

ZyXEL Prestige 310

Easy to set up, the ZyXEL Prestige 310 router has two Ethernet ports. Connect one port of the router to your hub or switch; connect the other port to your cable or your DSL modem. The port for your modem is labeled WAN, for wide area network.

You then install the Prestige Network Commander (PNC) software and restart your computer. You then start the Internet Setup Wizard that was placed on your Windows Start menu.

The router is set by default at the IP address of 192.168.1.1 and a subnet of 255.255.255.0. If your computer isn't set for dynamic addressing and is in a different subnet than the router, a screen like the one in Figure 13-8 appears. If you want to change your computer's settings to be compatible with those of the router, exit the program and change the settings using the Network icon in Control Panel. Otherwise, you can change the router's IP address and subnet so that they're compatible with your network.

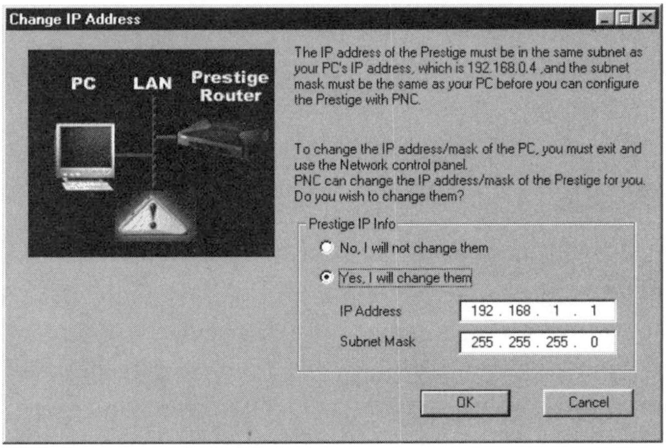

Figure 13-8.

Setting the network IP of the Prestige router.

Once your router can communicate with your computer, you configure it to work with your ISP using the options in Figure 13-9. For example, you can set it to accept a dynamic Internet IP address that the ISP assigns to it when you access the Internet, or you can enter the static IP address and subnet that your ISP assigned to you.

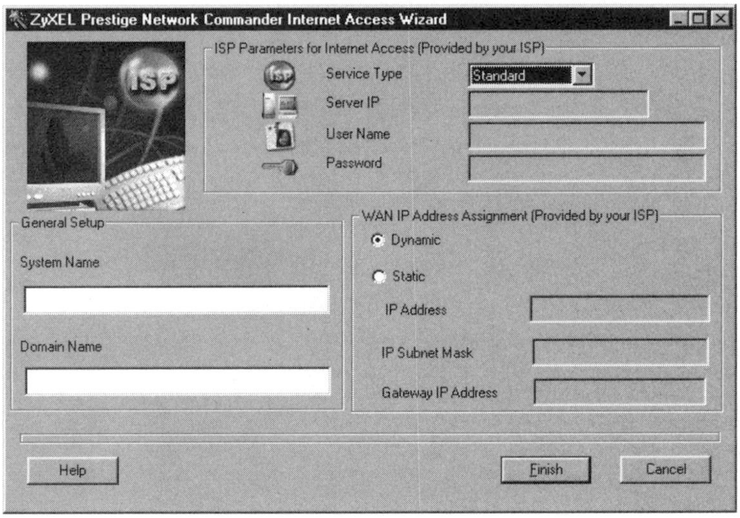

Figure 13-9.

Configuring the Prestige router.

Netopia 9100 Router

The Netopia 9100 router includes its own eight-port Ethernet hub that lets you perform both the hub and routing functions. Plug the Ethernet cable from each computer into the router's ports and plug your DSL or cable modem into the port provided for it on the router. If you already have a hub or switch that you want to continue using, connect it to the router's uplink port.

The router includes an installation and configuration program called SmartStart. The program guides you through the setup process using either a dynamic or fixed IP Internet address, and either a dynamic or fixed network address. When you start the program, for example, you'll be asked whether you want to perform the Easy installation using the default router address and settings, or the Advanced installation. If you select Advanced, you'll be able to enter the IP address you want to assign to the router on the network, as shown in Figure 13-10.

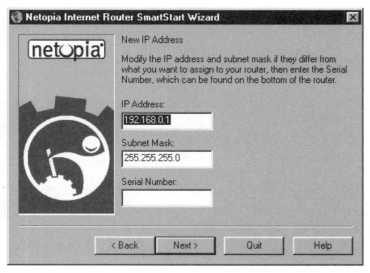

Figure 13-10.
Setting the IP of the Netopia router.

WatchGuard SOHO

The WatchGuard SOHO router includes its own four-port Ethernet hub, in addition to a WAN port for your DSL or cable modem. There's no uplink port to connect the router to another hub, but you can use a crossover cable between two regular ports, or a patch cable between the router and an uplink port on another hub.

This router is unique in that it doesn't include any software. Before you install the router on your network, you connect to the WatchGuard registration site on the Internet and get complete instructions for configuring your network to share the Internet. If you'd like to see how to set up this router, go to *http://bisd.watchguard.com/soho/install*. The configuration is basically straightforward.

Your first step is to determine whether your ISP uses a static or dynamic address. You do this using the Network icon in Control Panel by checking the TCP/IP properties for the NIC to which the modem is attached to your computer. If the properties show a static IP address, make a note of the address and the subnet mask.

The next step is to configure your computer to communicate with the router. The router is set by default to obtain its Internet IP address dynamically from your ISP and to serve as a DHCP host to assign IP addresses to computers on the network. So you have to use the Network icon in Control Panel to set your computers to obtain their IP addresses automatically.

Finally, if your ISP assigned you a static Internet address, you have to configure the router with that address. You perform this task by starting your Web browser and entering the router's address *http://192.168.111.1* to open a form built into the router. On that form, you clear the box labeled Use DHCP To Obtain Configuration and then enter the IP address and subnet mask that your ISP assigned.

Internet Security

Part of the reason you decided to create a home network is that you want to share your folders or disks with other family members. In Chapter 10, you learned how to turn on file sharing so family members could access your computer's resources.

When you connect to the Internet, however, sharing is not always advisable. Whenever you go online, you open the door to hackers and viruses that have the potential to damage your computer. High-speed Internet is even more susceptible to problems because DSL and cable modems are always connected, and hackers have a better chance of learning your IP address.

When you're networked, the potential damage is even greater. A hacker can reach not only into your own computer, but also into other computers that are connected to your network.

Turning Off Internet File Sharing

Before using your computer to connect to the Internet, you should turn off file sharing through the TCP/IP protocol that you use for the Internet. If you're using Consumer Windows, follow these steps:

1. Open Network in Control Panel.

2. Click TCP/IP –> Dial-up Adapter on the Configuration tab of the Network box.

3. Click Properties to open the TCP/IP Properties dialog box.

4. Click the Bindings tab.

5. Make sure the check box for the option File And Printer Sharing Using Microsoft Networks is not checked.

6. Click OK twice, and then select Yes if you are asked to restart your computer.

If you are using Windows 2000, follow these steps to turn off file sharing over the Internet:

1. Double-click My Network Places on the Windows desktop.

2. Click the underlined text, Network And Dial-up Connections, on the left side of the window.

3. Right-click on the icon representing your ISP connection and choose Properties.

4. Click the Networking tab.

5. Make sure the check box for the option File And Printer Sharing For Microsoft Networks is not checked.

6. Click OK, and then select Yes if you are asked to restart your computer.

Creating a Firewall

Most broadband routers have some firewall protection built in, and your DSL or cable ISP might offer some protection features. A firewall prevents unauthorized persons from getting into your computer from the Internet. If you have a regular dial-up Internet account that you share, however, you should consider installing security software to protect your network.

Internet Explorer has some protection features built in. To access the settings for these features, open the Internet Options icon in Control Panel and click the Security tab to see the options shown in Figure 13-11.

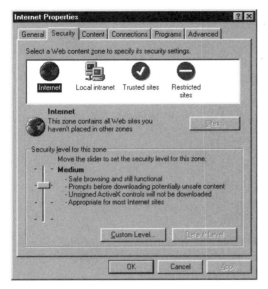

Figure 13-11.

Security settings in Internet Explorer.

At the top of the box are icons representing four zones:

- **Internet** determines security settings for all sites not in another zone.

- **Local Intranet** determines security settings for Web pages on your network.

- **Trusted Sites** determines security settings for Web sites that you know are safe to access.

- **Restricted Sites** determines security settings for Web sites that you don't trust.

I recommend that you leave the setting for the Internet zone at Medium, the Trusted Sites zone at Low, and the Restricted Sites zone at High. Select a zone and then drag the slider in the security level for this zone section to the level of security that you want. Moving it to the top sets security at High. The High setting provides the maximum security Internet Explorer offers, but it may cause some elements of Web sites to appear incorrectly.

To add a potentially hazardous site to the Restricted Sites zone, follow these steps:

1. Click Restricted Sites.

2. Click the Sites button.

3. In the box that appears, type the address of the site and click Add.

If you know that a particular Web site is safe, you can add it to the Trusted Sites zone by following these steps:

1. Click Trusted Sites.

2. Click the Sites button.

3. In the box that appears, type the address of the trusted site and click Add.

Although these security features are helpful, they can't protect you from all of the hazards on the Internet. Programs known as "Trojan horses," for example, can infiltrate your computer and transmit information about you to the hacker's Web site when you're online. So for greater security, consider any of the many security programs that you can download or purchase, such as Norton Internet Security and ZoneAlarm.

ZoneAlarm, from *http://www.zonelabs.com*, is free for downloading and nonbusiness use. ZoneAlarm prevents Trojan horses from sending information by prompting you to confirm whenever a program tries to access the Internet. It also prevents Web sites from obtaining information about you through requests to your system and can prevent access to the Internet after periods of inactivity.

Note

Some Internet security programs might interfere with normal network connections. If you have difficulty accessing a network computer after a security program has been installed on it, disable the program to confirm that it's the cause of the problem. If it is, check the documentation that came with the program for steps to solve the problem.

By sharing a modem and Internet connection, you can save a lot of money, even if you purchase a LAN modem rather than a purely software solution. You can also avoid having to wait for the telephone line in your home to be free. With the time you save waiting, you can play some of those cool computer games with other members of your family on the network. Playing games on the network is the subject of the next chapter.

Chapter 14

Playing Games

Playing games across a network encourages communication and competition and can be a great stress-reliever—especially if you win! But even if you don't win, network game playing can be a great family experience. You can share a virtual world with your family, fighting a common foe or going head-to-head in the spirit of friendly competition.

Solo vs. Network Games

Solo games on a computer can be fun and exhilarating, but you're playing against the computer. It's the computer that represents your foe—whether it's a galactic warrior, a World War II dogfighter, or a chess player at the other end of the board.

Although the computer can make all the right moves to keep a game interesting, it has no personality. When you're playing against a real person, you can try to anticipate your opponent's moves based on previous games or on what you know about his or her way of thinking. Human players provide more drama and a keener sense of competition. You can gently gloat over your win and someone else can gloat when you lose, making rematches all the more interesting.

Because many computer games allow more than two players, several members of the family can play. Usually, in fact, as many can play as there are computers on your home network. Games that require more players than you have available can sometimes create computer-generated competitors, so you can still practice your skills when other members of the family are busy.

When you don't feel competitive, you can play games that simply allow you to share experiences with other family members. With Microsoft Flight Simulator 2000, for example, you and another family member can soar over scenic landscapes and travel to distant lands in separate planes.

Preparing for Network Play

You can play hundreds of games over a network. Microsoft Windows 95, Microsoft Windows 98, and Microsoft Windows Millennium Edition (Me) even come with one, a game named Hearts. If you purchased a network kit, the accompanying CD might have network games on it, too. Check the documentation that came with the kit for a list of the games or insert the CD into the drive and browse through its folders to learn what games are included.

Note

Windows 2000 does not include any network-enabled games.

Selecting the proper games for you and your family and installing them on your network are the first steps toward network playing. But before you purchase or install any games, make sure your network is up and running.

To accommodate as many games as possible, you should make sure all three popular protocols are installed: TCP/IP, IPX/SPX, and NetBEUI. Check that all the computers on the network show up in Network Neighborhood (or My Network Places in Windows Me and Windows 2000) and that you can transfer information among them.

Selecting Games for Network Play

When choosing games, make sure that they fit your family's interests and standards and that they can be run on every computer on your network.

Many computer stores offer previews of popular games on special computers set up just for that purpose. You can play the game in the store before purchasing it to see whether it meets your standards. Bring your children with you and let them preview the game as well. You can also visit many sites online to read about games and download demonstration versions, such as *http://www.gamespot.com* and *http://www.gamecenter.com*.

You also need to make sure that your computers and network are capable of running the game you want. The minimum and recommended hardware requirements are usually listed on the game's box. The minimum requirements are those that are absolutely necessary for the game to play, although its performance might be unsatisfactory. The recommended requirements are those that the game's manufacturer suggests for good game play. The box might also list optional hardware, such as advanced sound and display systems, that will provide higher-quality video or audio.

Note

Network play normally requires greater resources than single-player action. For network play, your computers should meet the recommended speed and memory requirements rather than just the minimum requirements.

Here are some of the hardware requirements you'll need to consider:

- **Processor type and speed** Most of the sophisticated action games require at least a Pentium or a Pentium-compatible processor, running at a certain speed or above. Older Pentiums running at 90 MHz are often too slow for the newest games. In fact, new games are designed for high-speed processors, so don't be surprised to see 300 MHz or more listed as the minimum or recommended processor speed.

- **Amount of RAM** Some games, especially those with lots of graphics, require 32 MB or more of memory.

- **Available disk space** Programs that feature sound and video require a lot of storage space. A typical game might require 40 MB of disk storage or more, even when you run the program from the CD rather than installing it on your hard disk.

- **Sound card** To hear the sound effects that help make many computer games so exciting, you'll need a sound card and speakers in your computer. Most newer computer systems come with sound cards. Older computers might not be able to generate a game's sounds unless you add a sound card and speakers.

- **Display requirements** Look on the game's box for the minimum and recommended color and screen resolution settings. Many games require your system to be set at 256 colors or more, with a screen resolution of at least 800 by 600 pixels. In some cases, the game will start with lower settings, but the display won't be very clear. In other cases, you won't be able to start or play the game until the display is adjusted to the minimum settings. Although many games recommend advanced 3D or graphics accelerator cards, they're usually not part of the minimum requirements.

- **Joystick** For flight simulators, combat games, and other action games, a joystick or yoke is highly recommended. You can still play the game using the keyboard or mouse to control movement, but you won't experience the same sense of control.

If some of your computers don't meet a game's minimum or recommended requirements, consider playing the game on only the computers that do meet them. Or you can use the most advanced computers in the house to play the game on the network, leaving less sophisticated computers for solo action.

Most network games require that a single computer serve as the host, starting and organizing the game, and running its CD while the game is played. (The other computers on the network don't have to run the game CD during play.) For maximum performance, choose as the host the computer with the greatest memory, speed, and storage space.

Installing Games for Network Play

In most cases, you don't have to do anything special to install a game for network play. The usual setup process installs both the single- and multiple-player versions of the game. If you're presented with options to install the single- or multiple-player version, choose the multiple-player version.

Install the game separately on each computer on the network. For games on CD or floppy disk, insert the CD or disk into each computer and run the installation program. If you downloaded the game from the Internet, copy the file to each of the computers in Network Neighborhood or My Network Places, and then run the installation program on each machine.

At installation, most games present a series of dialog boxes that prompt you to select hardware options. Make sure you choose options appropriate for the machine on which you're installing the game.

If you're not asked to select options during the installation process, you might have to do so when you first start the game. For example, you might have to select from a menu of input devices used to manipulate objects, such as a keyboard, mouse, or joystick. Be sure to start and set up the game on each computer before playing it on the network.

Playing Games on the Network

To play a network game that was supplied on a CD, you usually need to insert the CD into the host computer's drive. Once the host starts the game and sets its options, other computers on the network can join in.

The procedure for starting games varies. The installation process might either place an icon on the desktop or add a listing to the Start menu. To begin playing, double-click the icon or select the program from the Start menu.

With some older games, the Start menu listing accesses the CD directly and can be used only on the host. To start the game on the other computers, each player has to find the game program in its folder.

Once you start the game, you'll be asked to choose whether you want the computer you're playing on to be the host or whether you want to join a game that's already in progress. Again, the process varies widely. In the dialog box shown here, from the game HyperBlade, you can select the type of network you're using, choose to host a new game, or wait until a game in progress appears in the Open Games list and choose to join that game.

Multiplayer Setup (Select Game)

NETWORK TYPE

WinSock IPX Connection For DirectPlay
WinSock TCP Connection For DirectPlay

OPEN GAMES

Update list of available games

Host   Join   Cancel

Status

SYSTEM: Waiting for you to JOIN a game, or to HOST a new one

To introduce some of the possibilities for network game playing, we'll look at two examples of network games.

Hearts

Hearts is a four-player card game that comes with Windows 95, Windows 98, and Windows Me. To see whether Hearts and the other Windows games are installed on your computer, click Start, and then point to Programs, to Accessories, and finally to Games.

If the Windows games aren't installed on your computer, follow these steps:

1. Insert the Windows CD into your CD-ROM drive.

2. On the Start menu, point to Settings, and then click Control Panel.

3. In Control Panel, double-click the Add/Remove Programs icon.

4. In the Add/Remove Programs Properties dialog box, click the Windows Setup tab.

5. Click Accessories. (Don't select the check box to the left of Accessories or you'll clear the check mark.)

6. Click Details to see a list of the items in the Accessories category.

7. In the list of components, click the Games check box to enable it.

8. Click OK to close the Accessories dialog box.

9. Click OK to close the Add/Remove Programs Properties dialog box. Windows then installs the games.

To start Hearts, point to Programs on the Start menu, point to Accessories and then to Games, and then click Hearts. You'll see the following dialog box.

Enter your name, if it's not already shown in the What Is Your Name? text box, and choose whether you want to connect to a game in progress or be the dealer (the host) of a new game.

To start a new game, choose I Want To Be Dealer, and then click OK. The Microsoft Hearts Network window appears as shown in Figure 14-1, with your name as the dealer at the bottom of the window. As other members join the game, their names are added to the window. If you want to play against three computer-generated opponents, you can press the F2 key.

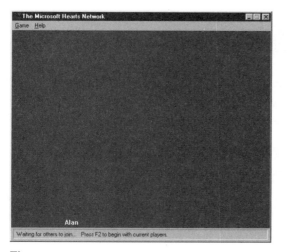

Figure 14-1.
The Microsoft Hearts Network window displays the name of the dealer when you start a new game.

To join a game that someone has already started, select I Want To Connect To Another Game, and then click OK to open the Locate Dealer dialog box. You must enter the name of the computer that the dealer is using and click OK to join the game. The Microsoft Hearts Network window appears and shows you as one of the players.

When another member joins the game, the new player's name appears in the Hearts window of all the other players. Once all the network players are signed in, the host presses the F2 key to start play. If there are fewer than four human players, the program adds its own players to bring the total up to four, as shown in Figure 14-2. (If four people are already playing, you will not be able to join the game, and you'll see a message saying, "The dealer is not ready or the game is already in progress.")

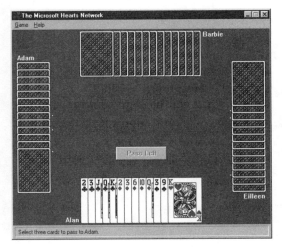

Figure 14-2.

Hearts can be played by a combination of human and computer-generated players.

To change the name of the computer-generated players for the next game, select Options from the Game menu to see the Hearts Options dialog box.

In the Hearts Options dialog box, you can also change the speed at which the animation runs in the game. Choose Sound from the Game menu to turn sound effects on or off, and choose Score to see the current score.

Flight Simulator 2000

Microsoft Flight Simulator has long been a popular game and learning program. If you enjoy flying or want to learn how, Flight Simulator 2000 lets you practice the skills you'd need to fly an actual airplane. Because the program so accurately depicts actual flying, many trainee pilots use Flight Simulator 2000, and programs like it, to supplement their time in the air. With its displays of detailed scenery from hundreds of locations around the world, Flight Simulator 2000 is great fun even if you just want to enjoy the view and leave the real flying to others.

If you're on a network, you can also fly with other members of the family, each network player in his or her own plane. You can do some sightseeing or try to outmaneuver each other through the skies and around the airport.

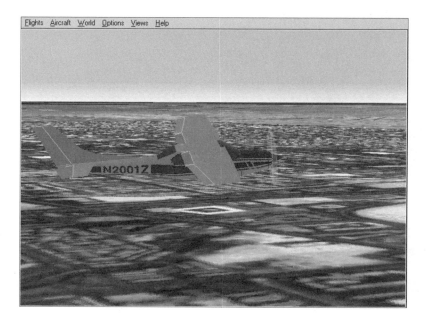

After you start Flight Simulator 2000, point to Multiplayer on the Flights menu and click Connect to see the Multiplayer Connect options, shown in Figure 14-3. Enter the name you want to use as your call sign. Next, select the type of network connection you're using from the following choices:

- Serial
- Modem
- TCP/IP
- IPX

Figure 14-3.
Before starting a Flight Simulator 2000 session, you need to choose your network protocol.

On a home network, choose either IPX or TCP/IP, depending on your network protocol. Now choose whether you want to host a session, join one that's already started, or search the Internet for a session in progress.

If you want to join an ongoing game on your network, the IPX protocol will automatically search for current sessions. If you're using TCP/IP, you can enter the computer name or IP address of the computer hosting the session or leave the address blank and click Search to have Flight Simulator 2000 search the network for a hosted session. Choose the session and whether you'd like to join as an observer, and then click Join.

Note

As an observer, you can lock into another aircraft's cockpit view to see that plane's instrument panel and view from the cockpit window.

If you choose to host a new session, you'll see the Host Options dialog box shown in Figure 14-4, in which you can set session options such as these:

- The session name and comments
- An optional password needed to join a game
- The maximum number of pilots
- The maximum number of observers
- Whether you want to host as an observer

You'll also be able to see the names of other network participants in the session you're hosting.

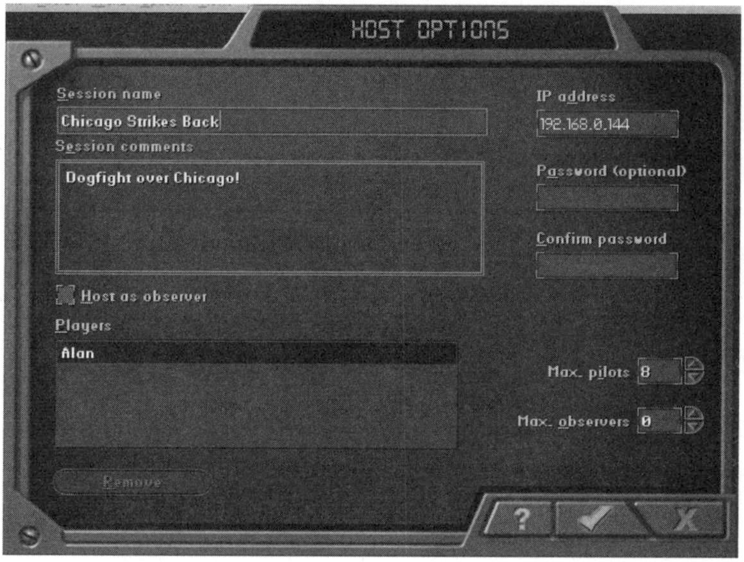

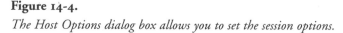

Figure 14-4.
The Host Options dialog box allows you to set the session options.

In addition to the Microsoft Flight Simulator 2000 window, you'll see a Chat window. You use this window to send messages to other planes. Enter your message in the text box at the bottom of the Chat window, and then press Enter or click Send.

Watching Out for Pitfalls

Because network games are played in real time, family members might want to practice on their own before joining a multiple-player game. They should learn the rules and be able to control movement and play. It's no pleasure to win too easily or to wait while a novice player stops the action to learn the rules.

Network playing requires a lot of system resources, so don't be surprised if the sound or video sometimes slows down during a game. The game might be accessing more information on the CD, or another player on the network might pause a game, which sometimes slows down the action for other players. Still, playing games on the network can be fun and challenging, and a great way to compete with the family.

In the next chapter, you'll learn another way to share with the family by setting up your own family Web using Microsoft's Personal Web Server.

Part 5

Extending the Network

Chapter 15
Setting Up a Web   **337**

Chapter 16
Networking PCs and Macs   **373**

Chapter 17
Networking for Road Warriors   **415**

Chapter 18
Your Future Home Network   **449**

Chapter 15

Setting Up a Web

Now that your home computers are connected on a network, you can easily set up your own Web. Your Web can have a Web site for each family member who wants one and a guest book for collecting messages. It can also offer each family member the capability to post documents that others can easily view with a Web browser. In a sense, it's like having your own version of the World Wide Web, but right on your home network so that you can share family news and information.

Each family member's Web site can have a customized *home page*, the first page people see when viewing that site with their Web browsers. Figure 15-1 shows how Dad's home page might look on the family Web. It includes information that Dad wants to share with the family and photographs of the family's award-winning son. The home page also provides three links to other pages that make up Dad's Web site. Anyone viewing the site can click a link to see vacation photographs, read Dad's favorite jokes, or return to Dad's home page.

Note

A private Web over a network, such as your own home Web, is called an *intranet*.

Figure 15-1.

Dad's Web site on the family Web.

Of course, Mom can have her own Web site on the family Web as well, as shown in Figure 15-2. On her home page, Mom shares an old photograph she found when rummaging through the attic and passes on some news about other relatives.

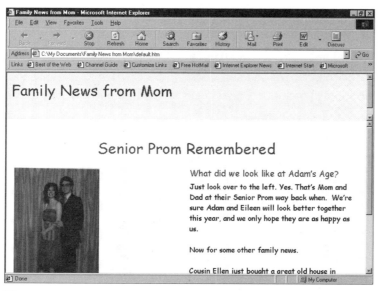

Figure 15-2.

Mom's Web site on the family Web.

Web sites aren't just for adults, so Beth has her own Web site on the family Web as well, which is shown in Figure 15-3. Of course, her Web site reflects her personality, with links to her schoolwork and to news about her most recent boyfriend as well as some graphics about her favorite subject, music.

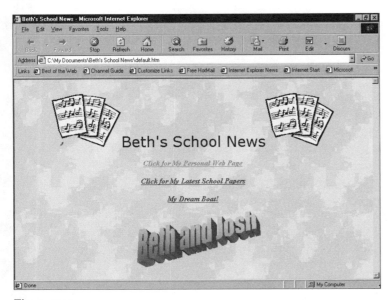

Figure 15-3.
Beth's Web site on the family Web.

What's in a Web Site?

Web sites, whether on the Internet or on your own home network, consist of one or more pages of text, specially formatted to enable Web browsers to display them on the screen. The formatting instructions for Web pages are called Hypertext Markup Language (HTML) tags. The pages are connected by *hyperlinks*, usually simply called *links*. A link is a word, phrase, or graphic that you click to jump to another page of the Web site, to send e-mail, or to go to another Web site on the Internet or intranet.

The first page that you encounter when you go to a Web site is called the site's home page. The other pages of the site are separate files that are retrieved and displayed on the screen when you click their associated links.

As you can see from the preceding examples, a family Web is a great way for everyone to share information, express themselves, and get to know a little more about one another. Although it's still not as personal as a good old family meeting, a family Web lets everyone be creative in a different way, and it serves as a terrific learning experience about the way the Web works.

If you have a personal Web site with your Internet service provider (ISP), you can also use your home Web to fine-tune and test your Web pages before uploading them to the ISP. This way, you can be sure your Web site looks right and works correctly before you expose it to the world.

Creating a Web Site with Personal Web Server

All the software you need to set up a Web server and create a home page comes with Microsoft Windows 98. The program, called Microsoft Personal Web Server (PWS), lets you set up and maintain a Web site on any computer on the network. In fact, each computer on the network can host its own Web site, as long as it has the PWS program installed. If you have three computers connected on a network, for example, you can have three separate personal Web sites, any of which can be viewed by the entire family. Microsoft Windows 95, Microsoft Windows Millennium Edition (Me), and Microsoft Windows 2000, however, don't include the PWS program.

Family members can then access everyone's pages using their Web browsers in much the same way as they access Web pages on the Internet. Instead of dialing in to an ISP to connect to the worldwide Internet, however, a user's browser connects to a personal Web server on the network. The personal Web server delivers the Web pages to the viewer's screen. As far as that browser is concerned, it's connected to a Web server just as if it were actually on the Internet.

Creating a Web Server with Windows 95 and Windows Me

PWS isn't included in Windows 95 and Windows Me, but users of those Windows versions can download from the Internet alternative shareware programs for creating a Web server. Some of the Web server programs include:

OmniHTTPd Professional from *www.omnicron.ab.ca*

Shambala Server from *www.evolvable.com*

TinyWeb Server from *www.ritlabs.com*

You'll find complete instructions for using these programs on the manufacturers' sites or with the program help files.

If you are upgrading from Windows 98 to Windows Me, you can also use the PWS program that was included in your Windows 98 CD. I've found that you can install and run PWS with Windows Me by following the same instructions for Windows 98. Because PWS is not included in Windows Me, however, Microsoft doesn't provide support for PWS in Windows Me.

See Also

See the section "Creating a Web Site with Windows 2000," later in this chapter, for information about setting up a Web server with Windows 2000.

Installing Personal Web Server

PWS is included on your Windows 98 CD, but it isn't installed as part of Windows. You have to install it yourself, directly from the CD, on the computer that you plan to use to create a Web site.

Note

If you use PWS to create a home page, it creates a file with the ASP (Active Server Pages) extension. Some computers on the network might not be able to access ASP Web pages unless you install PWS on them as well. If a user has trouble accessing your Web site from a computer on the network, install PWS on it.

Follow these steps to install PWS:

1. Insert the Windows 98 CD into your computer. If the Windows installation menu appears, click its Close button.

2. On the Start menu, click Run.

3. Type *D:\add-ons\pws\setup.exe*, and then press Enter. (If your CD-ROM drive's letter isn't D:, use the correct drive letter instead.)

4. When the setup program begins, click Next. You'll see three setup options: Minimum, Typical, and Advanced.

5. Click Typical, which supplies all the services you'll probably need. The next dialog box, shown in Figure 15-4, lets you set the location for the WWW Service (your Web site).

6. Accept the default for the location of the WWW Service by clicking Next.

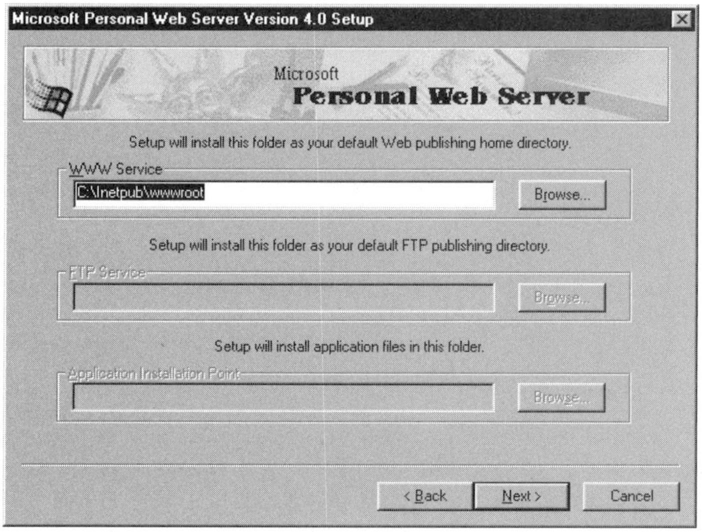

Figure 15-4.
This PWS dialog box lets you set your Web site's location.

7. Windows installs PWS and displays a final dialog box. Click Finish.

8. Click Yes when you're asked whether to restart your computer.

Now that PWS is installed, you're ready to create a home page and make it available to other family members on your own personal Web site.

Note

When you install PWS on a home network, you can ignore any error messages you encounter during setup that report problems with features called Microsoft Transaction Server (MTS) or Core Components, and just click OK. Both of them are business-oriented features that would not generally be used in a home network. These messages might appear if your Windows registry is full and the setup program is unable to add the necessary entries for Microsoft Transaction Server in your registry. If you want to learn more about these messages and how to correct the error, visit *http://support.microsoft.com/ support/kb/articles/q214/6/44.ASP.*

Using Personal Web Manager

When you restart your computer after installing PWS, you'll see a Publish icon on your desktop and a new icon in the system tray next to the clock. Double-clicking either of these icons opens Personal Web Manager, which helps you create and manage your Web site. If you right-click the system tray icon, you'll see Start Service and Stop Service options on a shortcut menu; these options allow you to turn PWS on or off or to pause or continue the service.

You can also open the Personal Web Manager window by clicking Start, pointing to Programs, Accessories, Internet Tools, and Personal Web Server, and then clicking Personal Web Manager.

The Tip Of The Day window appears first. You can click Close to close this window, or click Next to read another tip. You can also click to disable the Show Tips At Startup check box if you want to skip seeing tips each time you start the program. After closing the Tip Of The Day, you'll see the Personal Web Manager window, shown in Figure 15-5.

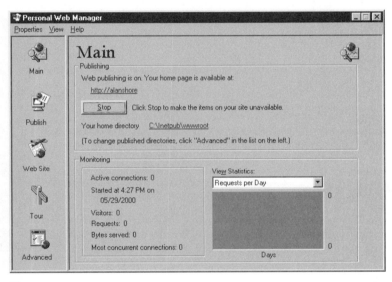

Figure 15-5.
Personal Web Manager helps you to create and manage your home page.

Along the left side of the window is a sidebar with five icons:

- **Main** displays the initial window that you now see.
- **Publish** lets you add documents to your Web site that you want to share over the intranet.
- **Web Site** runs the Home Page Wizard, which lets you create a personal home page.
- **Tour** takes you through a PWS tutorial.
- **Advanced** lets you change the directories in which your Web site is stored and the default home page document.

In the Personal Web Manager window, you'll see your home page address, which is *http://* followed by your computer's name and the name of the home directory in which the new Web site will be stored, such as C:\Inetpub\wwwroot. You'll also see a Stop button, which allows you to temporarily disable your Web server so it is not available to other network users. Once you click the Stop button, it changes to Start to allow other network users to access your Web server pages with their Web browsers. The number of times your Web site has been accessed over the intranet is listed at the bottom of the window along with other useful information, such as the number of people who are currently connected.

To access your Web site, just click the link to your home page. Until you create your own home page, you'll see a default home page in its place. Click the Home Directory link to display the subfolders and files in that location. To go to your site from My Computer or Windows Explorer, type your home page address in the Address text box, such as *http://alanneib*, and press Enter.

Note

When creating a Web address for your site, PWS substitutes dashes for the spaces and apostrophes in your computer's name. For example, the computer named *Barb's Room* becomes *http://barb-s-room*.

Creating Your Home Page

Your next step is to create a home page on your server. You can perform this task manually, using a Web page creation program, such as Microsoft FrontPage or FrontPage Express, or you can use the PWS program's Home Page Wizard.

Note

Windows 2000 doesn't include PWS, so you'll need to create a Web site using other programs and manually publish files to your Web site by copying them to the proper folders. For more information, see the section "Creating a Web Site with Windows 2000," later in this chapter.

Although it offers only a limited number of Web site design options, the Home Page Wizard is still great for creating a family Web site because it's easy to use and it lets you add two handy features to your site: a guest book and a drop box. A *guest book* displays messages from network users that all visitors to your site can view. You can use the guest book to hold family "conversations" and to leave messages for other people on the network.

A *drop box* contains private messages that only you can view. To read drop-box messages, you have to log on to your computer with your own user name and start PWS.

To create a home page with the Home Page Wizard, follow these steps:

1. In Personal Web Manager, click the Web Site icon to start the wizard. The Main dialog box is replaced by the Home Page Wizard dialog box, along with a small, animated figure of a wizard.

2. Click the animated wizard or the >> button. On the next page of the Home Page Wizard, you can select from a list of templates, shown in Figure 15-6, to set the design of your home page.

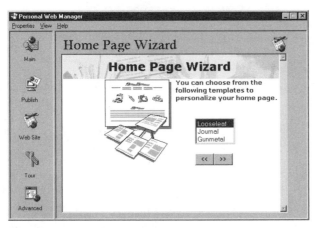

Figure 15-6.
Select a template for your home page in the Home Page Wizard.

3. Select one of the templates, and then click the >> button to move to the next page. You'll now be asked whether you want a guest book for public messages.

4. Click the >> button to accept the default response of Yes.

5. You'll now be asked whether you want a drop box for private messages. Again, click the >> button to accept the default response of Yes. A message appears in the Home Page Wizard reporting that you're ready to personalize your home page.

6. Click >> to open the PWS Quick Setup page in Internet Explorer, as shown in Figure 15-7.

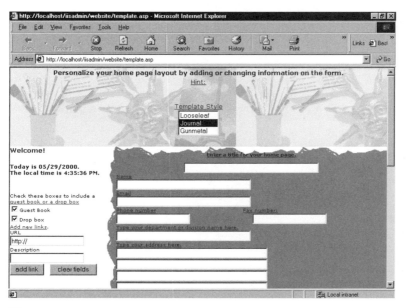

Figure 15-7.

By filling in the text boxes on the PWS Quick Setup page, you can personalize your home page.

You use the PWS Quick Setup page, which is actually a Web page in your browser, to create and edit your home page. Notice that the page contains an underlined link above each text box. To get help on the text box, click the link.

The PWS Quick Setup page shows the template you've selected and whether you've included a guest book and drop box. If you didn't change these settings in the Home Page Wizard, you can modify them here. Each template you select contains the same items; only their arrangement and background graphics differ.

On the PWS Quick Setup page, you can enter the following elements for your home page:

- A title

- Your name

- Your e-mail address

- A phone and fax number

- Your department or division name

- Your address

- Four headings and a paragraph of text under each heading

You can also enter links to favorite Web sites and documents on your computer. In the URL and Description text boxes, type the URL or path of a site, enter a brief description, and click Add Link.

Add new links.
URL
http://

Description

add link   clear fields

After you add your first link, it will be shown in a list box along with the Remove Link button.

Great old movies

remove link
Add new links.
URL
http://
Description

add link   clear fields

Note

If you want to change the information on your home page, click Web Site in the Personal Web Manager window, and then click Edit Your Home Page. After you make your changes, click Enter New Changes.

After you've entered information in as many text boxes as you'd like, click the Enter New Changes button near the bottom of the page. The Web page appears, as shown in Figure 15-8. Close the Browser window when you finish reviewing the page.

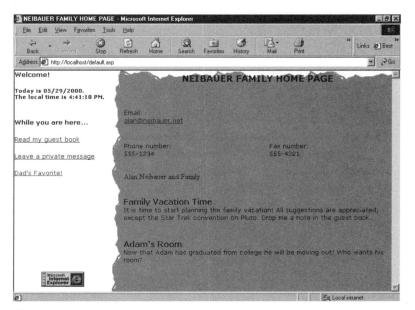

Figure 15-8.

Your completed Web page can be viewed by all network users.

Accessing Your Home Page

When you want to access your home page to see how it looks, enter its address in your Internet browser's address box or as the address in Windows Explorer. You can also choose Run from the Start menu, type your home page address (*http://your computer's name*), and then click OK.

Other family members on the network can access your home page in the same ways, from the Run box, their Web browser, or Windows Explorer. In some cases, however, a browser might try to dial in to the ISP rather than access the intranet. If it does, the browser has to be set to access the intranet using the local area network rather than the dial-up connection. Here's how you set up Microsoft Internet Explorer to access your intranet:

1. Right-click the Internet Explorer icon on your desktop and choose Properties. You can also double-click the Internet Options icon in Control Panel.

2. Click the Connections tab.

3. With Internet Explorer version 5, select Dial Whenever A Network Connection Is Not Present or Never Dial A Connection. With earlier versions of Internet Explorer, select Connect Through A Local Area Network.

4. Click OK.

Using Your Guest Book and Drop Box

The guest book serves as a bulletin board on which family members can leave their names, a short message, or even a favorite link. It's a great place to post important announcements or everyday information that you or another family member wants to share with everyone else on the network. Placing a message in the guest book is like sending e-mail, except that anyone who visits your site can view the guest book message.

To leave a message in someone's guest book, go to the home page on that person's computer and click the Read My Guest Book link. The guest book appears, formatted in three columns, as shown in Figure 15-9. Click a column heading to sort the list. To read a message, click its link.

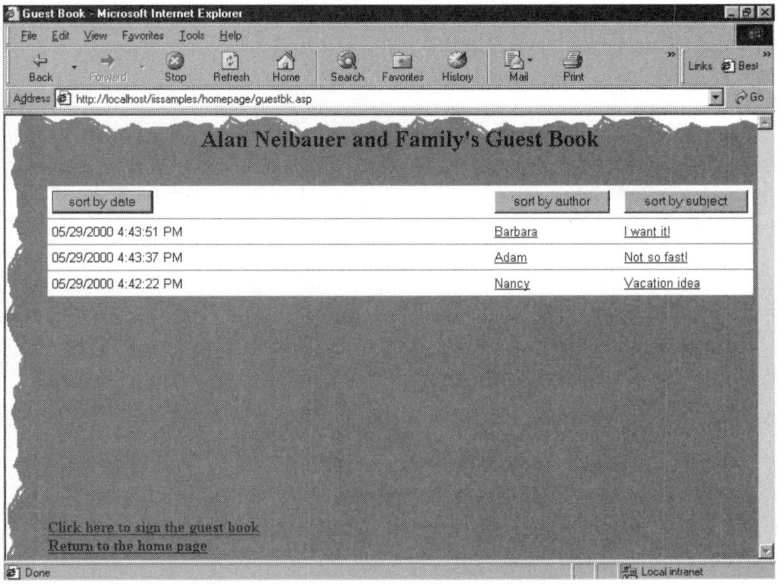

Figure 15-9.

Open a Guest Book message by clicking its link.

Leave a message by clicking Click Here To Sign The Guest Book. Type the information you want in the message window, as shown in Figure 15-10, and then click Send Message. To clear the message window and start again, click Clear Fields.

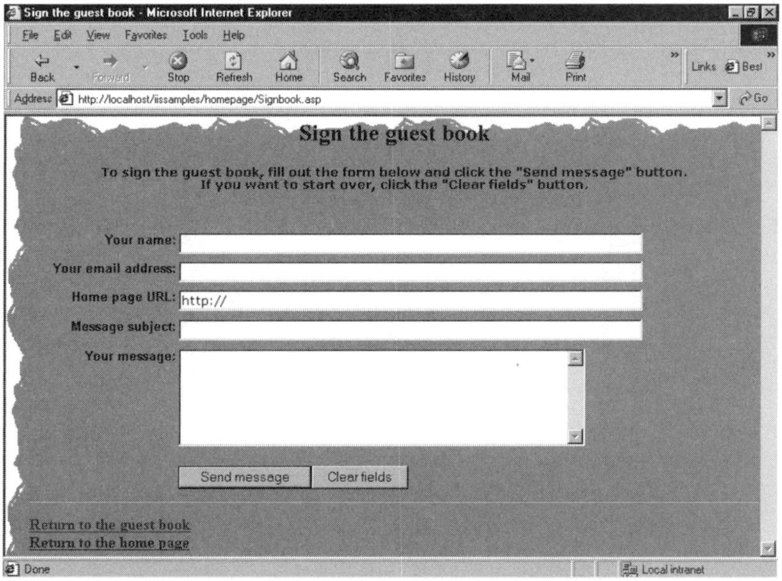

Figure 15-10.

Enter your message in the Sign The Guest Book message window.

If you want to leave a private message that only the owner of the home page can read, click Leave A Private Message. Type the message text, and then click Send Message. The message is stored in the drop box.

Once your guest book and drop box contain messages, you can view, sort, and delete messages. Open Personal Web Manager and click Web Site to see three options: Edit Your Home Page, View Your Guest Book, and Open Your Drop Box.

To read your guest book messages, click View Your Guest Book to access a wizard page such as the one shown in Figure 15-11. Use the options in this wizard page to construct a query that will find certain messages to display according to the criteria you supply. You can display messages by the date they were written, the person who sent them, their subject, or any combination of these categories. By default, the search is set to display all messages written before the current date and time. To view these messages, just click the Submit Query button.

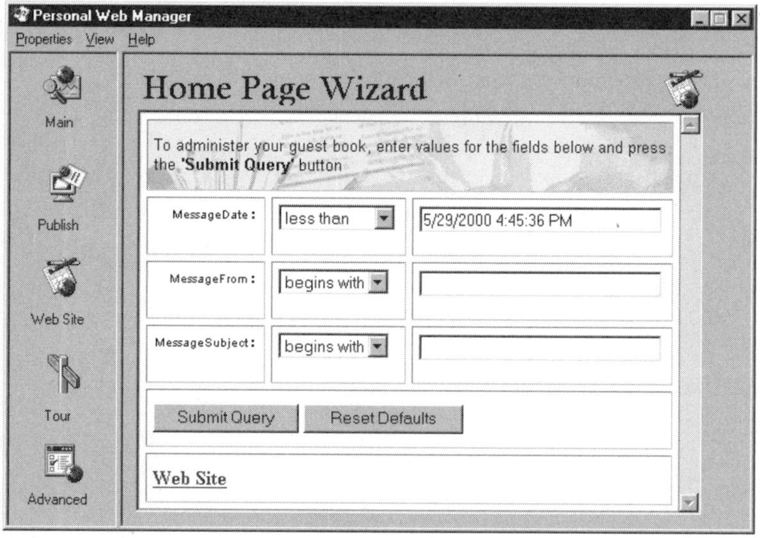

Figure 15-11.

This Home Page Wizard page lets you select messages by date, sender, or subject.

By using the drop-down lists and text boxes, you can fine-tune your search for specific messages. Next to the MessageDate option, you can choose Less Than, Equal To, or Greater Than, and then enter a certain date as the criterion. To display messages written after a certain date, for example, you'd choose Greater Than from the drop-down list and enter the date in the text box to its right.

With the MessageFrom option, you can choose to list messages from people whose names begin with, contain, end with, or are equal to the text you enter in the box. The MessageSubject option works the same way, except that it searches the Subject field of messages. For example, to look for messages whose subject contains the word "vacation," select Contains from the MessageSubject drop-down list and enter the word *vacation* in the text box to its right.

When you click Submit Query, you'll see a list of messages in the Home Page Wizard that meet the criteria you've entered. You can sort the messages by date, author, or subject by clicking the appropriate column heading. To read a message, click its link. Click Delete Message to erase the message from your guest book. You can also click New Query to change the search criteria, or you can click Web Site to return to the Web Site options.

Note

To update the time in a query to the current time, click the Web Site link, and then click View Your Guest Book again.

The drop box is similar to the guest book, except that it contains messages that only you can see, and you don't have the opportunity to create a query. When you click Web Site in the Personal Web Manager window and then click Open Your Drop Box, all messages in your drop box appear automatically.

Publishing Documents on Your Site

In addition to adding a home page, you can place all sorts of documents on your Web site and share them with family members. You can post scanned family pictures, information about vacations, or instructions on how the family can reach you when you're away on business.

One way to place a file on your Web site is simply to copy the file to the C:\Inetpub\Webpub folder. Or you can let the Publishing Wizard of PWS for Windows 98 do it for you.

Note

Windows Me and Windows 2000 don't include the PWS program. For information on maintaining a Web site in Windows 2000, see "Creating a Web Site with Windows 2000," later in this chapter.

The Publishing Wizard lets you select one or more files from any location on your hard disk to copy to the Web site folder. Here's how this wizard works:

1. Click the Publish icon on the Personal Web Manager toolbar on the left side of your screen. If you haven't yet used the wizard to publish a file on your Web site, the animated wizard figure appears.

2. Click the wizard figure or the >> button to see the page shown in Figure 15-12.

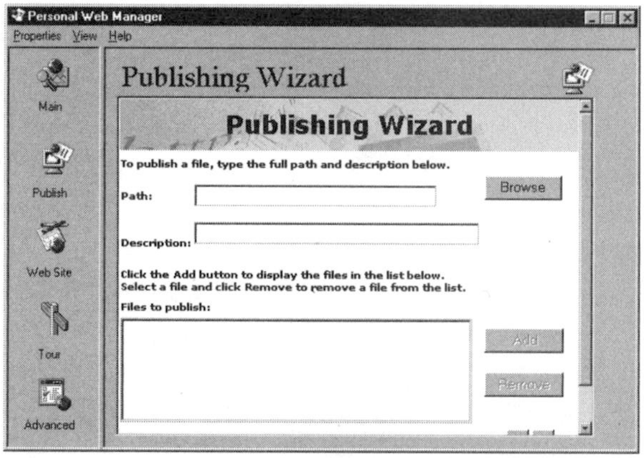

Figure 15-12.
The Publishing Wizard allows you to select files to publish on your Web site.

3. Enter the file's path and name or click Browse and locate the file using this dialog box.

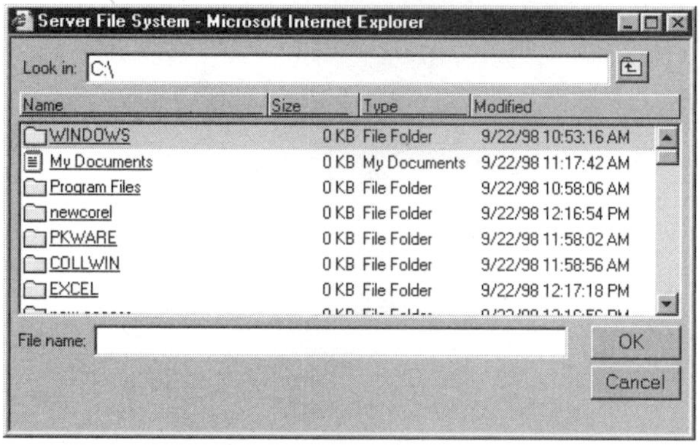

4. To locate a file, click the underlined link for the folder or subfolder containing the file, and then click the file itself.

5. Enter a description of the file in the Description text box.

6. Click Add.

7. Repeat the process for other files you'd like to add.

8. When you've added all the files you want, click the >> button.

Personal Web Manager copies the files to the C:\Inetpub\Webpub folder. Now they're available to anyone who clicks View My Published Documents on your home page. They'll see a list of files, as shown in Figure 15-13.

Note

As a shortcut, you can drag the file name to the Publish icon on the Windows desktop or to the Personal Web Manager toolbar to start the Publishing Wizard. You can also right-click a file, click Send To, and then click Personal Web Server to publish a file.

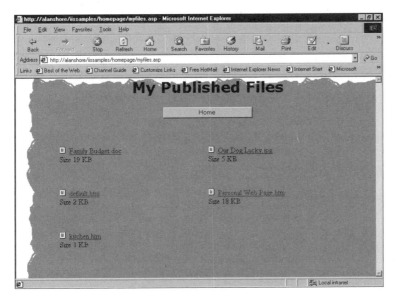

Figure 15-13.
Published files are available for anyone to open with a single click.

Once you publish the first file on your Web site, clicking Publish and then the >> button displays these options rather than the animated wizard.

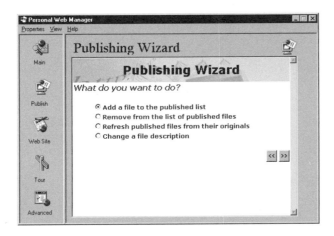

Make your selection, and then click the >> button to continue performing the action you selected.

Creating a Web Site with Windows 2000

Windows 2000 provides a feature named Internet Information Services (IIS) for creating and maintaining a home Web site. IIS is similar to PWS in that it handles requests from Web browsers to display Web site pages. However, IIS is a much more powerful and more complex program.

You can select which features of IIS you want to install during the installation of Windows 2000, or through the Add/Remove Programs feature in Control Panel. To use the Control Panel, follow these steps:

1. In Control Panel, open Add/Remove Programs.

2. Click Add/Remove Windows Components.

3. Select Internet Information Services (IIS), and then click Details to see the options shown in Figure 15-14.

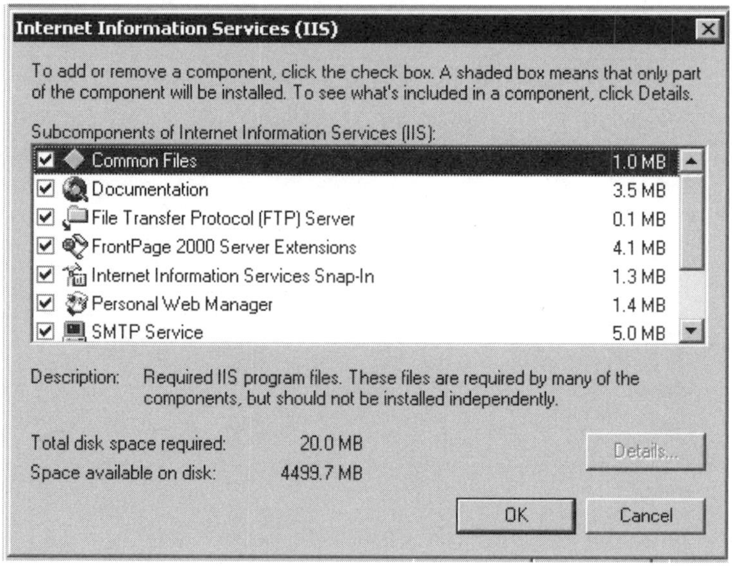

Figure 15-14.
Select which features of IIS to install.

4. Select the options you want to install, then click OK.

5. Click Next and then follow the instructions to complete the installation. You may need to insert your Windows 2000 CD in your computer so Windows can copy the necessary files to your disk.

Installing the services creates the Inetpub folder with your intranet site in the /Inetpub/wwwroot folder. Users can access your site in their browser by going to your computer, as in *http://Adam*, where your computer is named Adam. You can access your site and then folders by choosing Administrative Tools in Control Panel and selecting Personal Web Manager.

Click the Web site link to open your site in the browser or the folder link to display the folder contents. Click Stop to disable the Web server, or click Start later to restart it. Advanced users can manage their site by using the Internet Services Manager option in Administrative Tools.

You can publish your Web pages to your site by copying them to the \Inetpub\wwwroot folder. If you rename your home page default.htm, it will open automatically when a user accesses your computer by typing the computer's name in their browser. For example, if your computer was named Adam, a user could access your default.htm page by typing *http://Adam* in their browser.

Note

Regardless of the version of Windows you use to set up your Web server, your Web pages can be accessed by users of any version of Windows or by Apple Macintosh users.

Creating Web Pages with Microsoft Word

The Home Page Wizard is fast and fun, but it generates only one type of home page, even if it does come in three designs. Whether you're dealing with the Internet or your own home intranet, what makes creating pages for a Web enjoyable is that you can let your imagination go wild and create really personalized Web sites.

When you use the Home Page Wizard to create a home page, it automatically adds the HTML tags to the information that you enter. You don't see the tags in a Web browser; you just see the finished result in the form of a formatted Web page. If you want to, you can learn how to write the HTML tags yourself and create a Web page with even the simplest of text editors, such as Windows Notepad.

To create more personalized Web pages, however, you really don't have to rush out and take a course on HTML. You can use any of the dozens of programs that write the tags for you as you design Web pages. Programs such as FrontPage and FrontPage Express are specifically designed to create Web pages and manage all the pages that make up a

Web site. But you can also create Web pages with most of today's major applications, such as those that come with Microsoft Office 2000. Using programs included in Office, you can write documents, create spreadsheets and databases, and design slide shows. The programs then convert the formatting of your document, spreadsheet, or slideshow into HTML tags so that you can publish them on the Internet or to your home network Web. You can use Office 2000 programs to create Web pages on any version of Windows. You can then copy the files you create to the computer on which your Web site is kept.

Microsoft Word offers two ways to create a Web page. You can use Word's Web Page Wizard to design a Web page in much the same way you use the Home Page Wizard in PWS to design a Web page. You follow a series of pages to select the format and enter the contents of the page. Word then displays the resulting Web page so that you can further personalize it. You can also write and format a document using all Word's formatting features and then have Word convert the document into a Web page for you. Word will convert the formatting you've set up, such as boldfaced headings, into the HTML tags that your Web browser can understand.

Using the Web Page Wizard

The Web Page Wizard creates a small Web site of one or more pages with links that you can click to navigate between the pages.

One of the first decisions you'll have to make with the Web Page Wizard is to figure out where you want the Web page to be stored. If you choose to save it in C:\Inetpub\Webpub, network users can then access the Web page, and any other files you have stored in that folder, by selecting View My Published Documents on your home page. You don't have to use the Publish command in Personal Web Manager.

If you want to use your Word Web page as the PWS home page, you can delete all the files in the C:\Inetpub\Webroot folder and select that folder as the location of your Word home page. However, this will also delete your guest book and drop box, and your PWS home page will have only the features you've added in Word.

Now let's go through the process of creating a Web page in Word using the Web Page Wizard to see how it's done. You'll go step by step through creating your own Web page and placing it in the C:\Inetpub\Webpub folder to publish it.

Here are the generic instructions for using the Web Page Wizard to create a Web site.

1. From the File menu in Word, choose New.

2. In the New dialog box, click the Web Pages tab, shown in Figure 15-15.

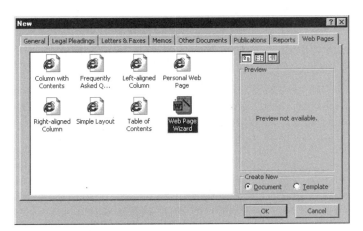

Figure 15-15.
Click the Web Pages tab to access the Web Page Wizard.

3. On the Web Pages tab, double-click the Web Page Wizard icon to begin a series of wizard pages.

4. Read the information on the first page of the wizard, and then click Next to see the page shown in Figure 15-16.

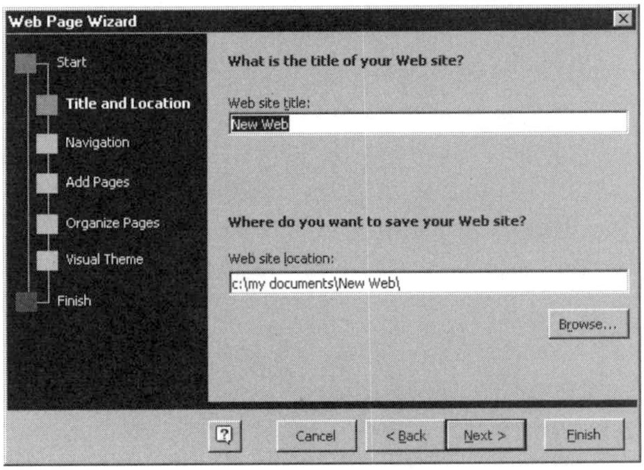

Figure 15-16.
This Web Page Wizard page allows you to set the title and location of your Web site.

5. Enter the title for the Web page and specify the location where you want it stored—usually C:\Inetpub\Webpub.

6. Click Next to see the options shown in Figure 15-17.

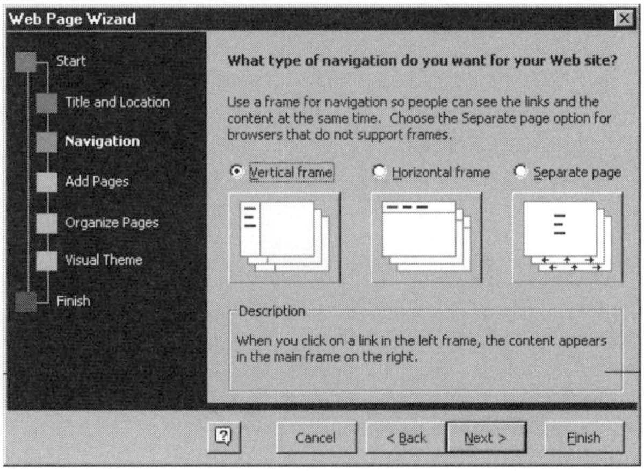

Figure 15-17.

Select the layout of your Web page from the options in this window.

You can select one of three navigation methods for your home page and the other pages you add to the Web site. The page can have hyperlinks in a vertical or horizontal frame, or it can have navigation buttons that link to other pages you add.

7. Select a navigation method, and click Next. You can now add more pages to the Web site, as shown in Figure 15-18.

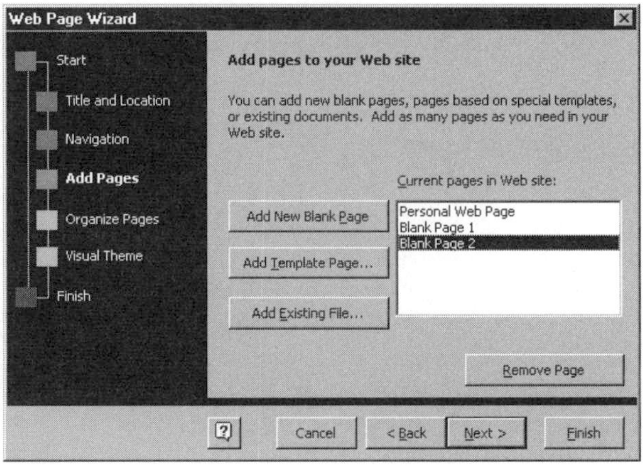

Figure 15-18.

The wizard allows you to add blank pages or template pages to your Web site.

The default option is a configuration of a Personal Web Page and two blank pages—Blank Page 1 and Blank Page 2. You can add additional blank pages or pages designed according to templates provided by the wizard.

8. Clicking Add Blank Page immediately adds a blank page to the Web site, but if you want to add a template page, click Add Template Page to see the list of templates shown in Figure 15-19. When you click a template in this list, a sample of the page appears in the background.

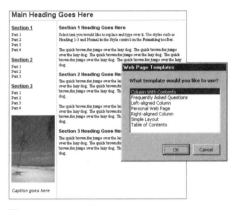

Figure 15-19.
Choose a page template from the list of templates.

9. When you've completed adding pages, click Next. You can now change the sequence of pages by selecting a page and then clicking the Move Up or Move Down button.

10. Click Next to display the next page of the wizard, which allows you to add a theme to your Web site, as shown in Figure 15-20.

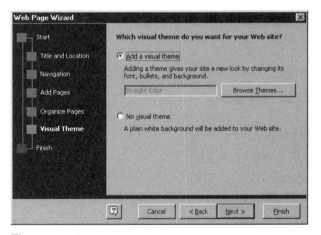

Figure 15-20.
Add a visual theme to your Web site.

11. To add a theme, select the Add A Visual Theme option, and then click Browse Themes to choose the theme.

Only some of the themes in the list are installed with Office 2000 when you perform the typical installation. If you select a theme that isn't installed, a message appears prompting you to install the theme at this time. Insert your Office 2000 CD into the CD-ROM drive and click Install.

12. From the list of themes, select a theme, such as Artsy or Blends, and then click OK.

13. Click Finish to display the Web page on the screen, as shown in Figure 15-21.

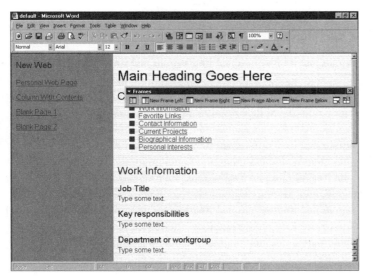

Figure 15-21.
After you add a visual theme to your Web page, click Finish to view the page.

Word adds sample text as a placeholder until you enter your own text on the page. Now you need to fill in only the sample text areas. You can click a link to another page or a topic to move to that page.

Now It's Your Turn

Now that you've read how easy it is to use the Web Page Wizard to create a Web site, here's a step-by-step example you can try to create a Web page for yourself. Just follow these steps:

1. Start Word.

2. From the File menu, choose New. Don't click the New Blank Document button on the Standard toolbar.

3. In the New dialog box, click the Web Pages tab and then double-click the Web Page Wizard icon.

4. Click Next.

5. Enter a title for your Web page. I've entered *Alan's Family Website*, but I'm sure you can be more creative.

6. Type *C:\Inetpub\Webpub* as the location for the Web site.

7. Click Next to select a navigation method.

8. Click the Horizontal Frame option button, and then click Next.

9. Click Next to accept the default number of pages, and click Next again to accept the default order of pages. You're now given the option of adding a visual theme.

10. Click the Browse Themes button to display the list of themes.

11. Select Blueprint in the Choose A Theme list, and then click OK.

12. Click Next and then click Finish to display your Web page, as shown in Figure 15-22.

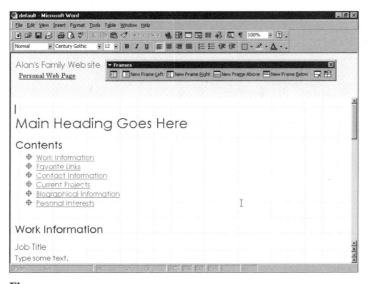

Figure 15-22.
The Web page you've created with the Home Page Wizard.

Working with Web Pages

Your Web page appears in Word's Web Layout view. In Web Layout view, your document appears just as it will when it's displayed in a Web browser. To actually use a browser to view your Word document, you can select Web Page Preview from the File menu. Office launches your Web browser, without connecting you to the Internet, and displays the document. Just close the browser to return to Word.

In Web Layout view, you also see the Frames toolbar. You can use this toolbar to change the way your page is divided into frames. A *frame* is a separate section of the page that contains its own text and hyperlinks, and it scrolls independently from the text in other frames. You won't be using the Frames toolbar in this example because your page already contains two frames, so click the toolbar's Close button to remove it from the screen.

When you're working in Web Layout view, you can continue formatting the document by using Word's formatting commands. To change the theme, for example, choose Theme from the Format menu to see the Theme dialog box shown in Figure 15-23. Choose the theme you want to apply, and then click OK.

Figure 15-23.
Choose a theme in the Theme dialog box to change the look of your Web page.

In the Theme dialog box, you can also apply various templates, which automatically format your text. Click the Style Gallery button in the Theme dialog box to display the Style Gallery dialog box shown in Figure 15-24.

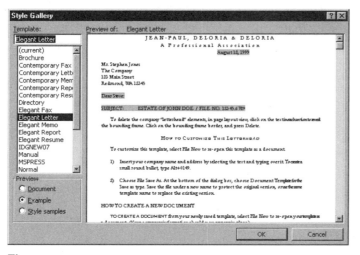

Figure 15-24.
Select a new style for your text from the Style Gallery dialog box.

Each template listed in the dialog box contains a collection of text formats that will be applied to certain areas of the document, such as titles, subtitles, and body text. To see how a template will affect your document, click a template in the list of templates, and then select the Document option in the Preview section. Your document will appear in the Preview Of panel. You can also select Example to see a sample document that uses most of the styles, or you can select Style Samples to see the name of each style set in that style. Click OK in the dialog box to apply the template to your document.

Of course, the sample text on the Web page isn't exactly what you'd like for your own family home page. So you can start changing it by beginning with the text of the headlines and then adjusting the hyperlinks.

1. Select the headline Main Heading Goes Here, and type *Get All of the News Here!*

2. Select the headline Work Information, not the underlined link, and type Family Vacation.

3. Select the next six lines, between Family Vacation and Back To Top, and replace them with some information about your most recent family trip.

You can leave the Favorite Links section as it is for now. You'll add several hyperlinks later.

4. Select the heading Contact Information and type *How to Reach Me*.

5. Select the next six lines, between How to Reach Me and Back To Top, and replace them with your daytime telephone number.

6. Now for the sake of brevity, delete the remainder of the text, from the heading Current Projects to the end of the document.

Working with Hyperlinks

It's now time to tackle the hyperlinks on the page. Go back to the top of the page where you see a series of six underlined hyperlinks, from Work Information to Personal Interest. You want to adjust the links for the new text.

1. Select the last three links and press Delete to remove them. You can't click a link to select its text because clicking a link actually goes to its associated location in the document or Web page.

2. To change the text of the Work Information link, right-click it, point to Hyperlink on the shortcut menu that appears, and select Edit Hyperlink to see the Edit Hyperlink dialog box shown in Figure 15-25.

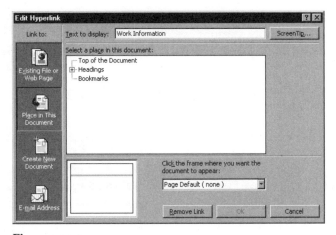

Figure 15-25.
Editing a hyperlink.

3. Change the text in the Text To Display text box from Work Information to Family Vacation. You now have to specify which heading in the document that clicking the link will jump to because you deleted the original heading, Work Information.

4. Click the plus sign next to Headings to see the item Get All of the News Here!

5. Click the plus sign next to Get All of the News Here! to see a list of the subheadings on the page.

6. Click Family Vacation, and then click OK.

When someone clicks the Family Vacation link in a browser, the section of the page starting with the heading Family Vacation will automatically scroll to the top of the page. Clicking the Back To Top link will scroll the window back to display the top of the page.

7. Change the Contact Information link so it reads How to Reach Me, and link it to the How to Reach Me heading.

Now it's time to add your favorite Web pages to the Favorite Links section.

1. Scroll to the Favorite Links section of the page.

2. Select the first line, Insert A Hyperlink Here, and then click the Hyperlink button on the toolbar, which looks like a globe with a link of chain.

3. In the Insert Hyperlink dialog box, click Existing File Or Web Page to display the options shown in Figure 15-26. The Web site addresses shown in the list depend on the links you last inserted using Office.

4. In the Text To Display text box, type the text that will be the link.

5. In the Type The File Or Web Page Name text box, enter the address of a favorite Web site, such as *http://www.westerns.com*. If you don't know the address of the site, you can click Web Page in the Browse For section to go online and locate the site.

6. Click OK to close the Insert Hyperlink dialog box.

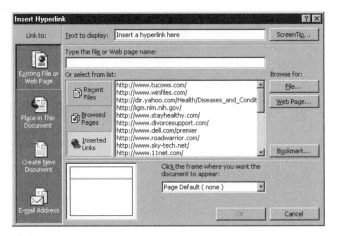

Figure 15-26.

Inserting a hyperlink.

Now let's add a link to a document that you've already created and saved on your disk.

1. Select the second line, Insert A Hyperlink Here, and then click the Hyperlink button on the toolbar.

2. In the Insert Hyperlink dialog box, click the Recent Files button to display a list of recently opened files. If the document you want to link to isn't shown, you can type its path and name, or click File in the Browse For section to locate the document.

3. In the Text To Display text box, type the name of a document.

4. Click one of the documents in the list of recent files, and then click OK.

When someone clicks this hyperlink, the linked document will open. Now let's add a link to a Web site that you've recently visited with your Web browser.

1. Select the third line, Insert A Hyperlink Here, and then click the Hyperlink button on the toolbar.

2. In the Insert Hyperlink dialog box, click the Browsed Pages button to display a list of recently visited Web sites.

3. In the Text To Display box, type the name of the Web site.

4. Click the site you want in the list of browsed pages, and then click OK.

Note

To add additional hyperlinks to your Web page, just type text where you want the link to appear. Select the text, click the Hyperlink button on the toolbar, and create the link the way you've just learned.

The Web page also has hyperlinks in the top frame. These links jump to the pages of the Web site and return to the page that serves as the site's home page, Personal Web Page. Let's change the text of these links and then look at one of these other pages.

1. Right-click the link Blank Page 1, point to Hyperlink on the shortcut menu, and click Edit Hyperlink to open the Edit Hyperlink dialog box.

2. In the Text To Display text box, change the text from Blank Page 1 to Family News, and then click OK.

3. Now click the Family News link to open the Web page.

The Family News page has the same upper frame as the Personal Web Page but the lower frame contains only the text This Web Page Is Blank Page 1. The actual name of the file in which the page is stored is Blank Page 1.htm. You can leave the filename the same, because it's the content of the page that you're interested in.

You can now add and format any text and hyperlinks that you want to appear on the Family News page. When you're done designing the page, click the link Personal Web Page to return to the site's home page. Using the same procedure, you can change the text of the link Blank Page 2 and the contents of that page.

Adding Graphics

Office also includes a collection of graphics called ClipArt, which you can use to illustrate your Web pages. To insert a ClipArt graphic, follow these steps:

1. Click the Personal Web Page link to display the home page.

2. Click in the document to place the insertion point where you want the graphic to appear.

3. From the Insert menu, point to Picture, and then click ClipArt to display the Insert ClipArt dialog box shown in Figure 15-27.

Figure 15-27.

The Insert ClipArt dialog box allows you to view and select graphics for your Web pages.

4. Click a category to display the ClipArt choices in that category.

5. Click the graphic you want and then click one of the four options on the short-cut menu:

- **Insert Clip** places the ClipArt selection in the document.

- **Preview Clip** displays the ClipArt selection in a separate window.

- **Add Clip To Favorites Or Other Category** adds the clip to the Favorites category, where you can keep the clips you use most often. It also lets you place a copy in a different category.

- **Find Similar Clips** displays ClipArt selections that are similar in theme to the clip you've chosen.

You can also insert a graphic from your hard disk, perhaps a picture that you downloaded from the Internet. To do so, point to Picture on the Insert menu and click From File to open the Insert Picture dialog box. Locate the picture you want to insert, and then click the down arrow on the Insert button to pull down the Insert list and choose from these options:

- **Insert** places the graphic in the document so that it will be saved within the Word file.

- **Link To File** saves a link to the graphic in the Word file, but not the graphic itself. This option reduces the size of the file and lets you use graphics that you might want to change later. When you open the document, Word automatically displays the current version of the graphic that's on your hard disk.

- **Insert And Link** inserts the graphic and saves a link to it. The graphic is actually saved in the Word file.

After you insert a graphic in a document, you can customize it in a number of ways. To work with a picture, click it so that small boxes, called *handles*, surround it. The Picture toolbar also appears, as shown in Figure 15-28. If the Picture toolbar doesn't appear, right-click any other toolbar and choose Picture from the shortcut menu.

Figure 15-28.
Use the tools on the Picture toolbar to customize an inserted graphic.

To delete a picture from your document, select it and then press Delete or choose Clear from the Edit menu. If you have selected a picture and no longer want it selected, click elsewhere in the document.

To change the size of a picture, place the mouse pointer on one of the handles so that the pointer changes to a two-headed arrow, and then drag the handle. Which handle you drag depends on how you want to change the picture's dimensions (a dotted box will show the size of the picture as you drag):

- Drag the handle on the left or right side to change only the width of the picture.

- Drag the handle on the top or bottom to change only the height of the picture.

- Drag a corner handle to change the height and width of the picture while maintaining its original proportions.

Just to see the number of files that make up a Web site, you can open the C:\Inetpub\Webpub folder. You'll see all the files shown in Figure 15-29. You'll also see a separate folder containing the graphic elements that were part of the theme for each of the pages, a separate file for each frame, and a file for each page. All the files are linked together by the hyperlinks on the page.

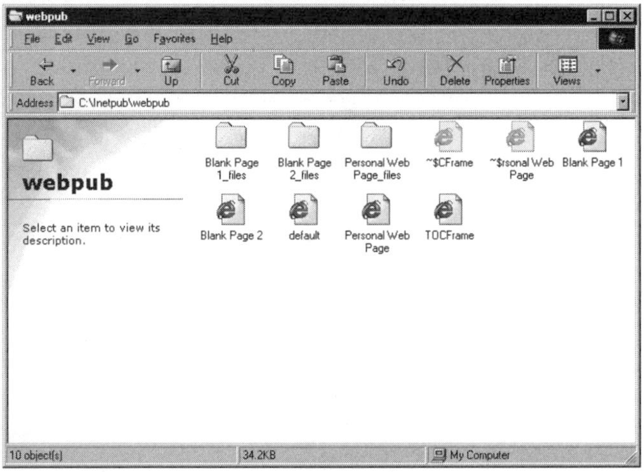

Figure 15-29.

The files that comprise a typical Web site created in Word.

To view the Web page you created in Word and access all its links, click the View My Published Documents link on your PWS home page, and then click the link for default.htm.

We've just touched on the formatting features of Word that you can use to create your Web site. By using other formatting techniques and features, such as WordArt, you can develop your Web page further, as shown in Figure 15-30.

Figure 15-30.
A formatted Web page in Word.

Converting a Word Document to a Web Page

If you've already created a document that you'd like to add to your Web site but it isn't in HTML format, you can easily convert it to a Web page. Just follow these steps:

1. Open a document that you've typed and formatted.

2. From the File menu, choose Save As Web Page.

3. In the Save As dialog box, click in the Save In box and locate the C:\Inetpub\Webpub folder.

4. In the File Name text box, enter the filename you want for the Web page.

5. Click Save.

   Word converts the document to Web page format and displays it in Web Layout view. A message appears whenever there are Word formats in the document that don't have HTML equivalents. Click OK to convert the document anyway. The file will be stored in the C:\Inetpub\Webpub folder so it can be accessed using the View My Published Documents link on your PWS home page.

   Home Web pages are a great way to share information over your computer network. But when you're away from home on a business trip, vacation, or perhaps at school, you can still keep in touch with the family network, as you'll discover in Chapter 17.

   In the next chapter, you'll learn how to include PCs and Apple Macintosh computers in the same network.

Chapter 16

Networking PCs and Macs

Many families these days have both Windows and Apple Macintosh (Mac) computers in the home. Although the two types of computers are quite different, fortunately, they can be connected on the same network. Windows and Mac users can share files, printers, and an Internet connection.

In this chapter, you'll learn how to add Mac computers to your Windows network, or vice versa. Any Mac with an Ethernet port works because the port is totally compatible with Ethernet hubs and switches on your Windows network. The popular Apple iMac computer—and all other new Macs, in fact—even come with an Ethernet port built in so you don't need to install an Ethernet card or worry about add-in adapters.

Planning for Networking

There are two major steps in networking a Mac with a Windows computer: configuring the protocols and sharing and accessing resources. Setting up and configuring a protocol will enable the Mac to send and receive signals that are compatible with the other computers on the network using the same protocol. Mac computers use three main protocols: AppleTalk, TCP/IP (Transmission Control Protocol/Internet Protocol), and IPX (Internetwork Packet Exchange).

AppleTalk is the original protocol developed for Apple computers, and it's usually used for an all-Mac network. The protocol is easy to set up and can be used to network older Mac computers to the newer models.

TCP/IP is the protocol that the Internet and many Windows networks use. Macs include TCP/IP support through a control panel. Most Windows computers can run several instances of TCP/IP at the same time—one TCP/IP for connecting to the Internet and another for the network, for example.

Mac computers, on the other hand, use one instance of TCP/IP at a time. So if you use TCP/IP, you might not be able to connect to the Internet through your Mac's modem and share files over the network at the same time. You can get around this limitation, however, by letting your Mac connect to the Internet via the network using Internet Connection Sharing.

And finally, the IPX protocol on the Mac is used primarily to connect to Novell Netware networks but might be required in Mac networks to play some multiple-player games such as Doom II and Netmech.

The Windows and Mac operating systems and file structures are totally different. Therefore, just because the protocol is set up for a physical connection doesn't mean that either machine will be able to access the resources on the other. In fact, neither type of computer can even recognize that the other is on the network.

To actually communicate with each other and share resources, you'll need to use one of two techniques:

- Install software on one of the machines to make it compatible with the others.
- Share files using a Web browser by using your Mac and Windows computers as Web servers.

The software solution takes one of two approaches. In one technique, you install a program on the Mac that enables it to be part of a Windows network using TCP/IP. In the other approach, you install a program on the Windows computer that enables it to be part of a Mac network using AppleTalk. In both cases, all the computers on the network will then be able to share disks and files, communicate, and perhaps even share printers.

MacIPX

The software to use IPX on a Mac, known as MacIPX, isn't included with the Mac operating system. If you want to use the IPX protocol, you have to download it from the Internet. It's available at many locations, including *http://www.prosofteng.com/ download.asp.*

Because the IPX protocol isn't included with the Mac, it's not covered in this chapter. However, if you're interested in learning more about MacIPX networking, check out these sites on the Internet:

- *http://www.macledge.com/netgames/configIPX.html*
- *http://ftp.cioe.com/~galanti/mac.html*

The software solution you choose depends on the number of Windows and Mac computers in your home. If you have only one Mac and one Windows machine, for example, either solution is just as effective. If you have several of one type of computer and just one of the other, however, you should choose the solution that requires you to install less software.

For instance, if you have one Mac and several Windows computers, select the Mac-based software. This way, you have to install the program only on the Mac. On the other hand, if you have one Windows computer and several Macs, choose the Windows-based software. This way, you have to install the program only on the Windows machine.

If you want to share files without purchasing additional software, consider the Web-server approach. In this solution, you configure your Mac as a Web server and connect it to the network using TCP/IP. Any other computer on the network that also uses TCP/IP can then access the Mac using a Web browser. This solution is limited only to file sharing, however, and no other network services.

Because the setup and configuration of the protocol depends on the solution that you choose, we'll look at three kinds of Mac and Windows networking solutions: Mac-based networks, Windows-based networks, and Web-server networks.

Files That Can Be Shared

While you can easily network a Mac and Windows computer and make their files available to each other, not all types of files can be shared.

Program files designed for one type of computer can't be run on the other. If you download a program that runs under Windows, for example, you won't be able to run it on the Mac, and vice versa. Many programs, however, come in both Windows and Mac versions. With some programs, both versions will come on the same CD, but with others, you might have to purchase separate versions for each type of computer.

You can use most graphic files on both types of computers. If you have a JPEG or GIF graphic on one computer, for example, you'll be able to copy it and display it on the other. One popular Mac graphics format, known as PIC or PICT, isn't supported by most Windows programs, but you can download programs that will display these graphics formats on your Windows computer.

You can open plain text files on either computer, as well as Web pages in the HTML format using a Web browser. Other types of files depend on the programs you've installed. Microsoft Office, for example, comes in both Windows and Mac versions. If you have Office installed on both computers, you can share Word documents, Excel worksheets, PowerPoint presentations, and Access databases.

DAVE: A Mac-Based Solution

If you have one Mac that you'd like to connect to a Windows network, consider the program DAVE, from Thursby Software Systems, Inc., at *http://www.thursby.com*. The program is remarkably easy to set up and requires no special configuration or setup on the Windows computers on the network.

DAVE configures your Mac so it appears on the network as another Windows computer. You'll be able to share files, access the Mac from the Windows computers, and even place a shortcut to network resources on the Mac desktop. You'll also be able to share a PostScript printer that's connected to Windows computers. PostScript is a language used by some printers. *If you want to share a non-PostScript printer, see the section "Sharing a Windows Printer," later in this chapter.*

To use DAVE, you have to configure TCP/IP on your Mac, and then install and configure the DAVE program.

Note

To connect to a Mac computer running the DAVE software, your Windows computers should be configured to use TCP/IP with static IP addresses. Refer to Chapter 8, "Installing the Software," for details on setting up TCP/IP.

Configuring TCP/IP on the Mac

You can set up TCP/IP as part of installing and configuring DAVE. In this chapter, however, you'll first learn how to manually configure TCP/IP on the Mac for a peer-to-peer home network. Just follow these steps:

1. Open the Apple menu, point to Control Panels, and click TCP/IP to open the TCP/IP control panel, as shown in Figure 16-1.

   Let's assume that you already have your Mac set up for connecting to the Internet, so you'll see the TCP/IP settings for your Internet service provider (ISP). You have to add and configure a new instance of TCP/IP to use for your network connection. If you're not using TCP/IP for the Internet, skip ahead to step 7 to configure the existing default setting.

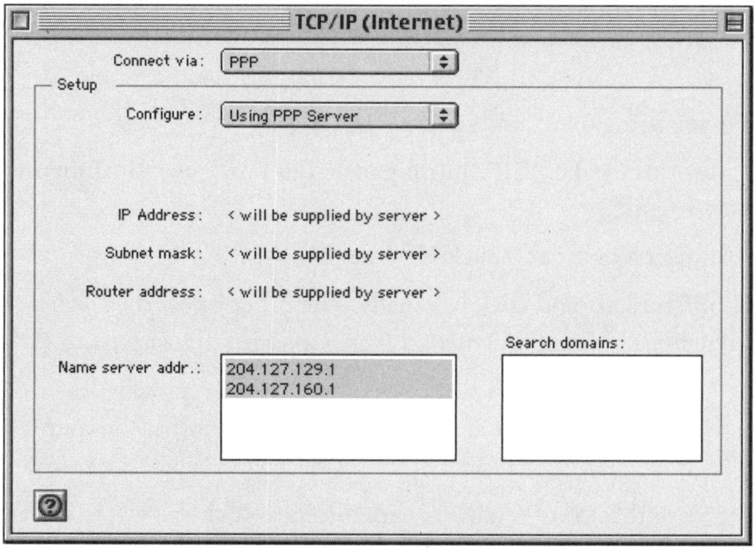

Figure 16-1.
The TCP/IP Control Panel.

2. Choose Configurations from the File menu to open the Configurations window, shown in Figure 16-2.

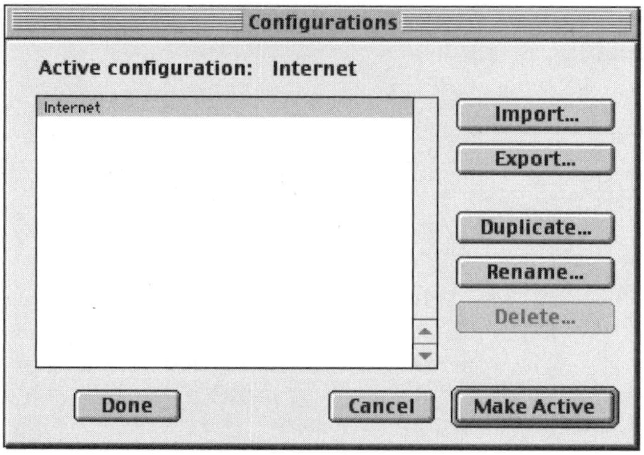

Figure 16-2.
Configuring TCP/IP for networking.

3. Select the default active configuration and then click the Duplicate button. A box appears in which you can change the name of the copy.

4. Type a name to identify the setting for your network, such as *Network,* and then click OK.

5. Select the setting you just created and click Make Active.

6. Click Done to return to the TCP/IP control panel. You now have to configure TCP/IP for your network.

7. Pull down the Connect Via list and click Ethernet Built-In.

8. Pull down the Configure list and click Manually. The other options let you assign the IP address dynamically using a Dynamic Host Configuration Protocol (DHCP) server.

9. Enter a valid network IP address not already being used by another computer on the network.

10. Enter the subnet mask that your Windows network uses, such as 255.255.255.0.

11. Delete any addresses in the Router Address and Name Server boxes that might be left over from the Internet configuration. The completed configuration appears as in Figure 16-3.

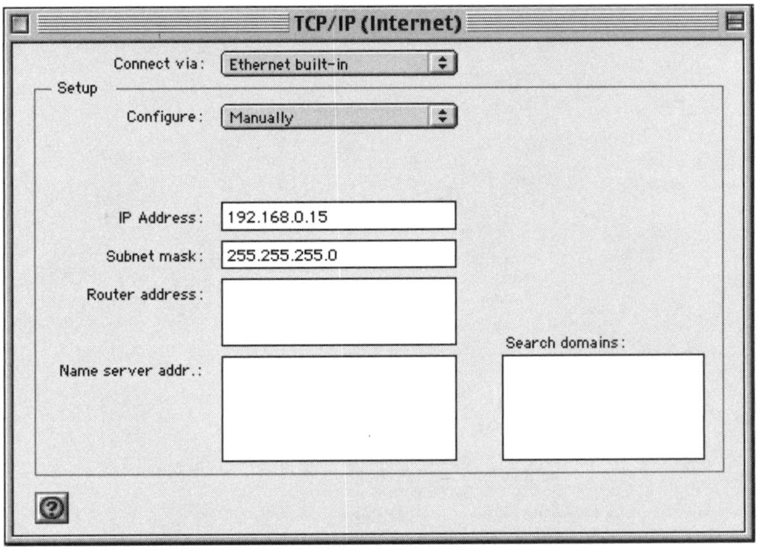

Figure 16-3.
Network configuration for TCP/IP.

12. Close the TCP/IP control panel and click Save when prompted.

Switching TCP/IP Configurations

You now have two TCP/IP settings. When you want to connect to the Internet using your Mac's modem, you'll need to make the TCP/IP that's configured for your ISP the default. To connect to the network again, you'll need to make the TCP/IP that's configured for your network the default. To select which configuration you want, follow these steps:

1. Open the TCP/IP control panel.

2. Choose Configurations from the File menu.

3. Select the configuration you want to use and click Make Active.

4. Click Done and close the TCP/IP control panel.Installing DAVE

Installing DAVE

The next step is to install DAVE software. Insert the DAVE CD, run the DAVE installer (Install DAVE), and follow the directions that appear on the screen.

1. After your Mac restarts, the DAVE Setup Assistant program begins, as shown in Figure 16-4. Click the right arrow at the bottom right of the window to move from page to page.

Figure 16-4.
The DAVE Setup Assistant program.

2. The next page asks whether you want to configure TCP/IP. Because you just configured it, select the option TCP/IP Is Already Configured, and then click the right arrow.

3. The next page asks for your name, organization, and license code provided on the DAVE license and registration form. Enter the information and click the right arrow.

4. The page asks whether you're using Windows NT Server. Click No, and then click the right arrow.

5. Enter a name that the Mac will have on the Windows network, called the *NetBIOS name*. The name can be up to 15 characters and must not already be used by another computer on the network. Enter the name and click the right arrow.

6. You now have to specify the peer-to-peer workgroup being used by the network, as shown in Figure 16-5. The usual workgroup name is WORKGROUP, and it can be found on the Identification tab of the Network icon in Control Panel on a Windows computer. DAVE will display WORKGROUP by default. Change the name as needed, and then click the right arrow.

Figure 16-5.
Specify the network workgroup.

7. Enter a short description of your computer, such as *Alan's Mac*, and then click the right arrow.

8. The computer name, workgroup, and description appear. Click the right arrow if they're correct, or click the left arrow to go back and make changes.

9. You're now asked whether you want to share your files on the network. Select I Want To Set Up DAVE To Share My Local Files, and then click the right arrow to open the DAVE Sharing control panel, shown in Figure 16-6.

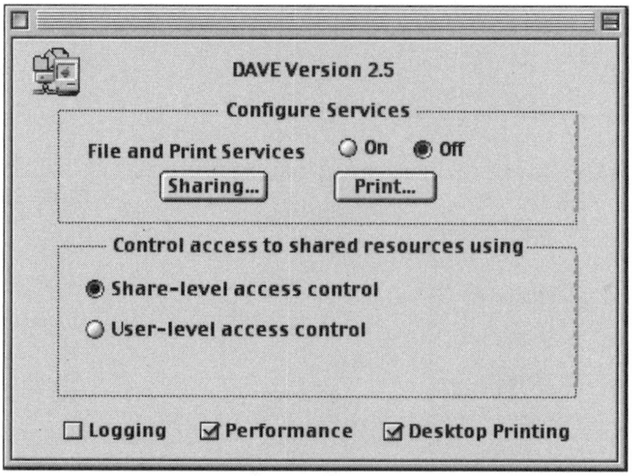

Figure 16-6.
The DAVE Sharing control panel.

Note

You can later share files or turn sharing off using the DAVE Sharing control panel from the Apple menu.

10. Click On to enable file and print services, and then click the Sharing button to see the Shared Resources dialog box.

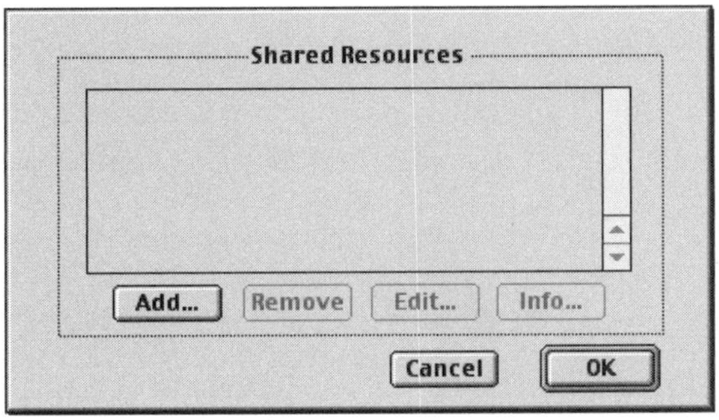

11. Click Add to see a list of resources on your Mac, as in Figure 16-7.

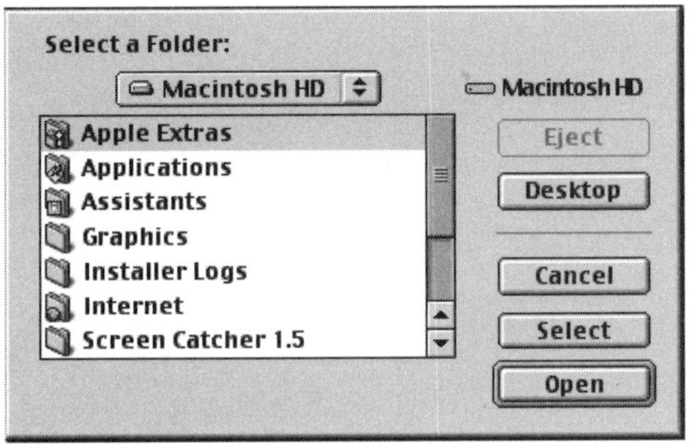

Figure 16-7.
Select a resource to share.

12. Select a folder you want to share, and click Select to open the Password box.

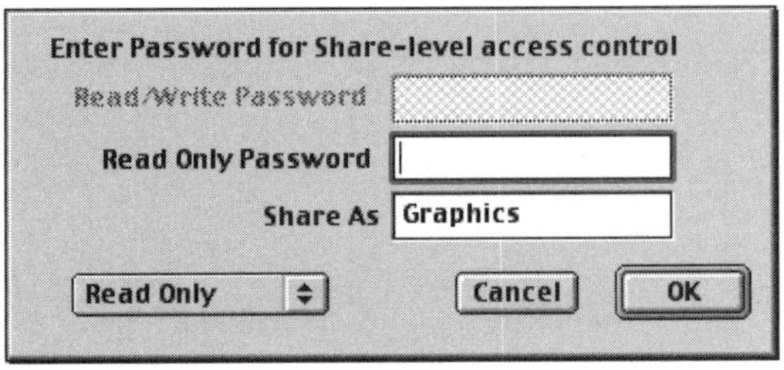

13. Pull down the list that says Read Only and choose the type of sharing: Read Only, Read/Write, or Both Passwords.

14. Enter a password if you want to use one.

15. Change the name in the Share As box if you want, and then click OK to return to the Shared Resources box. Repeat the steps to share any additional folders.

16. Click OK to return to the DAVE Sharing icon in Control Panel, and then select from these options:

- **Logging** creates a text file in the System folder that keeps track of who uses the shared folders.

- **Performance** allots CPU time to DAVE Sharing. If your network appears to be running slower with DAVE installed, clear the Performance option.

- **Desktop Printing** lets you share Mac desktop printers with the network.

17. Choose Share-Level Access Control. (Choose User-Level Access Control if you're on an NT network.)

18. Close the DAVE Sharing control panel to return to the DAVE Setup program, and then click OK.

You can always change the options or share other folders. Open the Apple menu, point to Control Panel, and click DAVE Sharing to open the DAVE Sharing control panel. Click OFF if you no longer want to make your files available on the network.

Accessing the Mac from a PC

Accessing the shared files on your Mac from a Windows machine is easy. Just open Network Neighborhood (or My Network Places in Microsoft Windows Millennium Edition and Microsoft Windows 2000) to see an icon for your Mac:

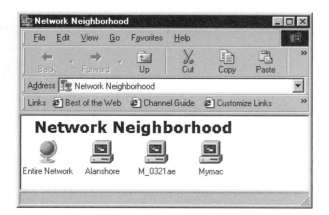

Note

Remember, a computer might take a few minutes to show up on Network Neighborhood or My Network Places. Rather than wait, however, you can use the Find or Search feature on the Start menu to locate a computer.

Double-click the icon to see the shared folders, and open a folder to access its files. You can now copy files in either direction or open files that are on the Mac.

Note

After copying a folder from your Mac to the Windows computer, you might see some new folders on your Windows computer, such as Resource.frk and DesktopFolderDB. Don't delete these folders—you'll need them if you decide to copy the original folder back to the Mac later.

Accessing the PC from a Mac

You can also access shared folders on a Windows machine from the Mac. In fact, there are two ways to do it:

- Browse the network to locate the folder.
- Mount the Windows resource as an icon on the Mac desktop.

Browsing the Network

Browsing the network means to display each computer on the network and then locate the disk and folders you want to access. To browse the network to access a folder, follow these steps:

1. Open the Apple menu and click DAVE to see a list of computers on the network, as shown in Figure 16-8.

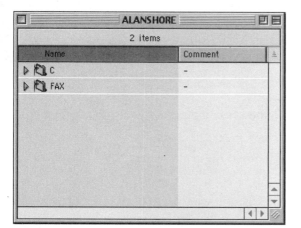

Figure 16-8.
Browsing the Windows network.

2. Double-click a computer to display its shared resources.

3. Double-click a folder to display its contents, as in Figure 16-9. You can now drag files from the list to your Mac desktop or a folder on your hard disk.

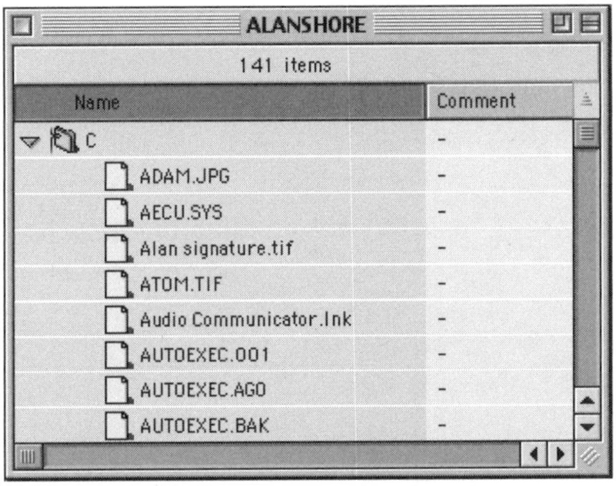

Figure 16-9.
The contents of a Windows folder.

Note

If you close the DAVE window, you can reopen it by choosing DAVE from the Application menu. If the browser window doesn't open when DAVE is shown on the Application menu, select Browse from the File menu and select one of the following options: Your Workgroup, Entire Network, or Location.

Mounting Resources

When you mount a resource, you place an icon for it on the Mac desktop. Mounting a disk drive on a Windows computer, for example, will display an icon for it on your Mac desktop so you can then access the drive by opening the icon, without the need to browse through the network to locate the resource.

You can mount a resource temporarily so it doesn't appear the next time you start your Mac, or you can mount the resource so it appears automatically each time you start your Mac and it's connected to the network.

To mount a shared drive from a Windows computer on your Mac desktop, follow these steps:

1. Open the Apple menu and click Chooser. An icon for the DAVE Client appears in the Chooser window.

2. Click the DAVE Client icon in the Chooser window to display the network resources in the Select A Server window, as shown in Figure 16-10.

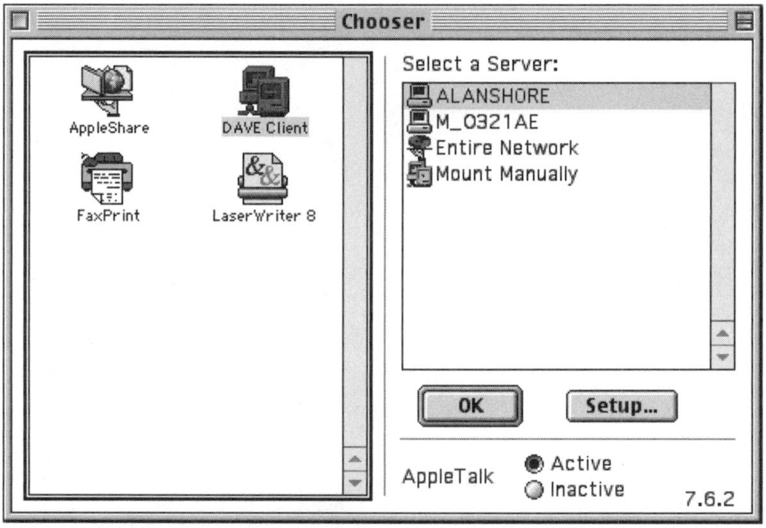

Figure 16-10.
The DAVE Client in the Chooser window.

3. Double-click the computer you want to mount to open its resource window, as in Figure 16-11.

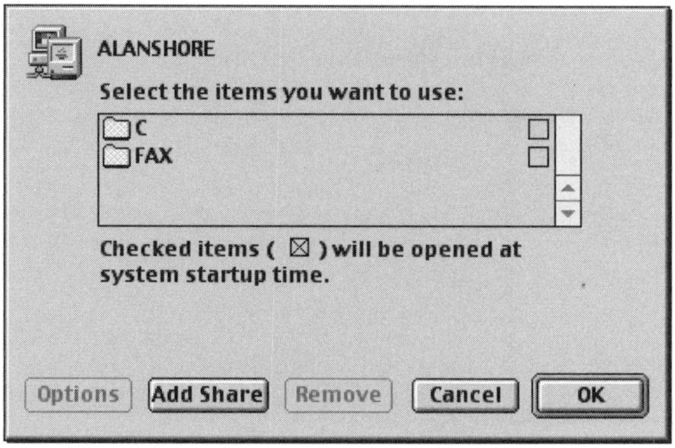

Figure 16-11.
Selecting the resource to mount.

4. Click the resource you want to mount.

5. Select the check box on the right for the resource if you want to mount it automatically when your Mac starts.

6. Click OK. An icon for the resources appears on the Mac desktop.

7. Double-click the icon to open its contents.

Communicating on the Network

DAVE includes a pop-up messaging feature that's compatible with the WinPopup program on Windows computers. Using DAVE and WinPopup, you can send and receive instant messages among network users.

Note

WinPopup must be running on the Windows computer. For a review of how to run WinPopup on Windows computers, see "Sending and Receiving Pop-up Messages," in Chapter 12, on page 251.

Here's how to use WinPopup. First, set DAVE to accept WinPopup messages from Windows computers by following these steps:

1. Open the Apple menu and click DAVE to open the DAVE browser.

2. Open the Edit menu and choose Messaging Preferences to open this box:

```
╔═══════════ DAVE Message Preferences ═══════════╗
║                                                 ║
║   Default name:  │ALAN NEIBAUER          │     ║
║  ┌ Message Reception ─────────────────────┐    ║
║  │ ☐ Display received messages            │    ║
║  │ ☐ Beep when message received           │    ║
║  │ ☐ Read messages aloud                  │    ║
║  │ ☑ Notify when names conflict           │    ║
║  └────────────────────────────────────────┘    ║
║              [ Cancel ]  [[ OK ]]               ║
║                                                 ║
╚═════════════════════════════════════════════════╝
```

3. Select the option Display Received Messages.

4. Choose Beep When Message Received if you want to hear a sound when a new message is received.

5. Choose Read Messages Aloud if you want the Mac voice feature to read the text of the message to you.

6. Click OK. An incoming message sent from a Windows computer will appear like this:

DAVE Message received from: ALAN NEIBAUER
Yes..the printer is ready.

Now when you want to send a message from the Mac to a Windows computer running WinPopup, follow these steps:

1. Open DAVE if it isn't already open. Open the Apple menu and choose DAVE.

2. Open the Access menu and choose New Message to open the window shown in Figure 16-12.

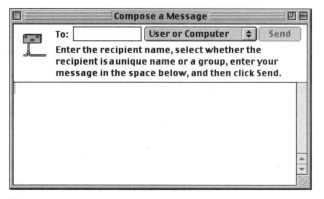

Compose a Message

To: [   ]   User or Computer ⬍   Send

Enter the recipient name, select whether the recipient is a unique name or a group, enter your message in the space below, and then click Send.

Figure 16-12.
Sending a message to another network user.

3. To send the message only to a specific computer, select User Or Computer in the second pull-down list, and then enter the user or computer name of the recipient in the To box. To send the message to everyone in the workgroup, select Workgroup in the list and enter the workgroup name if it doesn't automatically appear in the To box.

4. Enter the text of the message and click Send.

Sharing a Printer

Sharing printers across a Mac/Windows network is a little more complicated than sharing files. Using DAVE, you can share printers as long as all the printers use the PostScript method of printing. All printers designed for Macintosh systems use PostScript, so only PostScript printer drivers are provided with the Mac operating system.

To make a Mac printer available to Windows machines, follow these steps:

1. Open the Apple menu, point to Control Panels, and click DAVE Sharing to open the DAVE Sharing control panel.

2. Click Print in the DAVE Sharing control panel.

3. Click Add to open the Desktop Printers box.

4. Select the printer you want to share and click OK. You can now access the printer from a Windows computer.

See Also

To use a network printer in Windows, see "Accessing a Shared Printer," in Chapter 11, on page 241.

Letting the Mac access a printer connected to a Windows computer isn't as straight-forward as sharing a Mac printer with a Windows system. If the Windows computer uses a PostScript printer, you'll be able to access it from a Mac by following the instructions in the DAVE manual. You can also use a program or hardware device to share a Windows printer. *Sharing a Windows printer on the network is explained in the section "Sharing a Windows Printer," later in this chapter.*

A Windows-Based Solution

If your goal is to connect a Windows computer to a network that's primarily made up of Macs, consider a Windows-based software solution. You can choose from two excellent programs: TSStalk from Thursby Software Systems (*http://www.thursby.com*), and PC MACLAN from Miramar Systems (*http://www.pcmaclan.com*). Because we looked at Thursby's DAVE program in the last section, we'll discuss using PC MACLAN for a Mac/Windows network here.

Preparing Your Macintosh

Before you can connect your Mac to a Windows network running PC MACLAN, you have to set up your Mac for networking. If you have an AppleTalk network running between two or more Macs, the network is already set up. You just have to add the person who'll be networked on the Windows computer as a user and set his or her privileges. *If you have this setup, you can skip ahead to the section "Configuring File Sharing," later in this chapter.*

If you don't already have networking set up on the Mac, your first step is to follow the directions in the section "Configuring TCP/IP on the Mac" earlier in this chapter to assign your Mac an Internet Protocol (IP) address.

Setting Up AppleTalk

The next step is to set up AppleTalk on your Mac. AppleTalk is a popular protocol for all-Mac networks and the protocol used by the PC MACLAN program. Follow these steps on your Mac to set up AppleTalk:

1. Open the Apple menu and click Chooser to open the Chooser window, shown in Figure 16-13.

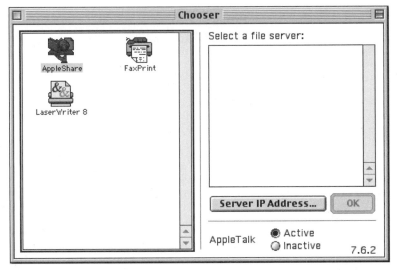

Figure 16-13.
Activate AppleShare in the Chooser window.

2. Click AppleShare.

3. Click the Active option button if it isn't already selected.

4. Close the Chooser window.

5. Open the Apple menu, point to Control Panels, and click AppleTalk to open the AppleTalk control panel.

6. Make sure that the Connect Via option is set at Ethernet Built-In.

7. Close the AppleTalk control panel.

Configuring File Sharing

Now you must identify your Mac on the network, determine who can access it on the network, and specify which resources can be shared. Follow these steps:

1. Open the Apple menu, point to Control Panel, and click File Sharing to open the dialog box shown in Figure 16-14.

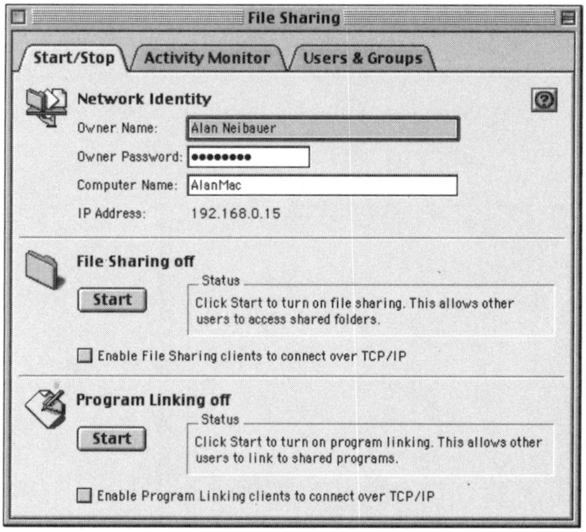

Figure 16-14.
File Sharing settings.

2. Click the Start/Stop tab if it isn't already selected.

3. Enter your name as the owner of the computer, type in your password, and enter a name for your computer that will appear to Windows users.

4. Click Start in the File Sharing section.

5. Select the option Enable File Sharing Clients To Connect Over TCP/IP.

Note

The option Enable File Sharing Clients To Connect Over TCP/IP is available only in version 9 and later of the Macintosh operating system.

6. Click the Users & Groups tab, shown in Figure 16-15.

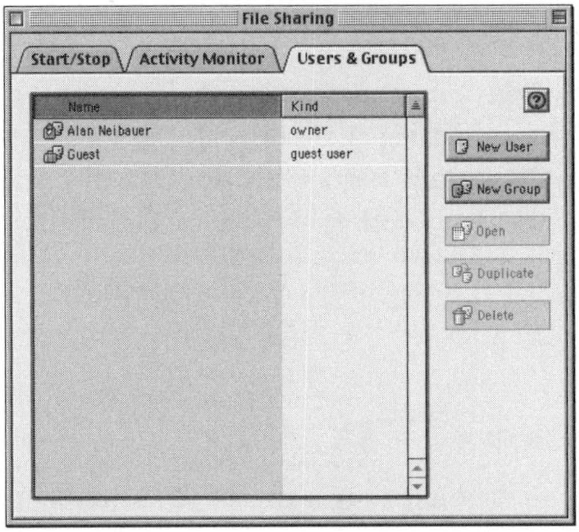

Figure 16-15.

Creating a user account.

7. Click New User to open the New User dialog box.

8. Choose Identity in the Show list if it isn't already selected.

9. Enter the name of a Windows user who'll be sharing the Mac files in the Name text box.

10. Specify a password the user will have to enter to access the Mac in the Password text box.

11. Close the New Users dialog box, and then close the File Sharing dialog box.

12. Click the Hard Drive icon on the desktop.

13. Open the File menu, point to Get Info, and click Sharing to open the window shown in Figure 16-16.

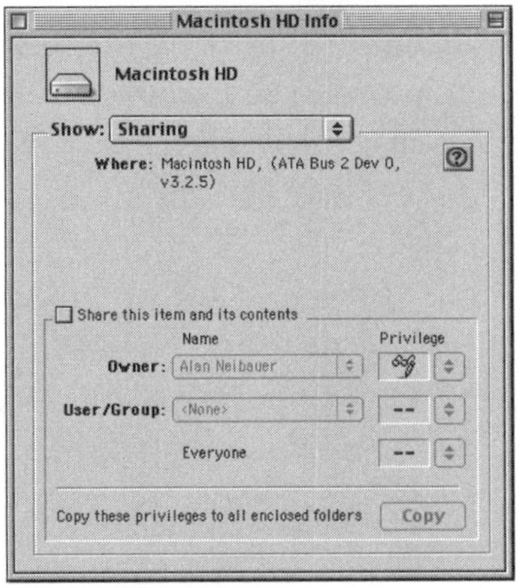

Figure 16-16.

Allowing your Mac hard drive to be shared on the network.

14. Select the check box labeled Share This Item And Its Contents.

15. If you want to assign privileges to everyone on the network, pull down the Privilege list next to Everyone and select the type of sharing allowed.

    The options are Read & Write, Read Only, Write Only, and None. You can also assign privileges to a specific user by choosing his or her name in the User/Group list and then setting privileges.

16. Close the window.

Using PC MACLAN in Windows

When you choose a Windows-based solution, you must perform two tasks on the Windows computer:

- Configure the computer to communicate using the AppleTalk protocol.

- Configure the computer to be an AppleTalk file server so that Macs can access its files.

    When you install PC MACLAN, you perform both of these tasks automatically. PC MACLAN adds the AppleTalk protocol to the Windows Network icon in Control Panel and binds it to your Ethernet network adapter. The installation program then restarts your computer.

Note

If you see an AppleTalk error message when you restart your computer, just click OK.

You can now access the shared drive on the Mac in almost the same way you can access files on any networked computer. Follow these steps:

1. Double-click Network Neighborhood on the Windows desktop. (Use My Network Places in Windows Me and Windows 2000.) You should see an icon for the Mac computer. If the icon doesn't appear in a few moments, double-click Entire Network and wait until the icon appears.

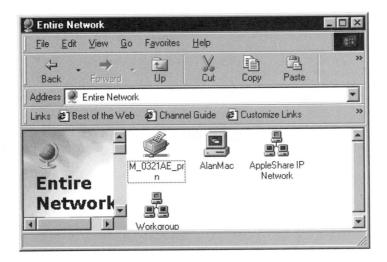

2. Double-click the icon for the Mac computer. You'll be asked for the user name and password that was specified for you as a Mac user.

3. Enter your user name.

4. Enter your password.

5. Click the option Save This Password In Your Password List if you don't want to enter the password each time you connect.

6. You'll now see an icon for the shared resource. Double-click the icon to open and access the folders and files being shared on the Mac, as shown in Figure 16-17.

Figure 16-17.

Available folders and files on the shared Mac drive.

Setting the PC MACLAN File Server

PC MACLAN also lets a Mac user access files on the Windows computer. To provide this capability, you have to first enable the File Server function of PC MACLAN on your Windows computer and then designate which Mac users have access to the Windows resources.

On a Windows computer on which you installed PC MACLAN, follow these steps to enable the file server:

1. Click Start, point to Programs and then PC MACLAN, and click File Server to open the dialog box shown here.

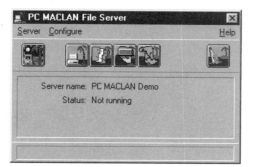

2. Click the Start Server button, the button on the far left of the File Server toolbar.

3. Click the Users & Groups button to open the Users & Groups window.

4. Click New under Users to open the dialog box shown in Figure 16-18.

Figure 16-18.
Creating a new user account.

5. Enter the name of the user's Mac.

6. Click Set Password to open the Password box.

7. Enter the user's password, press the Tab key, and retype the same password.

8. Click OK to return to the User dialog box.

9. Click Admin, All Privileges, or both, and leave the Can Login box selected.

10. Click OK and then click Done to return to the File Server box.

11. Click the Share Directories button to open the box shown in Figure 16-19.

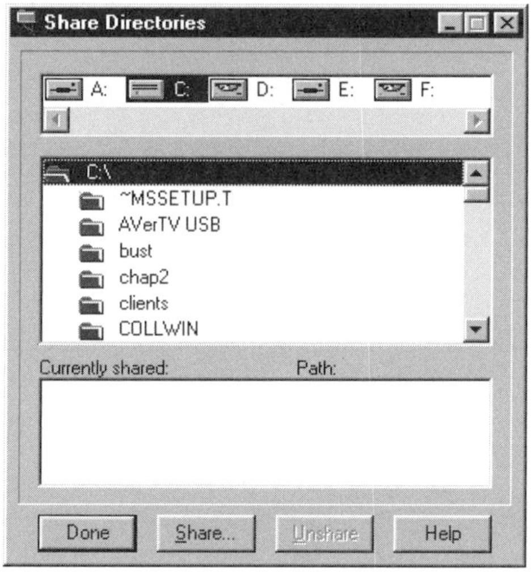

Figure 16-19.
Select a resource to share with the Mac.

12. Select the drive you want to share or a specific folder within a drive.

13. Click the Share button to open the Shared Directory box shown in Figure 16-20.

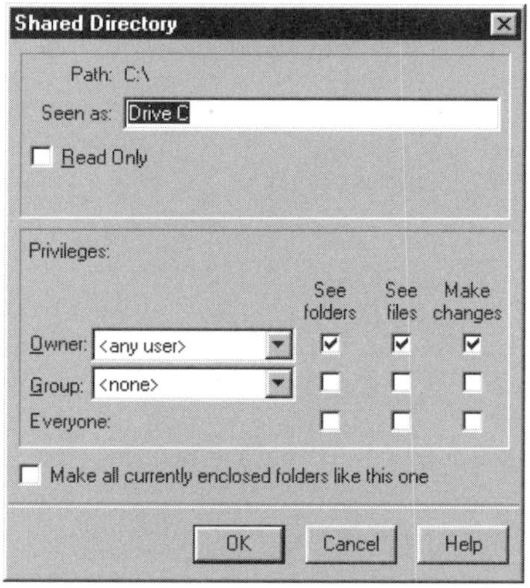

Figure 16-20.
Specifying share privileges.

14. Enter the name of the resource as it will appear on the Mac desktop.

15. Set the privileges for the Mac user. You can specify privileges for everyone or just for a specific group or user. To allow everyone to access the files, choose the options next to Everyone: See Folders, See Files, and Make Changes. To set privileges for a specific user, choose his or her name in the Group list and then determine the type of access.

16. Select the option Make All Currently Enclosed Folders Like This One to assign the same access to all folders.

17. Click OK.

18. A dialog box asks if you want to change all of the enclosed folders. Click Yes, and then click Done.

Connecting with the Mac

Your Windows computer is now ready to be accessed by the Mac. You can access the PC MACLAN file server just as you would any Mac file server on the network, using the Chooser. Follow these steps to access the PC MACLAN file server:

1. Open the Apple menu and click Chooser.

2. Click AppleShare to display a list of servers on the right as shown in Figure 16-21.

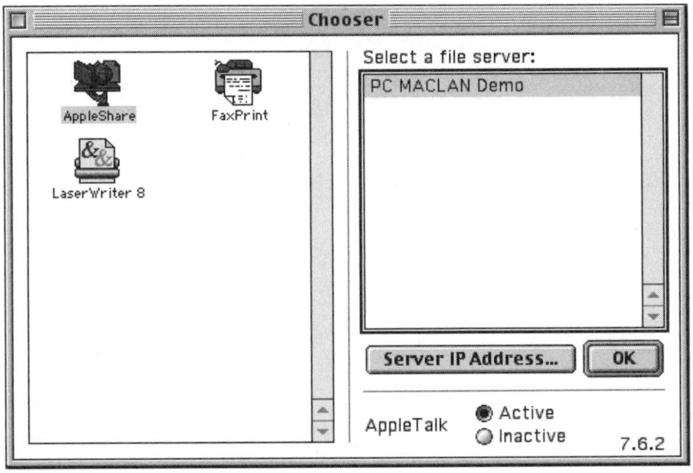

Figure 16-21.
Select the PC MACLAN file server in the Chooser window.

3. Click the PC MACLAN server name (it might take a moment for it to appear), and click OK to open this box:

Connect to the file server "PC MACLAN Demo" as:

○ Guest
● Registered User

Name: Alan Neibauer

Password: [   ]   ☐ Add to Keychain

2-way Encrypted Password

[Change Password...]   [Cancel]   [Connect]

3.8.6

4. Click the Registered User button.

5. Enter your user name and password.

6. Click Connect to see a list of the resources that are being shared by the PC MACLAN file server.

PC MACLAN Demo

Select the items you want to use:

Drive C   ☐

Checked items will be opened at system startup time

[Cancel]   [OK]

3.8.6

7. Click the resource to access.

8. Select the check box to the right of the resource to make it available each time you start your Mac.

9. Click OK and then close the Chooser window.

10. Now you'll see an icon for the PC MACLAN resource on the Mac desktop. Double-click the icon to access its folders and files.

You can also access the Windows resource using the Network Browser. Choose Network Browser from the Apple menu, and click the arrow next to AppleTalk in the box that appears to list the PC MACLAN file server. Click the arrow next to the file server name to display its shared resources.

The PC MACLAN Print Server

If you have a PostScript printer connected to your Windows computer, you can provide access to it from the Mac. PC MACLAN includes a separate print server program for setting up your printer on the AppleTalk network.

1. Click Start, point to Programs and PC MACLAN, and then click Print Server to open the dialog box shown in Figure 16-22.

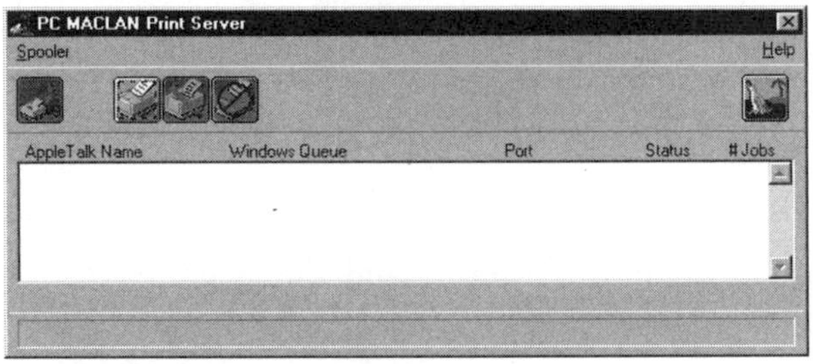

Figure 16-22.
Creating a print server on the Windows computer.

2. Click the Create New Spooler button to open the Spooler Configuration window shown in Figure 16-23.

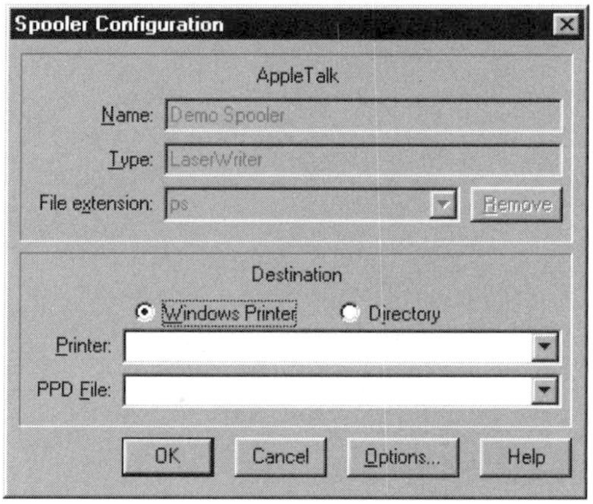

Figure 16-23.

Configuring a print spooler.

3. Pull down the Printer list and choose the printer that's attached to your computer.

4. Pull down the PPD File list and select the appropriate PPD file. The PPD file contains the driver information required to use the printer.

5. Click OK. A Mac user can now select the printer in the Chooser window the same way he or she would set up a printer attached to his or her own computer.

Once PC MACLAN is set up, you can use the file server to send an instant message to a Macintosh computer. Here's how:

1. Open the PC MACLAN file server.

2. Choose Connections from the Server menu.

3. Select the name of the person to whom you want to send a message.

4. Click Message.

5. Type the message and click Send. The message will appear on the Mac desktop.

Note

PC MACLAN doesn't provide a mechanism for the Macintosh to send an instant message to a Windows computer.

Sharing Files as a Web Server

If you don't want to purchase any additional software, you can still share your Macintosh files by setting up Web Sharing. The Web Sharing feature creates a Web server on the Macintosh and allows Windows users to access the Mac using their Web browser or a File Transfer Protocol (FTP) program.

Web Sharing also works both ways. If you set up Personal Web Server on a Windows computer, as you learned to do in Chapter 15, you can access the Windows Web site from a Mac by pointing the browser to the Windows machine's IP address. The Mac has complete access to the Web site.

To set up Web Sharing on your Mac, first make sure that file sharing is enabled for the folder you want to use as your Web server location. This is the location containing the files you want to share with Windows users. The default folder for Web Sharing is called Web Pages, but you can select any folder you want. Then follow these steps to set up Web Sharing on your Mac:

1. Open the Apple menu, point to Control Panels, and click Web Sharing to open the window shown in Figure 16-24.

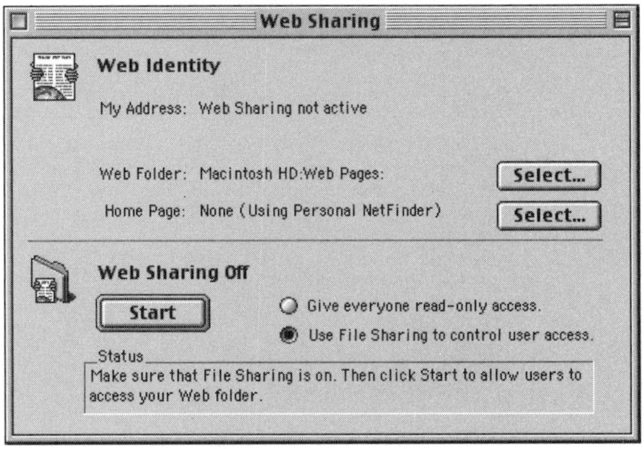

Figure 16-24.

Setting up Web Sharing.

Your computer's address is shown at the My Address prompt when Web Sharing is active. This is the address users will enter into their Web browser to access the Web Sharing folder.

2. To select another folder for the Web server location other than Web Pages, click the top Select button, choose the folder from the box that appears, and click Select.

3. If you want people to be able to read files but not change them, select Give Everyone Read-Only Access. If you want to provide full access, select Use File Sharing To Control Access, and then create user accounts in the File Sharing icon in Control Panel.

4. Click Start.

A person on a Windows computer can now start his or her Web browser and enter your computer's IP address to access the shared folder, as shown in Figure 16-25. If your Mac has the IP address of 192.168.0.15, for example, just enter *http://192.168.0.15* in the browser's address box and press Enter. Others on the network can also use FTP to transfer files from the Mac to their Windows machine.

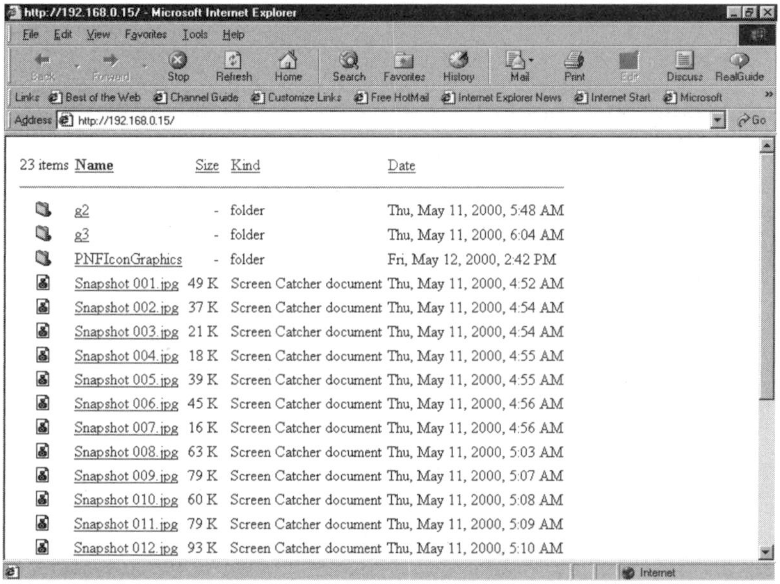

Figure 16-25.

A Mac folder shown in the browser.

Sharing a Windows Printer

As mentioned earlier, the Macintosh computer is designed to be used with PostScript printers connected to the Mac's serial or universal serial bus (USB) port. If your network is primarily made up of Windows computers, however, you probably have printers that aren't PostScript compatible and that use a parallel printer port. Using a non-PostScript parallel port printer with a Mac requires some additional software and hardware.

A company named Infowave (*http://www.infowave.com*) markets popular PowerPrint products that allow you to use a parallel printer with a Mac. The products include a set of Macintosh drivers for more than 1500 parallel printers and the hardware necessary to connect a parallel printer to your Mac. The drivers give your Mac the software capability to print documents and graphics on a Windows-compatible printer.

The PowerPrint Serial-to-Parallel kit includes a CD with the Mac printer drivers and a special cable that connects the printer's parallel port to the Macintosh serial port. The PowerPrint USB-to-Parallel kit includes the driver CD and a special cable that connects the Macintosh USB port to a parallel printer. Using either kit, you can connect the printer directly to your Mac.

PowerPrint for Networks is designed to share a Windows printer with the Mac and the Windows computers on the network. The product includes the driver CD as well as a network print server, like those discussed in Chapter 11. You connect the print server to your network hub or switch and the parallel port of your printer to a parallel connection on the print server.

When you install the software on your Macintosh, you choose the drivers for your Windows printer, as shown in Figure 16-26, and complete the installation process.

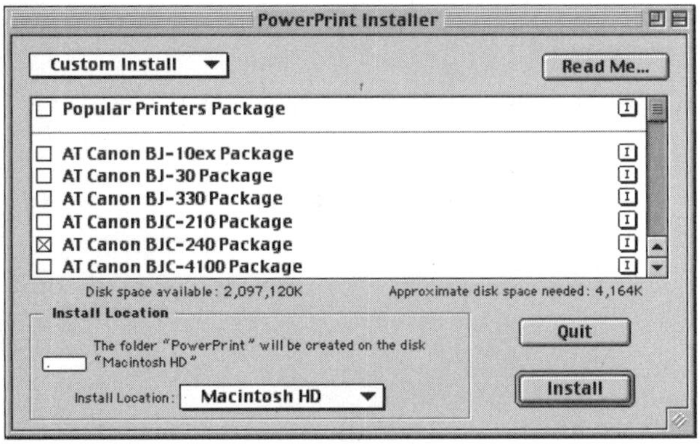

Figure 16-26.
Selecting a printer driver.

Now you'll see an icon for the printer in the Macintosh Chooser. Click the icon to see a listing for the print server in the Select A Printer list, like this:

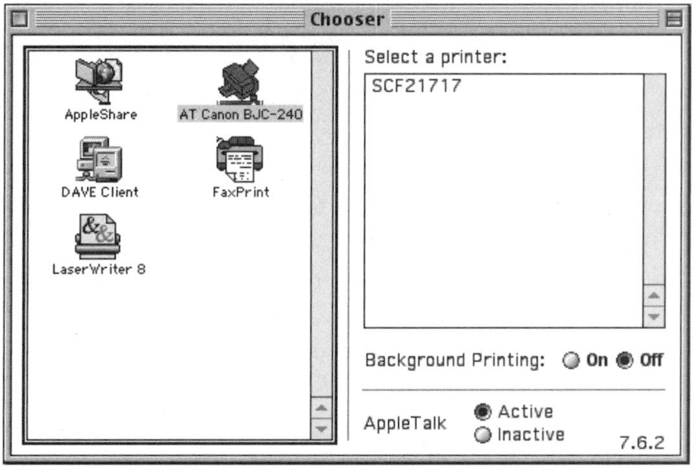

Select the print server and then close the Chooser window to use the printer as the default.

When you print a document, you'll see the Print dialog box shown here, although the options in the dialog box depend on your printer. Click Print to print your Mac document or graphic on the parallel printer attached to the network print server.

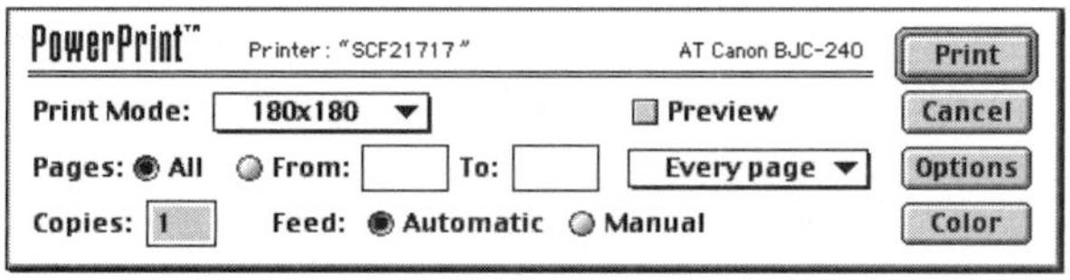

The PowerPrint print server is compatible with all popular network protocols—AppleTalk, TCP/IP, IPX/SPX, and NetBEUI—so you can configure Windows to access the print server as well. The installation CD includes a program named BiAdmin, shown in Figure 16-27, that lets you configure the server for connection to the Windows computer.

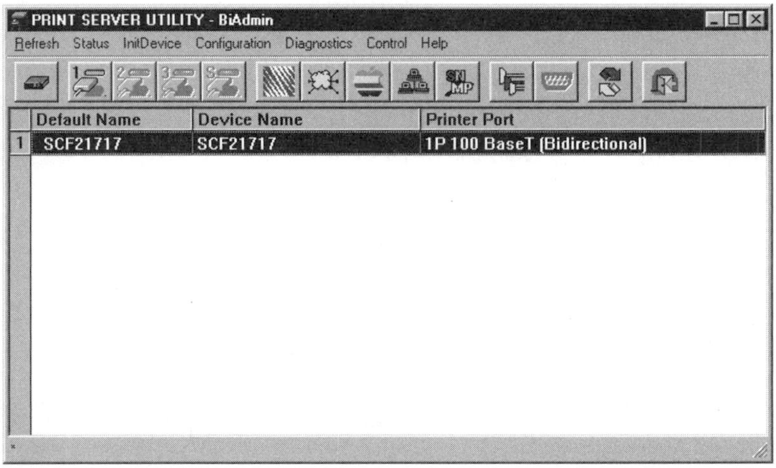

Figure 16-27.
Configuring the print server for Windows.

Notice that the device name in both the Macintosh Chooser and the Windows BiAdmin program is the same: in this case, SCF21717. You'll also find the device name on the bottom of the server.

> **Note**
>
> PowerPrint for Networks includes a Macintosh application called Infowave Name in the PowerPrint folder that lets you change the name of the print server.

The general procedure for configuring the server on a Windows computer using BiAdmin is as follows:

1. Open the InitDevice menu and choose Connected Protocol.

2. In the dialog box that appears, select the protocol you want to use to connect to the server from your Windows computer—TCP/IP, IPX/SPX, or NetBEUI.

3. Click OK.

4. Open the Configuration menu and choose the protocol you selected.

5. Set any options that are necessary.

Usually, you need to set options only if you select the TCP/IP protocol, such as the IP address and subnet mask to assign to the print driver. You can then install the printer on your Windows computer by following these steps:

1. With Windows 95 and Windows 98, open the Start menu, point to Find, and then click Computers. With Windows Me and Windows 2000, on the Start menu, point to Search, click For Files And Folders, and then click Computers in the Search For Other Items section of the Search Results window.

2. Type the device name (such as SCF21717) and click Find or Search Now. A listing for the device appears in the Find: Computer window.

3. Double-click the listing for the device to see an icon for the print server, as shown in Figure 16-28.

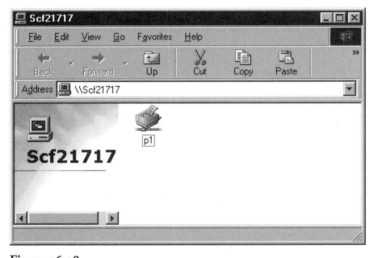

Figure 16-28.
Installing the print server in Windows.

4. Double-click the print server's icon and follow the instructions that appear for installing the necessary printer drivers. You'll now be able to select the print server from the Print dialog box in any Windows application, or make it the default printer in the Printers windows.

Sharing an Internet Connection

Sharing a modem and Internet connection, as you learned in Chapter 13, is a popular use for many home networks, and you can share the Internet with your Mac as well.

Sharing an Internet connection is actually more important when you add a Mac, in fact. Remember, with a Mac, you have to choose to use TCP/IP for either the Internet or your network, but not both. So if you use TCP/IP to connect the Mac to your PC network, you can't use the Mac to connect to the Internet using its own modem through TCP/IP at the same time.

By letting Mac share a connection on the Windows network, you can connect to the Internet and to the network at the same time. The Internet connection is made using TCP/IP on the PC that shares its modem, so the Mac can access the Internet and the network at the same time. How you set up the Mac to share an Internet connection depends on the type of software that the PC acting as the Internet server is using.

Windows Internet Connection Sharing

If you're using Microsoft Windows Internet Connection Sharing (ICS) on your PC, you have to configure TCP/IP on the Mac to access it. In Chapter 13, you learned how to configure a Windows computer to use ICS. If you used dynamic IP addressing, you ran a program installed on a floppy disk when you installed and configured ICS on a host computer. You can't run this program on a Mac because it's designed only for Windows. If you used static IP addresses, you manually configured your Windows computer to use ICS.

To share the Internet account with a Mac, you have to use static addressing on your network and manually configure the Mac's TCP/IP. Assuming that you have ICS completely installed on a PC and you're using static IP addresses, configure the Mac to access the Internet through the network by following these steps:

1. Open the Apple menu, point to Control Panels, and click TCP/IP to open the TCP/IP control panel.

2. If the network configuration isn't displayed, choose Configurations from the File menu, select the network configuration you want to use, and click Make Active.

3. Click Done to return to the TCP/IP Control Panel.

4. Be sure that TCP/IP is set up as explained earlier in this chapter in "Configuring TCP/IP on the Mac." It should be set for the built-in Ethernet, with the appropriate IP address and subnet mask.

5. In the Router Address box of the TCP/IP control panel, enter the IP address of the PC acting as the Internet server.

6. In the Name Server box, enter the Domain Name Server (DNS) address that your ISP provided you. A sample of settings will appear, as shown in Figure 16-29.

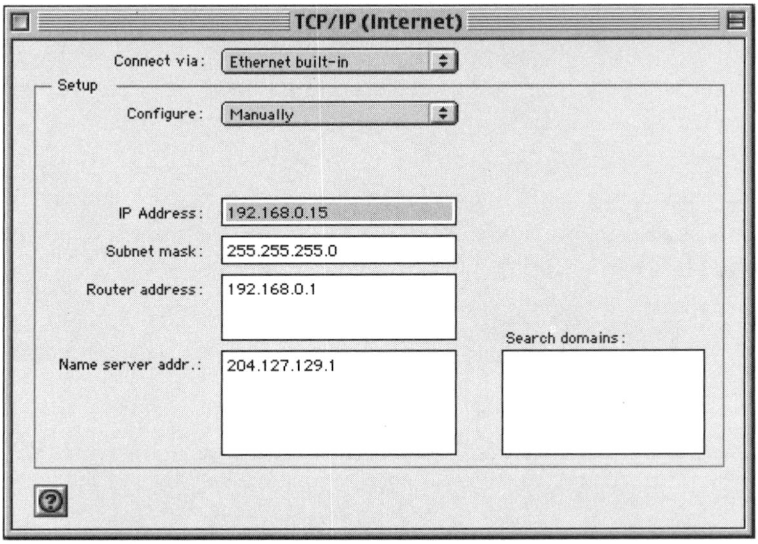

Figure 16-29.
A Mac set up to use Internet Connection Sharing on a PC network.

Now when you connect to the Internet using your Mac, it will access the modem and Internet connection of the ICS server computer on the network. If the ICS server isn't yet connected, it will dial into the ISP and make the connection.

Note

As with a PC using ICS, you might get an error on your Mac browser when it first connects through the server. If an error message tells you that the Web site cannot be opened, just enter the address of a site you want to access in the browser's address box and press Enter.

Using a Proxy Server

Some other Internet sharing software works using a proxy server. A proxy server looks for requests coming over the network to access an Internet site. It does so by watching a *port*—an electronic connection between the network computers. The server then gets the site using the modem and Internet account on the computer in which the proxy server is installed but sends it across the network to the computer that made the request.

If you're using proxy server software, you'll need to know the IP address of the server computer and the port to which the proxy server is connected. You'll get the IP address from the PC's Network icon in Control Panel and the port number from the proxy server's documentation.

When you have that information, start the Mac's Web browser but don't connect to the Internet. Open the browser's Preferences or Options dialog box. Using Microsoft Internet Explorer for the Mac, for example, click Preferences on the browser menu bar and then select Proxies in the Network section to see the options in Figure 16-30.

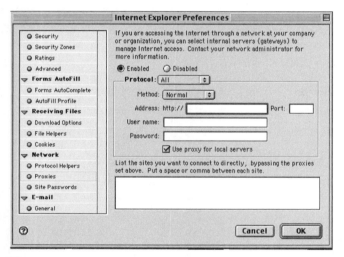

Figure 16-30.

Setting the Mac to access the Internet through a proxy server.

In the Address text box, following *http://*, enter the IP address of the PC being used as the Internet server. Enter the proxy server port in the Port text box, and then click OK.

Now when you connect to the Internet using the Mac, it will send its request for a Web site to the computer containing the proxy server. The proxy server will access the modem and Internet connection on its computer and then send the retrieved site through the network to the browser on the Mac.

If you're using Netscape Communicator as your Mac Web browser, set it to connect through a proxy by choosing Preferences from the Edit menu. In the box that appears, scroll the list on the left and choose Proxies in the Advanced section to display the options in Figure 16-31.

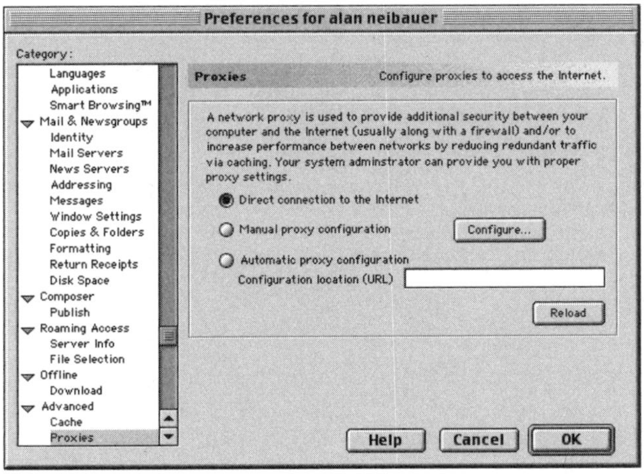

Figure 16-31.

Proxy options in Netscape Communicator.

Select Manual Proxy Configuration, and then click the Configure button to open the dialog box shown in Figure 16-32. In the HTTP Proxy text box, enter the IP address of the PC being used as the Internet server. Enter the proxy server port in the Port text box, and then click OK.

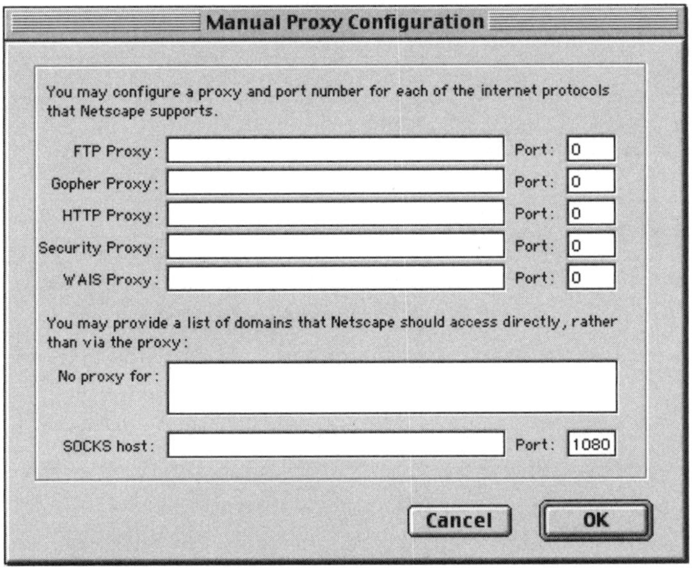

Figure 16-32.

Setting the proxy address and port.

The Best of Both Worlds

Windows and Mac computers have their own loyal groups of fans. Each camp touts its system as the better of the two, but most people agree that PCs and Macs both have their strengths and weaknesses. If you have at least one of each type of computer in your home, you can take advantage of the strengths of each.

Once you feel comfortable with using either Windows or the Mac, you can easily learn how to operate the other type of machine—the operating systems are not really that different. For example, where Windows has a Control Panel containing icons for various features that you can customize, the Mac offers similar features in the Control Panels list on the Apple menu. Where Windows has device drivers that must be loaded when your computer starts, the Mac has extensions that are loaded at start-up. Newer Windows and Mac computers both have USB ports, and can often now share the same peripherals, such as Zip drives and scanners.

Macintosh computers also have wireless Ethernet networking capability through AirPort technology. You can install a wireless AirPort network card into most Macs, including iBooks, iMacs, and PowerMacs. Some Macs even have a special external slot to accommodate the card.

See Also

Chapter 5, "Non-Ethernet Networks," discusses wireless networking with Windows computers.

AirPort-equipped Macs can communicate with each other without the need for cables. You can even link AirPort-equipped Macs with a wired network using the AirPort Base Station. This device has a built-in 56 Kbps modem for Internet sharing and a port for connection to a wired Ethernet network. A program called AirPort Setup Assistant helps you install and configure the base station.

Don't be intimidated by the differences between the Windows and Macintosh systems. As it turns out, it's easy to use both Macs and Windows computers on the same network—and Windows and Mac users can learn a lot from each other.

Chapter 17

Networking for Road Warriors

At some point, you'll probably hit the road for either business or pleasure. As you'll learn in this chapter, even when you're traveling, you can still communicate with the family back home on the home network and take advantage of all the benefits the network offers, such as sharing files and printing documents.

As countless computer-toting travelers—road warriors—already know, it's easy to stay in touch with a home computer from any place that's within reach of a telephone. In this chapter, you'll learn how to set up and use a process called *remote computing* to dial in to your home network to access its resources the same way you dial in to an Internet service provider (ISP) to access the Internet.

You'll also learn how to use Microsoft NetMeeting, a program that allows you to talk to and even see a family member on your home network or at a remote location, as long as each computer is equipped with a video camera (which can be inexpensive and easily added) and a microphone.

NetMeeting not only allows you to hold long-distance meetings, but it also provides *remote desktop sharing*, a handy feature that allows you to take over another computer on the network and actually operate it from your keyboard and screen, no matter where you are. As you'll see later in this chapter, remote desktop sharing gives you the opportunity to troubleshoot problems someone might be having with a computer on the network or even show someone how to perform a specific task on the computer.

Packing for the Road

Suppose you're on a trip away from home and you're relaxing in your hotel room going over the day's events. You'd like to dial in to your home computer to check e-mail messages from your family, send a file home, or perhaps print a note to your spouse on one of your home printers. At home, your modem is probably already plugged into the phone jack, so going online is simple. But when you're away from home, connecting to a phone line isn't always that easy. Even if your hotel room or a conference center has a standard, modular phone jack, the jack might not be in a location close enough to the spot at which you'd like to use your computer.

To avoid some potential hassles, you should start by packing a few essentials along with your laptop:

- Two telephone extension cables, each with a length of 6 feet or more
- A telephone cable coupler
- A two-to-one or three-to-one telephone adapter

The telephone cables, coupler, and adapter weigh practically nothing and they take up little space in your computer case or briefcase, but they can be lifesavers when you want to connect to a home network or to the Internet. You can purchase all these items at a hardware store, your local Radio Shack, or even at your local "Nothing over $1" store. They'll allow you to reach a phone jack, even one that's in an out-of-the-way place.

The coupler lets you connect two lengths of telephone cable to lengthen your reach even farther. If a telephone is already connected to the phone jack, the two-to-one adapter lets you plug in both the phone and your modem.

Note

In a pinch, the adapter can also be used as a coupler—just plug both extension cables into the adapter and plug one end of the cable, rather than the adapter, into the jack.

Most hotels cater to travelers who are now, more than ever, equipped with laptop computers. But not every hotel you stay in will be set up to facilitate remote computing.

The first hurdle you might encounter, especially if you're traveling abroad, is the lack of a standard RJ-11 modular phone jack in your room. This receptacle is the standard type that's used as a phone jack in North America. Even with the extra cables, couplers, and adapters that you've packed, you'll be stuck if there's no place to plug in your modem.

The second hurdle might be the phone line itself. The telephone lines in your home are regular analog lines. Your modem converts the digital information in your computer to analog signals that these regular phone lines can carry. But many hotels and offices have special digital telephone systems. In a digital system, voice and fax communications are transmitted through the system as digital information, so your analog modem won't work. What's worse is that if you connect your laptop to a digital network, the voltage from the digital lines might damage your laptop's modem permanently.

With a little preparation before your trip, however, you can overcome both of these hurdles. When you make hotel reservations, find out whether the hotel's telephone system is analog or digital. Even if it's digital, you might be able to request a room with an analog phone connection and an RJ-11 jack that you can use with your laptop.

You can also purchase an *acoustic coupler*, a device that fits over the telephone handset and connects to your modem. Instead of plugging directly into the phone system, you connect to the acoustic coupler, which sends and receives signals through the telephone handset. Another device that you can use with a digital system allows you to connect your modem to the jack into which the phone's handset is plugged. Both of these devices overcome the problems of not having access to a jack and to an analog phone system. Devices such as these are sold by Road Warrior (*http://www.roadwarrior.com*), and are shown in Figure 17-1. These devices enable you to connect easily and safely to digital phone lines when you're on the road.

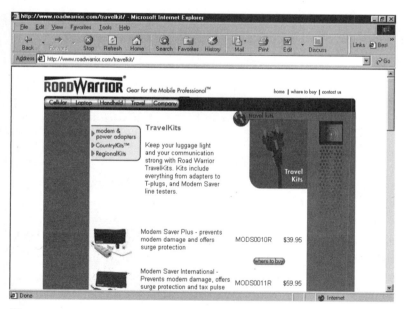

Figure 17-1.

These Road Warrior devices allow you to connect your modem to digital phone lines when you're traveling.

If you're traveling abroad, you can purchase jack adapters, which let you connect your modem to the type of jack used in the country you're visiting. To order the correct adapter, you'll have to find out which type of jack you'll be using, but most mail-order companies that specialize in remote computing hardware, such as Hello Direct (*http:// www.hello-direct.com*) and Road Warrior, can help you with that.

For maximum protection, you might want to consider buying a *line tester*, a device that indicates whether a line is analog or digital, and a *surge protector*, which protects a modem against power surges while you're connected. Road Warrior, for example, offers a product called the Modem Saver Plus. You plug this device into the phone jack before plugging in your modem. A green light indicates that the jack is safe to use; a red light indicates that it could damage your modem. A surge protector is also built into the Modem Saver Plus.

Dialing In to Your ISP

One other important item you should have for your trip is a local phone number for your ISP in the area in which you'll be staying. You've probably set up your computer to dial in to your ISP from home using the local number that's available where you live. You could use that same number when you travel, but you'd have to do two things first:

- Adjust Microsoft Windows so that it dials the area code as well as the number.
- Take out a loan to pay the long distance charges, especially at hotel rates.

Note

Some ISPs require that you install special software to connect to them. If that's the case with yours, you'll need to follow the instructions that came with the software to change the access number that your modem dials.

Fortunately, large, nationwide ISPs have local phone numbers in or near most major cities, so you should find out from your ISP ahead of time the local phone numbers for the areas in which you'll be staying. Call the ISP's support number and request the local access numbers, or connect online before you leave and look for the numbers on the ISP's Web site. When you arrive at your destination, you can change the phone number that your system dials to connect to the ISP. Be sure to make a note of the original number so you'll be able to restore it when you return home.

Tip

If you use a program such as Microsoft Outlook Express to check your e-mail, you'll need to change the connection it uses to dial in to your ISP to send and receive mail.

You can change the telephone number your computer dials by following these steps:

1. Double-click My Computer on the Windows desktop. With Microsoft Windows Millennium Edition (Me), choose Settings from the Start menu, click Dial-Up Networking, and then go to step 3.

2. In the My Computer window, double-click the Dial-Up Networking icon. In Microsoft Windows 2000, double-click Control Panel and then double-click Network And Dial-Up Connections.

3. Right-click the connection you normally use and choose Properties from the shortcut menu. You'll see a connection dialog box, much like the one shown in Figure 17-2.

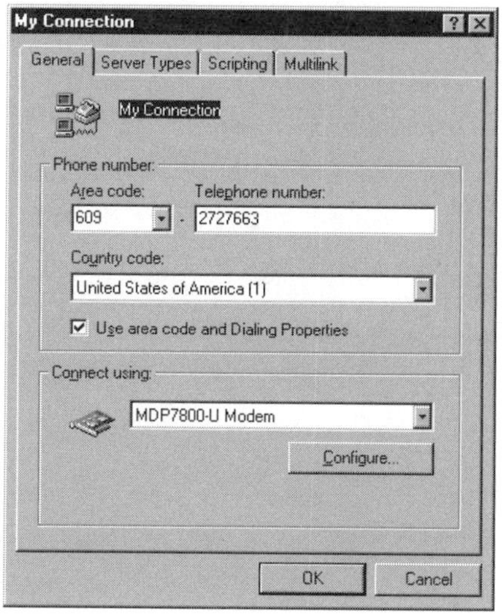

Figure 17-2.
Change your dial-up phone number to connect to your ISP from the road.

4. On the General tab, replace the existing area code and telephone number with the new numbers.

5. If you must dial 9 or some other number to get an outside line, add the number and a comma before the phone number, as in *9,5551212*. The comma causes the modem to pause after dialing the number 9 so the outside dial tone can be obtained.

6. Click OK.

Note

Remember to change the phone number again when you return home.

Creating an Additional Dial-Up Networking Connection

If you travel frequently to the same location, such as a branch office in a different city, changing and restoring the telephone number of your ISP can be an annoyance. So instead of changing the number in your dial-up connection, you can create a new connection that will have all the settings required to dial in to your ISP from the road. You can choose to use that connection when traveling and then switch back to the original when you get home.

Making a New Connection in Consumer Windows

First, you need to check the existing settings, including the primary and secondary Domain Name System (DNS) numbers. *If you're using Windows 2000, see "Making Connections with Windows 2000," later in this chapter.* If you're using Consumer Windows (Microsoft Windows 95, Microsoft Windows 98, or Microsoft Windows Me), just follow these steps:

1. Double-click My Computer on the Windows desktop. With Windows Me, choose Settings from the Start menu, click Dial-Up Networking, and then go to step 3.

2. In the My Computer window, double-click the Dial-Up Networking icon.

3. Right-click the connection you use to dial in to your ISP, and then choose Properties.

4. Click the Server Types tab in Windows 95 and Windows 98 or the Networking tab in Windows Me.

5. Make a note of the settings, including the Type Of Dial-Up Server setting, and the check boxes that are selected in the Advanced Options and Allowed Network Protocols sections.

6. Click the TCP/IP Settings button.

7. In the TCP/IP Settings dialog box, write down any numbers that appear in the Primary DNS and Secondary DNS text boxes. You should also make a note about the other settings in the box, although these are usually already set for you by default when you make a new connection.

8. Click Cancel to return to the Dial-Up Networking window, and click Cancel again to close the dialog box for the connection.

Now you can make a new connection by following these steps:

1. In the Dial-Up Networking window, double-click Make New Connection to open the Make New Connection dialog box.

2. Type a name for the connection, such as *Branch Office.*

3. If you have more than one modem, click the down arrow next to the Select A Device drop-down list and choose the modem you'll use to connect to the ISP.

4. Click Next.

5. Enter the ISP's local phone number at the remote location.

6. Click Next, and then click Finish.

While the Dial-Up Networking window is still open, you need to configure the connection for the proper protocols and server settings. Here's how to do it:

1. Right-click the connection you've just created, and choose Properties.

2. In the connection dialog box, click the Server Types tab in Windows 95 and Windows 98 or the Networking tab in Windows Me.

3. Set the options on the tab so they match the settings you noted earlier. Be sure to check that you've matched the Type Of Dial-Up Server, Advanced Options, and Allowed Network Protocols settings.

4. Click the TCP/IP Settings button.

5. In the TCP/IP Settings dialog box, enter the primary and secondary DNS numbers that you copied down earlier. Also, look at the other settings to make sure they're the same as your main ISP connection.

6. Click OK to close the TCP/IP Settings dialog box.

7. Click OK to return to the Dial-Up Networking window.

Now when you're away from home and want to dial in to your ISP, you can choose the new connection you've just made. When you want to connect to the Internet, you can open the Dial-Up Networking window and double-click the connection to dial in to your ISP. The first time you connect with the new connection, you'll have to enter your user name and password. Select the Save Password check box so Windows will remember the password for later connections. When you see a message reporting that the connection has been made, you can start your Web browser.

Making Connections with Windows 2000

If you're using Windows 2000, follow these steps to create an additional dial-up connection for your ISP:

1. Double-click My Network Places on the Windows desktop.

2. Click Network And Dial-Up Connections.

3. Right-click the connection you use to dial in to your ISP, and then select Create Copy. This action makes a new copy of the connection icon.

4. Right-click the copy of the connection icon and choose Properties to open the connection's Properties dialog box.

5. In the Phone Number text box on the General tab, type the ISP's local phone number at the remote location. If you need to enter a new area code, select the Use Dialing Rules check box, and enter the area code in the Area Code text box.

6. Click OK.

Now when you're away from home and want to dial in to your ISP, you can choose the new connection you've just made. When you want to connect to the Internet, you can open the Network And Dial-Up Connections window and double-click the connection to dial in to your ISP. The first time you use the new connection, you'll have to enter your user name and password. Select the Save Password check box so Windows will remember the password for later connections. When you see a message reporting that the connection has been made, you can start your Web browser.

Setting the Default Connection in Microsoft Internet Explorer 5

If you're using Internet Explorer 5, you can easily change the default connection.

1. Right-click the Internet Explorer icon on the desktop.

2. Choose Properties from the shortcut menu.

3. On the Connections tab of the Internet Options dialog box, click the connection you want to use and then click the Set Default button.

4. Click OK.

Now whenever you start your browser, it'll dial in to the ISP using the new connection. Using this technique means you'll need to change the connection again when you get home.

Connecting to Your Home Network

As long as you can connect your modem to a phone line, you can dial in to your home network to transfer files or print documents when you're away. But whether you want to connect to your home network to share or print files or just access your home computer to get messages, you need to set up your home computer so that it will allow you to dial in from the road. You perform this task by installing Dial-Up Server, a Windows feature that sets up a computer so that its modem answers the phone when you call in from a remote location, such as from a hotel room when you're traveling with a laptop computer.

When you set up your computers for dial-up networking, you can choose to password-protect your system so that only authorized persons can access your files. Password protection is optional but it's highly recommended. *You should also consider using password protection to restrict access to sensitive folders, as explained in "Sharing and Accessing Network Resources," in Chapter 10, on page 189.*

Installing Dial-Up Server

Although it comes with Windows 98 and Windows Me, Dial-Up Server isn't installed by default. Installing Dial-Up Server, however, requires only a few simple steps.

Note

If you have Windows 95, you'll find Dial-Up Server is part of the add-on program called Microsoft Plus!

Preparing to Install Dial-Up Server

Your first step is to make sure that all three network protocols are installed and that your hard disk is shared. If you haven't performed these tasks already, go back to "Installing Protocols" in Chapter 8 on page 152 and "Sharing and Accessing Network Resources" in Chapter 10 on page 189 of this book and follow the instructions there.

You'll need to install TCP/IP because Microsoft's Dial-Up Server software requires TCP/IP to connect to the remote computer. If your home network uses TCP/IP as its protocol, you can dial in to the dial-up server and access its files, but you won't be able to access the other computers on the network. To dial in to your dial-up server and access your entire home network, you must have installed either IPX/SPX or NetBEUI as a network protocol. In other words, you should install all three of the protocols—IPX/SPX, NetBEUI, and TCP/IP—on the computer you want to use as a dial-up server, but only IPX/SPX and NetBEUI on the other computers on the network.

You also need to set the Primary Network Logon to Windows Logon and enable file sharing through the dial-up adapter, which is usually a modem. If you just use your modem to connect to the Internet, file and printer sharing over the modem will be disabled, which helps prevent Internet hackers from accessing your files when you're connected to the Internet. To access your own files when you dial in to the network, however, you have to enable file sharing.

Here's how you enable file sharing in all versions of Windows:

1. On the Start menu, point to Settings, and then click Control Panel.

2. In Control Panel, double-click the Network icon.

3. From the Primary Network Logon drop-down list, shown in Figure 17-3, choose Windows Logon.

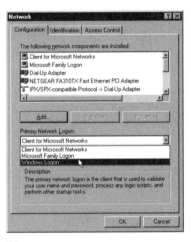

Figure 17-3.
Choose Windows Logon from the Primary Network Logon drop-down list.

4. Scroll the network components list and click the setting TCP/IP–> Dial-Up Adapter.

5. Click Properties and then click OK in the message box that appears.

6. Click the Bindings tab.

7. Select the check box labeled File And Printer Sharing For Microsoft Networks.

8. Click OK.

9. Click OK again to close the Network dialog box.

10. Click Yes when you're asked whether to restart your computer.

Installing the Dial-Up Server Software in Consumer Windows

To install the Dial-Up Server software in Consumer Windows, follow these steps:

1. On the Start menu, point to Settings, and then click Control Panel.

    If you're using Windows 95, you must first install the Windows add-on called Microsoft Plus! before you can set up and configure Dial-Up Server. If you run setup from the Microsoft Plus! CD, the Dial-Up Server will be installed as another connection in the Dial-Up Networking window. The Dial-Up Networking (DUN) 1.3 Performance and Security Update (available at *http://www.microsoft.com/ windows95/downloads*) also contains the Dial-Up Server.

2. In Control Panel, double-click the Add/Remove Programs icon.

3. In the Add/Remove Programs Properties dialog box, click the Windows Setup tab.

4. In the list of components, click Communications, but be careful not to remove the check mark in the check box to its left.

5. Click Details.

6. In the Communications dialog box, select the Dial-Up Server check box, as shown in Figure 17-4.

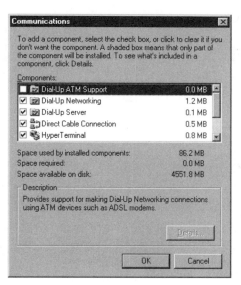

Figure 17-4.
If the component's check box is selected, the component, such as Dial-Up Server, is installed.

7. Click OK to close the Communications dialog box.

8. Click OK again to close the Add/Remove Programs Properties dialog box.

At this point, you might need to insert the Windows CD. On some computers, the files that Windows needs are already stored on the hard disk. In either case, Dial-Up Server will be installed and you'll be ready for the next stage of the setup process.

Activating Dial-Up Server

Now that Dial-Up Server is installed, you have to activate it. This procedure sets up your computer to answer the telephone when it rings and establish the connection to the remote computer. Follow these steps to activate Dial-Up Server:

1. Double-click My Computer on the Windows desktop. (With Windows Me, choose Settings from the Start menu, click Dial-Up Networking, and then go to step 3.)

2. In the My Computer window, double-click the Dial-Up Networking icon.

3. From the Connections menu, choose Dial-Up Server to open the Dial-Up Server dialog box shown in Figure 17-5.

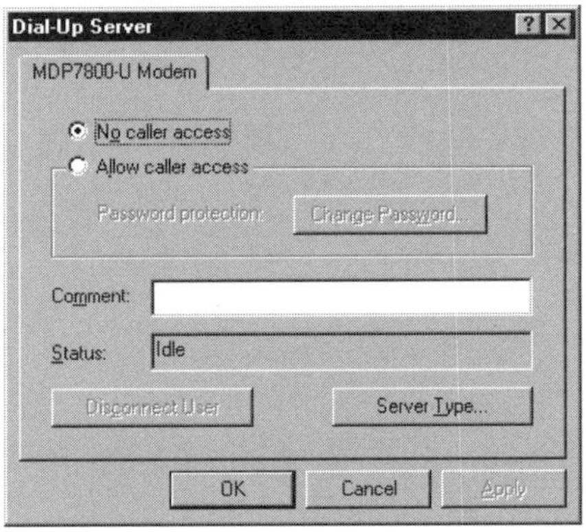

Figure 17-5.
The Dial-Up Server dialog box allows you to set up a modem to answer incoming calls.

If you have more than one modem, you'll see a tab for each modem in or connected to your computer. Click the tab for the modem you want to use to answer incoming calls.

4. Select Allow Caller Access.

5. To password-protect your system so that only authorized persons can connect to the network, click Change Password to open the Dial-Up Networking Password dialog box.

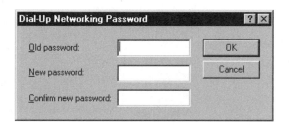

6. If you haven't yet set a password, leave the Old Password text box blank. Type your password in both the New Password and Confirm New Password text boxes, and click OK.

7. Click Apply. You'll now see a new icon next to the clock on the right of the Windows taskbar, indicating that Dial-Up Server is running.

Installing the Dial-Up Server Software in Windows 2000

If you're using Windows 2000, follow these steps to allow your computer to accept incoming calls:

1. Open Control Panel and double-click Network And Dial-Up Connections.

2. Double-click Make New Connection, and then click Next.

3. Click Accept Incoming Connections and then click Next to see a list of devices on your computer for accepting calls:

4. Select the check box for your modem and click Next.

5. Select the option Do Not Allow Virtual Private Connections and click Next. You'll see the Allow Users list showing all the users set up to access your computer.

6. Select the check boxes for the users you'll allow to call in and click Next. (You can also use the dialog box to add other users, delete users, or change their properties.)

7. You'll see a list of networking components, such as Internet Protocol, File And Printer Sharing For Microsoft Networks, and Client For Microsoft Networks. Select the components you want to use for the dial-up server, and then click Next.

8. The name for the connection will be shown as Incoming Connections. Click Finish. You can now right-click the connection and choose Properties to adjust any of the server settings.

Preparing Your Consumer Windows Laptop

Now you have to set up your laptop by creating a connection that'll call the number for your home network. *If you're using Windows 2000, see "Preparing Your Windows 2000 Laptop," later in this chapter.* If you're using Consumer Windows, just follow these steps:

1. Double-click My Computer on the Windows desktop. With Windows Me, choose Settings from the Start menu, click Dial-Up Networking, and then go to step 3.

2. In the My Computer window, double-click the Dial-Up Networking icon.

3. Double-click Make New Connection to open the Make New Connection dialog box, shown in Figure 17-6.

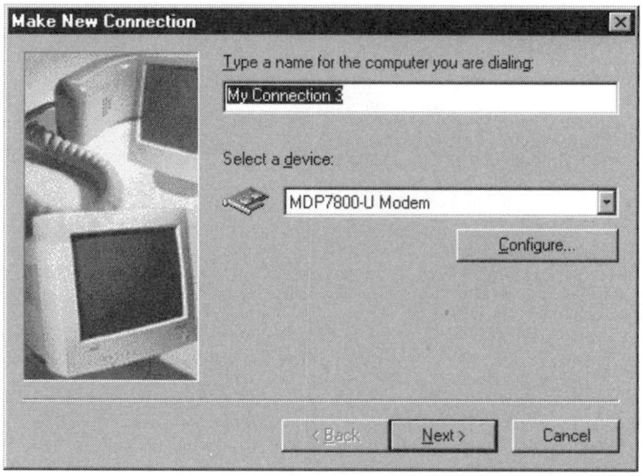

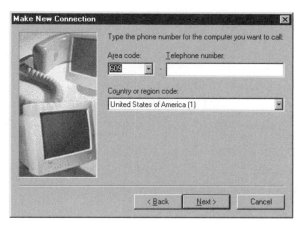

Figure 17-6.
The Make New Connection dialog box.

4. Type a name for your connection, such as *Road Warrior.*

5. If you have more than one modem, click the down arrow next to the Select A Device drop-down list, and choose the modem you'll use to connect to your computer.

6. Click Next to see the dialog box in Figure 17-7.

Figure 17-7.
Specify your computer's telephone number.

7. Type your computer's area code and telephone number.

8. Click Next, and then click Finish.

While the Dial-Up Networking window is still open, you need to configure the connection for the proper protocol. Here's how to do it:

1. Right-click the connection you've just created, and choose Properties.

2. In the connection dialog box, click the Server Types tab to see the options shown in Figure 17-8.

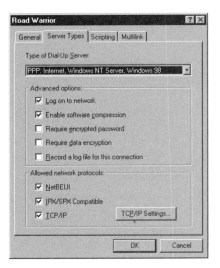

Figure 17-8.
Configure your dial-up connection from this set of options.

3. Make sure the Type Of Dial-Up Server option is set to PPP: Internet, Windows NT Server, Windows 98. If you're using Windows 95, make sure the option is set to PPP: Windows 95, Windows NT, Internet.

4. Select the Log On To Network check box.

5. Select all three protocols listed in the Allowed Network Protocols area of the dialog box: NetBEUI, IPX/SPX Compatible, and TCP/IP.

6. Click OK.

Note

You don't need to configure an IP address or set any other TCP/IP options.

Preparing Your Windows 2000 Laptop

If you're using Windows 2000 on your laptop, follow these steps to create a dial-up connection to use when you travel:

1. Double-click My Network Places on the Windows desktop.

2. Click Network And Dial-Up Connections.

3. Double-click Make New Connection to start the Network Connection Wizard, and click Next.

4. Select Dial-Up To Private Network, and click Next.

5. If you're asked to select a device, select the modem that you'll use to dial out.

6. Type the phone number of your home network, and click Next.

7. Select Only For Myself, and click Next.

8. Type the name of your dial-up connection, and click Finish.

9. In the Connect dialog box, click Cancel because you are not quite ready to dial into the network.

While the Network Dial-Up Connections window is still open, you need to configure the connection for the proper protocols. Here's how to do it:

1. Right-click the connection you've just created, and choose Properties.

2. In the Properties dialog box, click the Networking tab.

3. Make sure the Type Of Dial-Up Server I Am Calling option is set to PPP: Windows 95/98/NT 4/2000, Internet.

4. In the Components Checked Are Used By This Connection box, make sure that all these protocols are present: Internet Protocol (TCP/IP), NetBEUI Protocol, and NWLink IPX/SPX/NetBIOS Compatible Transport Protocol. If all three are present, click OK.

If one or more of the three protocols aren't present, you'll need to install them. Continue with these steps:

1. Click Install.

2. Select Protocol, and click Add.

3. Select the protocol you want to install in the Select Network Protocol box, and click OK.

4. If you need to install another protocol, follow steps 1 through 3 again.

5. Once you've installed all the necessary protocols, click Close.

Accessing a Home Computer Remotely

You're now ready to dial in to your computer from the road. Open the Dial-Up Networking window in Consumer Windows, or the Network And Dial-Up Connections window in Windows 2000, and double-click the Remote Dial-Up Connection icon. Click Connect to make the connection. Windows will dial in and make the connection to your computer. Enter your password if you're asked for it.

To access the files on a computer on your network, you must enter its name, as follows:

1. On the Start menu, click Run.

2. In the Run dialog box, type two backslashes followed by the name of the computer you're dialing in to, and then click OK. If the computer is named *adam*, for example, you'd enter *adam*.

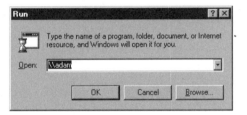

After you enter the computer name, you can access the computer just as if you were connected to the network at home. You'll see a window showing all the shared resources on the computer.

To access a file, double-click the shared drive and navigate to the file just as if you were using the My Computer window on your home computer. Copy and move files by dragging them between windows. For example, to get a copy of a file from your home computer onto your laptop, simply locate the file and drag it to your laptop's desktop.

Printing a document on a shared printer that's connected to the network is just as easy. Locate the document using My Computer or Windows Explorer on your laptop and drag it to the icon for the shared printer. The document will be waiting for you when you return home.

Keeping in Touch with Family

NetMeeting allows you to communicate with your family in a variety of ways when you're away from home. It's also a good way to keep in touch with other family members who are at remote locations.

Let's say you're on a business trip or your child is away at school. Instead of simply sending and receiving e-mail, you can use NetMeeting to talk to each other just as you would over the telephone. You can also send and receive files, work on programs together, and share drawings, as shown in Figure 17-9. If your computers are equipped with video cameras, you can even see each other as you're talking.

Figure 17-9.
NetMeeting in action.

If you have version 4 or later of Internet Explorer, NetMeeting is already installed on your system. If NetMeeting isn't installed, you can download a free copy of it from the Microsoft Web site at this address: *http://www.microsoft.com/windows/netmeeting/*.

The information in this chapter is based on NetMeeting 3, the version of the program that's installed with Internet Explorer 5 or later. If you have an earlier version of NetMeeting, you should download the newest version from the Microsoft Web site to obtain all the latest features.

To start NetMeeting in Consumer Windows, point to Programs on the Start menu, and then click Microsoft NetMeeting. The program might also be listed in the submenu that appears when you point to Internet Explorer on the Programs menu, or when you point to Accessories and then point to Internet Tools. In Windows 2000, point to Accessories and the Communications menu and click Microsoft NetMeeting.

The first time you run NetMeeting, you'll see a series of dialog boxes that help you set up the program on your system. Depending on your system's configuration and on the version of NetMeeting that you're using, the order and content of these dialog boxes might be somewhat different from the following description, which is based on NetMeeting 3. Respond to the prompts in each dialog box, and then click Next to move to the next dialog box.

1. Click Next in the first dialog box, which explains the features available in NetMeeting.

2. In the next dialog box, enter your name, e-mail address, city, state, and country, and a brief comment about yourself that will identify you onscreen to other NetMeeting users.

3. Click Next to continue.

4. In the next dialog box, shown in Figure 17-10, choose whether you want to log on to a directory server whenever NetMeeting starts, and select the default server.

   A directory server lists people you can call and helps NetMeeting users find each other over the Internet. The server acts like a gigantic telephone switchboard, maintaining a directory of everyone who is logged on and ready to accept calls. The member of your family that you plan to contact over the Internet with NetMeeting should choose the same server.

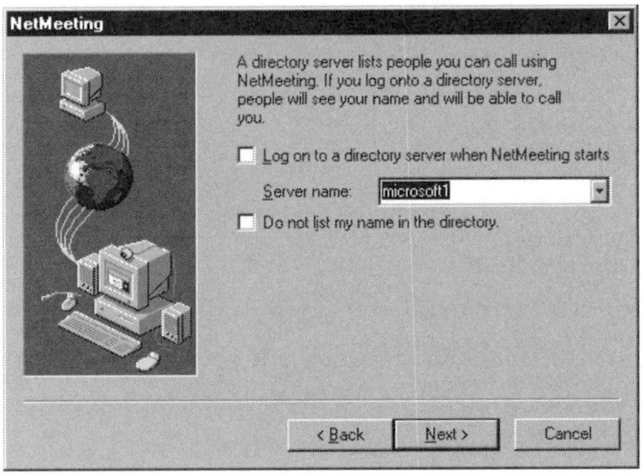

Figure 17-10.
This NetMeeting dialog box allows you to log on to a server.

Note

When you're home, you can also use NetMeeting directly over your home network as a family intercom. Since you don't need to log on to a server if you'll be using NetMeeting over your home network, don't choose to log on to a server when NetMeeting starts.

5. Click Next to continue.

6. If you have a video capture board installed in your computer, you'll see a dialog box that asks you to confirm its use.

7. Click Next to continue.

8. If a dialog box appears asking for the speed of your connection, select the speed of your modem and click Next.

Now you're halfway there. Continue by following these steps:

1. To make NetMeeting easier to start, select both check boxes in the next dialog box to place shortcuts for NetMeeting both on your Windows desktop and on the Quick Launch toolbar, just to the right of the Start button, and then click Next.

2. Click Next in the following window, when NetMeeting informs you that the Audio Tuning Wizard is about to help you tune your audio settings. It also instructs you to close all other programs that play or record sound.

    Now you might see a dialog box that asks you to select the devices that will record and play back sound on your system. Generally, your sound card performs both functions.

3. Select the sound card you have, and click Next.

4. Test the volume of your speakers by clicking the Test button in the dialog box shown in Figure 17-11 and by adjusting the slider to set a comfortable listening level. Click Stop to stop the sound, and then click Next.

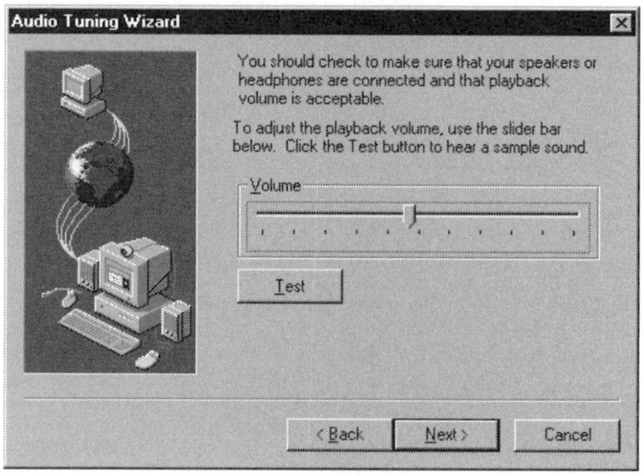

Figure 17-11.
Use the slider to adjust the sound volume.

5. To set the sensitivity of your microphone, speak into the microphone and watch the color bar that indicates the volume of your voice. Adjust the Record Volume slider so the bar reaches about the halfway mark, and click Next.

6. Click Finish when the Audio Tuning Wizard reports that you've successfully tuned your settings. When you click Finish, you'll see the NetMeeting window, shown in Figure 17-12.

Figure 17-12.
The NetMeeting program allows you to call other network users.

Note

After you start NetMeeting, you can change all the setup options and fine-tune calling, audio, and video settings by choosing Options from the NetMeeting Tools menu.

Starting a Meeting

If NetMeeting is set to log on to a directory server automatically, it will dial in to your ISP each time it's started. If it doesn't dial automatically, choose Log On To from the Call menu, which is followed by the name of the server, such as ils.Microsoft.com.

To place a call, choose Directory from the Call menu to open a dialog box listing the people logged on to the server. If many people are logged on, the list might take a few moments to appear while their names are downloaded. Scroll through the list to locate the person you want to speak with and double-click that person's name.

NetMeeting on a Network

Although NetMeeting is initially set to work across the Internet, you can call someone on your home network by adjusting the program so that it places the call through the network instead of through the Internet.

Note

If your computer tries to dial in to the Internet when you're placing a network call, just close the Dial-Up Networking box to stop the call.

To adjust the NetMeeting program, follow these steps:

1. Find out the IP address or name of the network computer you want to dial. You must be using TCP/IP on the network to make NetMeeting calls across the network.

2. Click the Place Call button or choose New Call from the Call menu to see the Place A Call dialog box.

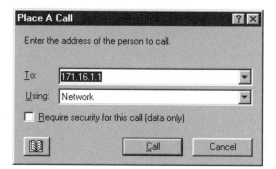

3. From the Using drop-down list, choose Network.

     In the To box, enter the IP address or the name of the computer you're trying to reach, and then click Call. The person at the computer you're calling will hear a telephone ring sound, and a message box will open to ask whether the user wants to accept or ignore your call.

     If the person chooses to ignore the call, a message appears on your screen reporting that the other user didn't accept your call.

Note

NetMeeting might also display a message reporting that the person you've called is currently in another meeting and can't accept your call, or it might inform you that the person is in a meeting and ask whether you would like to join.

When your call is accepted, the names of the people in the meeting are displayed in the NetMeeting window and you can start communicating. If each computer has a microphone and speakers, you can each speak into the microphone to talk to one another. If your computer is equipped with a camera, the person you're talking to will also be able to see you, as shown in Figure 17-13.

Figure 17-13.
In a NetMeeting, it's possible to see the people you're talking to.

To end the meeting, click the End Call button or choose Hang Up from the Call menu.

Using the Microsoft Internet Directory

Rather than log on to a directory server, you can connect to the Microsoft Internet Directory and search for the person you want to contact.

1. In NetMeeting, choose Options from the Tools menu to open the Options dialog box.

2. On the General tab of the dialog box, click the down arrow next to the Directory drop-down list, choose Microsoft Internet Directory from the list, and then click OK.

3. Select Log On To Microsoft Internet Directory from the Call menu. You'll see the search form shown in Figure 17-14. Enter the name or e-mail address of the person you want to contact and click Search.

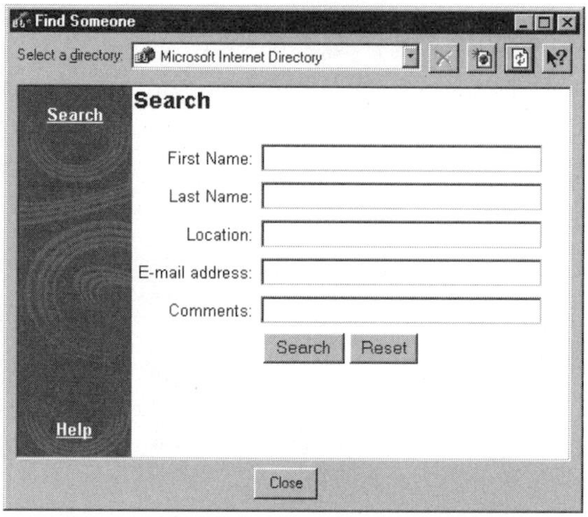

Figure 17-14.
Use the Microsoft Internet Directory to search for the person you want to contact.

4. You'll see a list of people who meet your search criteria. To place a NetMeeting call, click the person you want to contact.

Chatting in NetMeeting

Even with the proper equipment, the audio quality of a NetMeeting call can be poor. Instead of actually speaking over the network, you might want to open a chat window and type messages to the other participants in the meeting. Follow these steps to open a chat window:

1. Click the Chat button or choose Chat from the Tools menu to open the Chat window. The Chat window also opens on the other participants' screens.

2. Read the chat messages as they appear in the large text box, as shown in Figure 17-15.

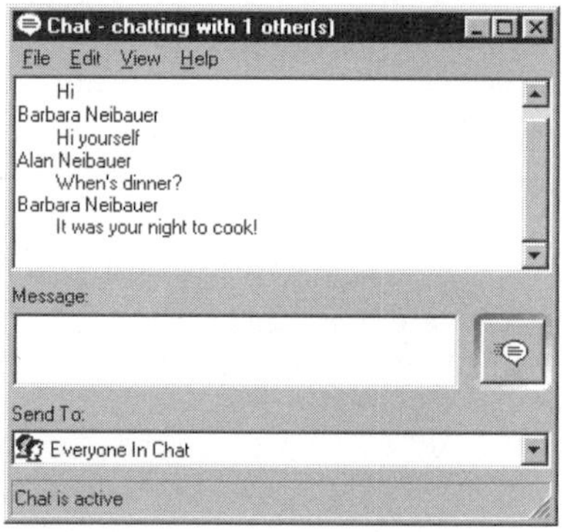

Figure 17-15.
With NetMeeting, you can create your own chat room on the network.

3. Type your messages in the Message text box and press Enter to transmit them.

4. If you want to send a private message to a particular chat participant, select the participant's name from the Send To drop-down list before clicking the Send Message button. To resume sending public messages to everyone in the chat, choose Everyone In Chat from the Send To drop-down list.

5. To exit the chat, close the Chat window or choose Exit from the File menu.

Using the Whiteboard

Sometimes you might need to communicate about something online that you can't easily express in words. Suppose, for example, that you want to communicate with a very young member of your family by drawing pictures rather than writing in a chat box. The solution in such situations is a handy NetMeeting feature called the whiteboard.

The *whiteboard* is a drawing window that you can share with everyone at the meeting. Whatever you draw on the whiteboard appears on the whiteboards of all the other participants. They, in turn, can use their whiteboards to add to your drawing, as long as you permit it. A NetMeeting whiteboard is shown in Figure 17-16.

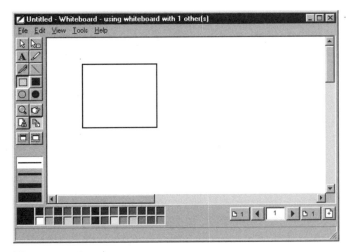

Figure 17-16.
The whiteboard feature in NetMeeting allows meeting participants to view and make changes to drawings.

To use the whiteboard, follow these steps:

1. Click the Whiteboard button or choose Whiteboard from the Tools menu.

2. Draw on the whiteboard using tools from the whiteboard tool palette, shown in Figure 17-17.

Selector			Eraser
Text			Highlighter
Pen			Line
Unfilled rectangle			Filled rectangle
Unfilled ellipse			Filled ellipse
Zoom			Remote pointer
Lock contents			Unsynchronize
Select area			Select window

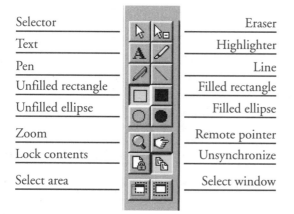

Figure 17-17.

The items in the whiteboard tool palette allow you to work on shared graphics and text.

The tool palette contains everything you need to create and edit drawings and text on the whiteboard. The same features are also available on the Tools menu.

Here's how to use the whiteboard tools:

- **Selector** Click this tool on an object you want to select, choose Delete, Copy, or Cut from the Edit menu, or drag the selected object to move it on the screen.

- **Eraser** Click this tool on an object you want to erase. You can also use it to drag a rectangle around an area. All objects even partially within the rectangle will be deleted.

- **Text** Click this tool to use your keyboard to type on the whiteboard. Choose a color from the color palette, or click the Font Options button that appears when you select the tool to change the font, font size, and font style. The Colors and Font commands on the Options menu also allow you to change the color, size, and style of your text.

- **Highlighter** Choose a line width and a color, and then drag this tool over the area you want to highlight.

- **Pen** Click this tool and then drag it in the whiteboard area to draw freehand on the screen.

- **Line** Click this tool to draw straight lines by dragging the mouse pointer from one point to the next. Select a line width and choose a color from the color palette shown in the Whiteboard window. You can also use the Colors and Line Width commands on the Options menu.

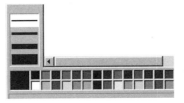

Note

You can use the Bring To Front or Send To Back commands on the Edit menu to change how objects overlap.

- **Rectangle** Choose a line width and color from the palette, and then click the Unfilled Rectangle button and draw the outline of a rectangle by dragging, or click the Filled Rectangle button and draw a solid rectangle of the selected color.

- **Ellipse** Click one of the two ellipse buttons and then drag on the whiteboard to draw filled or unfilled circles or ellipses in the line width and color of your choice.

- **Zoom** Click this tool, or use the Zoom command on the View menu, to switch between normal and enlarged views.

- **Remote Pointer** Click this tool to display a pointer, and then move it to the area of the whiteboard you want others to look at.

- **Lock Contents** Click this tool to prevent others from changing the whiteboard contents. Deselect it to allow others to change the whiteboard.

- **Synchronize/Unsynchronize** This tool lets you determine whether other whiteboard users can see the same pages you are viewing. To synchronize the pages, click the tool so that it appears depressed. To unsynchronize the pages, click the tool so that it appears released.

- **Select Area** Click this tool to drag a rectangle over an area of the screen outside the whiteboard that you want to copy to the whiteboard.

- **Select Window** This tool works in much the same way as the Windows clipboard. Click any window on your screen, even a partially obscured one, to copy the contents of the window to the whiteboard. The whiteboard will show the contents of the window inserted as a graphic.

Adding and Changing Whiteboard Pages

If a meeting you were conducting were held in person, you might use a flip chart to draw images and highlight important points. When you fill up one page, you just flip it over and start a fresh sheet. You can use the whiteboard in the same way, adding pages and changing them as needed.

Use the buttons at the lower-right corner of the whiteboard window to insert a page and to switch from page to page.

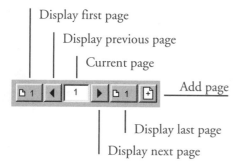

Display first page
Display previous page
Current page
Add page
Display last page
Display next page

Choose Clear Page from the Edit menu to erase the current page, or choose Delete Page from the Edit menu to delete the page. Erasing a page removes the page's contents on the screen of all NetMeeting participants but leaves the page in place. Deleting a page actually removes it from your whiteboard and from those of other participants as well.

Note

Normally, everyone in the meeting can see the same page that you have displayed on your screen. If you want to change pages without letting everyone see what you're doing, clear Synchronize on the View menu.

Saving and Printing the Whiteboard

When your meeting is over, you don't have to lose the contents of the whiteboard. While it's still displayed, each participant in the meeting can print a copy of the whiteboard by choosing Print from the File menu. Each participant can also save the whiteboard by choosing Save from the File menu. Whiteboards are saved in a special format, with a .wht extension. To reopen saved whiteboard files, choose Open from the File menu.

Note

Closing your own whiteboard doesn't close the whiteboards of other participants, who can continue to draw on theirs. If you open the whiteboard again, NetMeeting will locate and display the same whiteboard the other participants see. If you try to close a whiteboard before saving it, NetMeeting asks whether you want to save it.

Working Together on Programs

In addition to sharing a drawing on the whiteboard, you might want meeting participants to share a program as well. When you share a program with others, the meeting participants can see the program, but they can't control it unless you specifically allow them to do so. The person running the program is called the *owner*, and only the owner has control over who can work with the program. Here's how to use NetMeeting to share a program:

1. Start the program you want to share, and then switch back to NetMeeting.

2. Click the Share Program button or choose Sharing from the Tools menu to see the Sharing dialog box in Figure 17-18.

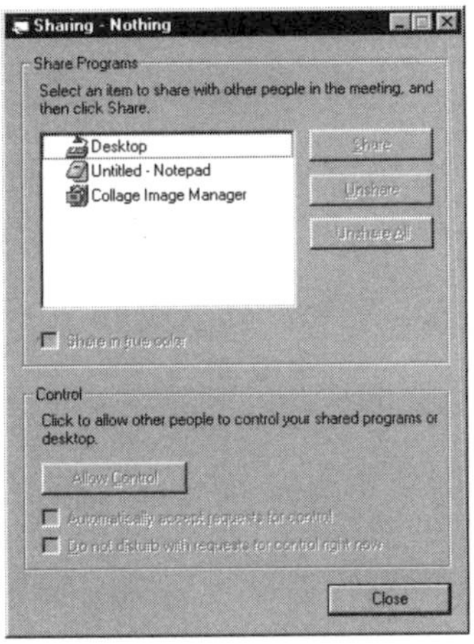

Figure 17-18.
The Sharing dialog box allows you to share programs with other meeting participants.

3. In the list of programs that are running, select the program you want to share, and then click Share. Other meeting participants will now be able to see exactly what you're doing with the shared program.

If you want to allow meeting participants to use the shared program, rather than just view it, click the Allow Control button in the Sharing dialog box. You'll be offered these two options:

*   **Automatically Accept Requests For Control** lets a meeting participant use the program without your express permission.

- **Do Not Disturb With Requests For Control Right Now** prevents requests for sharing from appearing on your screen.

To gain control of a program, a meeting participant must double-click the program window on the screen. This action either gives the person control of the program or, if you haven't turned on automatic acceptance in the Sharing dialog box, displays a dialog box asking whether you want to reject or accept the request.

By clicking Accept, you transfer control of the program to the participant, and you'll no longer be able to use your pointer onscreen. To regain control over the program and your cursor, and to stop any participant who's currently working with the shared program, press Esc or click the mouse button. To stop sharing the program, click Unshare or Unshare All in the Sharing dialog box.

Sending and Receiving Files

While you're in a meeting, you can exchange files with other participants. Click the Transfer Files button or choose File Transfer from the Tools menu to view the File Transfer dialog box.

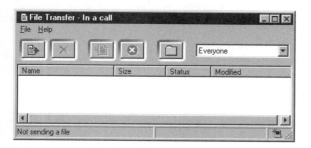

Click Add Files (the button on the far left side of the toolbar) and, in the Choose Files To Send dialog box, choose the files you want to transfer. Then click Send All to send the files to everyone or, from the drop-down list of meeting participants in the File Transfer dialog box, choose the participant to whom you want the files sent, and then click Send All.

When you receive a file from someone else, you'll see a dialog box, similar to the one shown here, giving you the option to close the dialog box, open the file, or delete the file.

Files that you receive are stored in the C:\Program Files\NetMeeting\Received Files folder. Click the View Received Files button—the one that shows an icon of a folder—to open that folder.

Controlling a Home Computer Remotely

NetMeeting includes a powerful feature that lets you actually control one of the other computers on the network. For example, suppose a family member is having trouble changing a setting in Control Panel or needs help performing some Windows task. You can take control of another person's computer from your own system and perform tasks as though you were sitting in front of the other computer.

To set up a computer to accept remote control, you have to use the Remote Desktop Sharing Wizard on that computer.

1. Start NetMeeting on the computer you want to be able to control and choose Remote Desktop Sharing from the Tools menu.

2. Click Next after reading the first Remote Desktop Sharing Wizard page.

3. With Consumer Windows, enter a password of at least seven characters that will allow access from the controlling computer. To access a Windows 2000 workstation, the user has to log on with an account that has administrative privileges on the computer that's being accessed remotely. In such a case, just read the information shown by the wizard at this point, and then click Next to proceed to step 5.

4. Reenter the password to confirm it, and then click Next.

5. You can now choose to password-protect a screen saver as an extra security feature. Make your choice and click Next.

6. Click Finish.

7. Close NetMeeting. The Remote Desktop Sharing icon will appear in the computer's system tray, to the left of the clock on the taskbar.

8. Right-click the Remote Desktop Sharing icon and select Activate Remote Desktop Sharing from the shortcut menu.

9. Start NetMeeting on the computer that will be in control and call the computer you want to share.

10. In the Place A Call dialog box that appears, select the Require Security For This Call (Data Only) check box, and then click Call. You'll be asked to enter the password.

11. Enter the password and click OK.

    You'll see a window that contains the other computer's desktop, as shown in Figure 17-19. You can now control the remote computer just as if you were sitting at its keyboard.

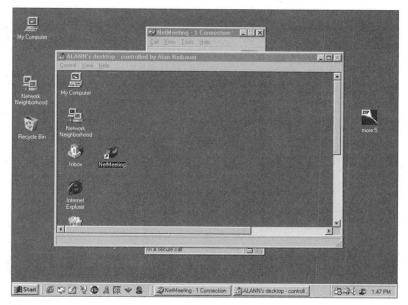

Figure 17-19.

With Remote Desktop Sharing, you can operate a remote computer from your own keyboard and screen.

12. To stop sharing, right-click the Remote Desktop Sharing icon on the desktop of the computer you're sharing and select Exit.

Dialing in from the road, remotely controlling a computer, and seeing the folks you're talking to over the Internet—it all seems like something out of the future, but these options are available to you today. In the next chapter, you'll learn which other futuristic features are available right now or are soon headed your way.

Chapter 18

Your Future Home Network

In previous chapters, you learned how to set up a home network using the latest available technologies: Ethernet networks, telephone and power-line networks, and wireless systems. Although computers and their peripherals are constantly changing, the technologies and techniques described in this book will see your home network well into the future.

In this chapter, however, we'll take a look at some emerging and alternative technologies and see what the future might hold for you and your home. A wired home, as you'll learn, will no longer be one that simply has an Ethernet network.

Controlling Your Wired Home

Imagine controlling every appliance, light, and security device in your home from your computer, or walking through the front door and saying, "Lights on. Television channel 6." Before going to sleep, you'd activate a system to automatically check that the lights and stove are turned off, that the refrigerator is working, and that your pet has come in for the night. You'd feed the dog, cat, or fish by calling in from the office or while on vacation, and you'd turn on the heating or air conditioning from your car phone on the way home.

Well, if you think complete home automation is a dream of the far-distant future, think again. The technology for home automation is here today, and thousands of homes have already led the way to the future.

Much of today's home automation is performed through a power-line technology called *X10*. The communication between automated devices is carried through your existing home wiring, much like the power-line network discussed in Chapter 5. You simply plug the X10 devices into wall outlets and control the system from a control station or computer interface.

Note

You can use several other types of interfaces besides X10—CEBus is one example—but the X10 system is the most widely available one.

An X10 controller—either a wall-mounted device or a program that runs on your computer—can individually direct the operation of up to 256 devices. In addition, the technology is standardized, so you can control devices from various manufacturers through the same wiring and with the same controllers.

In an X10 system, you can use three types of units:

- A *transmitter* sends signals from a controller to another X10 device. An X10 switch, for example, sends a signal to an X10 device that turns on a light.

- A *receiver*, such as a device that turns on a light or television, accepts signals from X10 controllers.

- A *transceiver* can both send and receive signals. These devices are usually controllers that can send signals to units and simultaneously receive status information from other units.

X10 receivers can be given one of up to 256 different codes. The controller uses the code to send a signal to the receiver telling it to switch on or off. You can have up to 256 separate devices, each controlled separately. You can also set several devices to have the same code so you can control them as a group with one signal from the controller.

You can control almost any electrical device with an X10 system. For example, X10 can underpin a security system that monitors access to your home and detects unauthorized entry. X10 security devices can include underground driveway sensors that alert you when a car enters the driveway, remote-controlled doors and gates, and video surveillance and alarm systems.

The system is ideal for controlling internal and external lights and appliances such as coffee makers, microwaves, ovens, and refrigerators. X10 can also automate television and stereo home entertainment systems and communications devices such as telephones and intercoms. Just some of the X10 devices that are available from SmartHome (*http://www.smarthome.com*) for home entertainment are shown in Figure 18-1.

An X10 product named DVD Anywhere (available at *http://www.x10.com*) lets you broadcast digital video disc (DVD) movies from your computer's DVD player to any television in the house. The system requires that your PC DVD player or video card have an RCA-type output jack. Another product from X10.com, VideoSender, can broadcast cable, digital satellite system (DSS), or VCR signals to any room in the house.

Figure 18-1.

The SmartHome.com Web site shows a number of X10 home entertainment devices.

Note

The Leapfrog Home Network System, available at the SmartHome.com Web site, can transmit video signals through your existing telephone lines.

You can also use X10 to control heating and air-conditioning systems that automate temperature and ventilation control and that compensate automatically for changing weather conditions. You can install systems that will open and close windows, drapes, and blinds at the touch of a switch or by voice command.

X10 devices can also perform the following tasks:

- Alert you when mail has been delivered to your mailbox or when packages have been dropped off at the doorstep
- Dispense food to a dog, cat, or fish
- Water your houseplants
- Control lawn sprinklers by sensing heat and dryness
- Monitor and report current weather conditions

To get started with an X10 system, you can purchase X10 starter kits that control a few lights from a small panel for about $30. You can then add individual devices to build a complete home automation system. The most common and inexpensive of these (about $6) are switches, dimmers, and lamp modules that allow you to turn lights and small appliances on or off. Heavy-duty modules for 220-volt appliances such as air conditioners, dryers, hot water heaters, and pool pumps cost about $15.

Controllable thermostats are more expensive, costing more than $100. Among the available models is a telephone-controlled thermostat that you can remotely control from any phone. And multiple switch boxes exist for controlling speakers, sprinkler systems, and window treatments. For drapes and blinds, you'll need a motorized control that opens or closes the drapes or blinds when the X10 signal is detected.

An X10 system can be self-contained; wall-mounted or tabletop panels can control the devices on the system. But for the ultimate in control, you can use your computer to control the entire system from your network. In fact, when you use a computer to automate your home, you can turn on the coffeepot so that the coffee is ready when you wake up, turn lights on and off according to a predetermined schedule, control a DVD player from any computer in the house, or check for mail. To achieve all this, you have to install software and then connect a special controller to your computer that connects it to the X10 system. You can then work with the controller from any networked computer.

You can choose from among several programs that connect your computer with the X10 devices in your home. This control panel, for example, is from the program Plato for Windows.

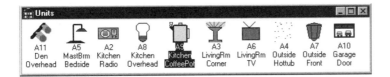

The icons in the control panel show that the coffeepot has been turned on to make coffee, the living room corner light is turned on, and the garage door is open. To add X10 units to the system, you use the Add An X10 Unit dialog box shown in Figure 18-2.

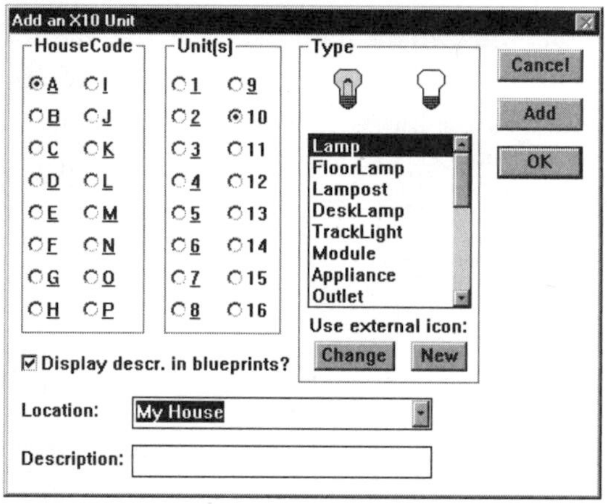

Figure 18-2.

You can add new X10 units in this dialog box.

So that you can control a particular device, you set its house and device codes. These codes identify the device and designate its type and location so it's controllable by the software. You can also create an onscreen blueprint of your home with icons representing each X10 device so you can visualize the location of each of the X10-controlled items in your house.

Getting Wired for the Future

In previous chapters, you learned how to run network cable through your home to create an Ethernet network. If you're building a new house or remodeling your current home, however, you might want to wire it for the future. Ethernet cable is certainly fine for a home computer network, but the future of your wired home goes far beyond Ethernet.

In addition to a computer network, you can wire your home for the following:

- Home entertainment
- Telephone and intercom
- Security
- Home automation
- Environmental controls

First, plan to have a central "wiring closet" somewhere in the house where all the wires can converge. This space can be any standard closet that provides enough room for you to get in and manipulate the wiring. As long as we're looking at the future, however, you might want to plan to use a small room, about the size of a small bathroom, that has heating and cooling vents and enough space for you to access all four sides of a central wiring cabinet. Make sure the wiring closet has enough electrical outlets and that all electrical outlets, telephone lines, and video cables are protected against surges.

In this wiring cabinet, you could have the following:

- An Ethernet hub

- A video distribution panel for a home entertainment system

- A telephone system

- A security panel

- Central home automation controllers

- A controller for multiple-zoned heating and air conditioning

- A broadband router or local area network (LAN) modem for sharing an Internet account

See Also

With modem sharing now so easy and popular, many Internet service providers (ISPs) have fine-tuned the small print in their customer agreements to discourage simultaneous sharing of an account. You shouldn't share an ISP account if the membership agreement forbids it.

When you plan the electrical system for your home, make sure your plan includes plenty of wall outlets. Carefully mark which outlets are connected to wall switches because you don't want to plug certain pieces of equipment into switched outlets. If you did, flipping the switch to turn off a light might also accidentally turn off a computer or hub.

If you plan on using X10 for home automation, have the electrician run a neutral wire to all wall switch boxes. Although some contractors don't bother running the neutral wire to all switches, it is needed for some X10 devices. Also make sure that the boxes themselves are extra deep to accommodate X10 switches, which are usually bulkier than standard switches.

Now run the following wires to each bedroom, den, and living room:

- Two coaxial video cables. You can use one for the television signal and the other for video cameras, VCRs, or DVD players. You can then watch a video or DVD playing from any other room in the house, or set up your own closed-circuit video system.

- Three Category 5 unshielded twisted-pair (UTP) cables. You can use one cable for your basic home network and reserve the others for maximum expandability so you can add networked printers, modems, and other equipment, as well as an intercom.

- Telephone cable for your telephone system, sufficient for two lines.

- Speaker cable for connecting stereo speakers throughout the home.

- Thermostat cable for use with a multiple-zoned heating and cooling system.

- Fiberoptic cable for future expansion.

Terminate all the cables into wall jacks, and label each of the jacks to identify its use. Plan the arrangement beforehand for each room, based on where you intend to place computer desks, entertainment units, and other furniture. You might decide, for example, to have speakers built into the walls or ceilings. You'll need to plan their location so the speaker wire can be run properly. Thermostats are usually located away from windows and other sources of drafts. Plan their location carefully with a heating contractor.

Bluetooth Wireless Technology

In Chapter 5, "Non-Ethernet Networks," we looked at ways to network your home without wires, including wireless, telephone-line, and power-line networks. Great strides are being made to improve these technologies, and in the future, telephone and wireless technologies will be able to match wired Ethernet in terms of speed and dependability. As mentioned in Chapter 5, some telephone and wireless networks currently operate around 10 Mbps, matching the low end of Ethernet, and their prices will drop into the range of Ethernet starter kits. In addition, standards are being developed to make these alternates to Ethernet more universal and more compatible with each other.

Broadband wireless technologies are in the forefront of this growth. An emerging standard called Bluetooth strives to enable mobile phones, computers, and other devices to communicate both voice and data in real time. Bluetooth is actually built into a microchip that will be installed in devices, while software will provide security to allow communications only between authorized devices.

Bluetooth calls for two levels of power. A low power level provides communications over small areas, such as within a room, while a higher power level is used over longer distances, such as throughout the entire house. The Bluetooth network, which is called a *piconet*, consists of one master device that controls the network and up to seven client or slave devices. By combining multiple piconets, you can extend the reach and number of devices in a Bluetooth network.

Home entertainment networks provide a centralized source for video and audio. For example, you might plan for a thin, wall-mounted television display and hidden speakers in every room. Using a universal, handheld remote control, you'll be able to tune into your favorite music or television show or watch a video or DVD. A video distribution panel will serve as a switchboard for video signals from your cable provider and also from your in-house video cameras and players. Much of this technology is available today. Some devices, for example, let you broadcast cable television signals, or output video from a VCR or DVD player, even a device in your computer, to any television in the house.

Wiring for High-Speed Internet Access

Most homes still connect to the Internet through a modem and standard telephone lines, often using an ISP. Since standard telephone lines are already wired into your home, they're the easiest and least expensive option. But when you plan your wired home, you can consider other options.

In the best of circumstances, when you've got good, clear phone lines, the maximum speed of a standard modem is 56 Kbps, but most connections are considerably slower. If you spend a lot of time surfing the Net and downloading software, these slow speeds might not be acceptable to you, so you might be willing to pay the higher cost of a faster connection. Even though you might pay more per month, your Internet experience will be much more pleasurable, and you can share one high-speed connection among all the members of your household.

Fortunately, if you want a faster connection, one or more of several technologies might be available in your area:

- Integrated Services Digital Network (ISDN)

- Satellite Internet access

- Digital subscriber lines (DSL)

- Cable modem

Of these, cable modems offer the fastest connections, but like DSL, they aren't yet available at every location. ISDN connections are more widely available, and satellite Internet connections are available just about anywhere, but they offer slower connections than cable and DSL, and they're more expensive to install and use. Table 18-1 compares these Internet access methods.

Table 18-1. **Comparison of Internet Access Methods**

Device	Initial Cost	Monthly Cost	Download Speed	Pros	Cons
Analog modem	Included with most computers, less than $100 to purchase and install otherwise	ISP charges of about $20, in addition to monthly telephone line charges	56 Kbps or less	Least expensive option; most widely available service; wide choice of ISPs	Requires a telephone line; slowest Internet option
ISDN	Up to $800	Phone line, $19–$50 for the ISDN line, plus a per-minute usage charge in some locations, plus ISP charges	128 Kbps	Next most widely available option	You must be located near the phone company's central office
DirecPC satellite	$300–$800	$30–$100	400 Kbps download, 56 Kbps upload	Widely available	Requires outside satellite dish; uploading via standard modem and telephone line
DSL	$500–$1,000	$40–$200	128 Kbps– 4 Mbps	Always connected to the Internet	Costly; not universally available; you must be located near the phone company's central office
Cable modem	Up to $600 with Ethernet card and modem	$30–$59	500 Kbps– 20 Mbps	High speed, always connected to the Internet	Not universally available; performance can be affected by the number of users

ISDN

The original attempt to provide a faster connection speed was a service called *Integrated Services Digital Network* (ISDN). ISDN uses three separate frequencies, called *channels*, on a special, dedicated telephone line. One channel (called the D channel) operates at a slow 16 Kbps, while the two remaining channels (the B channels) connect at up to 64 Kbps each. By binding the two B channels together, ISDN can achieve speeds of up to 128 Kbps.

ISDN is available at many locations in the United States, but your home must be within 18,000 feet of the local telephone company switching equipment. You'll also need a special modem or network interface that can cost between $200 and $500. With installation costs of $100 to $300, the total initial cost for setting up an ISDN line can be as high as $800. In addition, you must pay a monthly service fee to the phone company for the ISDN line, and you also might have to pay a penny or two for each minute you use the line. On top of that, many ISPs charge a premium for an ISDN connection.

Unless you set up your network for modem sharing, you'll need to buy a special ISDN modem for each computer you want to connect to the Internet and install a separate ISDN telephone line for each, which can get quite expensive. For most people, the increased speed of an ISDN connection doesn't justify the additional cost, especially when other, faster alternatives are available.

Satellite Internet Access

Hughes Network Systems, the company that offers DirecTV for satellite television, also offers DirecPC for your Internet connection, which provides downloads of up to 400 Kbps, quite a bit faster than ISDN. You must have a DirecPC dish installed on your roof, though, and a cable that runs from the satellite dish to your computer. The cable connects to an internal card or to an external universal serial bus (USB) modem. Unless you share the modem over a network, which requires a more expensive network option, you'll need a separate satellite dish, cable connection, and an internal card or an external USB modem for each computer you want connected to the Internet.

DirecPC works in conjunction with the modem and phone line you already have. You establish a modem connection to your regular ISP or to Hughes, which can be your ISP if you don't already have one. When you enter a Web site address into your browser, the request goes through your phone line at regular speed to Hughes. Then the data is sent back to your system by the satellite at high speed.

The great advantage of DirecPC is that you can use it anywhere in the continental United States, even in remote, rural areas. The dish and the card or USB modem cost about $200 plus an installation fee, and you must pay a monthly charge for a certain number of hours each month. This fee ranges from about $20 to $110, depending on the number of hours you choose. Hughes also sells DirecDuo, which combines DirecPC and DirecTV in one satellite dish. You might also be able to find a promotion that gives you free installation if you sign up for the DirecPC ISP service. You can also save money by installing the dish yourself, but it's not easy. You'll need an installation kit that costs about $30 to $40, the ability to climb onto your roof, and the patience to aim the dish and find the satellite. It's possible to do the installation yourself, but you're better off leaving it to your local expert.

The main disadvantage of DirecPC is that it offers high-speed access in only one direction, relying on your regular modem for uploading data and sending e-mail. So although you can download Web sites and software over the satellite at high speed, you can upload no faster than your regular modem connection. If you play games over the Internet, which requires fast two-way communication, the combination of DirecPC and a regular modem won't be any faster than a regular modem by itself.

DSL

Another high-speed Internet option is a DSL, which can let you download from the Internet at speeds up to 3 to 4 Mbps, although about 1 Mbps is more common. Most DSL lines are asymmetric, though, which means that the downloading speed is much faster than the uploading speed. Usually, the uploading speed of a DSL line is limited to about the speed of an ISDN line, 128 Kbps.

DSL modems are always connected to the Internet; you don't have to dial in to make a connection. As long as your computer is turned on, you're online and ready to send and receive mail and surf the Internet. They also have a fixed bandwidth, which means that the speed of your connection won't vary with the number of other people also connected to the Internet through their own DSL lines. DSL is available only in certain locations, however, and it works only when you live within a few miles of the local telephone company's office.

To get DSL service, you'll need a special line installed, a special telephone jack, a DSL modem, and an Ethernet card to which the modem connects. Installation costs are generally from $100 to $500, and the modem can cost up to $400, although many DSL companies will rent the DSL modem to you for a minor fee each month. Companies that provide DSL connections generally start at around $40 to $50 per month for the connection, plus the cost of ISP service.

As with ISDN, you'll need a special DSL line and modem for each computer you want to connect to the Internet, which can get quite expensive, or you'll need to set up your network for modem sharing. Having a high-speed, full-time connection to the Internet, though, is a great benefit to any family.

Cable Modems

If you have cable television service in your area, you might also be able to get cable Internet access. The Internet connection is made through the same coaxial cable that brings the television signal into your home, at two-way speeds between 500 Kbps and 20 Mbps, although about 1 Mbps is most common. The coaxial cable connects to a special cable modem that connects, in turn, to an Ethernet network interface card (NIC) in your computer. Because you're permanently connected to the Internet through the cable modem, you don't have to dial in to reach your ISP. Unlike ISDN and DSL, you can have cable modem service regardless of how far you live from the telephone company switches.

Installation usually costs less than $100, not including an Ethernet NIC, if you need to buy one, and the cost of buying or renting the cable modem. You can purchase Ethernet NICs for less than $50, but cable modems can cost up to $400. Monthly Internet charges are usually about $30, plus an additional fee if you rent rather than purchase the modem. You can set up your home network to share the Internet connection (subject to your ISP agreement), or you can purchase additional IP addresses to allow more than one computer to log on at the same time. The number of additional IP addresses you can buy varies with the cable provider and might cost an additional $10 or so per month for each address.

Not every cable TV provider currently offers cable modem service, and those who do might not yet offer it in their entire service area. In addition, the speed of your Internet connection depends on the number of other subscribers in your area who are online at any given time because everyone in the neighborhood (and possibly surrounding neighborhoods) shares the same bandwidth. Still, cable modems are a good alternative if you want a high-speed Internet connection. Call your local cable company to find out whether they offer cable Internet service or to inquire about when the service will become available in your area.

The Everyday Web

Many family members find that Internet access is the primary use of their home computer. In fact, recent research has shown that of the 45 million U.S. households that don't use a computer, more than 11 million still want some form of Internet access. To reduce the overall cost and complexity of Internet access for these individuals, manufacturers are developing special Internet devices—low-cost devices dedicated to providing Web access and e-mail without a computer.

Microsoft, along with hardware manufacturers, is working toward the vision of the *Everyday Web*. The Everyday Web means that Web access and e-mail will be made available inexpensively to everyone in the household, at any time, and from any place. The focus of the Microsoft effort is in the MSN-based Web Companion. Linked to the Web through the MSN Internet service, a *Web Companion* is a small, inexpensive plug-and-play Internet device.

A Web Companion will provide Internet access and e-mail without the user having to worry about configuration, ISPs, operating systems, or other hardware and software issues. Setting up a Web Companion will be as easy as plugging in the power cord and phone line, or connecting the device to a broadband cable or DSL modem or home network.

Because of the low cost, a family could easily have Web Companions located throughout the house—in the kitchen, family room or den, and all the bedrooms. You could take a small, handheld Web Companion on business trips so you could stay in touch with the family, and wireless Web Companion devices could provide connectivity from any location.

Convergence Appliances: Devices of the Future

The natural extension of the Internet device and Web Companion is a single device that serves all your personal communications needs. Toward that end, manufacturers are developing devices named *convergence appliances*, which combine television, the telephone, and the Internet. Products such as WebTV and mobile telephones that access the Internet are converging two or more communications media.

The home of today, however, has at least six devices that provide communications and entertainment:

- Telephone
- Computer
- Television, along with VCR and DVD
- Radio
- Stereo
- Alarm system

As we approach the future, all these devices might converge into a single communications and entertainment device some futurists generically call the *teledevice*. Straight out of a sci-fi movie, the teledevice will connect you to the Internet, serve as a videophone and answering machine, and bring movies, information, and music into every room of your home. It will be integrated into every major appliance in the home, including a home control and security system, and even your refrigerator and coffee maker.

Barcode readers, for example, will be able to detect when you've removed the last bottle of something from the refrigerator or pantry and automatically order more from your local store. You'll use the same display screen to watch movies, to surf the Internet, and to see your friends and relatives as you speak with them.

The teledevice falls right in line with Microsoft chairman Bill Gates's vision of a future in which "the boundary between what is a TV and what is a PC will be completely blurred" and "Americans will live a Web lifestyle." If this dream is realized, you'll be able to get your entertainment and communications needs through one device. You'll no longer need a television to watch entertainment programs and movies, a VCR to watch videos, and a computer to run programs, send and receive mail, and surf the Internet. One device will serve all these functions.

In a "Web lifestyle," getting information online and communicating through e-mail will become a standard fact of life. Just as most people consider the telephone a basic necessity today, the teledevice will become a ubiquitous household fixture.

Currency and charge cards might eventually be replaced completely by smart cards that automatically debit your accounts for purchases and identify your personal needs. When you come home, you'll swipe your smart card through the reader on the teledevice to automatically get your e-mail and other messages, update your bank accounts and portfolio, get the latest headline news that matches your interests, and set the temperature for your personal comfort level. You can see examples of personalized news, investment information, and retailing on the Internet. Amazon.com, for example, can track your interests and buying habits and use that information to recommend new books as they're published.

Smart-card technology promises to extend this personalization into many other areas of your life. In fact, some of the technology is already available. Microsoft's Smart Card for Windows provides a smart-card interface for the Windows environment. You can use it, for example, to authorize logon to a PC or to a computer network.

All this technology will be possible because of advances in hardware and home wiring. In the future, homebuilders will probably routinely install Ethernet, coaxial cable, or fiberoptic cable in all new houses. The home network you're setting up now is just the beginning. You'll have a jump on the future by planning for the complete wired home today.

Index

*Italicized page numbers
indicate figures or tables.*

Numbers and Symbols
4-bit parallel cable, 30
10BaseT cable, 74. *See also*
   twisted-pair cable
10Base2 thin Ethernet coaxial
   cable, 76–77. *See also* thin
   Ethernet coaxial cable
@MailGate mail server, 288–89, *289*

Access
access levels for shared resources,
   36, 190
   configuring network, 163–65,
      163, 164
   passwords for shared resources,
      199–200, *199*
   for peer-to-peer networks, 60
   setting file, 36
   setting up direct connection, 42
   for shared disks and folders,
      193–98, *194–97*
   for shared printers, 241–43, *242*
acoustic couplers, 417
active hubs, 136
Active Server Pages (ASP), 341
address book for Outlook
   adding to profile, 277–79, *278*
   opening, 276, *276*
   using, 275–76
AGP (Accelerated Graphics Port)
   slot, 109
analog telephone connections, 416–17
AppleTalk
   adding protocol to Windows Con-
      trol Panel, 394–95, *395–96*
   setting up for PC MACLAN,
      391, *391*
applications. *See also* software
   default locations for data files
      in shared, 221–22
   enabling MS-DOS programs to
      share network printers, 241
   limitations in sharing Mac and
      PC, 375
   opening remote files within,
      205–6, *206*
   running remotely, 220
   saving remote files from, 206–
      7, *207*

security for shared, 221
working jointly in NetMeeting,
   444–45, *444*
ASP (Active Server Pages), 341
attaching e-mail files, 269
automatic printer switches, 25–
   27, *26–27*

Backing up shared files, 222–27
backup copies of documents, 13
   with Microsoft Backup, 224–
      27, *225–27*
   onto removable disks, 223–24
   overview, 222–23
   storing files remotely, 224
backup jobs, 226, *226*–27
bandwidth, 136
bidirectional printer cables, 23
BNC connector
   female, 128, *128*
   joining male and female, 128
   male, 127, *127*, 128
   T-connectors, 128–29, *128, 135*
bridges
   about, 136
   connecting network types,
      100–102, *101–2*
   defined, 101
   illustrated, *102*
broadband Internet connections,
   312–15, *313–14*
broadband routers, 314, *314*
broadband wireless technologies, 455
browsers
   accessing home page with
      Internet Explorer, 348–49
   browsing network from PC to
      locate Mac folders, 385–86,
      385, 396
   errors finding Web sites with
      Internet Connection Shar-
      ing, 308
   setting default connection in
      Internet Explorer, 422
   sharing Mac and Windows files
      with, 374
   using Web Sharing feature for
      PC/Mac networks, 403
   viewing Mac folders with Win-
      dows, *404*
buffers, adding to printer switch,
   27–28, *28*
bulk cable, 126, 130

Cable Internet service. *See also*
   cable modems
   about, 459–60
   compared with other Internet
      access methods, *457*
   costs and setup for, 6–7, 460
cable modems. *See also* cable
   Internet service
   costs of installation and ser-
      vices, 6–7, 460
   Ethernet connections for, 67
   IP addresses for, 159
   sharing, *294*
   TCP/IP settings for, 160
cables, 121–37. *See also* thin
   Ethernet coaxial cable;
   twisted-pair cable
   adding raceways and floor
      cable covers to, 131–32, *132*
   categories of twisted-pair, 123
   crossover, 124
   for direct cable connections,
      30–31
   drilling holes in walls for, 122, 131
   expanding networks, 132–35,
      133–35
   fiberoptic, 78–79, *78, 79*
   fishing through walls, 131
   installing Ethernet networks in
      the home, 74
   for laptops and remote connec-
      tions, 416
   locating hub, 124–25, *125*
   making network, 126–27, *127*
   networking with USB, 98–99, *99*
   preventing bends in, 130
   printer, 21, 23
   for print servers, 244, 245
   running between rooms, 121–22
   running twisted-pair, 123–24, *123*
   running within room, 121
   tidy installations of, 130–31
   types of Ethernet, 74–77, *74–77*
   using continuous lengths of, 130
   using thin Ethernet coaxial
      cable, 127–31, *127–29*
   wiring homes for high-speed
      access, 456–60
cards. *See* network interface cards
CD-ROMs. *See also* drives
   advantages for networking, 14, 16
   playing games from, 326–27

CD-RW, 15
Centronics port, 245
changing passwords, 175, 178–79, 181
channels for ISDN, 457
chatting in NetMeeting, 439–40, *439*
client computers. *See also* client/server networks
  in client/server networks, 62–65, *62–64*
  configuring Internet access through network, 303–8, *303, 306*
  configuring modem access to Internet, 305
  illustrated, *62*
  sharing modems with host computers, 293
Client for Microsoft Windows, 150–51
clients, e-mail, 258–59
client/server networks
  blending peer-to-peer and, 65
  peer-to-peer networks vs., 59
coaxial cable
  about thin Ethernet, 76–77, *77*
  combining with twisted-pair networks, 135, *135*
  connectors on NIC card, *104*
  selecting NIC cards for, 108
collaborating on shared files, 12–13
combo cards, 108
communications over network, 251–89. *See also* e-mail; mail servers; pop-up messages; WinPopup
  creating network post office, 258–71
  messages on PC/Mac networks with WinPopup, 388–89, *388–89*
  with Outlook, 271–82
  sending and receiving pop-up messages, 251–57
  sticky-note software, 17, *17*
  with VPOP3 shareware mail server, 282–89
computers. *See also* client computers; host computers; Macintosh computers; PC computers
  accessing Mac from PC, 383–84, *384*
  checking for network interface cards, 103–4, *104*
  choosing bus slot for NIC installation, 109–10, *109*
  configuring host with Home Networking Wizard, 301, *301*

connecting old CPUs to other, 54–55, *55*
connecting printers via network, 9–10
creating shortcut to remote, 200
energy-saving features and networking, 61
hardware requirements for playing network games, 325–26
identifying on network, 156–58, *157*
indicating host or guest connections, 37, *37*, 40
installing network printer on, 241–43, *242*
linking to printer via switch box, 24, *24*
in peer-to-peer networks, *60*
performance with gigabyte Ethernet, 73
sharing printers with switch box, 21–25, *22–25*
two people sharing at once, 54
computer superstores, 113–14
configuring Windows for networking, 148–63. *See also* TCP/IP
  adding network client, 150–51
  configuring TCP/IP, 158–63, *161–62*
  identifying computer on network, 156–58, *157*
  installing protocols, 152–54, *153*
  overview, 148–49
  selecting network services, 155–56
connecting network USB devices, 58
connecting printers to network, 232, 244–49
  about, 244–45
  print server manufacturers and models, *249*
  setting up external print servers, 247–49, *248*
  setting up pocket print server, 245–47, *246*
connecting without networks, 21–56. *See also* direct cable connections; networking
  adding buffers to printer switch, 27–28
  with direct connections, 29–46
  extending distance to switch, 28–29, *29*
  with infrared ports, 52–54, *52, 53*
  sharing printers with printer switches, 21–25, *22–25*

software for sharing files and printers, 47–52
two people sharing computer at once, 54
using automatic printer switches, 25–27, *26–27*
using old CPUs, 54–55, *55*
connections. *See also* connecting without networks; Internet Connection Sharing; sharing Internet connections
  choosing type of network, 65–67, *66*
  creating additional dial-up network connections for travel, 420–22
  dialing in to ISP from remote laptops, 418–19, *419*
  dial-up, 308–9, *309*
  Dial-Up Networking, 4, *41*
  with infrared ports, 52–54, *52–53*
  reentering ISP passwords after deleting password file, 179
  sharing Internet, 4–7
connectors
  coaxial, *104*
  twisted-pair, *74, 104*
Consumer Windows. *See also* Microsoft Windows 95; Microsoft Windows 98; Microsoft Windows Millennium Edition
  activating Dial-Up Server in, 426–27, *426–27*
  adding network client in, 150–51
  client/server networks on, 64–65
  deleting all profiles in Registry Editor, 179–81, *180*
  direct cable connections for, 30–35, *32, 34, 35*
  dual-boot configuration for client/server systems, 65
  electronic intercom software in, 16
  enabling MS-DOS programs to share network printers, 241
  enabling printer sharing, 233–34
  identifying computer on network, 157, *157*
  installing Dial-Up Server in, 425–26, *425*
  installing drivers manually in, 143–44, *143–44*
  installing printer drivers on computer in, 234–36, *235*
  installing protocols in, 152–54, *153*
  installing TCP/IP on, 295–96, *296*
  making new dial-up connections for traveling, 420–21

selecting network services in, 155–56

setting IP addresses in, 160–61, *161*

setting IRQ and I/O settings in, 119

setting up remote connections to home network on, 428–30, *429, 430*

troubleshooting undetected hardware in, 142

turning on file sharing, 187–88, *188*

using profiles in, 170–72, *171*

using USB port with, 58

Control Panel, adding network users through, 173–74, *175*

convergence appliances, 461–62

cookies, 170

copying and moving remote files, 209–14, *211–13*

copying and pasting, 212–14, *213*

dragging files, 210–12, *211, 212*

Core Components, 342

costs

of automatic printer switches, 26

of buying DSL and cable modems, 6–7

of cable modem installation and services, 460

of crossover cable, 124

of DSL installation and services, 459

of getting someone to install NICs in your home, 107

of LAN modems, 312

for manual printer switch and cables, 23

for networking starter kits, 67

of network kits, 112–13

for phone-line network systems, 83

savings for multiple users on one ISP account, 6

savings for shared printers, 10

of switches, 136

of USB cable and software kits, 98

couplers, 123, *123*

crossover cables, 124

cross-pinned cable, 124

crosstalk, 75

currency and charge cards, 462

Data files

default locations in shared applications for, 221–22

sharing, 220–22, *222*

DAVE, 376–90

about, 376

accessing Macs from PCs, 383–84, *384*

browsing network from PC to locate Mac folders, 385–86, *385, 396*

communicating on network, 388–89, *388–89*

configuring TCP/IP on Mac, 376–78, *377–78*

installing, 379–83, *379–82*

mounting resources from PC to Mac desktop, 386–88, *387–88*

sharing printers, 389–90

switching TCP/IP configurations, 379

default printers, 238

deleting

all profiles, 179–81, *180*

remote files and folders, 214–15

users, 175

delivery receipt, 269

Depends On Password access, 36, *36*, 190

desktop

creating shortcuts for shared resources on, 200

mounting PC resources to Mac, 386–88, *387–88*

remote sharing of, 415, 446–48, *447*

diagnosing hardware conflicts, 167

Dial-Up Server, 423–28, *424–28*

about dial-up networking, 4

activating in Consumer Windows, 426–27, *426–27*

enabling connection sharing for Windows 2000, 308–9, *309*

installing in Consumer Windows, 425–26, *425*

installing in Windows 2000, 427–28, *427–28*

preparing to install, 423–24, *424*

direct cable connections, 29–46

about, 29

cabling for, 30–31

choosing protocol, 33–35, *34–35*

designating paths for, 45

installing Consumer Windows software for, 31–33, *32*

selecting, 65, *66*

setting up, 35–39, *36–39*

shared resources displayed for, 39–40

for Windows 2000, 40–45, *40–44*

Disable Internet Connection Sharing option, 302, *302*

disabling DHCP, 307

disconnecting network USB devices, 58

diskettes, 11

disks. *See* drives

disk space for network gaming, 325

display requirements for network gaming, 325

DNS server address, 306

documents

backing up copies of, 13

converting to Web page in Word, 372

formatting for Web, 363–65, *363–64*

publishing on home page, 352–55, *353, 354*

setting sharing for My Documents folder, 193

Drafts folder, 281

dragging

activating shortcut menu with right mouse button and, 211

copying and moving files with right mouse button and, 214

copying remote files by, 210–12, *211–12*

moving remote files by, 214

drilling holes in walls for cables, 122, 131

drivers. *See also* network drivers

installing printer, 234–36, *235*

for older or unlisted printers, 236–37

selecting for printers on PC/Mac networks, 405, *405*

using PostScript for shared PC/Mac network printers, 389–90

drives

accessing shared, 193–98, *194–97*

mapping network folders and, 201–4, *202, 204*

mounting PC resources to Mac desktop, 386–88, *387–88*

removable, 15–16, 223–24

sharing, 189–90, 190–92, *191*

sharing on Windows 2000, 216–18, *216–18*

drop box, 345

DSL (digital subscriber line) services

about, 459

buying DSL modems, 6–7

compared with other Internet access methods, *457*

connecting to, 6–7

Ethernet connections for, 67

IP addresses for, 159

sharing modems, *294*
TCP/IP settings for, 160
using USB Ethernet adapters
for network and high-speed
modem, 105
dual-boot configuration for client/
server systems, 65
DVD disk drive. *See* drives
dynamic addressing, 159
Dynamic Host Configuration Protocol (DHCP), disabling, 307

ECP **(Extended Capabilities
Port) parallel cable,** 30
educational advantage for
networkers, 20
EISA (Extended ISA) slots, 109
electronic intercom, 16–17
e-mail. *See also* Outlook; pop-up
messages; Windows Messag-
ing Service
adding Microsoft Mail to profiles, 266–67, *267*
attaching files, 269
creating and addressing, 268–
69, *268*
creating mail profiles, 265–66,
265, 273
creating post office, 262–63, *263*
filing in folders, 271, *271*
mail servers and, 258–59
message options for, 269, *270*
opening Windows Messaging
Inbox, 267–68, *268*
on peer-to-peer networks, 61
reading, 270–71, 282
saving incomplete Outlook
messages, 281
selecting services on Outlook,
272–73
sending, 17, 270, 279–81, *280*
server computers as message
center for, 64,
setting up network post office, 260
setting up Windows Messaging,
264–66, *264–65*
Entire Network option (Windows
2000), 165
erasing passwords, 192
errors
with AppleTalk when installing
PC MACLAN, 394
error messages for Microsoft
Transaction Server or Core
Components, 342
in Windows Messaging Service
for Windows 98, 266

Ethernet cabling for entertainment
and home needs, 453–56
Ethernet networks, 73–79
bridging network types, 100–
102, *100–1*
converting phone-line networks to, 84
defined, 67
Fast Ethernet, 108, 112, 123,
fiberoptic cables, 78–79, *78–79*
gigabyte Ethernet, 73, 108
locating hub for, 124–26, *125*
pros and cons of home installations, 73–74
types of cable for, 74–77, *74–
77*
Ethernet sockets, 126, *127*
Everyday Web, 460–61
Extended Capabilities Port (ECP)
parallel cable, 30
Extended ISA (EISA) slots, 109
extending distance to printer
switch, 28–29, *29*
external print servers, 247–49, *248*

Faceplate, **connecting cables to,**
126, *127*
family games. *See* games
family Web sites, 337–40, *338–39*
FastLynx software, 45–46, *46*
Favorites list, adding shared resources to, 201, *201*
FDM (frequency-division multiplexing), 82
female BNC connector, 128, *128*
fiberoptic cable
with gigabyte Ethernet NICs, 108
using, 78–79, *78–79*
file server function in PC
MACLAN, 396–99, *396–98*
file servers, connecting PCs to
Macs with PC MACLAN,
399–401, *399*, *400–1*
file sharing, 11–14. *See also* remote files
about network, 189–90
accessing shared files, 44–45, *44*
attaching to e-mail, 269
backing up shared files, 222–27
between PCs and Macs, 19–20, 375
cautions with TCP/IP protocol, 188
collaborating on shared files,
12–13
copying remote files by dragging, 210–12, *211–12*
default locations for shared
files, 221–22

deleting remote files and folders, 214–15
designating direct cable connection paths to file, 45
for direct cable connection,
35–40, *40*
enabling, *424*
keeping track of current files, 12
moving remote files by dragging, 214
in NetMeeting, 445–46, *445–46*
one-person-at-a-time rule for,
208–9, *208–9*
opening remote files within
applications, 205–6, *206*
organizing and finding files, 11
protecting files, 13, 158
with remote computers, 204–15
restoring files, 226–27
saving read-only files, 207, *207*
saving remote files from applications, 206–7, *207*
sending files to remote drives,
213, *213*
setting up access to, 36, *36*
sharing data, 220–22, *222*
software for, 47–55
storing on remote computers, 224
transferring via infrared, 53, *53*
Find command, accessing shared
resources with, 198–99, *198*
firewalls
creating, 319–21, *320*
defined, 92
routers and, 312
Flight Simulator 2000, 330–32,
331–33
floppy diskettes, 11
folders. *See also* file sharing
accessing shared, 44–45, *44*,
193–98, *194–97*
deleting remote, 214–15
designating direct cable connection paths to, 45
filing e-mail in, 271, *271*
locating Mac folders from PC
browser, 385–86, *385*, *396*
locating for profiles, 177, *177*
mapping network drives and,
201–4, *202*, *204*
networking, 11–14
setting sharing properties for, 37
sharing, 43–44, *44*, 189–90,
192–93, 218–19
forgotten passwords, 178–79, 181
4-bit parallel cable, 30
frequency-division multiplexing
(FDM), 82

Full access, 36, *36*, 190
future of home networks, 449–62

Games

Flight Simulator 2000, 330–
32, *331, 332, 333*
Hearts, 327–29, *328, 329*
installing for network play, 326
overview, 326–27
playing over network, 18–19, 333
selecting for network play,
324–26
setting up for network play, 324
solo vs. network, 323–24
gigabyte Ethernet
about, 73
NICs and fiberoptic cabling
for, 108
graphics
adding to Web sites, 368–71,
369–72
sharing files for PCs and Macs, 375
groups for Windows 2000 profiles, 182
guest book
defined, 344
PWS drop box and, 349–52,
349–52
guest computers
accessing shared files and folders on host, 44–45, *44*
designating passwords for, 38
finding out status of computer
as, 40
setting up for direct cable connections, 42–43
specifying for direct cable connections, 37, *37*

Hardware. *See also* cables; com-
puters; hubs; printers

Centronics ports, 245
choosing bus slot for NIC installation, 109–10, *109*
compatibility of non-Ethernet, 67
connecting and disconnecting
network USB devices, 58
diagnosing conflicts for, 167
incompatibility for types of
wireless network systems, 89
infrared ports, 52–54, *52–53*
installing drivers for manually
in Windows, 142, 143–45,
143–45
Internet sharing, 311–18
preparing to install NICs, 114–15
purchasing network kits, 112–13
purchasing NICs, 107, 113–14

requirements for playing network games, 325–26
selecting network interface
cards, 108
sharing keyboard, monitor, and
mouse between computers,
55, *55*
superdrives, 15
troubleshooting conflicts for
NIC drivers, 147–48
troubleshooting undetected, 142
uplink ports, 112, 133–34, *134*
Zip drives, 15, 27
Hearts, 327–29, *328–29*
home alarm systems, 453, 454, 461
home entertainment
convergence appliances for,
461–62
using Ethernet cabling for,
453–56
home installations. *See also* cables;
home networks
appearance of cabling in, 130–31
cabling between rooms, 121–22
drilling holes in walls for
cables, 122, 131
of Ethernet networks, 73–74
fishing cable through walls, 131
of phone-line networks, 83, *83,*
84, 84
running cables within room, 121
using surface-mounted jacks
in, 127
of wireless network systems,
87–88, *88*
home networks. *See also* home
installations
controlling home environment
with, 449–53, *451–53*
convergence appliances, 461–62
dialing from remote computers, 423
using Ethernet cabling for entertainment and home
needs, 453–56
using NetMeeting on, 437–38,
437–38
vision of Everyday Web, 460–61
wiring for high-speed access,
456–60
with X10 power-line technology, 449–53, *451–53*
home pages
accessing, 348–49, *348*
creating, 344–47, *345, 346,*
347, 348
defined, 337
editing information on, 347

publishing documents on your,
352–55, *353–54*
PWS guest book and drop box,
349–52, *349–52*
home phone line connections. *See*
phone-line networks
host computers
accessing shared files and folders on, 45
configuring with Home Networking Wizard, 301, *301*
finding out status of computer
as, 40
setting up ports for direct cable
connections, 41
setting up for shared broadband Internet connections,
312–15, *313–14*
sharing modems with client
computers, 293
specifying for direct cable connections, 37, *37*, 39
HTML (Hypertext Markup Language), 339
hubless networking, 124
hubs. *See also* routers
about, 111–12
defined, 75, *76*
expanding networks with uplink ports, 133–34, *134*
Fast Ethernet, 108, 112
linking together with twisted-
pair cable, 132–34, *133–34*
locating, 124–26, *125*
replacing with switches, 136
shared resources for uplink
ports, 134
types of, 135–136
USB, 96–97, *97*
hyperlinks, 339, 365–68, *365–67*
Hypertext Markup Language
(HTML), 339

Icons

fitting on Quick Launch
toolbar, 253
shared file, 37
WinPopup message, 257, *257*
IEEE 1284 compliant printer
cables, 23
IIS (Internet Information Services), 355–56, *355*
iMacs
adding superdisks to, 15
Ethernet port on, 373
Industry Standard Architecture
(ISA) slots, 109, 110
infrared ports, 52–54, *52, 53*

installing
DAVE, 379–83, *379–82*
external print servers, 245
games for network play, 326
Internet Connection Sharing,
298–302, *298–302*
ISA network cards, 117–19, *118*
Microsoft Backup, 224–25
Microsoft Mail Postoffice,
260–62, *260*
network client software, 150–51
network drivers, 141–48, *143–45*
network interface cards, 106,
115–17, *116–17*
PC Card NIC for laptops,
110–11
Personal Web Server, 341–42, *342*
printer drivers on computer,
234–36, *235*
TCP/IP on Consumer Win-
dows, 295–96, *296*
instant messaging (IM), 16
in-store installations of NIC
cards, 107
Integrated Services Digital Network. *See* ISDN
internal cards. *See* network interface cards
Internet. *See also* Internet Connection Sharing; Internet sharing hardware; ISPs
configuring client computers
for network access to, 304–5
configuring clients to access
through own modem, 305
connecting to through Internet
Connection Sharing, 307–8
disabling connection sharing,
302, *302*
downloading MacIPX, 374
firewall, 92, 312, 319–21, *320*
protecting files on shared connections, 158
satellite access to, 458–59
security for shared connections,
318–21, *320*
sending Outlook mail in RTF
format, 279
setting up client computers to
access through network,
303–4, *303*
sharing broadband connec-
tions, 312–15, *313–14*
sharing ISP connections, 4–7, 112
turning off Internet file sharing, 319
Internet Connection Sharing
adjusting, 302, *302*

configuring clients to connect
to Internet via, 306–7, *306*
connecting to Internet
through, 307–8
disabling DHCP, 307
installing, 298–302, *298–302*
for PC/Mac networks, 409–10, *410*
specifying static network addresses for clients, 305–6
Internet Engineering Task Force
(IETF), 159
Internet Information Services
(IIS), 355–56, *355*
Internet service providers. *See* ISPs
Internet sharing hardware, 311–18
overview, 311–12
sharing broadband Internet,
312–15, *313–14*
Internetwork Packet Exchange/
Sequenced Packet Exchange.
See IPX/SPX
intranets, 337
I/O addresses
checking available, 146
checking IRQ and I/O ad-
dresses in Windows, 146–47
setting for NIC cards, 117–19, *118*
IP (Internet Protocol) addresses.
See also static network addresses
about, 159
assigning to Mac, 390–91
attaching modem to communicate over, 7
changes to when installing
Internet Connection Shar-
ing, 299–300
checking network settings for, 166
configuring clients to obtain
automatically, 303
getting mail server's, 286
network address translation, 314
setting, 160–61, *161*
shared broadband connections
using multiple, 313–14,
313–14
for TCP/IP pocket print servers, 245
tips on entering, 161
using broadband routers, *314*
IPX protocol, downloading for
Macs, 374
IPX/SPX (Internetwork Packet
Exchange/Sequenced Packet
Exchange)
choosing for direct cable connections, 33
installing protocols, 152–54, *153*

IRQ (interrupt request)
checking addresses in Consumer Windows, 146
checking addresses in Windows
2000, 146–47
setting for NIC cards, 117–19, *118*
unavailable addresses for, 146
ISA (Industry Standard Architecture) slots, 109, 110
ISA network cards
checking IRQ and I/O ad-
dresses in Windows, 146–47
installing, 117–19, *118*
ISDN (Integrated Services Digital
Network)
about, 457–58
compared with other Internet
access methods, *457*
modems for, *294*
ISPs (Internet service providers)
agreements for sharing accounts, 4, 5, 291, 454
assigning IP addresses, 159
connecting to, 4
dialing in from remote computers, 418–19, *419*
displaying DNS server address
of, 306
getting money's worth from, 6

Jacks
phone, 83, *83*
surface-mounted, 127
joysticks for network gaming, 325
jumper settings for IRQ, 118, *118*

Keyboard sharing between computers, 55, *55*
KVM (keyboard, video, and
mouse) switch, 55

LAN modems, 312
laptops. *See also* remote files
accessing home computer remotely from, 432, *432*
connecting with infrared ports,
52–54, *52–53*
creating additional dial-up
network connections for
travel, 420–22
dialing home network from, 423
dialing in to ISP from, 418–
19, *419*
installing PC Card NIC for,
110–11
preparing for remote computing, 416–18, *417*

remote desktop sharing, 415,
446–48, *447*
setting up remote connections
to home network, 428–31,
429–30
suspend state, 61
line testers, 418
links, 339, 365–68, *365–67*
logging on
adding user profiles when,
172–75, *173–74*
as different user or switching
profiles, 175–76
with Microsoft Family Logon,
150–51, 176

Macintosh computers. *See also*
**AppleTalk; iMacs; PC and
Mac networks**
accessing from Network Neighborhood, 383–84, *384*
assigning IP addresses to, 390–91
configuring TCP/IP on, 376–
78, *377–78*
MacIPX, downloading, 374
mail order purchases of hardware,
107, 113–14
mail servers, 258–71. *See also*
Microsoft Mail Postoffice;
VPOP3 mail server
@MailGate, 288–89, *289*
e-mail clients and, 258–59
function of, 258
getting IP address for, 286
Microsoft Mail Postoffice as
network, 260–71
VPOP3 shareware, 282–89,
283–85, 287–89
making cables, 126–27, *127*
male BNC connector, 127, *127*, 128
manual printer switches, 22–23, *22*
mapping network drives and folders, 86, *86*, 201–4, *202, 204*
messaging. *See* communications
over network
Microsoft Backup, 224–27, *225–27*
installing, 224–25
starting and restoring files,
226–27
for Windows 95 and 98, 224
for Windows 2000, 225, *225*
Microsoft Exchange, 259. *See also*
Windows Messaging Service
Microsoft Family Logon, 150–51, 176
Microsoft Internet Directory,
438–39, *439*
Microsoft Internet Explorer
accessing home page with,
348–49

setting default connection in, 422
Microsoft Mail
adding to Outlook profile, 274
adding to profiles, 266–67, *267*
Microsoft Mail Postoffice, 258,
260–64. *See also* Outlook;
Windows Messaging Service
adding post office users, 263–
64, *264*
creating post office, 262–63, *263*
installing, 260–62, *260*
Outlook Express incompatible
with, 259
setting up network post office
with, 260
setting up Windows Messaging, 264–66, *264–65*
Microsoft NetMeeting, 251, 432–46
about, 432–33, *433*
chatting in, 439–40, *439*
connecting to Microsoft
Internet Directory, 438–39, *439*
sending and receiving files,
445–46, *445–46*
starting and adjusting, 433–36,
434–36
using on home network, 437–
38, *437–38*
using whiteboard in, 440–43,
440–43
working together on applications with, 444–45, *444*
Microsoft Personal Web Server
(PWS), 340–55
accessing home page, 348–49, *348*
creating home pages, 344–47,
345–48
guest book and drop box for,
349–52, *349–52*
IIS and, 355
installing, 341–42, *342*
publishing documents on your
site, 352–55, *353–54*
using Personal Web Manager,
342–44, *344*
Microsoft Transaction Server, 342
Microsoft Windows 95. *See also*
Consumer Windows
accessing network in, 163–64,
163–64
accessing shared disks and folders in, 194–95, *194–95*
Microsoft Backup for, 224–27,
225–27
using USB port with, 58
Web servers for, 340
Microsoft Windows 98. *See also*
Consumer Windows

accessing network in, 163–64,
163–64
accessing shared disks and folders in, 194–95, *194–95*
electronic intercom software in, 16
installing Internet Connection
Sharing for, 300
Microsoft Backup for, 224–27,
225–27
modem-sharing features in, 5, 7
Microsoft Windows 2000
accessing network in, 165
adding network client in, 151
cabling for direct cable connections, 30–31
choosing protocol for direct
cable connections, 33–35,
34–35
configuring TCP/IP in, 162–
63, *162*
creating Web sites in, 355–56, *355*
electronic intercom software in, 16
enabling Internet connection
sharing for, 308–9, *309*
identifying computer on network, 158
installing Dial-Up Server, 427–
28, *427, 428*
installing drivers manually in,
144–45, *145*
installing printer drivers for
computer in, 234–36, *235*
installing protocols in, 154
making new dial-up connections for traveling, 422
Microsoft Backup for, 225, *225*
modem-sharing features in, 5, 7
selecting network services in,
155–56
setting IRQ and I/O settings
in, 119
setting up direct cable connections, 40–45, *40–44*
setting up remote connections
to home network on, 431
sharing drives, 216–18, *216–18*
sharing printers in, 240, *240–41*
troubleshooting undetected
hardware, 142
turning on file sharing for,
215–16, *216*
user profiles for, 182–86, *183–85*
using USB port with, 58
using VPOP3 mail server with, 258
verifying TCP/IP installation, 297
Microsoft Windows Millennium
Edition. *See also* Consumer
Windows

accessing network in, 165
accessing shared disks and folders in, 195–96, *195–96*
configuring host with Home Networking Wizard, 301, *301*
electronic intercom software in, 16
installing Internet Connection Sharing for, 300–1, *301*
modem-sharing features in, 5, 7
using Home Networking Wizard, 149
using VPOP3 mail server with, 258
Web servers for, 340
Microsoft Word, 356–72
adding graphics to Web sites, 368–71, *369–72*
converting document to Web page, 372
creating Web sites with Web Page Wizard, 357–61, *358–61*
formatting Web documents in Web Layout view, 363–65, *363–64*
steps for creating Web sites, 360–61, *362*
Web design in, 356–57
working with hyperlinks, 365–68, *365–67*
modems. *See also* modem-sharing software
comparison of Internet access methods for analog and cable, *457*
DSL, 6–7, 105, *294*
ISDN, *294*
sharing, 5–6
sharing vs. connecting to hub, 111
software and hardware alternatives for shared, 293–95, *294*
software preparations for sharing, 295
USB Ethernet adapters for high-speed, 105
using acoustic coupler with, 417
modem server, 312
modem-sharing software, 297–311. *See also* Internet Connection Sharing; modems
adjusting Internet Connection Sharing, 302, *302*
installing Internet Connection Sharing, 298–302, *298–302*
Internet Connection Sharing with Windows 2000, 308–9, *309*
listing of, 309–10, *311*
overview, 297–98
running Internet Connection Setup Wizard, 304–8, *306*

setting up client computers for, 303–4, *303*
monitors
display requirements for network gaming, 325
sharing between computers, 55, *55*
mounting resources from PC to Mac desktop, 386–88, *387–88*
mouse
dragging file holding down right mouse button, 211, 214
sharing between computers, 55, *55*
Move Here command, 214
moving remote files, 214
MS-DOS programs and printer sharing, 241
multiplayer games, 18–19
My Computer
accessing remote files in, 204–5
dragging and copying file between Network Neighborhood and, *212*
shared network resources displayed in, *87*
My Network Places
accessing Mac from, 383–84, *384*
accessing remote files in, 204–5
accessing shared disks and folders in, 195–97, *195–97*
checking network settings with, 166

NAT (network address translation), 314
NetBEUI (NetBIOS Enhanced User Interface)
choosing for direct cable connections, 33
installing, 152–54, *153*
troubleshooting, 167
using in case of TCP/IP conflicts, 160
network cable connections, 65, *66*, 67
network clients
adding, 150–51
client computers, *62*
in client/server networks, 62–65, *62–64*
client/server and peer-to-peer networks, 59, 65
defined, 148
network drivers, 141–48, *143–45*. *See also* drivers
about, 68

checking hardware conflicts with NIC, 147–48
installing manually in Windows, 142, 143–45, *143–45*
installing for non-plug-and play NICs, 145–47
loading automatically, 142–43
types of installations for, 141–42
networking, 3–20. *See also* configuring Windows for networking; PC and Mac networks; planning networks; *and specific network types*
about peer-to-peer and client/server networks, 59
bridging Macs and PCs, 19–20, 375
bridging network types, 100–102, *100–1*
CD-ROMs and removable drives, 14–16
educational advantage for, 20
expanding networks, 132–35, *133–35*
files and folders, 11–14
hubless, 124
identifying computer on network, 156–58, *157*
ISP customer agreements and shared accounts, 4, 5, 291
network interface cards, 57–59, *58*
planning, 57–66
playing family games, 18–19
sending mail, messages, and reminders, 17–18
sharing Internet connections with, 4–7, 112
sharing modems, 5–6
sharing printers, 7–10, 405–8, *405–8*
software licensing agreements and, 219–20
suspend state and, 61
using electronic intercom, 16–17
network interface cards (NICs), 103–19
about, 57–59, *58*
checking computers for, 103–4, *104*
checking hardware conflicts with drivers for, 147–48
choosing bus slot for installing, 109–10, *109*
connecting phone cables with, 83, *83*
for Ethernet connections, 67
finding someone to install, 106–7

with hubs and switches, 111–12
installing, 106, 115–17, *116–17*
installing drivers for non–plug-and-play, 145–47
ISA card installation, 117–19, *118*
loading drivers automatically for, 142–43
with non-Ethernet networks, 81–82
PC Card NICs for laptops, 110–11
plugging into USB or printer port, 104–5, *105*
preparing to install, 114–15
for printers, 244
purchasing in network kits, 112–13
selecting, 108
shopping for, 113–14
network kits, 112–13
Network Neighborhood
accessing Mac from, 383–84, *384*
accessing remote files in, 204–5
accessing shared disks and folders in Windows 95 and 98, 194–95, *194–95*
checking network access in, *163*, 164
dragging and copying file between My Computer and, *212*
troubleshooting, 166
network operating systems, 68
network post office. *See* Microsoft Mail Postoffice
network services, 149, 155–56
non-Ethernet networks, 81–102
about, 81
bridging network types, 100–102, *100–1*
phone-line networks, 82–84, *86–87*
power-line networks, 91–96, *93–95*
USB direct cable networks, 96–100, *97*, *99*
wireless systems, 87–91, *88*, *91*
non–plug-and-play NICs, 145–47
null modem serial cable, 30

Office 2000 repairs after installing Windows Messaging Service, 261
one-person-at-a-time file sharing rule, 208–9, *208–9*
opening
remote files within applications, 205–6, *206*
Windows Messaging Inbox, 267–68, *268*
organizing and finding files, 11

Outlook, 271–82
about, 271–72
adding address book to profile, 277–79, *278*
adding Microsoft Mail to profile, 274
creating mail profile, 273
for Internet and network e-mail, 272
opening address book, 276, *276*
reading messages, 282
removing profiles, 275
saving incomplete messages, 281
selecting mail service on, 272–73
sending messages with, 279–81, *280*
using address book for, 275–76
using different profiles, 274–75
versions of, 272, 273
Outlook Express
configuring access to through client modem, 305
incompatibility with Microsoft Mail Postoffice, 259
setting up for VPOP3 mail server, 286–89, *287–89*
using for Internet and network e-mail, 272

Passive hubs, 135
passwords
for accessing shared resources, 199–200, *199*
changing, 175, 178–79, 181
designating access for shared resources with, *191*
erasing, 192
for guests on direct cable connections, 38
setting for network users, 172
patch cable
crossover cable vs., 124
defined, 123
installing connectors on, 126
path
designating for direct cable connections, 45
typing to remote files, 198–99
PC Card NICs, 110–11
PC computers. *See also* PC and Mac networks
bridging Macs and, 19–20
file sharing between Macs and, 19–20, 375
text files on Macs and, 375
PCI (Peripheral Component Interconnect) slots, 109, 110
PC and Mac networks, 373–413

bridging, 19–20
communicating with WinPopup, 388–89, *388*, *389*
DAVE software for, 376–90
files that can be shared, 375
Internet Connection Sharing for, 409–10, *410*
overview of, 373, 413
planning, 373–75
shared Internet connections with proxy servers, 410–12, *411–12*
shared Windows printer, 405–8, *405–8*
sharing files, 19–20, 403–4
using PC MACLAN, 390–403
peer-to-peer networks
about, 59–62, *60*, *62*
blending client/server and, 65
client/server networks vs., 59
configuring TCP/IP on Mac for, 376–78, *377–78*
performance
of DSL and cable modems, 7
of Ethernet networks, 73
of phone-line networks, 83
switches improving, 136
of USB direct cable networks, 97
using continuous lengths of cables, 130
Peripheral Component Interconnect (PCI) slots, 109, 110
permissions
changing in Windows 2000, *218*
setting for groups, 186
setting for sharing in Windows 2000, *217*
for shared printers, 240, *241*
personalizing user profiles, 172–75, *173–74*
Personal Web Manager, 342–44, *343–44*
phone jacks, 83, *83*
phone-line networks, 82–87, *82*, *86–87*
bridges for, *101*, 102
characteristics of, 65, *66*
choosing system for, 85
pros and cons of, 83–84, *83–84*
piconet, 455
pitfalls of network game playing, 333
planning networks, 57–69
about network interface cards, 57–59, *58*
blending peer-to-peer and client/server networks, 65

choosing peer-to-peer or client/
server networks, 59
client/server networks, 62–65,
62–64
peer-to-peer networks, 59–62,
60, 62
types of network connections,
65–67, *66*
understanding network drivers
and operating systems, 68
plug-and-play compatibility
network drivers for plug-and-
play NICs, 142
of PCI cards, 110
pocket servers
defined, 244
setting up, 245–47, *246*
POP (Post Office Protocol),
about, 259
pop-up messages, 251–57. *See also*
e-mail; WinPopup
ports. *See also* printer ports; USB port
Centronics, 245
connecting printer to parallel, 10
infrared, 52–54, *52–53*
selecting for direct cable connections, *38*
setting up for host direct cable
connections, 41
setting up to connect computers, 48–49, *49*
uplink, 112, 133–34, *134*
PostScript drivers, 389–90
power-line networks, 91–96, *93–95*
about, 91–92
characteristics of, 65, *66*
pros and cons of, 92
preventing bends in cables, 130
printer cables, 21, 23, *23*
printer ports
network interface cards that
plug in, 104–5, *105*
plugging NIC into, 105
printers, 7–10, 231–49
accessing shared, 241–43, *242*
adding buffers to printer
switch, 27–28
benefits of shared, 231–32
cables for, 21, 23, *23*
cautions sharing with TCP/IP
protocol, 188
connecting directly to network,
9–10, 244–49
connecting to parallel ports, 10
drivers for older or unlisted,
236–37
enabling sharing of, 233–34,
237–38, *238*

extending distance to switch,
28–29, *29*
installing drivers on computer,
234–36, *235*
linking computers to multiple,
24–25, *25*
MS-DOS applications with
shared, 241
parallel or USB printer connections to network, 232
permissions for shared, 240, *241*
preparing for printing, 232–33
reasons for networking, 7–9
selecting network, 243
separating print jobs, 238–39, *239*
setting default, 238
sharing on PC/Mac networks,
389–90
sharing with printer switches,
21–25, *22–25*
sharing Windows, 405–8,
405–8
shortcuts for, 243–44
software for sharing, 47–55
using automatic printer
switches, 25–27, *26–27*
Windows 2000 shared, 240,
240–41
printer switches
adding buffers to, 27–28, *28*
automatic, 25–27, *26, 27*
costs for, 23
extending distance to, 28–29, *29*
manual, 22–23, *22*
using, 21–25, *22–25*
printing
preparing shared printers for,
232–33
separating print jobs, 238–39, *239*
whiteboard, 443
print servers
connecting printers to network
with, 244–45
enabling in PC MACLAN,
401–2, *401–2*
installing external, 245
manufacturers and models of
external, *249*
setting up external, 247–49, *248*
processors for network gaming, 325
profiles, 169–86
adding Microsoft Mail to,
266–67, *267*
adding and personalizing user,
172–75, *173–74*
changing passwords for, 178–
79, 181

changing user settings, 175
configuring Windows 2000,
182–86, *183–85*
contents of, 169–70
creating mail, 265–66, *265*
creating and modifying Outlook, 273, 274, 275
defined, 169
deleting all, 179–81, *180*
locating folders for, 177, *177*
logging on as different user or
switching, 175–76
turning on for Consumer Windows, 170–72, *171*
using different mail, 274–75
program sharing, 219–22
running programs remotely, 220
sharing data files, 220–22, *222*
software licensing agreements
and, 219–20
pros and cons
of phone-line networks, 83–84,
83–84
of power-line networks, 92
of wireless network systems,
88–89
protecting original files, 13
protocols. *See also* IPX/SPX;
NetBEUI; TCP/IP
choosing for direct cable connections, 33–35, *34–35*
defined, 149
indicating in Flight Simulator,
331, *331*
for installation on dial-up
server, 423
installing, 152–54, *153*
for network games, 324
for print servers, 245
setting up for direct cable connections, 42, *42*, 43
troubleshooting problems with, 167
used by Macs, 373–74
proxy servers
defined, 310
sharing Internet connections
for PCs and Macs with,
410–12, *411–12*
purchasing
NICs, 107, 113–14
NICs with network kits, 112–13
raceways and cable covers,
131–32, *132*

Queuing printing, 232–33
Quick Launch toolbar, 253
Quick Logon feature, 203–4

Raceways, 131–32, *132*
RAM requirements for network gaming, 325
reading e-mail, 270–71
Read-Only access, 36, *36*, 190
read-only files, saving, 207, *207*
Read Receipt button, 269
receivers
  with printer switches, 28, *29*
  for X10 power lines, 450
receiving
  NetMeeting files, 445–46, *445–46*
  pop-up messages, 251–57
Recycle Bin, deleting remote files in, 214
Registry Editor, 179–81, *180*
remote computers, 415–48. *See also* remote files
  accessing home computer from, 432, *432*
  creating dial-up network connections for travel, 420–22
  creating shortcut to, 200
  dialing in to ISP, 418–19, *419*
  installing Dial-Up Server, 423–28, *424–28*
  preparing laptops as, 416–18, *417*
  remote desktop sharing, 415, 446–48, *447*
  setting up connection to home network on laptop, 428–31, *429*, *430*
  storing files on, 224
  using NetMeeting, 251, 432–46
remote desktop sharing, 415, 446–48, *447*
remote files, 204–15. *See also* file sharing
  accessing with Network Neighborhood, My Network Places, or My Computer, 204–5
  copying and moving, 209–14, *211–13*
  deleting, 214–15
  moving, 214
  opening within applications, 205–6, *206*
  saving from applications, 206–7, *207*
  sending files to remote drives, 213, *213*
  sharing with one-person-at-a-time rule, 208–9, *208–9*
  typing path to, 198–99
removable drives
  advantages for networking, 15–16
  backing up shared files onto, 223–24

repeaters, 136
restoring files, 226–27
revision marks, 12, *13*
RJ-11 connectors, *74,* 416, 418
RJ-45 connectors, *74*
routers. *See also* hubs
  about, 311–12
  broadband, 314, *314*
  configuring, 315
  network address translation and, 314
rules for installing cables, 130–31
Run command, accessing shared resources with, 198–99, *198*
Run dialog box
  accessing files on home computer remotely with, *432*
  accessing home page from, 348, *348*
running applications remotely, 220

Satellite Internet access, 458–59
saving
  incomplete Outlook messages, 281
  read-only files, 207, *207*
  remote files from applications, 206–7, *207*
  whiteboard, 443
security, 318–21, *320*
  about shared Internet connections and, 318
  creating firewalls, 319–21, *320*
  home alarm systems, 453, 454, 461
  for program sharing, 221
  turning off Internet file sharing, 319
selecting games for network play, 324–26
selecting network printers, 243
sending
  e-mail, 17, 270
  files to remote drives, 213, *213*
  messages with Windows Messaging Service, 270
  NetMeeting files, 445–46, *445–46*
  Outlook messages, 279–81, *280*
  pop-up messages, 254–57, *255–57*
separator pages, 238–39, *239*
serial port devices, network interfaces for, 105
server computers in client/server networks, 62–65, *62–64*
shares, 189
shareware
  for creating Web servers, 340
  for mail servers, 282–89, *283–85, 287–89*

sharing, 187–228. *See also* access; file sharing; printing
  accessing resources with Windows Explorer, Run, and Find commands, 198–99, *198*
  accessing shared disks and folders, 193–98, *194–97*
  access levels for, 190
  adding shared resources to Favorites list, 201, *201*
  backing up shared files, 222–27, *225–27*
  creating desktop shortcuts for, 200
  data files, 220–22, *222*
  disks, folders, and files, 189–90
  drives, 190–92, *191*
  folders, 192–93, 218–19
  Internet connections, 4–7
  mapping network drives and folders for, 201–4, *202*, *204*
  modems, 5–6
  network performance and, 4
  printers, 7–10, 389–90
  printers with printer switches, 22–25, *22–25*
  programs, 219–22
  remote files, 204–15
  selecting network services to configure, 155–56
  software for sharing files and printers, 47–55
  turning on file, 187–88, *188*
  turning on for Windows 2000, 215–19, *216–18*
  Windows printer, 405–8, *405–8*
sharing Internet connections, 4–7, 112, 291–321
  alternatives for, 293–95, *294*
  hardware for, 311–18
  installing TCP/IP, 295–97, *296*
  ISP agreements for, 4, 5, 291, 454
  modem-sharing software, 297–311
  overview, 291–92, *291*, 292–93
  security and, 318–21, *320*
  software preparations for sharing modem, 295
shortcut menu, 211
shortcuts
  creating for printers, 243–44
  creating to files on remote computer, 213
  for shared resources on desktop, 200
slots
  choosing bus slot for installing NICs, 109–10, *109*
  removing cover plates for, *116*
smart cards, 462

software, 141–67. *See also* applications; network drivers; *and specific software*
about network drivers, 68
accessing network from computer, 163–65, *163–64*
adding network client, 150–51
adding new hardware manually in Windows, 142
checking hardware conflicts with NIC drivers, 147–48
configuring Windows for networking, 148–63
for direct cable connections, 45–46, *46*
drivers for older or unlisted printers, 236–37
installing network drivers, 141–48, *143–45*
installing printer drivers, 234–36, *235*
listing of modem-sharing, 309–10, *311*
for networking PCs and Macs, 374–75
for non-Ethernet networks, 81
for phone-line networks, 85–87, *86–87*
selecting printer drivers on PC/Mac networks, 405, *405*
for sharing files and printers, 47–55
troubleshooting network, 166–67
using PostScript drivers for shared PC/Mac network printers, 389–90
software licensing agreements and program sharing, 219–20
solo vs. network game playing, 323–24
sound cards for network gaming, 325
speed
of Fast Ethernet, 108
of hubs, 112
wiring homes for high-speed access, 456–60
spread spectrum, 89
stackable hubs, 136
starting NetMeeting, 433–36, *434–36*
static electricity, 115
static network addresses
assigning to client computers, 305–6
changes to with Internet Connection Sharing, 299–300
configuring routers for, 315
defined, 159
for PCs networking with Macs, 376

sticky-note software, 17, *17*
storing files remotely, 224
STP (shielded twisted-pair) cable, 75, *75*
subnet masks, 159–60
checking network settings for, 166
configuring for ZyXEL Prestige 310 router, 315
tips on entering, 161
superdisks, 15
surface-mounted jacks, 127
surge protectors, 418
suspend state, 61
switches. *See also* printer switches
defined, 112
increasing performance with, 136
printer, 21–25, *22–25*
switching profiles, 175–76

T-connectors, 128–29, *128*, *135*
TCP/IP (Transmission Control Protocol/Internet Protocol), 158–63, *161–62*
about IP addresses, 159
cautions for file/printer sharing with, 188
configuring client computers to obtain IP addresses automatically, 303
configuring on Mac, 376–78, *377–78*
configuring in Windows 2000, 162–63, *162*
for direct cable connections, 33
installing, 152–54, *153*
installing on Consumer Windows, 295–96, *296*
Mac support for, 373–74
required for Dial-Up Server, 423
setting IP addresses in Consumer Windows, 160–61, *161*
switching configurations for Mac ISPs and network connections, 379
troubleshooting, 160, 166
verifying installation for Windows 2000, 297
teledevices, 461
telephone cable coupler, 416
telephone connector, *74*
telephone-line networks. *See* phone-line networks
terminators, *129, 135*
text editing in shared files, *13*
text files on Macs and PCs, 375
thin Ethernet coaxial cable, 127–31, *127–29*

about, 76–77, *76*
connectors for, 103, *104*, 127–29, *127–28*
making, 130
terminators for, *129, 135*
ThinNet. *See* thin Ethernet coaxial cable
transceivers
defined, 87–88, *89*
for X10 power lines, 450
transformers, 92
transmitters
with printer switches, 28, *29*
for X10 power lines, 450
traveling. *See* remote computers
troubleshooting
AppleTalk errors when installing PC MACLAN, 394
changes to Windows Registry, 179
checking network settings, 166–67
computers not appearing in Network Neighborhood window, *163*, 164
conflicts with TCP/IP, 160
diagnosing hardware conflicts, 167
error messages for Microsoft Transaction Server or Core Components, 342
hardware conflicts for NIC network drivers, 147–48
Network Neighborhood, 166
problems accessing ASP Web pages, 341
unavailable IRQ addresses, 146
undetected hardware in Windows, 142
turning off Internet file sharing, 319
turning on
Consumer Windows profiles, 170–72, *171*
file server function on Windows computer, 396–99, *396–98*
file sharing for Consumer Windows, 187–88, *188*
file sharing for Windows 2000, 215–16, *216*
Mac file sharing, 392–94, *392–93*
printer sharing, 233–34, 237–38, *238*
Quick Logon feature, 203–4
twisted-pair cable
about, 123–24, *123*
categories of, 123
combining with coaxial networks, 135, *135*

illustrated, *75*
linking hubs together with,
132–34, *133–34*
running, 123–24, *123*
selecting NIC cards for, 108
twisted-pair connector
illustrated, *74*
for NIC card, *104*

UCM (**Universal Cable Module**)
parallel cable, 30
UNC (Universal Naming Convention), 45, 198-99
uplink ports
defined, 112
expanding network with, 133–
34, *134*
USB (universal serial bus) devices
Ethernet adapters for network
and high-speed modem, 105
hubs, 96–97, *97*
transceivers for wireless networks, 88
USB direct cable networks, 96–
100, *97*, *99*
about, 96–98, *97*
ActionLink, 98, 100–101
EZLink system, 98, 99
USB Direct Connect system,
98–99, *98–99*
USB port, 15, 58
adding to older computers, 96
connecting and disconnecting
network devices to, 58
connecting printers to network
with, 232
network interface cards that
plug in, 104–5, *105*
phone-line networks for, 85
users
adding and personalizing profiles, 172–75, *173–74*
adding to post office, 263–64, *264*
adding for VPOP3 mail server, 285
passwords for, 172, 175
setting up access for direct connections, 42
UTP (unshielded twisted-pair)
cable, 75, *75*

Video with NetMeeting, *438*
virtual computers, 54
VPOP3 mail server, 282–89
installing and adding setting
up, 283–85, *284–85*
setting up Outlook Express for,
286–89, *287–89*

using for Outlook Express
Internet e-mail, 272
using Outlook Express with, 259
with Windows Me and Win-
dows 2000, 258

Web browsers. *See* browsers
Web Companion, 460–61
Web design in Microsoft Word,
356–57
Web Layout view, 363–65, *363–64*
Web servers. *See also* Microsoft
Personal Web Server
IIS and Personal Web Server, 355
installing Personal Web Server,
341–42, *342*
Internet Information Services,
355–56, *355*
as means of networking Macs
and PCs, 374–75
sharing PC/Mac files as, 403–
4, *403–4*
Web sites, 337–72. *See also*
Microsoft Word
about hyperlinks and HTML, 339
adding graphics to in Word,
368–71, *369–72*
converting Word document to
Web page, 372
creating with Personal Web
Server, 340–55
creating in Word, 356–72
designing with Web Page Wizard,
357–61, *358–61*
developing in Windows 2000,
355–56, *355*
family, 337–40, *338–39*
for modem-sharing software, *310*
for power-line network products, 92
publishing documents on,
352–55, *353–54*
shareware for creating, 340
vision of Everyday Web, 460–61
whiteboard for NetMeeting, 440–
43, *440–43*
Windows CD, installing Direct Cable
Connection from, 32–33
Windows computers. *See* PC and
Mac networks; PC computers
Windows Explorer
accessing shared resources
from, 198
copying by dragging remote
files, 210–12, *211–12*
Windows Messaging Service (WMS)
about, 259

attaching files, 269
creating and addressing messages, 268–69, *268*
creating mail profiles, 265–66, *265*
filing messages in folders, 271, *271*
fixing error in Windows 98
Second Edition, 266
message options, 269, *270*
opening inbox, 267–68, *268*
reading messages in Inbox,
270–71
running after installing Office
2000, 261
sending messages, 270
setting up, 264–66, *264–65*
WinPopup
about, 252
communicating on PC/Mac networks with, 388–89, *388–89*
installing, 254, *254*
message icons in, 257–57
sending and receiving messages,
254–57, *255–57*
starting, 252–53, *253*
wireless network systems, 87–91,
88, *91*
about wireless connections, 65, *66*
bridges for, *101*, 102
choosing, 89–91, *91*
enabling infrared ports, 52–54,
52–53
installing NICs for, 116
pros and cons of, 88–89
transceivers and, 87–88, *89*
wiring homes for high-speed access, 456–60
workgroups, 149
working copies of files, 13

X10 power-line technology, 449–
53, *451–53*

Zip drives
about, 15
adding to automatic printer
switches, 27
backing up shared files onto,
223–24
zones for security settings, 320–
21, *320*

Alan Neibauer

Alan Neibauer has written several best-selling computer books, including *Running Microsoft Outlook 2000*. With a master's degree from the Wharton School, he has helped organizations of all sizes network their business information systems. Neibauer served as chairperson of Computer Management Information Systems at Holy Family College in Philadelphia, and has been an active corporate trainer and consultant. He and his wife Barbara, both black belts in Tae Kwon Do, enjoy practicing martial arts on the beaches of New Jersey and riding the summertime waves.

The manuscript for this book was prepared and galleyed using Microsoft Word 2000. Pages were composed by nSight (nSightworks.com) using Adobe PageMaker 6.52 for Windows, with text in AGaramond and display type in Garamond Condensed. Composed pages were delivered to the printer as electronic prepress files.

Cover Art Director:	Patrick Lanfear
Cover Illustrator:	Todd Daman
Cover Designer:	Tom Draper Design
Interior Graphic Designer:	James D. Kramer
Illustrator:	Joel Panchot
Principal Compositor:	Joanna Zito
Principal Proofreader:	Jan Cocker